GRAPHICSTUDIO

GRAPHICSTUDIO

Contemporary Art from the Collaborative Workshop
at the University of South Florida

Ruth E. Fine
Mary Lee Corlett

National Gallery of Art, Washington
Prestel

Exhibition Dates
National Gallery of Art, Washington
15 September 1991–5 January 1992

This book was produced by the Editors Office, National Gallery of Art
Editor-in-Chief, Frances P. Smyth
Editor, Tam Curry
Designer, Phyllis Hecht
Production assistant, Robyn Lash

The type is Sabon, with Helvetica, set by BG Composition, Baltimore, Maryland
Printed on Vintage Velvet by Schneidereith & Sons, Baltimore, Maryland

Trade edition distributed by Prestel-Verlag, Mandlstrasse 26,
D-8000 Munich 40, Germany
Tel:(89)38-17-09-0; Telefax:(89)38-17-09-35

Distributed in continental Europe by Prestel-Verlag, Verlegerdienst München GmbII & Co. KG, Gutenbergstrasse 1, D-8031 Gilching, Germany
Tel:(8105)2110; Telefax:(8105)55-20

Distributed in the USA and Canada by te Neues Publishing Company,
15 East 76th Street, New York, NY 10021, USA
Tel:(212)288-0265; Telefax:(212)570-2373

Distributed in Japan by YOHAN-Western Publications Distribution Agency,
14-9 Okubo 3-chome, Shinjuku-ku, J-Tokyo 169
Tel:(3)208-0181; Telefax:(3)209-0288

Distributed in the United Kingdom, Ireland, and all other countries by Thames & Hudson Limited, 30-40 Bloomsbury Street, London WC1B 3QP, England
Tel:(71)636-5488; Telefax:(71)636-4799

Library of Congress Cataloging-in-Publication Data
National Gallery of Art (U.S.)
    Graphicstudio: contemporary art from the collaborative workshop at the University of South Florida / Ruth E. Fine and Mary Lee Corlett.
    Catalog of an exhibition held Sept. 15, 1991–Jan. 5, 1992, to celebrate the formation of the Graphicstudio Archive at the National Gallery of Art, Washington, D.C.
    Includes bibliographical references and index.
    1. Graphicstudio—Exhibitions. 2. Group work in art—Florida—Tampa—Exhibitions. 3. Prints, American—Florida—Tampa—Exhibitions. 4. Prints—20th century—Florida—Tampa—Exhibitions.
    I. Fine, Ruth, 1941–. II. Corlett, Mary Lee.
    III. Graphicstudio. IV. Title.
    NE538.T35N37   1991
    769.9759′ 65′ 074753—dc20   91-27201
                                           CIP

Cover: Jim Dine, *The Heart and the Wall*, 1983 (cat. 11)
Frontispiece: James Rosenquist, *Sister Shrieks* (detail), 1987–1989 (cat. 59)
Page 6: Robert Rauschenberg, *Study for Chinese Summerhall*, 1982 (app. 204)

ISBN 0-89468-164-8 softcover
ISBN 3-7913-1282-4 hardcover (trade edition)

CONTENTS

RAUSCHENBERG   USF PROOF

FOREWORD

During the past decade, the National Gallery of Art has greatly expanded its program of collecting and exhibiting contemporary art. Among notable gifts received in this field are the archive collections of two major print and sculpture workshops, Gemini G.E.L. and Graphicstudio U.S.F. With initial gifts of selected publications, both the Gemini and Graphicstudio archives have been brought up to date periodically, enabling the Gallery's international audience to keep abreast of the recent works created at two of this country's most experimental ateliers.

Donald J. Saff, founding director of Graphicstudio at the University of South Florida, was among the artists represented in the National Gallery's 1984 exhibition *Gemini G.E.L.: Art and Collaboration*. Enthusiasm for that show prompted discussions among Saff and our senior curator, Andrew Robison, and curator of modern prints and drawings, Ruth Fine, about establishing a Graphicstudio Archive at the Gallery similar in concept to our Gemini collection. This proposal received the support first of then-president of the University of South Florida, John Lott Brown, and more recently of his successor, Frank Borkowski. We are deeply grateful to both of these men for their interest. We would also like to thank the workshop's current director, Alan Eaker, and the renowned artists who have contributed to Graphicstudio's success and generosity.

The Graphicstudio Archive has grown to include prints and sculpture editions of great diversity: more than 250 works by thirty-seven artists working in collaboration with the workshop's talented printers and craftspeople. The archive also includes numerous unique proofs, preparatory drawings, and sculpture maquettes. These lithographs, etchings, screenprints, woodcuts, multi-media prints, and three-dimensional pieces greatly enrich this national collection's representation of the far-reaching art of our time.

Graphicstudio: Contemporary Art from the Collaborative Workshop at the University of South Florida presents a selection of Graphicstudio's publications between 1969 and 1990 as well as some of the related studies. The exhibition celebrates the formation of the Graphicstudio Archive and suggests its extraordinary range. It is particularly fitting that this splendid gift be celebrated in 1991, which marks the fiftieth anniversary of the founding of the National Gallery of Art. A time of great festivity, the anniversary has been commemorated by an outpouring of generosity on the part of the Gallery's donors, many of whom are the artists themselves. We extend our warmest appreciation to all of them.

The Graphicstudio exhibition was enthusiastically organized by Ruth Fine, assisted by Mary Lee Corlett, who has made a major contribution to this catalogue about an exemplary collaborative workshop. Exhibitions are complex collaborative undertakings as well. Thus many colleagues at the University of South Florida and the National Gallery of Art have offered their time and expertise to the project, as noted in the acknowledgments that follow.

J. Carter Brown
Director

ACKNOWLEDGMENTS

Our foremost appreciation is to the artists in this exhibition. Their work has provided inspiration, challenge, and pleasure. They have given abundantly of their time and hospitality, supplying answers to questions and providing valuable insights. We thank them all. In addition, Jim Dine, has generously donated to the Gallery from his own collection *The Metamorphosis of a Plant into a Fan* and *The Tampa Tool Reliefs*, and for this we are most grateful.

Donald J. Saff, the founding and long-term director of Graphicstudio, whose commitment to the National Gallery of Art over several years inspired the formation of our Graphicstudio Archive, has welcomed us to the workshop on numerous occasions and shared our enthusiasm for the project. Don and his wife, Ruth, have made donations of prints to the Graphicstudio Archive from their private collection; and Don's support has continued since he stepped down as the workshop's director. His successor, Alan Eaker, has also made every effort to provide information as needed.

We would like to extend special thanks to the printers and fabricators who willingly shared their technical expertise and knowledge: Paul Clinton, Nick Conroy, Ken Elliott, Patrick Foy, Alan Holoubek, Tom Pruitt, and Charles Ringness. Deli Sacilotto was especially helpful in demonstrating printmaking techniques and answering questions about processes.

Other Graphicstudio staff dedicated to this project include Brenda Woodard, assistant director, who provided the link between us and the moving target that is Don Saff; Susie Hennessy, shop manager, who shared her knowledge of the workings of the shop during the 1980s; Michael Harrigan and Marcia Brown, curators, who supplied vital documentation sheets about the works of art; George Holzer, whose photographic documentation of the workshop's activities was invaluable; also Apple Bass, Wendy Elias, Jill Livermore, and Kelly Anne Medei, who maintained the flow of information during the change in Graphicstudio's directorship.

In addition to university presidents John Lott Brown and Frank Borkowski, many colleagues at the University of South Florida were helpful during the formation of the Graphicstudio Archive, including Barbara Ann Blue, August L. Freundlich, Michelle Juristo, Willard McCracken, Margaret Miller, George Newkome, Gregory O'Brien, and Ann Ross.

Elizabeth Armstrong, curator of prints at the Walker Art Center, Minneapolis, offered many thoughtful comments on the catalogue manuscript. Several artists' staff members were particularly helpful: Blake Sommers for Jim Dine; Jane Samuels for Nancy Graves; Bradley Jeffries and David White for Robert Rauschenberg; Beverly Coe, Michael Harrigan, and Cindy Hemstreet for James Rosenquist; and Pat Poncy for Edward Ruscha.

We gratefully acknowledge the assistance of our colleagues at the following galleries and workshops, especially Pat Caporaso and Jodi Scherer at Castelli Graphics; Olivia D'albis and Constance Kao at Leo Castelli Gallery; Marcia Corbino at Corbino Galleries; Valerie Wade at Crown Point Press; Dart Gallery, Inc.; Jackie Roeser and Joëlle Rabion at Richard L. Feigen & Co., Inc.; Susan Young at Ronald Feldman Fine

Arts, Inc.; Jay Tobler and Alexis Summer at Barbara Gladstone Gallery; Betty Cunningham, Frank Del Deo, and Amy E. Harte at Hirschl & Adler Modern; Laurence Miller Gallery, Inc.; Marla Goldwasser at Robert Miller Gallery; Richard Bellamy and Jeanie Blake at Oil & Steel Gallery; Pace/MacGill Gallery; Sally Lebwohl at the Pace Gallery; J. Rosenthal Fine Arts, Ltd.; Joanne D. Isaac at Bernice Steinbaum Gallery; Joe Pedoto at Styria Studios; Elyse Goldberg at John Weber Gallery; and Sperone Westwater.

Thanks are due to U.S.F. professor Thomas McLaughlin for his remembrances of the Alice Aycock project, and to former U.S.F. professor Oscar Bailey, who answered numerous questions about his participation at Graphicstudio. We thank U.S.F. student Jade Dellinger; photographer Jim Strong; Deborah Wythe, archivist for the Brooklyn Museum; Lindy A. Waites, registrar, Elvehjem Museum of Art; and the library staff at the National Museum of American Art/National Portrait Gallery, and the Art Students League, New York.

At the National Gallery, we thank J. Carter Brown, director, Roger Mandle, deputy director, and Andrew Robison, senior curator. In the department of modern prints and drawings, Carlotta J. Owens, Charles M. Ritchie, Thomas H. Coolsen, Kim Bockhaus, and former staff member Sarah Cash have assisted in countless ways. Matter/framers Hugh Phibbs, Virginia Ritchie, and Jamie Stout are responsible for the handsome presentation of the objects; and Gaillard Ravenel, Mark Leithauser, Gordon Anson, William Bowser, Barbara Keyes, Jane Rodgers, and their colleagues have provided the sympathetic exhibition design and installation. For assistance with the catalogue, we thank Frances Smyth, editor-in-chief, Tam Curry, for her astute editing, Phyllis Hecht, for her imaginative design, Chris Vogel, and Abigail Walker. For compiling the bibliography, we thank Lamia Doumato, head of reader services in the library.

We also thank assistant to the deputy director, Carol Kelley; curator of photography, Sarah Greenough; curator of twentieth-century art, Jack Cowart; Mary Suzor, Anne Halpern, John Poliszuk, and the art handlers in the registrar's office; D. Dodge Thompson and Heather Reed in the exhibitions office; Richard Amt, Ira Bartfield, Dean Beasom, Philip Charles, and Sara Sanders-Buell in photographic services as well as contract photographer Ed Owens; Shelley Fletcher, Pia Pell, Shelley Sturman in the conservation laboratories; Neal Turtell, Frances Lederer, Ted Dalziel, Thomas McGill, Jr., in the library; Linda Downs, Susan Arensberg, and Lorraine Karafel in the education division; Michael Sassani in media programs; Elizabeth A.C. Perry and Elisa Glazer in corporate relations; Genevra Higginson and Pauline Watona in special events; and Ruth Kaplan, Deborah Ziska, Tina Coplan, Keira Ellis, and Elizabeth Kimball in the information office.

Finally, we thank Larry Day and Thomas Corlett for their patience.

Ruth E. Fine
Curator
Modern Prints and Drawings

Mary Lee Corlett
Research Associate
Modern Prints and Drawings

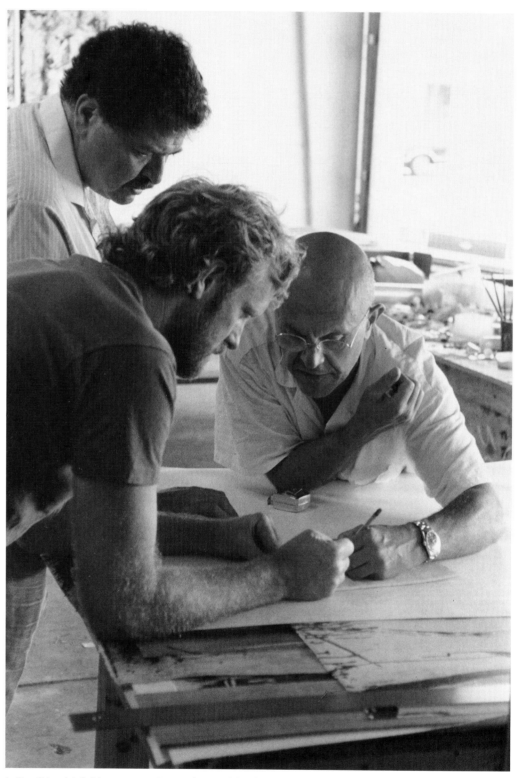

1. Jim Dine (right) in conversation with Donald Saff (rear) and Patrick Foy, September 1987

INTRODUCTION Ruth E. Fine

The making of prints in professional workshops has played a promi-
nent role in artistic activity in the United States during the past three
decades. Artists in this country have been involved in printmaking for generations, of course, often printing their etchings, lithographs, woodcuts,
screenprints themselves in their own studios or in cooperative artists'
workshops such as Stanley William Hayter's Atelier 17, the famous
Parisian-based shop that was temporarily set up in New York during and
immediately following World War II, and Pratt Graphics Center, which
came after it in the 1950s. In addition, artists working with professional
printers—for example, George Bellows with Bolton Brown—have played
a crucial role in printmaking for centuries. Nevertheless, the recent past
has been marked by an enormous growth in collaborative printmaking,
transforming the art of the print from an art of small-scale objects stored
in solander boxes and requiring intimate study to one that rivals painting
and sculpture in scale, technical complexity, and place of importance in
many artists' oeuvres.[1]

In any account of this transformation, the year 1957 is pivotal. It was
then that Tatyana Grosman started Universal Limited Art Editions (ULAE)
in the garage of her home in West Islip, New York.[2] This has long since
taken on the status of a landmark event in the history of contemporary
printmaking, in great measure because of Grosman's insistence on introducing the graphic media (screenprinting and lithography at first) to artists
who not only were principally interested in painting and sculpture rather
than printmaking but were in fact sometimes hostile to the meticulous
technical "cookery" that printmaking often requires.

In 1960, three years after ULAE was established, June Wayne, with support from the Ford Foundation, opened Tamarind Lithography Workshop
in Los Angeles, another mythic place in contemporary printmaking.[3]
Wayne's own experiences as an artist had taken her to Europe on several
occasions, seeking the skills of professional fine art lithographers. The
purpose of the workshop she founded was to train lithographic printers so
that artists would be able to work professionally in that medium in the
United States; she also hoped to generate increased interest on the part of
artists in doing so. This was accomplished by offering fellowships to artists with radically varied points of view—and often with little or no printmaking experience—to come and work at Tamarind, usually for periods
of two months, and to challenge the master printers and printing trainees
with a range of aesthetic and technical demands.

Wayne's goal has been handsomely met during the past thirty years, as
shops owned or staffed by Tamarind master printers have been established
throughout the United States and others have been inspired by the Tamarind example. Professional workshops—Gemini G.E.L. on the West
Coast, Tyler Graphics Ltd. on the East Coast, Landfall Press in the Midwest (all of which have extended their technical offerings well beyond
traditional lithography)—have worked with artists of virtually every persuasion to create prints of great beauty and power.[4] Tamarind Lithogra-

phy Workshop moved from Los Angeles to the University of New Mexico campus in Albuquerque in 1970, changed its name to Tamarind Institute, and changed its status, taking on contract printing as well as offering fellowships to artists. Publishing workshops have been opened on numerous other campuses as well, including Nova Scotia College of Art and Design (now closed), Arizona State University, and Rutgers University. Artist-in-residence programs at institutions across the country often offer their participants the opportunity to complete a print during their stay.

Within this wide range of possibilities, Graphicstudio at the University of South Florida (U.S.F.) in Tampa holds a special place. Located on the university campus and committed first and foremost to the importance and power (educational and otherwise) of works of art, Graphicstudio has aspired from the very outset to produce work of the quality and technical complexity that was the hallmark of professional shops such as Gemini G.E.L. Initiated in 1968, with its first visiting artist, Philip Pearlstein, arriving in January 1969, Graphicstudio flourished in its first phase for eight years, producing 121 prints in lithography, screenprint, woodcut, and photography, as well as a number of sculpture projects. In 1976 it was closed down in what was thought at the time to be a permanent move. Beginning in 1980, however, the workshop slowly reestablished itself and during the following decade it completed some of the most daring prints and sculpture of the period. A selection of works dating from 1969 to 1990 is presented in detail in this exhibition catalogue, followed by a checklist of Graphicstudio's publications during those years (see appendix).

Graphicstudio's Mastermind: Donald J. Saff

Graphicstudio was conceived and sustained by the energy and imagination of Donald Saff, chairman of the visual arts department at U.S.F. when the workshop was founded.[5] He later became dean of the newly established College of Fine Arts at U.S.F., a position he held until 1976, about the time the first phase of Graphicstudio closed down. Saff took on the directorship of Graphicstudio again in 1985, resigning in 1990 to open an independent workshop called Saff Tech Arts (S.T.A.).

A native New Yorker, Saff attended Queens College, Pratt Institute, and Columbia University, starting out as an engineering major but

2. Deli Sacilotto etching a gravure plate for Jim Dine's *Shellac on a Hand* (app. 68), for which proofs are hanging in the background, November 1975

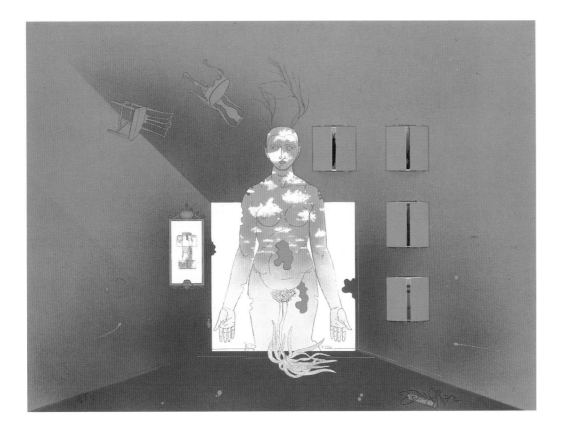

shifting to art in his sophomore year. Principally interested in drawing and sculpture, he also became involved in printmaking, first as an undergraduate—working with Louis Hechenbleikner, a transplanted Austrian wood engraver who traveled annually from New York to Paris to make lithographs—and later at the Pratt Graphics Center.

Saff's first significant experience with collaborative printmaking came while he was on a Fulbright Fellowship in Urbino, Italy. His collagraph plates, large for that time, were somewhat unwieldy compared to the more conservative landscape etchings that then dominated printmaking in Italy. Saff was fortunate enough to be introduced to some local printers willing to work outside of their traditions, a watershed event in Saff's life in several ways. The pleasures of working with skilled craftspeople were patently obvious to him, and his experience in Urbino sowed some of the seeds that eventually led to the Graphicstudio idea. Soon after his arrival in Italy, Saff met Deli Sacilotto, a young Canadian also interested in printmaking, and the two men have remained both professional associates and close friends, together exploring such arcane subjects as clock repair.[6]

In his own art Saff continues to work in painting, drawing, sculpture, and printmaking (fig. 3), and he has a considerable record as an author as well.[7] His skills as both craftsman and entrepreneur have also contributed to a variety of artistic enterprises in addition to Graphicstudio. His long-term association with Robert Rauschenberg, which started with their first Graphicstudio collaborations in 1972 (see cats. 64–69), led to his accompanying Rauschenberg to China in 1982, when, with support from Gemini G.E.L., the artist produced a series of 491 unique paper pieces together titled *7 Characters* as well as the photographs used in the hundred-foot-long *Chinese Summerhall* (cat. 76).[8] These travels in China were among the international working trips that developed into the Rauschenberg Overseas Culture Interchange (ROCI), an evolving exhibition that has been curatorially coordinated by Saff as it has traveled to eleven countries, including Mexico, Tibet, Cuba, the Soviet Union, and the United States.[9]

Saff's involvement specifically with printmaking projects has been wide ranging. Prior to assisting with Rauschenberg's China project for Gemini, Saff served as consultant when Gemini's directors, Sidney Felsen and Stanley Grinstein, decided in 1979 to add a fully equipped etching studio to the workshop's facilities; he traveled to Los Angeles to act as the liaison for both equipment suppliers and printers, also proofing a group of etchings by Saul Steinberg. And when Jim Dine was invited to make a print as artist-in-residence at Hartford Art School, Saff worked with him as he developed *Rachel Cohen's Flags, State I* (D'Oench and Fineberg 1986, no. 41).

After the early phase of Graphicstudio closed down, Dine urged Saff to open a workshop privately. With Alan Eaker, the present director of Graphicstudio and at that time a sculptor on the U.S.F. faculty who had contributed to several Graphicstudio projects, and attorney Arnold Levine, Saff started a new publishing venture, Pyramid Arts Ltd. During its approximately two years of existence, Pyramid Arts completed print and sculpture editions with Dine, Pearlstein, Rauschenberg, James Rosenquist, and Theo Wujcik, another U.S.F. faculty member who had printed for Graphicstudio in 1970–1971 before turning to teaching and who was called back temporarily in 1973. Wujcik's project with Pyramid consisted of several portraits of artists, including Dine, Rosenquist, and Rauschenberg.[10]

These various undertakings, while of shorter duration than Saff's involvement with Graphicstudio, nevertheless make vivid his enthusiasm for working with other artists in producing their work. This urge most certainly was central to his Graphicstudio idea, and as the chairman of the visual arts department and later dean of the College of Fine Arts, he was in a fortuitous position to put his thoughts about a collaborative printmaking workshop into action. His personal appeal brought others into the fold. As Rosenquist explains: "Don, he's a scholar, but he's also very innovative with ideas and materials and things, and he sees how they can work for other artists. . . . He's very generous, and he seems to be giving away ideas that he develops. They work very well for other artists, and they seem to be apropos."[11]

Phase I of Graphicstudio

When Graphicstudio was founded, Saff and his supporters thought the potential for artistic exploration at the workshop would be a logical extension to research programs that existed at U.S.F. Nevertheless, direct funding for research in art rather than the sciences was a radical idea.[12] In Saff's words, "If one believed in the value of art, one believed in its value to teach; and it was just as good as another professor standing in front of the class pontificating. . . . The object was to fund this teaching process through the same procedure that you would fund a faculty member except divert the funds into salaries for technicians and consultants and the purchase of paper and ink—whatever."[13]

Fortunately for all concerned, a supportive core for the Graphicstudio idea included university president, Cecil Mackey; former chair of the department of fine arts and then associate dean of the College of Liberal

Arts, Harrison Covington; and vice president for academic affairs, Carl Riggs, among others. Their support of Saff was courageous and far-sighted, not only within the university context but in the wider art community. In the late 1960s what has since come to be celebrated as a "print renaissance" was well underway; but it was far less pervasive with respect to the numbers of workshops in operation and the numbers of artists using them than it was to become in the decades that followed. Certainly the importance of this new interest in prints had yet to be fully assessed; it was noticed in the art press, but there was no body of literature then as there would be today to support the notion that printmaking plays a central role in the art of the time.

Saff's idea was also radical in that he maintained a quest for informality in the necessarily bureaucratic university setting. His thought was to encourage spontaneous rather than programmed interaction between students, faculty, and visiting artists by placing the Graphicstudio workshop in the middle of the university's teaching facility "so you simply had to bump into the artists in the halls." Inevitably students would come in and ask printers technical questions, and there was interaction back and forth among students, artists, faculty, and printers in a rather fluid situation.[14] Saff insisted, however, that the visiting artists were to have no formal obligation to the students unless the artists themselves initiated it, that the teaching would take place through the availability of the Graphicstudio printers to consult on technical issues with the students and faculty, and most important, through the art: the drawings and proofs produced in the development of the artists' work; and the printed editions that were completed on campus. In addition, under the auspices of the Florida Center for the Arts and the Art Bank, an impression of every print and sculpture published was turned over to the university, with the Center for the Arts acting as a liaison with the community in a variety of ways, including the organization of traveling shows drawn from the university's growing collection.

The Florida Center for the Arts, directed by James Camp, was a separate entity from the university's art department and coordinated the university's exhibitions program. The center's mandate included a charge to build a university collection. A program, not a place, the center was a key player during Graphicstudio's early years. In fact, Graphicstudio grew out of an idea that Camp had had for a one-time event, a ceramics workshop and symposium. Saff, whose interest in prints was greater than in ceramics, suggested an ongoing print workshop instead. Amusingly, one of the most ambitious projects undertaken at Graphicstudio during its early years was Robert Rauschenberg's series of Made in Tampa Clay Pieces (cats. 68A-D).

Saff's only models for Graphicstudio were the Pratt Graphics Center, which he knew firsthand, where artists either could work independently or could hire the services of a printer; Tamarind, which was familiar through its own miscellaneous publications on a variety of subjects; and Gemini, which Saff had visited. Ken Tyler, then a partner at Gemini, was cordial but did not invite Saff into the workshop itself. Thus Saff knew Gemini essentially from its reputation and from the art that was produced there: "The degree of ignorance that I had about how all of this worked was rather tremendous." Imagination conquered ignorance, however. The suggestion was put forth that initial funding for the workshop be requested from the Florida Arts Council. Everyone agreed, the grant was obtained, and Graphicstudio was launched. An embossed sunburst, a symbol of energy, was chosen as its logo (fig. 4).

4. Enlargement of embossed sunburst chop used to mark Graphicstudio publications

Graphicstudio's initial home was modest: a single converted classroom. Its funding was modest, too. In addition to the seed grant from the Florida Arts Council, Saff garnered a group of ten community supporters, asking them for a thousand dollars each in exchange for the promise of twenty prints, one of the great bargains of the century. As the workshop completed the last of the prints promised for a given series, a new subscription period would begin, the operative time frame being determined by the number of pieces produced, not by any calendar account. This community support was of crucial importance throughout Graphicstudio's history, although the subscription program's provisions changed over the years.[15]

With the initial subscription funds Saff was able to buy a Charles Brand lithographic press as well as papers, inks, and other supplies, and to pay the artists a modest honorarium, a practice that lasted only briefly. Two lithographic stones were borrowed from Syracuse China Corporation, which was switching from lithography to screenprinting. The pervasiveness of the Tamarind ideal at that time undoubtedly influenced Saff's choice of lithography as the medium with which to start his shop, his personal preference being etching. He also thought that lithography, with its potential for direct drawing, seemed most sympathetic to the ideas of the painters with whom he was hoping to work.

During its early phase (1968–1976) Graphicstudio received support for its work space and funding for its academic research positions from the state, through the university. The National Endowment for the Arts, at first through the Florida Development Commission and then directly to Graphicstudio, provided several grants ranging from $15,000 at the beginning to $3,000 at the end when it was wrongly believed the support was less needed.[16] Travel funds were occasionally provided by an artist's gallery; and Petersburg Press helped to support the equipment for production of Dine's ambitious sculpture *Metamorphosis of a Plant into a Fan* (cat. 7). Other private funding included a crucial advance of $30,000 from private collector Gordon Gund in exchange for which he was later able to acquire work from Graphicstudio on a continuing basis.[17]

It was the subscription program, however, that was the mainstay for Graphicstudio. In turn, the workshop provided an extraordinary resource for all of its participants, functioning as an inspiration for private collecting in the Tampa area.

The Artists

Saff's plan was to have artists come to Graphicstudio by invitation, one at a time, to do a specific number of prints, usually two, within a specific time span, usually two weeks. He had no set ideas regarding which artists he would ask, although he hoped to work with a range of aesthetic positions, presumably to provide U.S.F. students with exposure to a variety of approaches: "I wanted to demonstrate that I had catholic taste about all of this and was willing to give all schools a chance." Saff himself also relished technical challenges—"Inevitably I'd be confronting something I didn't know how to do"—and wanted to present the artists with new possibilities, a broader palette of materials and processes.

Collaboration between artists and craftspeople at Graphicstudio, as in other workshops, is structured in phases: 1) defining the project; 2) developing the ideas in the form of a proof for prints or a maquette or prototype for sculpture; and 3) completing the editions. The artists have

5. Printer Paul Clinton inking a lithographic stone, c. 1972

often developed their thoughts about a project in advance of their arrival at the workshop. Reaching the proof or prototype stage requires the intimate participation of the artist and workshop staff, often over a long period, with consultation sometimes taking place through the mail or by telephone. When a satisfactory solution is reached, the artist signs his or her approval, thus authorizing the production of an edition of a specified size. After an edition is completed, Graphicstudio's curator reviews it for consistency to ensure quality control of every sheet or piece. Once the artist signs the edition, the shop's blindstamp is affixed for identification.

Collaborative projects each have their own unique character, evolving according to the personalities of the artist and craftspeople as well as the nature of the project and the processes involved. Nevertheless, there are certain general parameters that seem consistent. Saff's role in all of his Graphicstudio projects was to contribute his technical expertise: "Everything started with protracted conversations with the artists that would offer clues as to the possibilities we'd encounter. Then I'd have conversations with the staff. . . . I was always there having a conversation and somehow nudging the project one way or another by asking the printers to do an experiment . . . or suggesting something hopefully in the subtlest of ways to the artist." Despite his extraordinary expertise and passion for technical experimentation, Saff usually functioned as an intensely involved coordinating consultant rather than a hands-on printer or fabricator of any sort. He enabled artists to explore various processes by focusing attention and opening up new options.

Even as a student at Pratt, Saff did not want to do his own printing. At Graphicstudio he said he did not want to "sweat printing and then have to change things," apparently feeling that if someone else undertook the labor he would be more intellectually daring. He wanted to be in a position to see that something was redone to get it right—again and again if necessary—and feared that he might otherwise compromise his sense of perfection and his desire to experiment: "I was more interested in be[ing] somehow able to orchestrate a group of people who maybe left to their

own devices would not necessarily communicate printer to printer or printer to artist, and somehow make music out of it. Of course, even if I wanted to do the actual printing, administrative issues, interaction with the university, was so consuming that I could never be [at Graphicstudio] hours and hours in a row as needed." Saff's primary concerns were: "How to rid yourself [of] or minimize preconceptions? And what's more important than minimizing preconceptions?"

The first artist to work at Graphicstudio was Philip Pearlstein. Known not only for his art but for his sympathy as a teacher, he was a splendid choice for setting the tone in this new professional workshop. Pearlstein recalls that "the studio was a raw space, cement-block walls, cement floor, a staircase with an iron railing students stood on so they could watch me ."[18] No special lighting or luxuries of any sort were available. In fact, Pearlstein's desire to work directly from the nude model, central to his work, presented quite a hurdle: "It was the first time they'd ever had [nude] models to work from. They didn't even know if it was legal. Somebody said it wasn't legal. And it was Donald's idea to turn it into a kind of student workshop. They didn't work, but they watched me work. . . . I worked directly on the stones from the models, with all the students standing around. . . . The models were art students. They were both very sophisticated young women . . . totally aware of what was going on in the art world."

Pearlstein's availability to the students, welcoming them into the studio while he was working, encouraged the interaction that Saff had desired. In addition to a group of drawings, the artist completed four lithographs during this first working session (see cats. 1, 2, app. 159, 160). Pearlstein returned to work with Graphicstudio again toward the end of the workshop's first phase, finishing two versions of *Two Female Models on Rocker and Stool* (figs. 7, 8, app. 162). He was among the artists with whom the workshop renewed contact as it was tooling up again in the 1980s, and he completed several projects then, including *Jerusalem, Kidron Valley* (cat. 5), one of the crowning achievements of Graphicstudio's most technically experimental phase.

6. Printers Paul Clinton, Dan Stack, and Charles Ringness, curator Michelle Juristo, and printer Julio Juristo (left to right) during a production meeting for Robert Rauschenberg's Made in Tampa Clay Pieces, 1972

As might be imagined, it was not particularly easy to get artists to travel to Tampa to work in an as-yet-unproven printshop, despite the great success of Pearlstein's first visit. Printmaking was still a somewhat novel idea, and Saff was faced with "Who are you? Why should we do prints?" Once again, however, serendipity combined with aggressive searching brought Saff an important contact: Jacqueline Chambord, graphics director at the Richard Feigen Gallery, was looking for a printer to work with some of the gallery's artists. From that association came a number of projects with artists of a very different persuasion from Philip

7. Philip Pearlstein, *Two Female Models on Rocker and Stool*, 1975 (app. 161)

8. Charles Ringness preparing a lithographic plate for Pearlstein's *Two Female Models on Rocker and Stool*, 1974

Pearlstein. Each artist completed several pieces over a period of a few weeks, the pattern during the early years of Graphicstudio. Although the styles of many of the artists—Richard Anuszkiewicz, Charles Hinman, Nicholas Krushenick, Richard Smith, Adja Yunkers—were rooted in abstraction, the work varied radically.

Every new artist presented new challenges for the printers—some major, some minor. Hinman's embossings (app. 120, 121), for example, brought the first atypical problem to be solved: that of compensating for the stretching and wrinkling the paper underwent because of the depth of the area etched into the plate. Smith's were the first sculptural prints with movable parts (cats. 30, 31); preliminary drawings were completed in Tampa, too (figs. 30a, 31a), and the demands of turning these elegant and sensuous works into prints sparked a new kind of awareness in Saff: "It was the complication, and somehow you were thinking about things other than just how good a black you could have or what the longevity of the ink would be."

The challenge of Anuszkiewicz' thin strips of pale, closely related colors was the need to mix and print inks in the artist's tight value scale and have them appear as intended when dry, the colors necessarily undergoing a subtle change during the drying process (see cats. 17, 18, app. 5, 6, 8). Theo Wujcik's great skill prompted Saff to lure him back to Graphicstudio especially for this project (he had by this time taken a faculty position at U.S.F.). In addition to taking extraordinary care with the mixing of inks, Wujcik had to pick imperfections from the papers, meticulously removing the "visual impurities" so as not to interfere with the overall delicacy of the images.

Of working with Krushenick's broad, brilliant color areas (see cats. 23–25, app. 125–127, 129–130), Saff has commented that "the flats were impossible." Krushenick came to Graphicstudio after working at Tamarind, where he apparently met resistance to his use of a certain color because of its fugitive nature. According to Saff, the issue struck a nerve with the artist, whose feelings apparently were echoed somewhat by Saff's own: "The longevity of a work is important up until the point that it begins to interfere with the creative process, at which time it becomes an absolutely ancillary issue. . . . I don't think an artist's obligation is to make something that lasts for a thousand years when that focus interferes with producing the art; and I think that Nick was right in raising that simple issue: he wanted the print to look the way he wanted it to look." The decision not to print Krushenick's flat color areas on the motorized flatbed presses that Graphicstudio had acquired meant that the shop would probably never use them. There was such a strong, ingrained tradition of hand-printing among the Tamarind-trained staff that even though the quality of printing on the flatbed press, which laid down an even layer of ink, was demonstrably better than that achieved using the handpress, which often produced streaks, and even though it was much less labor-intensive to use an electric press, there was steadfast refusal to do so: it would not be "hand-printing."[19]

A collaboration with Edward Ruscha (cats. 26–29, app. 235, 240) followed the work with Krushenick. Saff had visited Mel Ramos (another Feigen artist at the time) at his studio in Hayward, California, and had been captivated by one of Ruscha's works on Ramos' wall: "this tiny little Ed Ruscha drawing and I couldn't take my eyes off of it. Working with him was great. He just sat down and drew. . . . He did some tests, was open to trying different processes. . . . The project was so fluid and he was so affable, and the conversation ranged over everything and the

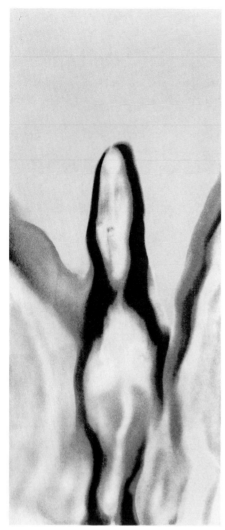

9. Larry Bell, *Untitled #6,* 1974 (app. 29)

20

technique was so logical that he was in total harmony with the printers. . . . There were trips to Tarpon Springs for dinner, where sponge fishing is done by the Greek community."

Ruscha showed Saff a film he was making with Larry Bell, which prompted Saff to invite Bell to work with him in Florida. The six *Untitled* prints that make up Bell's 1974 project (fig. 9, app. 24–29) were the first works completed at Graphicstudio entirely in screenprint. Printed in auxiliary studio space that had been acquired off campus, this series was overseen by an outside printer, the only such instance during the first phase of Graphicstudio's activity. William Weege came in from Wisconsin and joined the workshop staff temporarily, contributing his expertise in screenprinting and in the flocking techniques demanded by Bell's project. A person of indefatigable energy, Weege seemed willing to go wherever the artist's imagination might lead, offering his own specialized experience. Saff was "very impressed with Bill and felt at harmony with his style and passion."

Two lithographs by Mel Ramos (fig. 10, app. 167) were the first Graphicstudio prints in which photographic processes were used. These editions presented yet another combination of ingredients and called on the expertise of Oscar Bailey, a photographer whom Saff had hired to start the photography department at U.S.F., principally to provide backup for Graphicstudio projects. Bailey worked on several other prints with artists who came to Graphicstudio, including several by Rauschenberg and Rosenquist. In the following decade four of his own color Cirkut photographs became Graphicstudio publications (see cats. 34, 35, app. 20, 21). By that time photography and photogravure were very important in the workshop's program.

The development of Graphicstudio progressed on the basis of opportunities grasped as they came along rather than of long-range planning. Issues like the rejection of automated presses, social events like special dinners, and the temperaments of all participants determine the personality of the workshop at any given time. That personality changes. In collaborative undertakings more is involved than the work itself. Saff was hoping that Graphicstudio would establish a community of artists in the Tampa area, or more likely, bring one there on a rotating basis to

10. Mel Ramos, *Indian Rhinoceros*, 1970
(app. 168)

11. Adja Yunkers, *Untitled*, 1969 (app. 257)

provide intellectual stimulation. He has spoken with great warmth about working with Adja Yunkers, not only in terms of the development of Yunkers' three prints (fig. 11, app. 255–256) but also in terms of their conversations and the elder artist's old world elegance, broad connections to the New York art world, and passionate discussions of his work.

The character of Graphicstudio was virtually transformed when James Rosenquist came there to work in 1971 (fig. 12), partly because of his energy, partly because of his combined propensity to explore materials and great sensitivity to printmaking media, partly because of the circumstances of his life. Saff had contacted Rosenquist through a mutual friend, Bruce Barton. In their first telephone conversation Rosenquist immediately launched into a discussion about a project that would deal with ideas surrounding the fact that Americans were going to the moon. According to Rosenquist, "the idea of it was to pay attention to what goes on on the earth before you go over to the moon. Think about the earth again." Rosenquist's excitement was shared by Saff: "I had never spoken to anybody in terms of these projects who had talked so conceptually about what he wanted to do, and with as much enthusiasm. . . . He came down, immediately loved the light in Florida, loved the idea of the studio being a place for experiments. We started talking about possible objects related to prints—the idea that it didn't have to be a flat print started maturing."

Rosenquist, who was then based in New York but now divides his time between that city and Aripeka, Florida, made arrangements to come back to Tampa with his family, a visit that was disastrously interrupted by an automobile accident that hospitalized the artist for a brief period and placed his wife and young son in more threatening situations. Saff made Graphicstudio available to Rosenquist essentially as a personal studio, for as long as he wanted it and on whatever schedule was possible, hoping to provide temporary relief from the artist's preoccupation with his family's ordeal. Rosenquist came to the shop whenever he could between hospital trips. As a result of this terrible misfortune, Graphicstudio's program of artists working on projects of limited and predetermined duration was tossed to the wind, allowing for a far greater seriousness of purpose to unfold as part of the workshop's scheme. Rosenquist completed eleven multicolor lithographs during this period, ranging from postcard size to a few feet in either dimension (app. 209–219). Several of the works incorporated photographic processes, and two—*Mastaba* and *Earth and Moon* (cat. 54, app. 212)—had elements that were not only three-dimensional but movable as well.

Rosenquist's skills as a draftsman and his ability to explore yet control materials are evident in all of his Graphicstudio prints. One also senses in them the artist's fascination with all aspects of the printmaking processes. Working at Graphicstudio again in 1975, he completed seven prints that make these qualities even more vivid (cats. 55–57, app. 220, 221, 225, 226). Much larger in scale than the earlier group for the most part, two are screenprints, some incorporate screenprinting and lithography, some feature collage and three-dimensional elements. During that working session, Rosenquist rented a dime store to use as a studio in Ybor City, the older section of Tampa, also known as the Latin Quarter. He recalls it as a very productive period: "Came back, went to work with Don; it was fantastic. Worked hard; all I did was work, work, work, work, work. . . . The studio I had was a block from Arnold's Art Supply and a block from the post office. And you could buy pretty good Spanish wine around the corner, and *cafe con leche* was fifteen

12. James Rosenquist at work on his first Graphicstudio project, 1971

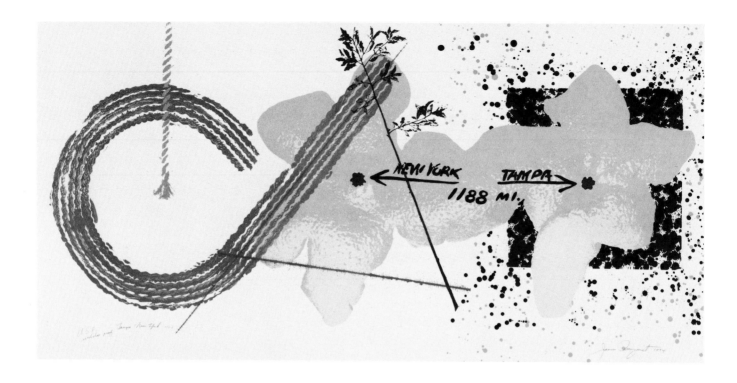

13. James Rosenquist, *Tampa–New York 1188*, 1975 (app. 226)

cents. . . . I had an old pick-up truck. It was no hassle, no traffic to deal with, no waits. You could just go right to it and get a lot done . . . a lot of different forays into the dark, a lot of different kinds of things instead of one kind of progression. . . . I'm very aware and anxious that they're different, and it continues that way." For Saff, Rosenquist's print entitled *Tampa–New York* (fig. 13) was an especially important symbol of Graphicstudio's coming of age. That Rosenquist had placed the two cities together suggested to Saff that "something of importance could be done in the provinces." This functioned as confirmation that an artist of considerable stature could find a confluence of significant artistic activity in Tampa.

The scale of Rosenquist's 1975 prints presented new technical challenges at every stage. These demands, particularly the factor of monumentality, excited Saff enormously, an excitement he intuitively shared (and shares) with Rosenquist and others, especially Rauschenberg. Watching paintings become increasingly expensive, Saff was eager to "provide works of art that, through scale as a logical extension, assuming all else was equal, would have more impact on the environment than portfolio art. . . . I like the idea of having the work occupy the same space as you, of being surrounded by something of artistic importance yet affordable. . . . Also, I've always had a greater inclination toward Masaccio than Jan van Eyck, to art in which the impact is somehow there immediately, in the first view, at a glance, as opposed to looking at the relationships of detail to detail and then moving away and seeing a totality—although I always admired *Multum in Parvo*."[20] Saff's interest in making large prints is among the factors that have placed Graphicstudio in the forefront of advanced printmaking during the past few decades, and this aspect of his concern was absolutely central to the workshop's efforts in the late 1980s. The sense of expansiveness generated during the Graphicstudio collaborations with Rosenquist suggests that the artist was having a wonderful time putting forward his ideas. In

Saff's mind, he was: "He knows what he's doing; he's not tentative; he surges ahead and sorts it out afterward; he tries more things than most other people."

Rosenquist's presence at Graphicstudio led to Saff's introduction to Robert Rauschenberg. Rauschenberg, by then based in Captiva, Florida, as well as New York, had come to visit Rosenquist in the hospital after his accident, and Saff, meeting Rauschenberg there, invited him to come out and see the shop. He responded enthusiastically, and came out the following day. After a few hours of showing the artist around, during which time Rauschenberg looked carefully at everything but made very few comments, Saff "gingerly," he says, asked if the artist might be interested in working there. As Saff recalls the visit, Rauschenberg replied, "God, I thought you'd never ask."

Rauschenberg's tenure at Graphicstudio was deferred because of Rosenquist's continued residency, but shortly after the workshop became available, Rauschenberg came to Tampa. His arrival prompted the next great shift in Saff's approach: "Bob changed the way I thought about everything. The whole nature of collaboration was clarified by him— what the potential was—just what the potential was in the material, or what kind of flexibility I'd have to have relative to doing projects was really I guess a product of working with him." Rauschenberg's residency in Captiva, where he was not able simply to walk around the corner and turn up art supplies or scavenge from the potentially rich refuse along New York City streets, had reinforced his notion that art could be made from anything. He began to turn increasingly toward ubiquitous materials: such as paper bags, cardboard boxes, and a kind of tar wrapping paper used in his first group of prints at Graphicstudio, the Made in Tampa series (cats. 64–67, app. 170, 173–177, 179, 181); newspapers used in his Crops series (cats. 70–72, app. 191, 192); and cheesecloth, a basic supply in lithography shops, used in his Airport series (cats. 73–75, app. 194, 197).

From the very start Rauschenberg's energy, authority, and excitement were an inspiration to everyone in the shop, and his interests provided new and fascinating challenges. His desire to find a way to have color

14. Dan Stack (left) and Charles Ringness unrolling an impression of Robert Rauschenberg's *Tampa 10* lithograph, 1972 (app. 179)

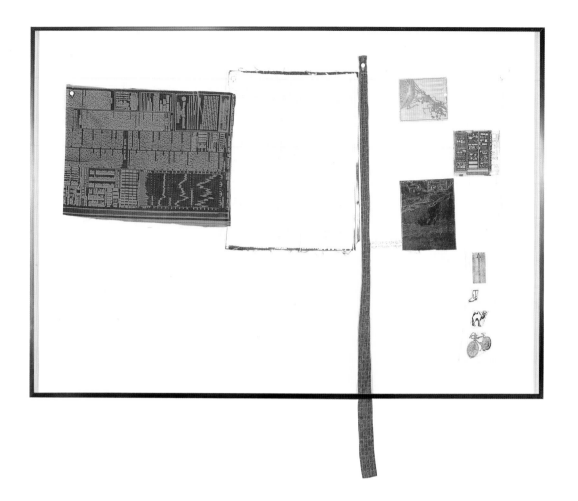

truly penetrate the paper, for example, to be a part of its fibers, led to experiments with blueprinting and sepiaprinting in the Made in Tampa suite, chemically impregnating the sheet with color rather than mechanically applying inks. For the Airport prints Rauschenberg wanted all of the colors to be printed in one run through the press. According to Saff, this idea developed from a conversation he and Rauschenberg had had about Picasso's color linoleum cuts, many of which were printed from a single block (although they generally were put through the press several times). For one of the prints, *Room Service* (fig. 15), several neckties that the artist had available for use in the composition act as a variable component.

Rauschenberg's Crops series had earlier challenged ideas of what an edition might be, just as using different neckties in *Room Service* had done. Eschewing the concept of slavish consistency, Rauschenberg wanted to ensure his creative participation not only in the conception of the images but in the process of printing as well. To that end, he laid out every one of the collages himself prior to its printing, and although the format is consistent for each impression in the edition, the details vary from print to print.[21]

Saff recalls that nothing seemed like a problem when working with Rauschenberg, not even when janitors irreverently discarded the cardboard boxes essential to the artist's Made in Tampa project (see cat. 64): "He saw the unexpected as opportunities rather than obstructions, ways to get you places you've never been before. What could be more interesting? . . . Everything was just a potential additional avenue in which he could investigate his art. . . . He had the ability to move with the problem at hand and somehow turn it around completely. If you were confronted by something, you solved it." Saff paraphrased Rauschenberg's attitude as: "If I can think of it, it can be done."

With Rauschenberg's Made in Tampa Clay Pieces, an outgrowth of his *Cardbirds* and *Cardbird Door* executed at Gemini G.E.L. in 1970–1971 (fig. 16), the artist went on to challenge Graphicstudio to move from making prints that included three-dimensional parts, like Rosenquist's *Mastaba*, to making three-dimensional works with printed elements. This thoroughly pleased Saff, as Rauschenberg's interest in sculpture reflected Saff's own first passion. One suspects as well that Saff was eager to outdo Gemini in the quest for new materials and methods for producing art in editions.

Just as the experience with James Rosenquist had drastically modified Saff's approach to scheduling artists in the shop, collaboration with Robert Rauschenberg helped to crystallize Saff's belief that the point and object of Graphicstudio—not merely a by-product of circumstances—was to be open to following opportunities, allowing one thing to lead to another. Saff had in fact been doing this, but he was then able to do so without worrying about attempting to hypothesize the future.

Jim Dine was one of the last artists to come to Graphicstudio during this phase who contributed significantly to the workshop's early character. Saff had long been interested in collaborating with him, and introductions were arranged by Paul Cornwall-Jones of Petersburg Press.

16. Robert Rauschenberg, *Cardbird Door,* 1970–1971, cardboard, paper, tape, wood, metal, offset lithography, screenprint, 80 x 30 x 11 (203.2 x 76.2 x 27.9), National Gallery of Art, Washington, Gift of Gemini G.E.L.

Conversations about art and gardening first took place in Paris. As ideas developed, Dine's projects turned out to be Graphicstudio's most technically ambitious to date, including two dramatic cast-aluminum multipart sculptures, *Metamorphosis of a Plant into a Fan* and *Tampa Tool Reliefs* (cats. 7, 9A–E), created both in Dine's studio in Putney, Vermont, and in Tampa. Also in Tampa, Dine completed a series of delicately drawn lithographs with screenprinted overgloss, called *The Plant Becomes a Fan* (cats. 6A–E). In an example of minimal collaboration, printers Charles Ringness and Paul Clinton delivered the lithographic plates for the prints to the artist, who was with his family at a hotel in Clearwater, and picked them up after the drawings were completed, a collaboration amusingly described by the two printers as lasting a total of three minutes.[22] At about the same time, Dine worked on two images of his signature *Bathrobe*, one of which was Graphicstudio's first woodcut (cat. 8), executed in combination with lithography and printed in thirteen colors.

The last artist Saff brought to Graphicstudio during this period was photographer Lee Friedlander, who had recently collaborated with Dine on a portfolio entitled *Photographs and Etchings*. Friedlander awakened a new interest in Saff, who had not previously considered a photographic project for the workshop. It turned out to be a prescient move, given the attention devoted to photography during Graphicstudio's second phase.

The Workshop's Operations

Graphicstudio started with one lithographic press in a classroom described by Philip Pearlstein as a raw, cement-block space. Saff, hardly one to slow down, quickly became impatient to expand, especially given Graphicstudio's early successes. Aware that Syracuse China Company, which had already lent the workshop some lithographic stones, had a great cache of equipment for sale, Saff and Florida Center for the Arts

17. Charles Ringness (left) with assistant Dan Stack in the first Graphicstudio workshop, c. 1971

director James Camp took a group of the prints already completed at the workshop by Pearlstein, Hinman, Smith, and Yunkers, and traveled north to explore the possibility of acquiring the equipment.

Two motorized flatbed lithographic presses were available, as were a Fuchs and Lang handpress, beautiful gray lithographic stones (the best quality), and stone racks. To their great good fortune, the vice president with whom they met, Richard Bessie, was sympathetic to art, even to the point of being on the board of the Everson Museum of Art, Syracuse. Bessie was apparently quite impressed with the work that had been accomplished at Graphicstudio and became convinced that a donation would be possible, rather than the sale that was the starting point for discussion. He undoubtedly saw that it would make a major contribution toward building an important workshop. In addition to the heavy equipment, which Saff and several graduate students soon drove from Syracuse to Florida—very slowly in an overloaded truck whose tires blew out on the New Jersey Turnpike—Graphicstudio also acquired miscellaneous items for which particular uses were unimagined at the time: the decal paper that eventually showed up in some of Rauschenberg's Made in Tampa Clay Pieces, for example.

Not all of the equipment was equally successful. Although Serge Lozingot, the great French printer with expertise in the use of flatbed presses, was brought from California to Graphicstudio to check the presses and explain their distinctive uses, motorized presses were not fully accepted by the younger, Tamarind-trained printers. These presses were eventually disposed of, which is unfortunate, for as printers became more experienced and art developed new traditions, such presses became exceedingly desirable.

With all of the new equipment, it became essential to expand Graphicstudio's space. By breaking through one of the studio walls, a second classroom was added, doubling the workshop's square footage. But as further equipment was acquired and projects increased in size, off-campus space was required as well: thus the workshop added what came to be known as the Florida Avenue studio north of town as well as another studio to the south. A few projects were even developed elsewhere, including Rauschenberg's Airport suite, conceived and printed at the artist's Captiva studio, and the beginning stages of Dine's *Metamorphosis of a Plant into a Fan* and *Tampa Tool Reliefs*, prepared in his Vermont studio.

For the most part, artists stayed at a Holiday Inn near the U.S.F. campus while they were in Tampa. Some rented cars, some were shuttled back and forth by Saff. Editions were divided between the artist and the workshop, with the number of impressions reaching as high as one hundred, plus proofs, although most editions were somewhat smaller. Each impression is stamped with the workshop sunburst, and often with the printer's blindstamp as well.

Anthony Stoeveken was Graphicstudio's first printer, and he stayed for about a year. Then Theo Wujcik came on board, along with Charles Ringness, who served as shop manager until the studio closed in 1976. Paul Clinton and Julio Juristo were added later, and Wujcik became a member of the art department faculty. Several other printers were on the staff for brief periods. Michelle Juristo was Graphicstudio's curator from 1971 to 1976, and faculty members Alan Eaker and Oscar Bailey were active participants as well. Editions were completed directly after each artist's visit, with students and other assistants taking turns on various projects as needed.[23]

18. Frank Rampolla, *Standing Man,* 1970
(app. 169)

Graphicstudio's role in the university community as well as the larger Tampa community was then, and remains, difficult to define. In some respects the workshop more readily caught the attention of the national art community, and in a 1973 issue of *Art in America*, art historian and critic Diane Kelder wrote that "print studios have been at the forefront of the decentralization of the New York art world, and Graphicstudio is surely one of the country's most progressive and open opportunities for local and big-name artists to work together in a situation of mutual benefit and respect."[24] Such national visibility would presumably have encouraged art students to apply to U.S.F. In 1980, at the start of the workshop's second phase, one Tampa reporter applauded the effort "to revive Graphicstudio, an operation that had brought nationwide fame to the University."[25]

The interaction of Graphicstudio artists with students, faculty, and the rest of the art community varied according to individual personalities. Several students have gone on to become assistants to some of the artists—Dan Stack working with James Rosenquist, and Peter Wirth with Robert Rauschenberg, for example. Still others rejoined Graphicstudio during its second phase or became printers elsewhere—for example, Mark Stock at Gemini G.E.L. Many have become independent artists as well. It seems likely that Graphicstudio played a considerable role in shaping the professionalism of its alumni, and the diversity of the images produced in the workshop would have served as permission to follow many different paths. Susie Hennessy has said that even as an undergraduate in the literature department at U.S.F., the excitement surrounding Graphicstudio drew her interests in that direction. By the time she entered the art department, the workshop had closed, but its reputation lingered, as did the university's strong commitment to prints and drawings. This led her to pursue studies in those areas, and she later became the shop manager for the revived Graphicstudio.[26]

Clearly, the university art collection was enhanced by donations of the Graphicstudio publications, and the university's circulation of the collection is ongoing. Sometimes there were special on-campus exhibitions for major projects as they were finished.[27] Graphicstudio was also the catalyst for other exhibitions at the university: in 1973 *Collaboration: Artist, Master Printer—Print*, was drawn from the collections of three Graphicstudio printers—Charles Ringness, Paul Clinton, and Julio Juristo—and included pieces they had printed at other workshops.[28] Private collections were begun in the Tampa area by workshop subscribers, and these collections have since been extended to include considerably more than the Graphicstudio publications.[29] Extensive coverage in the Tampa and St. Petersburg newspapers also suggests that Graphicstudio served to stimulate broader interest in the arts throughout the community.

In spite of all these successes, it was evident to Saff by 1974 that Graphicstudio was in danger of closing. In an article written for the fall issue of the *Art Journal* that year, featuring on its cover Rauschenberg's *Tampa Clay Piece 5* (cat. 69), Saff intimated that although he was eager to make available to younger artists the extensive collaborative ability of Graphicstudio's personnel, he was concerned that artists who were not yet well known might be less of a draw than "key names" for the subscription support on which the workshop depended. He went on to identify other problems he faced as Graphicstudio's director: "Perhaps most formidable of all is faculty ambivalence and equivocation with regard to continued support. It is difficult for an individual who may lose his teaching position because of low departmental productivity to support an area of excellence which does not directly aid in the production of student credit hours, which in turn generate budget dollars and faculty positions for his department. As positions decline, developing a priority for programs will evoke substantive discussion. These facts added to growing material and labor costs create what will perhaps be in the near future an insurmountable obstacle. One hope of the future is for a change in the budgetary system but, more realistically, additional aid will have to be sought through grants, individual donations, and, as has happened in recent projects, gallery and publisher support."[30]

Saff presented a grim picture. One suspects that many university administrators never fully appreciated the educational value of the Graphicstudio program, so that its needs might predictably be called into question at a time of greater budget restrictions. There may also have been growing resentment among some of the art department faculty. Many of them, all serious artists, executed only a single print at the workshop—Saff speaks of the lithograph by Frank Rampolla (fig. 18) as one he particularly admired. The faculty may well have thought their own work deserved more attention in Graphicstudio's publication program. They may also have felt they should have some say in determining which artists would be invited to Tampa and how they might interact with the students. Student disaffection may also have increased at a time when "relevance" was becoming more important and Graphicstudio was probably seen as "elitist."

The problem of funding was pervasive, however, not only for Graphicstudio, but for education generally at a statewide level. And when Saff stepped down as dean of the College of Fine Arts (concurrent with the closing down of the workshop's first phase), he no longer had as much influence in the allocation of funds.

The closing of Graphicstudio was gradual, not abrupt, with obligations to subscribers, commitments to artists, and contracts with printers all necessarily juggled. As prints were finished and contracts expired, the phasing out ended with a program of documentation in the workshop's final months. The Graphicstudio equipment was then turned over to the university's art department, which had in fact been the recipient of various valuable items throughout the workshop's tenure.

A great event in the life of the workshop, ironically occurring after its initial demise, was a major exhibition at the Brooklyn Museum in 1978. Accompanied by a catalogue raisonné of the prints that had been produced at Graphicstudio, the text of its introductory essay closed with Rauschenberg's comments on the workshop's fate: "It killed itself. We should have pretended that we weren't so interested in it. We should have done worse work. All the artists who came there—we should have gotten them aside and said, 'look, if you really do a good job here, this place is going to fold.'"[31] Another great irony following the Brooklyn exhibition was the designation of the then-closed workshop as a "program of distinction" within the state university system.

A Second Flowering

In 1980 Graphicstudio slowly rose like a phoenix from what might have been thought its ashes, responding to current university needs and desires, and with initial support from funds given by the Florida legislature

19. Alice Aycock, *Collected Ghost Stories from the Workhouse*, 1981, glass, steel, galvanized metal and wood sculpture

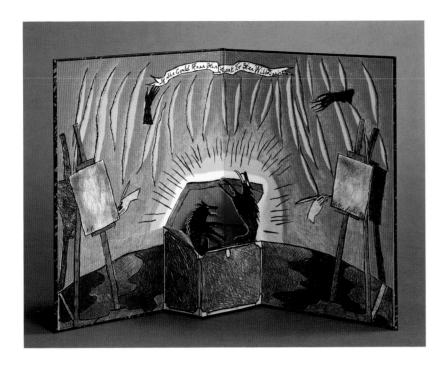

20. Hollis Sigler, *If She Could Free Her Heart to Her Wildest Desires*, 1982 (app. 243)

under its Quality Improvement Program, perhaps as a result of Graphicstudio's earlier status as a program of distinction. Indeed, even after the workshop had shut down, Graphicstudio continued to be associated with the university, a point that must have become clear to the new university president, John Lott Brown, as he traveled around the country, and to Gregory O'Brien, then the university provost. O'Brien, in fact, according to Saff, became one of the staunchest supporters of the second phase of Graphicstudio as it evolved, with the president's strong support of his efforts.

The new shop was at first run according to very different principles than the original shop had been; therefore, at Saff's request, it was temporarily called Graphicstudio II to distinguish it from the earlier phase. A double sunburst blindstamp identifies works made during this period.[32] The conception of what one writer called "son of Graphicstudio" was stimulated by an outdoor sculpture project for the U.S.F. campus by Alice Aycock (fig. 19).[33] Soon after the sculpture was underway, a lithograph project was initiated as well (it became an etching, cat. 33), presumably as a way to generate funds for the sculpture's completion. Both works were called *Collected Ghost Stories from the Workhouse*, but the sculpture, undertaken by Aycock with assistance from students and faculty alike, is unfortunately no longer standing.

Because Graphicstudio had given all its printmaking equipment to the university art department a few years before, Graphicstudio II functioned only as a publisher at first, subcontracting the work out to private printers as necessary. Aycock's etching was printed at Palm Press by Saff's former student, Betty Ann Lenahan; Hollis Sigler's lithograph, *If She Could Free Her Heart to Her Wildest Desires* (fig. 20), was printed at Topaz Press by Julio Juristo.[34]

At the outset of the revival of Graphicstudio, Saff had been asked to be part of the as-yet-only-loosely-defined undertaking, but he kept some distance, at least at first. Although he apparently maintained an advisory status, his role is difficult to pin down between 1980 and 1985, the year he resumed the position of director. Saff's technical expertise had been in demand from the start, with the Aycock etching project. Between Saff's terms as director, however, he seems not to have been involved with some projects: the Sigler lithograph, and works by Michael Glier and Miriam Schapiro (cats. 43A–E, 49), for example. Yet sometimes his role was more active: in the projects with Jim Dine and Robert Mapplethorpe, for example (cats. 6–13, app. 59, 60, 62; and cat. 45, app. 144–147). Evidence of this is seen in the fact that Saff's name appears on some documentation sheets in an editorial or collaborative capacity, whereas on others it does not.

Graphicstudio II was initially directed jointly by the chair of the art department, painter George Pappas, and the director of the university's Art Gallery, Margaret Miller. Pappas was described in a 1980 article by Charles Benbow as saying that the Aycock project was "a pilot project for Graphicstudio II . . . [and that] the new program will probably emphasize sculpture, will involve more students in the processes and will result again in editions of 'multiples' (maybe not always graphics). It will engage the artists with the academic program as teachers and will provide exhibitions and documentations for the artists." Miller, in another article, had set out their intentions to invite one sculptor and three printmakers to Graphicstudio each year, to have less isolation of the creative process than was perceived in the original Graphicstudio, and to have artists-in-residence at the workshop also involved in teaching and major exhibitions on campus. The plan also called for more students to be involved in producing the art.[35]

In addition to the Aycock sculpture, a collaboration with Robert Morris was proposed about this time though never brought to completion.[36] In fact, the Hollis Sigler lithograph appears to have been the only other work completed before the Graphicstudio directorship again changed hands, when a new department chair, photography professor David Yager, took over. Yager soon became the program's sole director, while Miller continued to coordinate exhibitions and other related events. Saff took an increasingly active role as consultant. Yager has described a productive relationship: "I loved working with Don; we had a great relationship, so as much as I could get him to work on things, I did. . . . It's always nice to have a sounding board."[37] Distinctive aspects of Yager's directorship are additional collaborations with women artists, with artists of a younger generation, and with photographers. As he described his plan, "there was a tradition established at Graphicstudio, and I wanted to maintain a certain amount of that tradition and broaden that tradition."

The first undertaking during Yager's directorship was Robert Rauschenberg's *Chinese Summerhall* (cat. 76), a hundred-foot-long color photograph that Saff had spurred the artist to do during their trip to China with Gemini in 1982. The only workshop staff at this time apart from Yager was George Holzer, who devoted several months to working with Rauschenberg to coordinate and print the monumental photographic scroll (and related projects), copublished with Gemini G.E.L. (app. 199–204). Along with the Hasselblad camera purchased for Rauschenberg's use, Graphicstudio acquired a color processor. Additional work space outside the art department complex became essential during production and was retained after the project was completed. In fact, Saff's own Tampa studio ("Nebraska Avenue") became essentially a Graphicstudio annex.

The color processing equipment was later put to further use by photographer Oscar Bailey, who had been the mainstay of photographic work during Graphicstudio's early years. At the time of Bailey's retirement from teaching at U.S.F., Graphicstudio celebrated his great contribution to its publications by giving him special film for his Cirkut camera and publishing four of his Cirkut photographs, among his first in color. It was the one instance when Graphicstudio II resurrected the earlier practice of publishing examples of work by the university faculty.

It was clear, however, that if Graphicstudio II was to operate seriously, it needed even more space, specifically a home of its own. Quite a picturesque lodging was obtained: an unused observatory adjacent to a golf course at the edge of the university campus. Among the most distinctive characteristics of the building was its roll-back roof. According to Deli Sacilotto, who later joined the staff, "the observatory was great. The whole idea was fascinating. Not entirely practical—you opened the roof, and it could be windy. Sometimes bugs would come in. Or the sun would shine directly on certain things, like the paper would dry very quickly. But it was great on certain days when you could open it up and it wasn't that windy. It was fantastic."[38]

On Saff's recommendation, Yager formally hired Susie Hennessy, who had coordinated the Aycock project, to be shop manager in 1982, a position she stayed in for about a year, returning again in 1985 when Saff resumed the directorship. Her first charge was to contact Jim Dine and invite him to return to Tampa to work at Graphicstudio II. He agreed to a visit a few months from that time, in December 1982. Hennessy's next charge was to see that Dine would have printers with whom to work and a shop that was fully equipped to meet his needs.

Graphicstudio reclaimed some of the equipment it had turned over to the art department a few years earlier. Saff was again tapped for advice concerning other matters. He had recently been working with Gemini as a planning consultant for their new etching shop. Through him, Hennessy was in touch with Patrick Foy and Doris Simmelink, formerly with Crown Point Press in San Francisco, the preeminent workshop for inta-

21. Jim Dine applying acid directly to the plates for *The Heart and the Wall* (cat. 11), with Susie Hennessy and Stephen Thomas behind him, December 1982

22. Philip Pearlstein working on *View of Rome* (cat. 4) in the Graphicstudio observatory, 1986

glio printing in the United States, but at that time working at Gemini G.E.L., where Hennessy met with them.[39] Foy agreed to oversee the fabrication in Southern California of a large aquatint box and hot plate as well as special sinks capable of handling large etching plates. Simmelink put Hennessy in contact with her network of printers, one of whom, Steven Thomas, was able to take on a temporary job in Tampa.[40] When the aquatint box, hot plate, and sinks were ready to travel across the country, Thomas hired a truck, drove east to Tampa, and set up the shop just in time for Dine's arrival.

Three prints resulted from this session: *Swaying in the Florida Night*, the monumental, four-part *The Heart and the Wall* (cats. 10, 11), and *The Robe Goes to Town* in which the etched bathrobe is combined with a screenprinted border based on a flowered fabric (app. 62). The open roof of the observatory turned out to be a splendid asset, allowing for greater ventilation in the studio when Dine was using a mop to swab undiluted nitric acid onto the four large copperplates for *The Heart and the Wall* (fig. 21), an activity that created considerable noxious fumes. Dine's projects suggest some idea of the potential complexity of coordinating these collaborations. Once the plates for the three works were completed in Tampa, they were printed at various points around the country: *The Heart and the Wall* was completed in Tampa by Thomas, working with Susan McDonough, another former U.S.F. student of Saff's; the etching plate for *The Robe Goes to Town* was shipped to the West Coast to be printed by Thomas after his return, but the screenprinting and assembling of the two parts was carried out in Tampa; and *Swaying in the Florida Night*, after proofing by Saff, was sent off to Boston to be printed by Robert Townsend.

Dine was followed at Graphicstudio a few months later by Vito Acconci. About this time Townsend essentially took on the etching responsibilities at Graphicstudio. He traveled from Boston to Tampa to oversee the proofing for several projects, including Acconci's *Building-Blocks for a Doorway* (cat. 32) as well as his *End Mask, People Mask,* and *Red Mask* (app. 1–3), generally taking the plates back to his New England studio to print the editions.

The year 1984 was quite busy at Graphicstudio. Collaborations with Arakawa, Robert Fichter, Robert Gordy, and Miriam Schapiro were all engaged, with Townsend coming to Tampa as necessary to proof the etching projects and Julio Juristo back on the staff for work in lithography. Schapiro's *Children of Paradise* (cat. 49) is certainly among the works Graphicstudio produced that entailed the maximum student participation, as Margaret Miller earlier had envisioned, with the collage elements applied in a more or less assembly-line manner as the print was passed from one participant to another. Fichter's photographs (cats. 39–41, app. 88–92), by contrast, involved virtually no activity at Graphicstudio: the transparencies were selected by Yager and Fichter in the artist's Tallahassee studio and sent off to a cibachrome processor in Minnesota for developing. Fichter did work on prints in-house at Graphicstudio, completing three of them (app. 83, 87, 93). The artist also enjoyed the attention of a university exhibition.[41]

The following year, in another long-distance relationship, Graphicstudio II and 724 Prints in New York copublished Philip Pearlstein's *Models with Mirror* (cat. 3), completed in New York over a period of several years and coordinated by Graphicstudio only during the work's final stages. This enterprise led to collaboration on Pearlstein's delicate aquatint *View of Rome* (cat. 4), the technical preparation being accomplished in Tampa (fig. 22).

It became clear during this period that Graphicstudio needed a full-time, in-house etching printer. Attention was fractured in too many ways, for example, when Arakawa's plates for *The Sharing of Nameless* (cats. 20, 21) had to be sent for the edition printing to Simmelink/Sukimoto Editions, an etching workshop set up in Marina Del Rey, California, by Doris Simmelink and Chris Sukimoto, who had left Gemini. Yager's own expertise being more specifically in photography, in 1984 Saff recommended his long-time friend and master printer Deli Sacilotto, who took on the etching duties of Graphicstudio II and eventually became the workshop's technical director in 1985 when Saff again took over the helm. Sacilotto brought a host of new possibilities to the shop. Exceedingly knowledgeable in the history of prints, especially the history of early lithography, Sacilotto had written a most useful book on photographic printmaking processes and was highly respected for his expertise in the demanding process of gravure. Most significant for Graphicstudio's specific needs at the time, he had a longstanding reputation as a gifted printer not only of lithographs, the first technique he had mastered, but of etchings as well; and during his many years in New York he had come to know a wide range of artists and to have forged other useful professional associations.

Among Sacilotto's early undertakings was the completion of Acconci's *Building-Blocks for a Doorway*, which had been languishing although almost finished. Other early projects were the first group of three fingerprint gravure portraits by Chuck Close, all entitled *Georgia* (app. 39–41), and the set of five gravures by Michael Glier in the Men at Home series (cats. 43A–E). Both Close and Glier seem to have taken naturally to the gravure process. Glier's preliminary drawings on mylar were rich in their tonal range, taking advantage of the gravure process' potential to translate a drawing's detail with extraordinary fidelity. He could also rework the plates after examining proofs, enhancing the images with drypoint and roulette. Close, too, by varying the quality of the impression of his thumbprint, achieved portraits that are splendidly varied in their tonal richness.

Sacilotto's New York connections were tapped as rapidly as was his technical expertise. Shortly before he had been approached by Saff about shifting his base to Florida, he had copublished with the Barbara Gladstone Gallery a portfolio of ten flower prints in photogravure by Robert Mapplethorpe, an artist with whom Yager had been eager to work. Yager and Saff visited Mapplethorpe's studio, at which time the artist agreed with great enthusiasm to undertake a series of figure prints (cat. 45, app. 144–147) because of Sacilotto's presence at the shop. Mapplethorpe warmly referred to Sacilotto as "the mad scientist," according to Saff. These figures were later followed by the larger format flowers (cats. 46–48, app. 148, 149, 152, 154), the first of which was the *Tampa Orchid*, an image shot in Yager's studio. Obviously because of Sacilotto's special expertise and his penchant to experiment, gravure became an integral part of the Graphicstudio II menu. Following Mapplethorpe's flower prints, another photogravure project was pursued with Joel-Peter Witkin, an artist about whom Yager had had conversations with Mapplethorpe. Witkin completed seven photogravure plates, all of which were issued in proof impressions only (cats. 50–52, app. 248, 249, 252, 253); none were formally published.

David Yager's tenure as department chair and director of Graphicstudio ended in 1985, and responsibilities for the department and the workshop were divided. Alan Eaker took over the departmental chairmanship, and Don Saff took over the directorship of Graphicstudio. The battles to secure funding that had plagued Saff's earlier tenure continued; and the need to increase the workshop's visibility in the community was always on his mind. But there were differences between these later years and his experience of the early 1970s. During the first phase of Graphicstudio, Saff had had so many administrative duties that he was only able to be involved with Graphicstudio projects sporadically—at the outset, at various points in the working process, and again at the end. Starting in 1985, however, Saff's full-time work as director was incredibly exciting and time consuming, even given such other responsibilities as the coordination of Rauschenberg's ROCI exhibition program.

Almost immediately Saff began acquiring additional space for the workshop, adding equipment, and forming a large, imaginative, expert staff on-campus. In addition, within months of his resuming the directorship, Graphicstudio became a separate administrative entity from the art department, with responsibility directly to the university provost.[42] Saff's program was an ambitious one, and the work produced during his second term as director became increasingly large and complex. The idea of the workshop as a research program within the university was much more dramatically at the core of the projects undertaken, and by early 1988 the workshop's letterhead featured "Institute for Research in Art" above and in larger type than "Graphicstudio." Saff's own penchant for tinkering, finding new ways of using traditional materials, or using new materials to establish new traditions, led him in a variety of directions. He was able, then, to provide greater leadership for technical experimentation.[43] Moreover, the artists with whom Graphicstudio worked both inspired the experimentation and engaged in the dialogues Saff started, the needs of their art always playing the central role in the workshop's investigations and in the way its program developed.

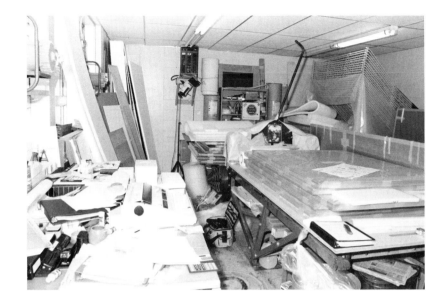

23. The lithography space in the observatory, shared by curating, photography, and the studio manager, 1987

24. The cramped curating area in the observatory, showing prints stacked along the wall at left waiting to be shipped and paper storage shelves at right. The lithography studio may be glimpsed through the door at the far left, 1987

When Jim Dine returned to Graphicstudio in 1985, he incorporated the gravure method into his images, including *Yellowheart and a Devil* (cat. 12), using drawings on mylar as a starting point for copperplates, which he then considerably reworked using the power tools that he has so masterfully exploited.[44] Dine's use of the gravure process at so large a scale, the largest Sacilotto had ever undertaken with an artist, eventually demanded that a separate workshop be set up to process them. Saff once again converted what had been his own Nebraska Avenue studio, off-campus about two miles from the observatory, into another Graphic-studio printmaking shop, where Dine's large gravure plates were processed (experiments with screenprinting and other techniques later took place there as well). Saff has described Dine's approach to his projects: "He would come and work intensely—working for about three or four hours, during which time he did more than most people would do in a full day of work. . . . There was so much work before he arrived—he had thought it out and talked it out and in many cases drawn it out."

Even if there had been no special demands such as those the large Dine plates presented, the observatory would have been cramped. Lithography was crammed into the smaller of two rooms (measuring about 15-by-20 feet), its strong point being that it was air-conditioned, which allowed for the temperature and humidity control that that process requires. Sharing that space was a desk that was called the Graphicstudio office. It served as a storage area as well. The etching shop was set up in the larger and more romantic of the spaces, the one with the roll-back roof and a large block of concrete at the center of the room on which a telescope had once been assembled. In the building's original entryway, a variety of curatorial functions took place, including the review of editions for consistency, storage of finished prints, and shipment of works out to artists and subscribers. Commodious the space was not. Eventually a storage crate was suspended from the ceiling, and standing under it caused many visitors (and probably staff as well) to hold their breath for fear the crate might fall at any moment.

Finally, there simply was no more room, so in 1988 the workshop relocated once again, this time to a two-story industrial building close to campus. This new space was essential for Roy Lichtenstein's Brushstroke Figures (cats. 81–83, app. 134, 135, 137–139), which required a controlled environment for printing with wax. Offices were segregated from printing shops, and the curatorial area was able, at last, to accommodate the increasingly large prints that the artists were producing. Before moving in, however, everyone on the staff pitched in to transform the raw space into something more suitable for their needs. Once settled, they continued to customize the shop, developing special facilities for drying printed editions, for example. The observatory was retained as well and was devoted in its entirety to sculpture editions that, like the prints, were becoming larger and more complex. In fact, by the time Saff stepped down again in 1990, yet another building had been secured for the production of Nancy Grave's multimedia sculpture, *Canoptic Legerdemain* (cat. 84).

The staff that Saff assembled was impressive. In addition to Sacilotto (who developed a course about Graphicstudio for students in the U.S.F. art department), he hired Patrick Foy to work in etching. Foy had by then left Gemini and now came to run the shop he had earlier helped equip and organize. Working with Foy was Greg Burnet. The lithography shop was run by Alan Holoubek, another former Gemini printer; and with him was Tom Pruitt, a Tamarind master printer. Marcia Brown, another Tamarind master printer, worked as a curator under head curator Michael Harrigan, also formerly on Gemini's staff. Having curatorial staff with training in printing was a boon: they could better understand the demands and effects of the processes involved. George Holzer continued as resident photographer and jack-of-all-trades during these years, with primary responsibility for the photographic aspects of particular prints and for the documentation of workshop activities through still photography and videotape. As edition sculpture took on increasing importance, a number of objects fabricators were hired: Ken Elliott and Nick Conroy, both former U.S.F. students, oversaw this part of the Graphicstudio operation. They also conducted various technical experiments—for example, working to develop the possibilities for

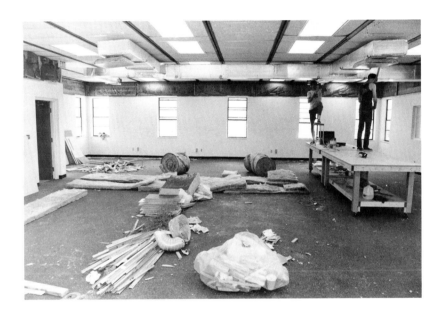

26. Alan Holoubek (left) and Greg Burnet modify the ceiling in the second-floor lithography workshop at the new Graphicstudio workshop, May 1988

27. Riggers moving the etching presses into the first floor of the new Graphicstudio workshop, May 1988

three-dimensional brushstrokes in glass, marble, and laminated wood that led to the curved wooden brushstrokes that form Roy Lichtenstein's *Brushstroke Chair* and *Brushstroke Ottoman* (cat. 80). Other technical staff, including Eric Vontillius, worked for shorter periods of time in a wide variety of roles. Susie Hennessy, who had resigned as shop manager to pursue her own work as an artist, was cajoled into returning to that position. And Brenda Woodard coordinated both Graphicstudio, which was no longer called Graphicstudio II, and the various ROCI projects. Woodard later became assistant director of Graphicstudio.

Overall, the workshop staff was excited about their abilities, individually and as a group, to contribute new ideas as part of the team. As Saff described them, "the wheels were always turning, looking for a new approach, doing something different." They were unacademic, perhaps antiacademic or antibureaucratic in their aspirations, and for the most part, unlike the earlier group of Graphicstudio printers who often went on to teach, this new group tended to move from workshop to workshop.

During Saff's second directorshop he was eager both to work with artists who had already produced ambitious and successful pieces at Graphicstudio and also to extend invitations to new faces as well. Among those returning during this period were Chuck Close, Jim Dine, Robert Mapplethorpe, Philip Pearlstein, Robert Rauschenberg, and Jim Rosenquist. Artists who came to the Florida workshop for the first time included Sandro Chia, Nancy Graves, Alfred Leslie, and Roy Lichtenstein.[45]

Although research had always been the mission of Graphicstudio, it was probably not until 1985 that this goal was truly at the center of the

28. The edition of Sandro Chia's *Father and Son Song* (cat. 79) hanging to dry in the observatory, November 1987

29. Eric Vontillius placing Roy Lichtenstein's newly screened waxtype prints on specially built curing racks in the Graphicstudio workshop, October 1988

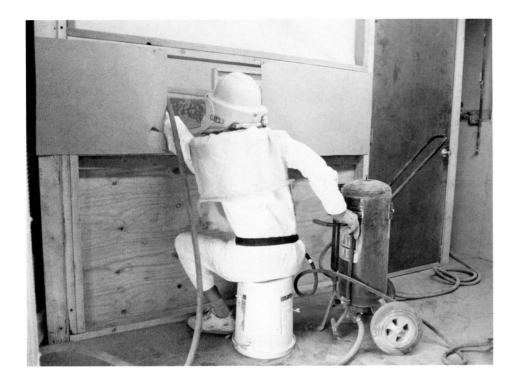

30. Tom Pruitt sandblasting a woodblock, September 1982

workshop's activities. Since that time staff research has often precipitated projects as well as responding to them. Earlier, Rauschenberg's desire to have clay look like cardboard and Dine's desire to have the forms of a plant metamorphose into the forms of a fan challenged workshop staff to solve particular problems by inventing procedures. By contrast, Graphicstudio's development of a photographic-based sandblasting method that could achieve meticulous detail in a woodblock image (fig. 30) actually led Philip Pearlstein to create his ten-foot-wide *Jerusalem, Kidron Valley* (see technical note at the end of this catalogue). The process was an outgrowth of blasting techniques used for the Vietnam Memorial in Washington, which were first shown to Saff by Luke Century, who had developed the method and had tried it on stone and glass, but not on wood. Graphicstudio essentially fine-tuned the technique in-house to meet its own specific needs.

Another technical experiment enabled workshop staff to present Roy Lichtenstein with a variety of material samples in two and three dimensions (fig. 31), which stimulated the artist to undertake the series of Brushstroke Figure heads employing screenprinted waxtype (see technical note) and the *Brushstroke Chair* and *Brushstroke Ottoman*. It was not uncommon, in fact, for Saff to encourage the development of processes with the interests of specific artists in mind. A less radical development during this period was the large-scale use of silk collé, first for Chuck Close's group of direct gravure portraits, then for Robert Mapplethorpe's flower pieces.

Size was an issue in almost all of the projects of this period in Graphicstudio's history, and each work seemed to prompt a new way of doing something. For Alfred Leslie's *Folded Constance Pregnant*, the eight-foot-high image was placed on three copperplates aligned one above the other and printed on a sheet of folded paper in a method developed specifically for that project (see cat. 44). Folded sheets were used again later for Jim Rosenquist's two extraordinary out-sized aquatints, *Welcome to*

31. Nick Conroy making a marble brushstroke sample for presentation to Roy Lichtenstein, October 1986

32. James Rosenquist, *Flowers and Females*, 1986 (app. 229)

the *Water Planet* and *The Prickly Dark* (cats. 62, 63), the former of which Saff described, commenting on Rosenquist's consummate skill, as "[going] from beginning to end, step by step, from an empty plate to a full plate without hesitation."

Rosenquist's prints called for other ways to achieve the sort of grandeur the artist seeks in his paintings as well as in his graphic work. For several Graphicstudio prints of the late 1980s, including *Flowers and Females* (fig. 32; see also cats. 58–60), the artist completed colorful monoprint fields, soft in character, and then had sharply defined lithographic elements collaged to them in order to work on sheets larger than the presses could carry. Indeed, pressing the scale issue even further, a thirty-five-foot-long unique piece, part painting and part collage print, was under discussion in 1989 but was dropped when Saff left the workshop.[46] Saff described working with Rosenquist by noting that basically all of the discussion about a project takes place before anything is started; once the artist sets to work, "then you get out of the way."

Jim Dine is not an artist who generally tends toward heroic scale, but more toward something the width of his outstretched arms and as tall as his own height. Nevertheless, he completed his largest print to date at Graphicstudio during this period: his six-and-a-half-foot-tall *Youth and the Maiden* (cat. 14). Printing from blocks that were found objects, hand-carved, or cut by the newly developed heliorelief process, and combining these with etching and hand-painting, Dine achieved a richness and diversity of surface characteristic of his paintings and drawings as well. The size of this three-part print enhances the mythic quality of its imagery. Dine's Graphicstudio prints from this period, as a group, are inventive in their combinations of media, with many works using several etching processes along with woodcut and hand-painting (fig. 33). The very nature of his combinations of processes sets a challenge to his printers, who must concern themselves, for example, with registration problems that come from dampening and drying papers as well as the varying pressures that different types of printing elements demand. For

33. Jim Dine hand-coloring a unique impression of *Yellowheart and a Devil* (cat. 12), December 1985

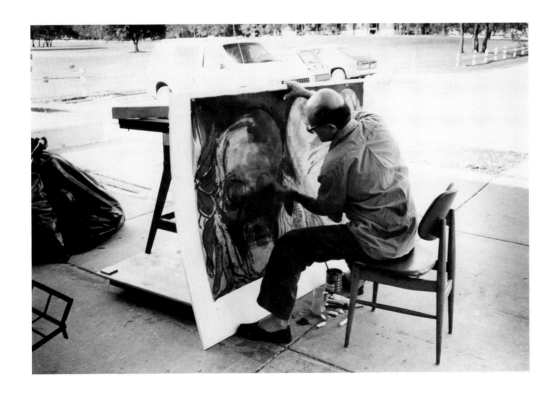

34. Sandro Chia positioning the wood elements for the frame of *Father and Son Song* (cat. 79), May 1987

an artist such as Dine, however, whose work as a whole is so tactile, the diverse surfaces produced by different printing processes is frequently a central component of his aesthetic, and the printer's task is to help achieve the essential mix.

Another sort of mix was sought by Roy Lichtenstein, one of the last names to be added to the Graphicstudio roster during Don Saff's tenure. His eight Brushstroke Figures (mixed-media heads and *Nude*) all incorporate waxtype, screenprinting, lithography, and woodcut to portray the artist's brushstroke imagery. The waxtype idea derived from Saff's interest in Jasper Johns' use of encaustic as a painting medium, and over a period of several months the Graphicstudio staff had been testing the possibilities of printing with wax.[47] For Lichtenstein, always intrigued by opportunities to explore new surfaces, the screenprinted wax provided a tantalizing palette. He determined that some strokes were to be left as printed, with the screen texture evident, while others were to be "burned in" for a smoother surface and burnished to a high sheen. These two distinct waxtype qualities were then enhanced by the use of traditional screenprinting, woodcut, and lithography. Like all of the artists who have worked at Graphicstudio, Lichtenstein had the run of the shop and the choice of working in two or three dimensions or both. In addition to his complex of prints, Lichtenstein also undertook both painted wood and painted bronze versions of *Brushstroke Chair* and *Brushstroke Ottoman*, the former edition fabricated under Graphicstudio's auspices in Vermont, the latter in Walla Walla, Washington, further expanding Graphicstudio's wide network of activity.

Sandro Chia's *Father and Son Song* was produced at Graphicstudio and provided a chance for the object makers on staff to coordinate with printers and complete a work that is part print/part sculpture, with the elements in each reflecting those in the other (fig. 34). Taking advantage of the full range of skills available in Tampa, Chia also completed a suite of hand-colored prints entitled *Surprising Novel* (app. 32–38), and a bas-relief scupture, *Flowers Fight* (app. 31), which employed the helio-relief process as an end in itself rather than to make blocks for printing. This must have delighted Saff, who earlier had felt "the block was as nice as its potential for a print."

Lichtenstein's and Chia's projects suggest the important focus of Graphicstudio at the time on developing sculpture editions. The Rauschenberg Overseas Culture Interchange exhibition (ROCI) provided another strong impetus in this direction. Traveling to several countries around the world over a period of years, with a new body of work created in each country visited, ROCI was to have Graphicstudio complete a sculpture edition for each venue. *Fifth Force* was the first, incorporating references to the leaning tower of Pisa, Galileo, and an article about a fifth force in the universe in accordance with which objects of dissimilar mass if dropped in a vacuum would fall at different rates. As it turned out, ROCI never did make a stop in Italy, so this particular piece marked a show that never happened. Both Rauschenberg and Saff were so busy at this time that most of the ROCI shows unfortunately passed without completion of a Graphicstudio project. Countries whose participation *was* so celebrated were Chile, Tibet, and Japan (see cats. 77, 78, app. 208). The Japanese piece, entitled *Bamhue*, was composed of a square stalk of bamboo into which a random light sequence was incorporated.

Production of the complicated Graphicstudio projects of all these artists required countless telephone conversations, express mail packages,

35. Robert Rauschenberg (right) and Donald Saff discussing the prototype for *Fifth Force* (app. 206), April 1986

36. At lunch outside the observatory: Patrick Foy, Greg Burnet, Marcia Brown, Alan Holoubek, and Tom Pruitt (left to right), summer 1987

and travel to and from Tampa by both the artists and the Graphicstudio staff. When there was something to do, the artist came to the shop; when there was something to see, it often would be shipped; and when there was something to discuss, the shop frequently went to the artist. Saff has indicated that he was "always playing catch-up" for every project: "I never had the funds in the bank." Yet he seems never to have seriously considered that the shop should try to maintain itself by the sales of a quantity of work. And production has never been geared in that direction.[48]

According to Saff there were many advantages to Graphicstudio's location as part of a university:

> There were any number of times when issues of chemistry were worked out by the chemistry department; the idea of sending George [Holzer] off with the engineering faculty for a month or two to work on software programs for Arakawa [for a project never realized]. Then, of course, there is the ability to tap into sculpture faculty like Alan Eaker, Ernie Cox, and Chuck Fager for ceramics, or photo people like Oscar Bailey—they were very helpful and they were right there, so you didn't have to research it or look for somebody. . . . [You could] get the input and find out immediately whatever you needed to know or get help. . . . More important, it was a place to know certain people [students] who either had the skills or had the aptitude, and you screened them over a period of time by having them in different circumstances; so you could get a Susie [Hennessy] or a Ken Elliot or a Nick Conroy. It's really hard to find people who have the skills, or you find people who have technical skills and they don't have interpersonal skills. . . . so [the university] is a fantastic place to find skills.

In fact, the full attention and skills of everyone on staff at Graphicstudio would often be directed to a single project, not only while the artist was in-house, but between the artist's visits and while the edition was being completed. For some artists, Nancy Graves among them, this opened up many doors. Graves was the very last artist Saff brought to the shop before leaving, and he had been eager to work with her for some time. As it turned out, Bjorn Wetterling, who represents her work in Sweden, was instrumental in bringing the two together. Once in touch, Saff held no resources in reserve. After an initial conversation with the artist, he took a team—including Marcia Brown, Nick Conroy, Ken Elliot, Patrick Foy, Tom Pruitt, Deli Sacilotto—to Graves' New York studio with boxes of material samples to illustrate processes they thought might be of interest to her. A free-for-all dialogue began that day and was continued soon after when the artist came to Tampa for the first of the four three-day trips that were necessary to complete two works: a three-dimensional lithograph, *Canoptic Prestidigitation*, and a wall sculpture, *Canoptic Legerdemain* (app. 117, cat. 84), the latter being incredibly dense—both formally and iconographically. Incorporated in the sculpture is an extraordinary variety of elements, one of which is a specially printed edition of her lithograph. Other components include a laser-cut design, several epoxies, found and bought materials of all sorts, located by everyone involved, all connected by a plethora of means. The rampant energy in the piece and its thematic complexity convey the artist's excitement in working on this, her first edition sculpture. She has also spoken enthusiastically of her experience at Graphicstudio: "The engineering was the crux of the problem. It was ultimately how we were going to hold this thing together that the problems rested on; and they devised something that was extremely ingenious. Techniques seemed to be coming out of their pores. Anything I would think of, they'd come up with ten solutions that I'd never dreamed about."[49]

Graves' print and sculpture were Don Saff's last project with Graphicstudio, and his comments, similar to Graves', suggest that he felt the work precipitated collaboration at its most rewarding: "I don't think there was a player in the studio that didn't contribute in a really powerful way." It was a grand finale. When Saff left, so did many on the team he had brought together. Sacilotto moved back to New York; several other staff members joined Saff at S.T.A.

In March 1990 Alan Eaker, whose association with the Graphicstudio goes back almost to its beginnings, resigned his chairmanship of the art department and took over as the workshop's new director. Among his first projects was to oversee an exchange of artists with the Soviet Union, an initiative that had been put in motion by Saff the previous year. Under Graphicstudio's new leadership, the key to productive collaborative undertakings remains the same. But the last word on that subject should go to Robert Rauschenberg, who probably knows more about it than anyone else around: "It takes trust, and it takes love."[50]

The bibliography at the end of this volume provides complete publication data for the abbreviated references used in the notes.

1. The bibliography lists several texts on American printmaking in general. The most comprehensive information about contemporary printmaking may be found in the pages of *The Print Collector's Newsletter* (hereafter called *PCN*), published since 1970. On the particular subject of professional printers, see Adams 1983. For a brief overview of the period from 1960 to 1984, see Bruce Davis, "Contemporary Printmaking Workshops" in Fine 1984; and Richard S. Field, "Printmaking Since 1960: The Conflicts between Process and Expression," in Field and Fine 1987. On Atelier 17, see Joanne Moser, *Atelier 17: A 50th Anniversary Retrospective Exhibition* [exh. cat., Elvehjem Art Center] (Madison, 1977).

2. On ULAE, see Sparks 1989.
3. On Tamarind, see *Tamarind*, Albuquerque 1985.
4. On Gemini G.E.L., see Fine 1984; on Tyler Graphics, see Gilmour 1986, and Friedman 1987; and on Landfall Press, see Moser 1981. For one overview on collaboration, see Antreasian 1980, 180-188. See also Saff 1981, 55–68.
5. For a biographical essay about Saff, see Ruth E. Fine, "Donald Saff: A Life in Art," in *Saff*, Tampa 1989, 10–15. The catalogue also provides a retrospective overview of Saff's art.
6. Sacilotto's role in the Graphicstudio story will be developed later in this essay. He has written extensively on print subjects: see Sacilotto 1982, Sacilotto and Saff 1978, and Sacilotto and Saff 1979.
7. In addition to works in note 6, co-authored with Deli Sacilotto, Saff's writings

include essays on Jim Dine, Robert Rauschenberg, and James Rosenquist, listed in the bibliography under the artists' names.

8. See Fine 1984, 122–125; and Saff, in *Rauschenberg*, Los Angeles 1983.

9. The ROCI exhibition opened at the National Gallery of Art, Washington, in May 1991. See the exhibition catalogue, Washington 1991.

10. For a portrait of Johns by Wujcik, see app. 254.

11. Jim Rosenquist, conversation with Fine, 8 October 1990. Unless otherwise cited, all quotations from Rosenquist in this essay are drawn from this conversation.

12. According to Saff (conversation with Fine, 28 June 1990), it was always a problem to obtain state funding for nonteaching programs such as Graphicstudio. Educational effectiveness in state institutions tended to be measured by the numbers of students taught in a particular course: research facilities were thought to reduce teaching productivity. For further comment on these issues, see Baro 1978, 15–25. This catalogue and Saff 1974, 10–18, have provided background material for this essay.

13. The author has had informal conversations about Graphicstudio with Saff over a period of several years. Lengthy taped conversations were held on 19 and 28 June 1990, however, and all quotations in this essay not otherwise cited are taken from those two sessions.

14. Charles Ringness, in a telephone conversation with Fine, 1 October 1990, spoke at some length of the interactions that took place.

15. As the prints became increasingly valuable, fewer were offered for more money. The last subscription fee under Saff's tenure was $5,000 for eight prints. All subscribers were private individuals, and the subscriptions were the only marketing that Graphicstudio did, committed as it was to refraining from competition with galleries.

16. A full accounting of National Endowment for the Arts grants may be found in Baro 1978, 270.

17. See Saff 1974, 76. Further information offered by Saff in conversation with Fine, 20 June 1990.

18. Philip Pearlstein, conversation with Fine, 12 October 1990. Unless otherwise stated, this is the source for all quotations from Pearlstein in this essay.

19. Such a stance is not unusual among craftspeople committed to traditional methods. Saff has suggested, however, that this was the only truly conservative stance his staff maintained, that generally there was an openness to new ideas and processes, which would have been essential for them in working with such artists as Robert Rauschenberg, who clearly has no patience for conceptual rigidity—for example, regarding the consistency of editions.

20. The reference is to Carl Zigrosser's book *Multum in Parvo* (New York, 1965), the title of which translates "much in little." Zigrosser illustrated his text with fourteen tiny prints, ranging from a work by Albrecht Altdorfer to one by Rockwell Kent.

21. This kind of variation is common for many of Rauschenberg's editions: he also laid out the 491 collages for the Gemini G.E.L. Works in the 7 Characters series, produced in China with Saff's participation, all vary in details.

22. Ringness, telephone conversation with Fine, 1 October 1990.

23. For a list of Graphicstudio staff during the first phase, see Baro 1978, 26–27.

24. Kelder 1973, 84–85.

25. Joanne Milani Rodriquez, "Extra Money Ignites Visual Arts," *Tampa Tribune Times*, 20 April 1980, in *Institute for Research in Art: Annual Report to the Provost, 1986/1987, Graphicstudio U.S.F.*, vol. 3, *Bibliography*, 168. This is one of six volumes of memoranda, correspondence, reports, and press clippings on file in the National Gallery's Graphicstudio Archive. According to Brenda Woodard, most other records devoted to Graphicstudio from 1968–1977 were discarded by the university after the workshop was closed.

26. Susie Hennessy, telephone conversation with Fine, 4 November 1990.

27. Exhibitions were held on campus and throughout the region. To cite one review of one show, Jeanette Crane, in "Imagination Runs Wild," *St. Petersburg Independent*, 11 January 1974, describes the "honest cause for jubilation" at the Florida Center for the Arts-sponsored show "Rauschenberg at Graphicstudio" in the U.S.F. Library Gallery (see Graphicstudio Archive, *Annual Report, 1986/1987*, 50).

28. See Bob Martin, "No Poorly Printed Images in Art Show," *Tampa Times*, 26 April 1973 (Graphicstudio Archive, *Annual Report, 1986/1987*, 39).

29. Bob Martin, "The Printmaker—As Much an Artist as the Artist," *Tampa Times*, January 1973, reports a sale of Graphicstudio prints by the Florida Center for the Arts to the community. Only forty-nine of sixty-nine available were sold, but Martin quotes James Camp as saying he planned to sell the others to galleries in New York where "they will snatch them up at $75 each" (Graphicstudio Archive, *Annual Report, 1986/1987*, 31). Among Graphicstudio's earliest Tampa supporters was Ann Ross, who is the coordinator of community relations at U.S.F. The collection that she and her husband James formed includes a strong representation of the workshop's prints, and it has been generously shared with the public. See Steve Turner, "Polk Public Museum Display Showcases Ross Art Collection," *Lakeland Ledger*, 19 April 1984 (Graphicstudio Archive, *Annual Report, 1986/1987*, 260–261).

30. Saff 1974, 82.

31. Baro 1978, 14.

32. The Graphicstudio II designation was

dropped in l985 when Saff resumed the directorship.

33. Rodriquez 1980.

34. Juristo had set up this press after leaving Graphicstudio. He became a staff printer at the workshop again for a period during the early 1980s.

35. Benbow 1980; and "Graphicstudio (II) Is 'Alive and Well' Here," *USF Today*, June 1980 (Graphicstudio Archive, *Annual Report, 1986/1987*, 166, 170). Exhibitions on campus featured works by Aycock, Robert Gordy, Robert Fichter, all of whom worked at Graphicstudio; but as mentioned in note 27, exhibitions of works by artists working at Graphicstudio had been undertaken during the early phase as well, so the sense that this was a new idea seems overstated in these articles.

36. Rodriguez 1980.

37. David Yager, telephone conversation with Fine, 26 October 1990. Unless otherwise cited, all quotations from Yager are from this conversation. The authors are grateful for Yager's help in clarifying several points about the art produced during these years. The documentation sheets for them are quite spare, presumably because of a lack of staff.

38. Deli Sacilotto, conversation with Fine, 13 October 1990.

39. On Crown Point Press, see Nancy Tousley, "In Conversation with Kathan Brown," *PCN* 8 (November–December 1977), 129–134; and Abner Jonas, *Kathan Brown, Publisher: A Selection of Prints by Crown Point Press* [exh. cat., Trisolini Gallery, Ohio University] (Athens, OH, 1985).

40. Susie Hennessy, conversation with Fine, 11 July 1989.

41. See Fichter 1984.

42. This action was reported in a memo of 17 May 1985, from provost Gregory O'Brien to the file, one of several memos and letters recording discussions among various university factions about the relationship between Graphicstudio staff and members of the art department. Regarding the need for office space and furniture, Saff wrote a letter to the provost on 7 October 1985: "It is not an exaggeration when I tell you that one person must sit on the floor when the other person has the chair"

(Graphicstudio Archive, *Selected Memoranda*, May 1982–March 1988).

43. Saff had recently gone back to school to study electronics, for example.

44. Dine had previously worked in gravure with Sacilotto in 1978 (D'Oench and Fineberg 1986, 23–25). He started using the Dremel on his plates in 1980. See Ellen D'Oench, "Jim Dine: Portrait of a Printmaker," D'Oench and Fineberg 1986, 15.

45. Saff was eager to work with Louise Bourgeois as well; a sculpture project was started but never brought to completion.

46. Rosenquist went on to do several enormous editions at Tyler Graphics, Inc. See *Rosenquist*, Mount Kisco 1989.

47. Wax screenprints had been executed earlier—by Brice Marden in the 1970s, for example—but the surfaces of Lichtenstein's prints are more varied and complex.

48. Generally, professional workshops seem to devote their full resources of equipment and staff as needed during the development and proofing stages of a project, whether the artist is in-house or elsewhere. And all seem eager to devote as much time and attention as needed to carry the projects to successful conclusion. At the most ambitious commercial shops, however, it is common for a number of projects to be worked on simultaneously, allowing for the production of a larger number of works each year to ensure the survival of the shop. Not all artists or projects are equally ambitious from the standpoint of technical challenges or demands. "Ambitious" in these terms tends to be synonymous with costly, however, and the style of each shop is closely related to what it is able to handle both technically and financially. Graphicstudio's not-for-profit status is distinctive for a shop working continuously with such successful artists. Because the publications were released directly to subscribers only, the galleries that handled the artists' copies often were credited for production and publication, thus obscuring Graphicstudio's identity.

49. Graves, telephone conversation with Corlett, 25 October 1990.

50. Rauschenberg, conversation with Fine, 7 October l990.

NOTES TO THE READER

All objects in the exhibition and all other works of art illustrated in this catalogue are in the collection of the National Gallery of Art, unless otherwise designated. Accession numbers are given in the checklist of the Graphicstudio Archive (see appendix) or in captions.

For both catalogue headings and checklist entries, media lines specify "one-color" or "color" for works printed in colors other than black and omit this designation if printed in black. Measurements for prints refer to sheet size and are given in inches followed by centimeters in parentheses; height precedes width (precedes depth when applicable). When an edition is divided and numbered separately with arabic and roman numerals, both sections are noted. Following the edition, proofs are listed according to the following abbreviations:

BAT: *bon à tirer*	PP: printer's proof
PrP: presentation proof	GP: Graphicstudio proof
CTP: color trial proof	TP: trial proof
AP: artist's proof	WP: workshop proof
NGAP: National Gallery of Art proof	USFP: University of South Florida proof
PuP: publisher's proof	ProdP: production proof
SP: special proof	CP: cancellation proof
CoP: copyright proof	

Some artists have additional proofs made—Robert Rauschenberg's Change, Inc., proofs, for example—and these are spelled out in full. For illustrations of variant proofs, the captions do not include information on size and medium if they are similar to those of the related work in the exhibition. Finally, if an up-to-date catalogue raisonné exists for an artist's prints, as for Jim Dine, reference numbers are provided at the end of the catalogue headings.

Uncommon technical terms and processes are explained in the text as needed, and innovative processes developed at Graphicstudio are described in a technical note at the end of this volume. But a basic knowledge of printmaking processes and the terminology of prints has been assumed, with a selection of general references given in the bibliography. The bibliography provides full publication data for the abbreviated references used in the notes to the catalogue entries.

Catalogue entries for works by Jim Dine have been written by Ruth E. Fine, and entries for works by other artists have been written by Mary Lee Corlett.

FIGURES AND LANDSCAPES

Philip Pearlstein applying hardground to a plate for *View of Rome* (cat. 4), June 1986

PHILIP PEARLSTEIN

Born in Pittsburgh, Pennsylvania, 1924
Lives and works in New York City

PEARLSTEIN ATTENDED Saturday art classes at the Carnegie Institute during high school and later enrolled there full time. His studies were interrupted in 1943 when he was drafted into the army. Pearlstein was first
assigned to the Training Aids Unit at Camp Blanding, Florida, where he
assisted in the production of signs, charts, and diagrams for the assembly
of weapons and was introduced to printmaking, specifically the screenprinting process. He was later stationed in Italy. After the war Pearlstein
re-enrolled at Carnegie (B.F.A. 1949), and in 1955 he earned his master's
degree in art history at the Institute of Fine Arts, New York, completing
a thesis on Francis Picabia. He has since written a number of articles on
art. During the summer of 1947 Pearlstein shared a barn-studio in Pennsylvania with Andy Warhol, Arthur Elias, and Dorothy Cantor (whom
he married in 1950). Soon after graduation from Carnegie, he moved to
New York City and briefly shared a residence with Warhol.

Pearlstein was a graphic designer early in his career, including a period
with *Life* magazine (1957–1958), which he left when he was awarded a
Fulbright Fellowship for a year's study in Italy. On his return, he became an
instructor at the Pratt Institute in Brooklyn, where he did his first experiments with lithography. In 1963 he joined the faculty at Brooklyn College, serving as distinguished professor at the time of his retirement in
1988. Known for his rapport with students, he has been invited to participate in numerous visiting artist programs, among them at the American Academy of Art in Rome, Navajo Community College in Tselei,
Arizona, Skowhegan School of Painting and Sculpture in Maine, and
Yale University's School of Art and Architecture.

In 1969 Pearlstein's first color lithograph was published by Brooke
Alexander. Since then he has produced many editions, working with
various printers and publishers in addition to Graphicstudio, including
Landfall Press in Chicago, Printmaking Workshop in New York (with
Robert Blackburn), Pyramid Arts, Ltd., in Tampa, Tamarind Institute in
Albuquerque, and the University of Nebraska at Omaha. Pearlstein is
also a collector of prints and folk art as well as antiquities, patterned
rugs, kimonos, and furniture, primarily for use in his studio.

Pearlstein was selected by Clement Greenberg for his *Emerging Talent*
show at the Kootz Gallery, New York, in 1954, and his first one-man exhibition followed the next year at the Tanager Gallery, New York. Other
important one-man shows, many of which traveled and several of which
featured prints, include those organized by the Georgia Museum of Art,
University of Georgia (1970–1971), Staatliche Museen Preussischer
Kulturbesitz, Kupferstichkabinett, Berlin-Dahlem (1972), Madison Art
Center, Wisconsin (1978), Springfield Art Museum, Missouri (1978–
1979), Davison Art Center, Wesleyan University (1979), John and
Mable Ringling Museum of Art, Sarasota (1981), American Academy,
Rome (1983), Milwaukee Art Center (1983–1984), Amherst College
(1986), and the Brooklyn Museum (1989).

1 Nude Curled Up, 1969

One-color lithograph on Arches Cover paper
18¹/₄ x 23¹/₁₆ (46.4 x 58.6)
Edition: 30 (I/X through X/X; 1/20 through 20/20); 1 BAT; 2 AP
Collaboration: Donald Saff, Anthony Stoeveken
Landwehr 1978, no. 8

When Philip Pearlstein came to Graphicstudio in 1969 as the first invited
artist to the new workshop, he had only been experimenting with
lithography for about a year. His experience had been at Pratt Graphics
Center, and some images had been lost in the process of printing, so he
was "prepared for the worst."[1] Happily, the artist successfully completed
four lithographs during two and a half weeks at Graphicstudio, and he
now credits his Florida experience with having spurred his deepening involvement with the graphic arts: "Like the rest of my work, everything
has become more complex as I learn more and more about capabilities of
the processes. I've worked with other printmakers as well, but I think
that really was my first experience in depth, not just superficial."[2]

Pearlstein began at Graphicstudio by executing a group of drawings
directly from the model: "I don't think of those as preliminary drawings
but as tries at layout—designing how the forms will divide that area, that
rectangle. So it's searching for a composition, I guess."[3] Each of these
drawings offers a different compositional alternative for the arrangement
of the curled nude figure. Cast shadows and modeling are broadly indicated, emphasizing their function as two-dimensional compositional elements rather than their role in defining volumetric form. In one study in
particular (fig. 1a) the contours and shadows seem to operate relatively
independently, which establishes a tension between the two-dimensional
composition and the three-dimensional form. The strokes used to indicate the shadow on the model's arm, for example, cross over the contour
line and extend onto the head to become the darker areas of her hair.

Major compositional adjustments are evident when one compares the
drawings with the final print, also worked directly from the model. One

*The volumetric torso, limbs, and other parts
of the figure have to move choreographically
through measurable three-dimensional space;
simultaneously they must be the primary architectonic units of the strongest possible two-
dimensional picture structure.*
Philip Pearlstein, in Perreault 1988

56

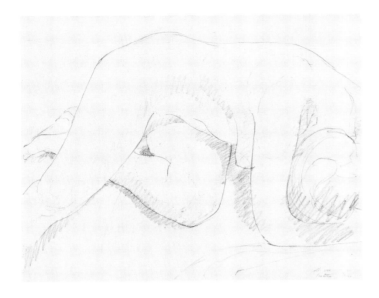

1a. Study for *Nude Curled Up*, c. 1969, graphite on paper, 18 x 24 (45.7 x 60.9), 1985.48.22

of the most obvious is the refinement in the print of the relationship between the model's head and her arm. In the drawing shown here, this relationship is indicated with an unarticulated, *L*-shaped pair of nearly parallel curved lines that surround the head rather than support it. The size and shape of the thigh and knee of the bent leg have also been adjusted in the lithograph.

In the lithograph of *Nude Curled Up* the picture plane is dominated by the form of a single figure that gracefully arches from the oval shape of the head upward along the neck and torso and back down to the left knee. This curved form, which has been compared to Maillol's figures,[4] is anchored by the opposing curves of the bent knee and arm. A firm touch with the lithographic pencil and a hardness in the rendering of both contours and shadows are typical of Pearlstein's lithographs of the 1970s.[5] Yet the line is not without subtlety, as can be seen in the contour that begins at the back of the left knee and travels upward along the leg to the back and right shoulder blade.

The tension between representation and abstraction that is a hallmark of Pearlstein's style is enhanced by the overall consistency of handling— in the strokes used to articulate the figure and the blanket, for instance: "In drawing, or in doing graphics, the point of the pencil or needle, or of the japanese silk brush I use for wash drawings is a much more precise instrument, establishing its own kind of gesture, which is quite different from my painting gestures. And so I can draw or work on graphics and enjoy the small, precise movement of the point, moving like the needle of a seismograph, recording every bump along the contour of a form."[6]

1. Pearlstein, conversation with Fine, New York, 12 October 1990. The catalogue raisonné of Pearlstein's prints by William C. Landwehr (Springfield, MO, 1978) identifies one lithograph produced before 1968. It should also be noted that the titles for the present cats. 1 and 2 are taken from Landwehr, but at the time the Graphicstudio documentation sheets were completed, the works were designated *Untitled*.
2. Pearlstein, unpublished interview with Jade Dellinger, 8 July 1987.
3. Pearlstein, conversation with Fine, 1990. Six of these drawings are part of the Graphicstudio Archive at the National Gallery of Art.
4. Field 1979, 16.
5. Jerome Viola, in *Pearlstein*, New York 1982, 151, noted: "Printed in brown ink on buff-colored paper, [the Graphicstudio prints] are more developed in chiaroscuro than his earlier prints, giving a full range of tones that completely describe the volumes of the forms in space. This subtlety of tone was a direct reflection of the fully worked-out figure drawings in pencil that Pearlstein had recently resumed."
6. Pearlstein, in Berlin 1972, 14.

2 Two Nudes, 1969

One-color lithograph on Arches Cover paper
22³/₈ x 29¹/₈ (56.8 x 74)
Edition: 40 (I/X through X/X; 1/30 through 30/30); 1 BAT; 1 CTP; 2 AP
Collaboration: Donald Saff, Anthony Stoeveken
Landwehr 1978, no. 9

Pearlstein began drawing the figure in 1958 in a group organized by fellow artist Mercedes Matter, whom he has credited with his involvement in this subject.[1] Indeed, the poses that Matter arranged—often using two models in relaxed, nonacademic attitudes—became a major influence on Pearlstein's developing style.[2] Pearlstein works in close proximity to his models, and the cropping of the head of the figure seated on the chair in *Two Nudes* is a characteristic compositional device. According to the artist, "The cropping is never planned. It results from the struggle to find the proper scale of forms within the rectangle."[3]

Comparison of the lithograph to a related drawing (fig. 2a) reveals that Pearlstein adjusted his point of view in the print to include the leg of the model seated on the floor. By doing so, he established a rectangular shape between her bent left leg and the bent left leg of the model seated on the chair, which echoes the rectangular space defined by the latter's bent elbows. The inclusion of the leg created a structure that reflects the artist's approach to composition as he described it in relation to another work: "The prime technical idea . . . was that large forms deployed across the canvas produce axial movements that clash and define fields of energy forces and that the naturalistic depiction of forms as they are in relation to one another in nature is capable of creating the axial movements and fields of energy forces."[4] In Pearlstein's figures contour takes precedence. But the artist also uses dots and dashes to define volume and shadow.[5]

Pearlstein explores a reality in his work that relates directly to the process of seeing, which explains why some of his forms appear distorted.

I concentrate on drawing the contours of shapes, seeing them for the moment as flat areas. If I get the contours of all the shapes, including the shapes of the empty spaces, correctly measured against one another, the drawing works itself out.

Philip Pearlstein, in Berlin 1972

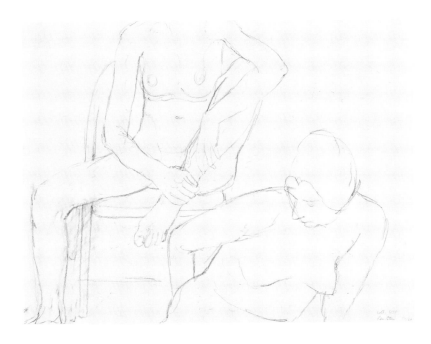

2a. Study for *Two Nudes*, c. 1969, graphite on paper, 18 x 24 (47.7 x 60.9), 1985.48.25

Here, for example, the left arm of the figure seated on the floor appears somewhat shrunken; and the forearms of the model seated on the chair are markedly different in size: "Complete verisimilitude . . . is not my goal. It is the process, my experience during the attempt to achieve the likeness, that is my purpose. For me the process is an intensely interior experience, a non-verbal experience of feeling rather than of analysis."[6]

The Graphicstudio prints may be the first in which Pearlstein used the pattern on a rug as a structural element in the composition: "The model brought her own blanket. It had a couple of big bold stripes on it. Immediately I saw that it became an organizing factor. It helped enrich this black-and-white medium; it brought additional coloristic values."[7]

As is the case in much of Pearlstein's graphic work of this period, the shadows in *Two Nudes*—those under the chair, for example—have a density that functions compositionally rather than naturalistically. Despite the importance of strong cast shadows, however, Pearlstein's earliest Graphicstudio prints do not yet display the triple shadows that became a signature of his style (see Introduction, fig. 7).

1. See Mainardi 1976, 74; quoted in Bowman 1983, xxvi.
2. In an interview with Paul Cummings (Cummings 1979, 169), Pearlstein stated: "Having more than one model was [Mercedes Matter's] idea. Of course, it increases the complexity. It makes it much more like a bunch of rocks lying around. If you get more than two, I find it becomes a problem in terms of subject matter. It gets out of hand. You have a party going on or a theatrical performance or something."
3. Pearlstein, in Berlin 1972, 14.
4. "Realism and Existentialism," *Allan Frumkin Gallery Newsletter* (spring 1978), 6; quoted in Bowman 1983, 10.
5. In an interview with Ralph Pomeroy (Pomeroy 1973, 39), Pearlstein discussed his development of the dot system:

"That's just finding an interior form. They begin to look like a symbol of some sort. . . . But it just means the form has changed and I don't have time to work it out."
6. Pearlstein 1976, sec. 2, p. D29.
7. Pearlstein, in Cummings 1979, 169. In an interview with Sanford Sivitz Shaman, however (see Shaman 1981, 213), Pearlstein stated: "The first time I used a patterned rug in a painting was after I had done the drawing in Bill [White]'s studio. The model was standing, and my drawing was from the waist down. I was doing a large 5-by-6 foot painting. The model fainted after the first couple of poses. It looked so nice with her lying on the patterned rug that I changed the painting to that. That was about 1964–65."

3 Models with Mirror, 1983–1985
Color etching and aquatint on T. H. Saunders hot-pressed paper
35⅝ x 54 (90.5 x 137.2)
Edition: 60; 5 PP; 1 PrP; 1 GP; 1 USFP; 9 AP; 3 PuP
Collaboration: Nancy Brokopp, with Greg Burnet, Deli Sacilotto, Susan
Steinbrock, Catherine Tirr, David Yager

Models with Mirror is based on a watercolor of the subject executed in
1983 (fig. 3a), which is in reverse of the printed image. In producing the
print, however, Pearlstein started over again, working directly from the
models. The emphasis on linearity in Pearlstein's early lithographs expands in later prints, such as *Models with Mirror*, to include decorative
color and pattern. In addition, the differentiation of textures, such as
those of skin, cloth, and furniture, became increasingly important: "At
the beginning I was much more interested in the overall scheme and
could even be satisfied with solving it on the two-dimensional level. I
think more and more the three-dimensional aspect has taken over, and it
has meant developing each surface much further so that, while I'm not
into a microscopic examination of what the difference is between, say,
cotton and satin, I have to deal with the look of those surfaces."[1]

In *Models with Mirror* Pearlstein set the brown skin tones of the
models against rich yet muted reds and greens. The color is crisp and
flat, and its uniform intensity contributes to its decorative quality. Pearlstein used a delicate line to define such details as the knuckles, veins, and
wrinkles in the hands of the figure seated on the bench. Often these con-

tours seem to have a life of their own, independent, yet related to the color around them.

Tension between the conceptual and the perceptual is a leitmotif in Pearlstein's art. The wood grain of the bench, for example, varies from the intricately rendered boards on the left-most portion, to the looser, more expressionistic strokes on the right. On the right, a single stroke describes the graining on both the seat and back of the bench, even though the boards would not actually be touching. Such passages recall Pearlstein's early commitment to abstract expressionism.

What Robert Storr has described as the "distinction between active space and passive figures"[2] became key in Pearlstein's work of the 1980s. In *Models with Mirror* space not only recedes but projects aggressively out toward the viewer, giving the whole composition a sense of urgency and immediacy that is intensified by the density of the pictorial elements. The composition is organized on a complex arrangement of diagonals, both parallel to the surface and penetrating space. The view from above accentuates the diagonal placement of the rug in relation to the bench, and the edges of the rug, the pattern within the rug, the angle of the bench, the direction of the slats of the seat, the wall and molding all define angles against which play the rounded forms of the figures. These compositional devices—the aerial point of view, strong diagonals, flat forms, animated patterns, dynamic space—reflect the artist's interest in Japanese prints.

Mirrors appear intermittently in Pearlstein's work, and here one provides a third figure fragment. Reflecting, in an almost claustrophobic way, the face of the reclining model and a small portion of the rug and floor, the mirror offers no wider view of the artist's studio and thus does not serve to extend space, as it often does for other artists. The appearance of the model's face, her eyes nearly meeting the viewer's, is rare in the oeuvre of an artist known for his arbitrary cropping of heads.

Models with Mirror was executed in New York at about the same time *View of Rome* (cat. 4) was undertaken in Florida.

1. Pearlstein, in Shaman 1981, 124.   2. Storr 1984, 98.

I became very conscious of furniture when I began using it in relation to the models, seeing it as sculpture and seeing how it works with the human body. Furniture designers are great artists. Their challenge is to create different ways of supporting the body.

Philip Pearlstein, in Sarasota 1981

3a. *Two Models with Green Bench and Mirror*, 1983, watercolor, 40 x 60 (101.6 x 152.4), private collection

4 View of Rome, 1986
Color direct gravure and sugar-lift aquatint with roulette work on Arches Cover paper
35⅝ x 47¼ (90.5 x 120)
Edition: 60; 1 BAT; 1 PP; 3 PrP; 1 NGAP; 1 GP; 1 USFP; 3 CTP; 13 AP
Collaboration: Greg Burnet, Patrick Foy, Deli Sacilotto, Donald Saff

Although Pearlstein is better known for his figures, landscape has been a recurring interest throughout his career: "Landscape ideas dominated my works of the fifties, at first in an emotionally charged manner. Technically I attempted to merge ideas from Chinese Taoist/Buddhist painting traditions, exemplified in the works of the Sung artists, with the expressionist, calligraphic style of the New York Action Painters (Abstract Expressionists), whose works then dominated the art scene. These two influences entwined with a third—that of Cézanne's landscape painting, particularly the watercolors and late oils."[1]

After focusing on the figure during the 1960s, Pearlstein returned to landscape subjects in the 1970s, applying the methodology of his mature style to the rendering of landscape and ruins. Pearlstein's fascination with ancient architectural sites was fueled by the time he spent in Italy on a Fulbright Fellowship in 1958, and he returned to Italy periodically during the 1970s and 1980s, serving for three months in 1982 as artist-in-

In dealing with the ruins I suppress all their romantic, expressive, and metaphorical overtones. Reconstructing them almost brick by brick, as a model on the paper or canvas, gives me the same kind of tension [as painting the nonerotic nude]. That tension is the result of suppression.
Philip Pearlstein, in Shaman 1981

4a. Proof of black plate for *View of Rome*, 1991.75.147

4b. Color trial proof for *View of Rome*, 1991.75.150

4c. Drawing for red plate of *View of Rome*, 1991.75.144

4d. Drawing for ocher plate of *View of Rome*, 1991.75.146

residence at the American Academy of Art in Rome. He has also traveled widely to depict such sites as Machu Picchu and Sacsahuaman in Peru, the Temple of Hatshepsut in Egypt, Stonehenge and Tintern Abbey in England, the Amalfi Coast in Italy, and Monument Valley and the Grand Canyon in the American West. Despite his intention to suppress romantic and metaphorical overtones, Pearlstein's landscape subjects nevertheless share a sense of historical preeminence.

While painting in oils at the Canyon de Chelly in 1974, Pearlstein was forced by high winds to secure his canvas to surrounding rocks. This experience led him to turn to the more manageable medium of watercolor for painting outdoors.[2] Pearlstein was also eager to extend his explora-

4e. Drawing for green plate of *View of Rome*, 1991.75.143

4f. Drawing for black plate of *View of Rome*, 1991.75.145

tion of aquatint to landscape subjects, and the transparency of water-color allowed for the layering of color in a way similar to the building up of aquatint tones.[3]

View of Rome is based on a watercolor Pearlstein painted from the roof of the American Academy when he was in residence there.[4] Using the watercolor as a model, Pearlstein made color separations on mylar for this aquatint, one sheet for each color, working in his studio in New York (see figs. 4c-f). He sent these to Tampa, where the images were transferred to the plates using direct gravure. In this process the mylar drawing is placed face up on sensitized carbon tissue and exposed to light; then the exposed carbon tissue is adhered face down to the plate.

This reverses the image, which will reverse again when printed so that the orientation of the final print will be the same as that of the original watercolor. Pearlstein then went to Tampa, where he extensively re-worked the plates. With a high-quality reproduction of the watercolor as a reference, he refined areas of tone and shape on the plates, using the sugar-lift aquatint process and working directly on the plates with hand tools, including the roulette wheel. Although several color trial proofs exist (figs. 4a–b), they were part of the process of refining the color, not the compositional structure.[5]

This panoramic view is a visually animated image. Diminution of scale rather than graying of color is used to establish the sense of depth, the greens and reds being nearly as vibrant along the horizon line as in the foreground. Colors define three-dimensional objects while function-ing compositionally as independent two-dimensional forms (Pearlstein's landscape equivalent to the triple shadows on his models; see Introduc-tion, fig. 7). Pearlstein did not employ academic perspective in the ren-dering of the architecture, but was as true as possible to his visual perceptions—in the same way he approaches the figure.

1. Pearlstein, "Foreword," in Perreault 1988, 13.
2. Pearlstein worked on lithographic plates for *Ruins at Gran Quivira*, 1978, on site at Canyon de Chelly (see *Print Collector's Newsletter* [Jan./Feb. 1979], 194), but this did not allow him to work with color separation.
3. For a general discussion of the devel-opment of Pearlstein's career, including the role of landscape, see Bowman 1983. For a discussion about his use of water-color, see Perreault 1988; and *Pearlstein*, New York 1981, with introductory essay by Jerome Viola.
4. According to Perreault, the watercolor *View of Rome* is in the collection of Roy M. Huffington, Inc., Houston (see Per-reault 1988, pl. 127, for a reproduction). It is one of four watercolors Pearlstein painted during this period with the inten-tion of translating them into prints. Only one other of the four was used for a print, *Temple at Paestum*, published by Conde-sco and Brokopp.
5. Technical information concerning this print was obtained in discussions with Deli Sacilotto and Patrick Foy.

5 Jerusalem, Kidron Valley, 1987–1989

Color heliorelief woodcut with hand-carving and roulette work, printed in two sections on Rives BFK paper
40⅛ x 119 (101.9 x 302.3)
Edition: 22; 1 BAT; 2 PP; 4 PrP; 1 NGAP; 1 GP; 1 USFP; 1 CTP; 1 SP; 9 AP
Collaboration: Alan Holoubek, George Holzer, Tom Pruitt, Donald Saff, Conrad Schwable, with Tim Amory, Marcia Brown, Eleanor Erskine, Michael Harrigan, Kelly Medei, Johntimothy Pizzuto, Eric Vontillius

Pearlstein traveled to Jerusalem for the first time in October 1986 with the intention of producing a watercolor of the city that could be used as the source for this print. While working on *View of Rome* (cat. 4), he began to think about doing a view of Jerusalem to go with the view of Rome, because "the two cities are so entwined historically."[1] He had already executed approximately twenty aquatint/etchings of historic views, including *View of Rome,* and Donald Saff suggested that he do "a real big [print] this time" in woodcut,[2] without the size constraints of the etching press. Saff originally planned to have Chinese woodcutters whom he had met in China come to Florida to cut and print the block. Subsequently, the idea of doing a "heliorelief" woodcut was developed and used (see technical note at the end of this catalogue). In this way Pearlstein began what was, incredibly, his first woodcut. At the same time, he was the first artist to explore the possibilities offered by heliorelief.

Pearlstein worked on location in Jerusalem to paint a remarkable watercolor panorama of the Kidron Valley that measures slightly more than ten feet in length. He used a separate sheet of paper for each half of the composition. The watercolor is the same scale as the final print and was executed during sixteen and a half days: "I stood on the edge of a precipice which was a lookout point for tourists because I didn't want to be in

Every little mark becomes a stylized representation of something out there in nature. But that's exactly what the challenge of realism is.

Philip Pearlstein, Graphicstudio videotape 22, winter 1988

5a. Pearlstein, leaning on press, discussing *Jerusalem, Kidron Valley*, with a group of University of South Florida students, February 1988

a real deserted place. But even so this was an Arab village that I was standing in."[3] Pearlstein used part of the crate in which his paper had been packed to fashion a temporary drawing board, taping it to a tripod and then to stable objects nearby such as a tree or his car. At the end of each day the entire contraption would have to be dismantled and loaded into the car. At the start of the next work day, it was set up all over again.

To render the details of such a vast subject, Pearlstein began by making a series of dots to establish reference points: "Then I picked out all the big trees that I could see . . . and the prayer tower, and those became my starting points. I just measured points in all directions from there and then gradually filled in the details. Gradually pattern establishes itself, and I became aware of what the actual compositional possibilities were; not that I could do anything about it. It's a matter of clarifying."[4] The difficulty was in keeping track of precisely where he was in the landscape compared to his rendering, particularly on the right half of the composition where the image is most dense. At the center of the panorama is a huge Jewish cemetery, and the lower hillside is the Mount of Olives. Pearlstein did not know that these specific sites were included in the view: "I just started working. There were only a few choices. You don't have to add anything to these places, they come equipped with their own meaning."[5]

The process of making the print began with an 8-by-10-inch color photograph of the watercolor, which was enlarged to full scale to serve as a guide for the creation of color separations. Pearlstein drew on

frosted mylar with pelican drawing ink to make the separations, working intermittently for about ten months with an assistant in his New
York studio: "The mylar was taped over the photograph, and the original watercolor was set up parallel to it so that it looked like a hallway.
[My assistant] and I just spent days and days picking out the color—each
one took roughly a month (not working full time). . . . Concentrating
on one color at a time . . . you got very conscious of, say, raw sienna, or
raw umber, or blue."[6] Pearlstein then sent the mylars to Tampa for technical preparation—the sandblasting and other basic cutting described in
the technical note—and came to Tampa himself when the first proofs
were pulled. Pearlstein further worked each of the blocks by hand, using
roulettes and other tools: "I knocked down edges, I cut away things that
were totally wrong, excess, and kept making the inks more and more
transparent. I wore gloves to keep my hands from getting blisters."[7]

During the proofing, the artist would correct the blocks after placing
a sheet of mylar on top of the proof, marking the areas that needed
changes, and tracing them onto the blocks: "One of the big things in my
mind was to keep it accurate. But it shouldn't end up looking like an ar-
chitect's rendering. . . . On the other hand, I didn't want it to become
too impressionistic or too expressionistic, and that happens automat-
ically anyway. When things get translated into a print, the areas become
a little exaggerated. . . . The print medium takes over at a certain
point."[8]

After the first proofs were pulled, Pearlstein elected to add another set
of hand-cut blocks (one pair of left and right halves) to the original nine,
"because I discovered I missed a whole area."[9] Four different woods were
selected for the blocks—birch, walnut, cherry, and gumwood—each
yielding subtle, individual textures that play an important role in the
overall scheme. The roulette work, too, added texture along the chim-
neys in the center foreground, for instance, and on rooftops.[10]

The overlaying of transparent hues and the use of the white paper as
an additional color suggest the watercolor source of the print and capture a sense of the atmosphere and the strong, clear light of the city.
Buildings emerge from washes of color—grays and ochers—yet seem to
dissolve when the print is viewed from a few feet away, paralleling the
way one perceives only limited detail when viewing an actual landscape
from a distance.

During the production of *Jerusalem, Kidron Valley*, Pearlstein completed a detail of the view to get a feel for the process and to decide
which colors to use in the full print. *Jerusalem, Temple Mount*, used nine
blocks, and Pearlstein had an edition made of it as well.

1. Pearlstein, conversation with Fine,
1990.
2. Pearlstein, Graphicstudio videotape 22.
3. Videotape 22. As Pearlstein commented to Fine in October 1990, "The
tragic thing is it could not be done now.
I was a totally exposed target on a bluff
overlooking that valley."
4. Videotape 22.
5. Videotape 22.
6. Videotape 22. In a letter to Corlett,
23 January 1991, Pearlstein noted: "The
work on the color separations done on

mylar was essentially the same as that
done for the color aquatint/etchings. The
work I did on the blocks—after the initial
cutting by a technician—was also related
to my work on the copperplates of
etchings."
7. Pearlstein, conversation with Fine,
1990.
8. Videotape 22.
9. Videotape 22.
10. In videotape 22, Pearlstein noted that
he had selected woods with the smoothest
grains, "except for the sky."

HISTORY AND MYTH

Jim Dine making painted additions to *Youth and the Maiden* (cat. 14), March 1988

JIM DINE

Born in Cincinnati, Ohio, 1935
Lives and works in New York City

JIM DINE'S MOTHER, a great lover of music, died when Dine was a teenager. Soon after, he went to live with his maternal grandparents; his
grandfather owned a hardware store where Dine developed a fascination
with tools. While in high school and for one year after graduation, Dine
studied at the Cincinnati Art Academy. He then attended the School of
the Museum of Fine Arts, Boston, for six months before enrolling at
Ohio University (B.F.A. 1957), where he met his future wife, Nancy
Minto, who has been an important subject in his art. He also enrolled in
the graduate program at Ohio University but left in 1958 for New York,
where he met Allan Kaprow and Claes Oldenburg.

Dine's mixed-media constructions and experimentation with "happenings" quickly earned him a reputation as an exceptional young talent. In
1966 he received a commission from Editions Alecto to do a series of
prints in London, and the following year he moved there with his family,
remaining until 1970 and concentrating on drawing and printmaking. In
1971 Dine returned to the United States, purchased a farmhouse in Putney, Vermont (where he lived until 1985), and while continuing his work
in drawing and printmaking, again took up painting. He presently maintains residences in New York City and Connecticut and travels extensively, spending long periods in Paris and Venice and maintaining studios
in London and Walla Walla, Washington.

Dine had experimented with printmaking as a student, and his first
professional prints were made at Pratt Graphic Center in 1960. Since
that time, his work in printmaking, as well as painting, drawing, and
sculpture, has been prodigious. He has completed over six hundred editions, working with numerous printers, workshops, and publishers, including Angeles Press, Atelier Crommelynck, Burston Graphic Center in
Jerusalem, Derrière l'Etoile Studios, Mitchell Friedman at Dartmouth
College and at Dine's own printshop, Kelpra Studios, Ltd., Petersburg
Press, and Universal Limited Art Editions, as well as Graphicstudio.

Dine has designed sets for Shakespeare's *A Midsummer Night's Dream*
for the Actor's Workshop in San Francisco (1965) and for Richard
Strauss' *Salome* for the Houston Grand Opera (1986). He also designed
sets and costumes for Oscar Wilde's *Picture of Dorian Gray* (1968),
which was never staged, but he produced a portfolio of prints using the
costume designs. Other special projects include his collaboration with
Lee Friedlander on *Photographs and Etchings* (1969) and with poet Ron
Padgett on *Oo la la* (1970). Dine has also completed a number of mural
projects and outdoor sculptures, including the *Double Boston Venus*
(1987), the *Cincinnati Venus* (1988), and *Looking Toward the Avenue*,
New York (1989).

In 1980 Dine was elected to the American Academy and Institute of
Arts and Letters, New York. One-man exhibitions of his work have been
held at Palais des beaux-arts, Brussels (1963, 1970), the Museum of
Modern Art, New York, (1967, 1978), Stedelijk Museum, Amsterdam
(1967), Whitney Museum of American Art, New York (1970), Staatliche
Museen, Nationalgalerie, Berlin (1971), Städtische Kunsthalle, Düsseldorf (1971), Institute of Contemporary Arts, London (1974), Los Angeles County Museum of Art (1983), Walker Art Center, Minneapolis
(1984), Albertina Museum, Vienna (1989), and the Isetan Museum,
Tokyo (1990–1991).

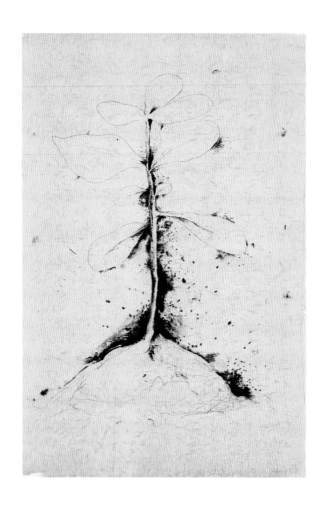

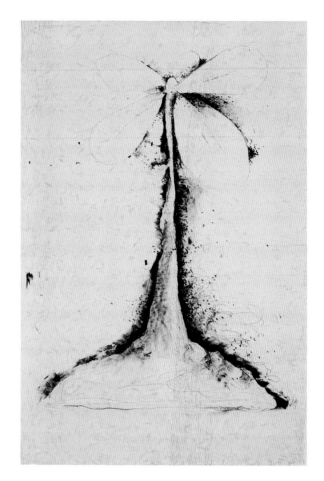

6A–E **The Plant Becomes a Fan #1** through
The Plant Becomes a Fan #5, 1974–1975
Five lithographs with screenprinted gloss varnish on Japanese Natsume paper
Each: 36 x 24 (91.4 x 61.0) irregular
Each edition: 80 (1/60 through 60/60; I/XX through XX/XX); 1 BAT; 4 PrP; 2 PP;
16 AP; 1 USFP; 1 CP
Collaboration: Julio Juristo, Charles Ringness, Donald Saff
Krens 1977, nos. 171–175

While Jim Dine was in Florida during the production of the sculpture edition of *The Metamorphosis of a Plant into a Fan* (cat. 7), this series of prints was undertaken. Closely related to that five-part sculpture in the gradual transformation of its forms, the details of the changes vary considerably. Here they metamorphose more swiftly than in the sculpture, from curvilinear leaves gracefully flowing from a spindly stem that arises out of a mound of earth, into sharply defined blades symmetrically attached to a broad and rigid mechanized base. It is clear that neither work in any specific sense served as a model for the other. The lithographic plates were delivered by Graphicstudio staff to Clearwater, Florida, where Dine was staying with his family, and he worked on them independently of any workshop interaction prior to the process of proofing and printing the editions.

Dine at heart is a draftsman, and his love of drawing is evident in this set of prints. His use of an incisive line coupled with areas of dark tone—mainly to enhance our sense of the outer shapes of individual forms of the subject but sometimes to imply space or volume—is similar to that seen in his extraordinary Untitled Tool Series drawings in the collection

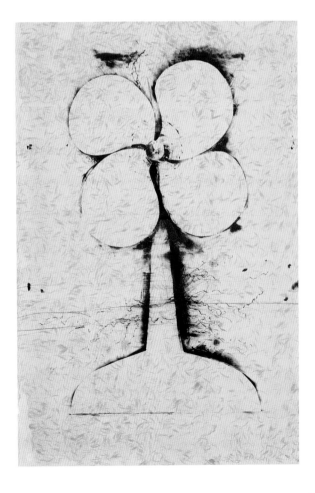

6a. Cancellation proof of *Plant Becomes a Fan #2*, 1985.48.8

of the Museum of Modern Art, New York, as well as in other prints and drawings from this period.[1]

Dine's fascination with dynamic surfaces is also clear here, in his use of a screenprinted gloss varnish to deepen the color and heighten the activity in the already visually enriched paper. It appears that more layers of gloss were added to the sheets as the image moved toward its mechanized self. With each image, the field color becomes slightly darker, the paper fibers become more visually active, and the sheet itself feels more fully impregnated.[2] Over time, Dine's interest in ever richer surfaces has been displayed by a variety of materials and means. Recently, for example, he has been using shellac (a liquid similar in color to these varnish-covered sheets) in his mixed-media works on paper as well as in his prints.[3]

The cancellation proof of *The Plant Becomes a Fan #2* (fig. 6a) reveals the original white color of the Natsume paper. The *X* across the fan's blades shows a common means of cancelling an image on a plate after the edition is printed. The heart drawn across the base, however, is a more personalized reference to Dine's own art.

The great failure is the lack of drawing. X would say there's no need for it in modern art, but I think that's the weakness in the art, the automatic quality of everything, the manufactured quality. What everyone thinks is great freedom is a lack of draughtsmanship. And the forced ugliness is true ugliness, I think.

Jim Dine, in Shapiro 1981

1. The Untitled Tool Series drawings are reproduced in Beal 1984, 60–63.
2. The effect of the varnish on the paper, especially in the more fully impregnated sheets, recalls the laminated waxed paper hand-made in Nepal that Tatyana Grosman had obtained for Edition A of Dine's *Flaubert Favorites* (see Krens 1977, nos.

95–98). One image, *The Marshal*, is very similar to this fan.
3. In a conversation with Fine, 20 September 1990, Dine spoke of his attraction to the color of shellac and connected its use with the use of the screenprinted gloss varnish in this series.

7 The Metamorphosis of a Plant into a Fan, 1973–1974

Cast aluminum in five parts
Each part: approximately 26 x 16 x 12 (66.0 x 40.6 x 30.5)
Edition: 26
Collaboration: Alan Eaker, David Martin, Donald Saff
Gift of Jim Dine, in Honor of the Fiftieth Anniversary of the National Gallery of Art

Jim Dine completed his first large body of freestanding sculpture in 1965, including works in aluminum, painted bronze, pewter and fiberglass, and fiberglass and iron.[1] The titles of the pieces included *Large Boot Lying Down* and *The Hammer Doorway*, suggesting surreal or dreamlike situations that employ common household objects. Intermittently, from that time through the mid-1980s, Dine has completed a substantial body of three-dimensional work. In the last several years, in fact, he has concentrated as steadily on sculpture, particularly in bronze, as he has on paintings, drawings, and prints. His activity in each of these media has had a considerable interactive impact on the others, a process that is readily apparent in two of his Graphicstudio projects, *The Metamorphosis of a Plant into a Fan* and *The Plant Becomes a Fan #1–#5* (cats. 6A-E).

  The idea for this metamorphosis of an object from nature into an object of industry was first set down in a lively graphite and ink sketch on graph paper, labeled "plant to fan growth" and dated 1961 (fig. 7a). There is also a 1962 painting of the subject. More than a decade later, thanks to Paul Cornwall-Jones of Petersburg Press, who arranged for Donald Saff to meet Dine, the idea for doing a sculpture project was initiated in a few brief discussions in New York. Later, in Paris, where Dine

Everything comes to me in dreams. I dream all the time. Continually. It's my most constant source of material. And if not night dreams, daydreams.

Jim Dine, conversation with Ruth Fine, 1990

for Don with love & thanks — Jim

Jim Dine 1961

7a. *Plant to Fan Growth*, 1961, graphite and ink on graph paper, 11 x 8¹/₂ (27.9 x 21.6), collection of Ruth and Don Saff

and Saff discovered their mutual interest in both cultivating and drawing plants and flowers, the details of the project evolved and Dine sketched out his idea for the five-part sculpture.[2] Initial work took place about a month later in Dine's studio in Putney, Vermont. From that point, technical challenges encountered in accomplishing Dine's idea—and there were many—were met step by step.

Saff sent the drawing from Paris to Graphicstudio for Alan Eaker's input into the possibility of casting it in aluminum. Eaker recalls the next stages:

> I cast a leaf from a ficus plant and some other examples. . . . We flew up to Vermont and showed [Dine] the examples. . . . Then it was a matter of deciding logistically how to go on from there, to figure out what we were going to do, which was to provide five wax ficus plants and five wax fans drawn to [Dine's] specifications, which he then was going to transform and bring together by merging the two, one into the other, [starting] with the two polarities. . . . You had these full-size wax plants hanging upside down . . . literally with wax bullet shapes and the blades all together, sitting in garbage cans in water so they wouldn't deform. . . . We arrived with our wax, our molds, our garbage cans, our plaster, everything, and

we set up a facility and spent a week preparing everything for him. Then we left, and he went into the studio and created the piece.[3]

Once an appropriate mold to use for casting was created, other challenges followed: transporting the pieces and molds to Florida, for example, and determining investment materials that would maintain the crucial fidelity to Dine's meticulous surface details throughout the casting process. Eaker constructed a large kiln lined with kaowool, a spaceship material, and developed a table that swiveled 360 degrees to facilitate the welding that was essential to the elegance of the piece. Working on campus, Eaker recalls, "the casting was done by students. And one beauty of that project was that seven students actually were supported through a year and a half of their education working on that project. . . . We had to design equipment that didn't exist in order to re-weld the leaves back on the bases of those pieces. . . . There were basically three patentable ideas that come out of that process."[4] Other special equipment—welders and sandblasters, for instance—was acquired as well, which brought the expenses for the project astronomically beyond what was originally anticipated.

But this extraordinary idea was given tangible form: the plant emerging from a mound of earth did indeed become a fan. The fan, moreover, was provided with an almost heart-shaped base, to include this human aspect in the most fully mechanized of the five units of the work. A heart was also employed in cancelling the lithograph *The Plant Becomes a Fan #2* (see fig. 6a). Humor and pathos are conceptually joined in this miraculous view of creation. Before our eyes, the life is wrung from a plant, its ten gyrating leaves turning to five steel blades, as it is transformed into an already obsolete product of the machine age.

1. See *Dine*, New York 1984, with introductory essay, "Methods and Metaphors: The Sculpture of Jim Dine," by Michael Edward Shapiro.
2. For Saff's account of the project, see

Baro 1978, 23–25.
3. Alan Eaker, conversation with Fine, 13 July 1989.
4. Eaker, conversation with Fine, 1989.

8 The Woodcut Bathrobe, 1974–1975
Color woodcut and lithograph
36¼ x 24½ (92.1 x 62.2)
Edition: 80 (1/60 through 60/60; I/XX through XX/XX); 1 BAT; 4 PrP; 2 PP; 16 AP; 1 USFP; 19 CTP
Collaboration: Paul Clinton, Donald Saff
Krens 1977, no. 198

Originally a self-portrait icon, over time Jim Dine's bathrobe has taken on more universal meanings.[1] *The Woodcut Bathrobe* is one of several prints Dine completed at Graphicstudio with this signature image. *Black and White Bathrobe* (app. 59), completed during the same working session and prior to this print, employs the same lithographic drawing printed in white on a solidly printed black field. Using a tracing from this lithograph, Dine made a pattern for the individually cut plywood sections that he used for the color panels of *The Woodcut Bathrobe*.

Of particular interest in studying this work is a series of trial proofs that document both the artist's and the printer's thought processes. Most informative is a proof of the lithograph alone (fig. 8a). Printed on a glossy proofing paper, it is annotated by Dine in graphite as to the colors to be used in the woodcut, and by Paul Clinton in blue ink as to which of

The only thing I care about is making art and doing art. In the first place I love doing it. It's a true pleasure. . . . I can't think of doing anything that has more dignity.

Jim Dine, in New York 1977

8a. Working proof for the lithographic element in *The Woodcut Bathrobe*, 1985.48.13

the three necessary woodcut runs would include each color panel. Cut from cedar plywood, panels that directly touch each other were not printed simultaneously. Along the bottom edge of this proof is Dine's notation: "Background-stone silver." Another proof (fig. 8b) shows the woodcut alone, without the black lithographic delineation, but with a silver background; a third proof (fig. 8c) shows the woodcut again without the lithograph, but also without the silver field, providing for a more dramatic image.

The final version of *The Woodcut Bathrobe* is printed on richly textured Japanese Natsume paper rather than the Arches used for the earlier woodcut proofs. The woodcut and lithograph are combined, with one further adjustment: responding to Dine's instructions on another proof not included here to "make this brown a bit different from orange," the printer has altered the hue of the right lapel to a cooler and darker brown than was used in the earlier versions.[2]

Among the prints Dine worked when Graphicstudio was starting up again is *Robe Goes to Town* (app. 62), for which etching and screenprint were used. From his 1986 Graphicstudio sessions, another work that combined printing processes is *Two Florida Bathrobes* (app. 70): segmented like *The Woodcut Bathrobe* into panels of color, *Two Florida Bathrobes* uses lithography for the panels, along with a black linear structure composed of marks in softground etching—many of them the

artist's own fingerprints and handprints—and lines made by power tool drypoint. This rich process is in keeping with other shifts in Dine's art. Over the years, for example, his work has become increasingly animated and expressionistic, regardless of image. Robes, specifically, have been marked by a greater sense of a human form within them than is evident in *The Woodcut Bathrobe*, and they are often combined with an active gestural stance.

8b. Color trial proof for the woodcut element of *The Woodcut Bathrobe*, 1985.48.14

8c. Color trial proof for *The Woodcut Bathrobe*, 1985.48.15

1. On Dine's bathrobes, see Beal 1984, 8.
2. Another proof in the National Gallery's Graphicstudio Archive not included here shows the woodcut with both the silver ground and the black lithograph.

Fourteen color trial proofs and three woodblocks used for this print are in the collection of the Library of Congress, Washington.

9A-E The Tampa Tool Reliefs, 1973–1974

Cast aluminum in five parts
Each part: approximately 27 x 29 x 2 (68.6 x 73.7 x 5.1)
Edition: 9
Collaboration: Alan Eaker, David Martin, Donald Saff
Gift of Jim Dine

Three-dimensional objects affixed to his canvases were a central feature of Jim Dine's paintings from 1959 to the mid-1970s. In recent years they have again assumed an important role. Often these objects have been tools of the sort employed in *The Tampa Tool Reliefs*. Indeed tools have been a major theme in Dine's art since 1962, with associations often made to his grandfather's hardware store in which he spent many hours as a child. One suspects, however, that the importance of tools among the materials and processes of making art, with all of the self-reflexive aspects—a pervasive theme in the contemporary vision—has played at least an equally significant role in Dine's attention to these implements. According to the artist, his "tools refer to people without having to deal with a human presence; they aren't monuments to American workers."[1] Dine's imaginative use of tools, and his sense that the most appropriate one for a given task might be taken from a totally unrelated realm, may be seen in his use of a mop for applying acid (see fig. 11a), a medium most often approached with a bath or a brush or a feather.

The tools featured in *The Tampa Tool Reliefs* include scissors, a painting spatula, various knives, and an awl. Dine began work on these pieces in Putney, Vermont, just after he had executed the waxes for *The Metamorphosis of a Plant into a Fan* (cat. 7) and while the Graphicstudio staff was preparing the molds used for transporting that sculpture to Florida. According to Alan Eaker, who assisted with the project, Dine "gathered up the tools and embedded the tools in wax and clay and Plasticine, and we set out a format. Every night we would cast another relief, and the next morning he would take that relief and either change it or start a new one. So the five reliefs grow out of his modifying the waxes each time."[2] In other words, once the mold was made for the first configuration, Dine reworked the composition, retaining some aspects and changing, adding, or deleting others to arrive at the second panel. A similar process was followed for the third and fourth panels. For the last, however, the sheet of wax was removed from the plywood and broken; then the fragments were reassembled to form a sharper, fractured field.[3]

These sculpture reliefs relate closely to works such as *Black Garden Tools* (1962), in which actual objects are suspended from a wood panel painted in oils.[4] And Dine's gate sculptures of the 1980s provide a similar sense of a flattened sculptural expanse. To press the comparison, Dine frequently has affixed tools to the gates. "Tools are somehow what one does and can do. Or, perhaps better, one can recognize things are done and these things do them."[5]

[Tools] are the link with our past, the human past, the hand.

Jim Dine, in Beal 1984

1. Dine, in Beal 1984, 64.
2. Eaker, conversation with Fine, 1989.
3. For a brief, not terribly clear account of the process, see the documentation sheet for the work in Baro 1978, 184.
4. Reproduced in Beal 1984, 21. Tools are one of the themes alluded to in the title of this book—*Jim Dine: Five Themes*—with other comments and illustrations in the introduction.
5. Robert Creeley, in Beal 1984, 49.

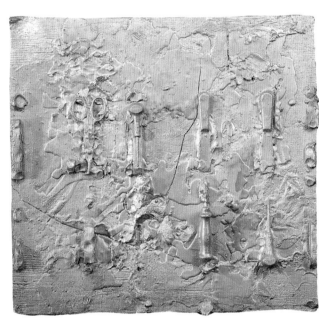

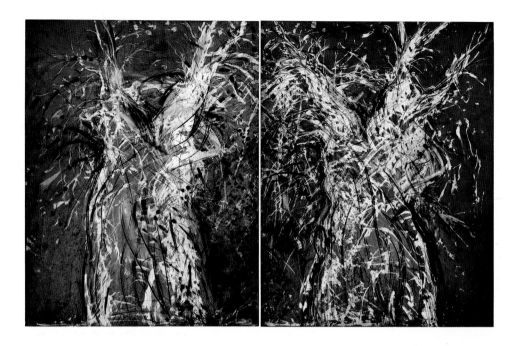

10 Swaying in the Florida Night, 1983

Etching, aquatint, and drypoint on Arches rolled paper, with some proofs on
Somerset paper
Two plates, each: 42³/₄ x 33³/₄ (108.6 x 85.7)
Edition: 65; 1 BAT; 10 AP; 1 PrP; 5 PP; 1 GII; 1 USFP; 1 WP
Collaboration: Susie Hennessy, Susan McDonough, Donald Saff, Stephen Thomas,
Robert Townsend
D'Oench and Fineberg 1986, no. 143

Although an interest in landscape had been implicit in Dine's art
throughout his career, it was not until 1980 that the artist began to use
trees as a specific landscape element in his paintings. He was inspired by
an old apple tree not far from his Vermont studio.[1] Within a year after
he started his tree paintings, the theme entered his printmaking repertoire as well, with a group of etchings drawn on the plates in Key West,
Florida, and then printed at Palm Press in Tampa, soon followed by explorations in woodcut and in a combination of screenprint and etching.[2]

With this subject, Dine's gestural propensities assumed free reign. His
trees tend to be mature, with broad, gnarled trunks and full, interlocking
branches, as here, in *Swaying in the Florida Night*. They are barren, suggesting winter, not spring, a metaphor for age, not youth—similar in
connotation, perhaps, to the skull image the artist increasingly examined
during the 1980s as well. With the trees, one is also given air, wind, fog.

The *Swaying in the Florida Night* diptych was energetically drawn
onto two copperplates with greasy lithographic crayon. The crayon thus
established the white areas of the image by resisting the action of the
acid, some of which Dine painted on the plates directly. By adding marks
with a wire brush and a variety of power tools, including an electric drill
and a Dremel (which provides a velvety and dramatic drypoint-like line),
the artist created an image of intense motion, representing the wind implied in its title.

Dine's mastery of the power tools he had been using for a decade is
evident from the array of strokes he produced here. In some places the

tool seems to have skipped across the surface of the plate, leaving what may be read quite literally as tracks. Elsewhere the deep, dark lines convey smoother gliding. The diversity of these blacks is echoed in the complex palette of whites, some of which were achieved with strokes of the lithographic crayon mentioned above, whereas others seem to have resulted from a more fluid acid resist. The variety of grays, generally lighter in the left-hand plate, reflects variations both in the acid resists and the length of time the plates were immersed in the acid baths or were directly painted with the liquid. The differences between the two panels—the left being more open and light, with less contrast and less activity; and the right having greater rhythmic intertwining, richer densities, and a darker atmosphere—suggest a shift in the time of day and the mood of the landscape setting.

Dine works in studios, hotel rooms, printshops, and sculpture foundries all over the world, and it is not uncommon for his titles to allude to the location in which a particular piece was made, or where an idea was instigated.[3] But the geography involved in producing *Swaying in the Florida Night* was more complicated than the title implies. Like *The Heart and the Wall* (cat. 11), it was one of three prints undertaken by Dine as Graphicstudio was starting up again but not yet fully organized. Although the proofing was completed in Tampa, the plates were shipped to Boston for edition printing at R. E. Townsend, Inc. For another print from this period, the etching/screenprint *Robe Goes to Town* (app. 62), the etched plate was proofed in Tampa by Stephen Thomas and printed by Thomas back at his home base in Berkeley; the screenprint was completed at a commercial shop in Tampa, and the assembly of the two parts was accomplished on campus at Graphicstudio. Together, this group of prints includes three of Dine's signature images: the heart, the robe, and the tree.

These strange trees take me back to my childhood fears of darker things, so working in this way exorcises my demons and keeps me in touch with unreality. In a primitive society I would maybe be a shaman, one of those guys who is a hit man for an unconscious civilization.

Jim Dine, in Beal 1984

1. Beal 1984, 43–49.
2. D'Oench and Fineberg 1986, cats. 79–85, 108, 147. Don Saff has recounted how he flew the plates for *Swaying in the Florida Night* back and forth between Key West and Tampa throughout the working process.

3. A 1981 triptych, for instance, was called *Three Trees in the Shadow of Mt. Zion*, and a 1983 triptych—which includes a tree, a heart, and a hand—was named *The Three Sidney Close Woodcuts* for Dine's London studio where the woodblocks were carved.

11 The Heart and the Wall, 1983

Softground etching, aquatint, and power tool drypoint on four sheets of Somerset textured paper
Two upper sheets, each: 43⅝ x 34¾ (110.8 x 88.3)
Two lower sheets, each: 45¾ x 34¾ (116.2 x 88.3)
Edition: 28; 6 AP; 4 PP; 1 GII; 1 USFP; 1 BAT; 1 WP
Collaboration: Susie Hennessy, Susan McDonough, Donald Saff, Stephen Thomas
D'Oench and Fineberg 1985, no. 145

In addition to the bathrobe and the tree (cats. 9A–E and 10), the heart is a theme closely associated with Jim Dine's art. As the bathrobe has been seen to function at least initially as a metaphor for the artist, the heart has been viewed as representing his wife, Nancy. Dine's hearts have also been suggested as a metaphor for creativity, for feeling, and for abundance.[1] Universal associations are a factor here, too: references to anatomy, romantic love, Valentine's Day, candy. Dine's heart images developed from his 1965 set designs for *A Midsummer Night's Dream* and have since appeared in his paintings, sculpture, and prints.[2] In the early

1970s, for example, working in Vermont, Dine completed a group of large paintings in which the heart form filled the entire canvas, as it fills the composition here.

The Heart and the Wall is printed in four quarters on four sheets of paper as an accommodation to the limitations in the size of available press beds. Dine created the work by painting, or more literally sweeping, acid onto the copperplates with great freedom (fig. 11a), an activity possible indoors only due to the roll-back roof of the observatory studio. The fumes would have been deadly otherwise. The fluidity of the aquatint Dine obtained by working in this fashion is a splendid counterpoint to the vigorous markings of the power tools and the elusive qualities of the softground etching, all of which have been increasingly important in Dine's etchings during the last decade. Printed in three colors—yellow, green-blue, and black—there is a clarity of layering enhanced by the mixtures of hue that result. The drips, blotches, strokes, scraping, incising, and rubbing in the print invest this heroic icon of Dine's art with all of the freshness, immediacy, and power of his drawings.

Closely related to this print, and also part of the National Gallery's Graphicstudio Archive, is a large pastel drawing on brown wrapping paper that is divided into four quarters with black chalk (fig. 11b). Drawn as part of the process of Dine's working on the etching, it is very differ-

11a. Jim Dine swabbing acid on plates for *The Heart and the Wall*, December 1982

11b. *Heart and Wall*, 1983, pastel, 91⁷/₈ x 72¹/₈
(233.4 x 183.2), 1986.26.220

ent in effect from its printed counterpart, especially in its use of a diverse
palette of vivid reds, yellows, blues, oranges, violets, and greens, as well
as grays and black. If the drawing is compared, in reverse, to the etching, it becomes clear that the drawing was developed while applying
marks to the softground plates, which echo the pastel strokes in all of
their rhythms and breadth. Indeed, it is likely that the layers of color in
the drawing reflect the different stages of etching, the color differentiation being a way for the artist to keep track of what he had done as
well as what he was doing at any given time as the work on the plates
progressed.

Although Dine's printmaking is interrelated in imagery and conceptual
approach to his work in other media, his ability to extend the means of
print technology is nevertheless both distinctive and distinguished, resulting in surfaces of supreme beauty. Among Dine's most recent prints is
a series of seven hand-painted screenprints entitled *The Hand-Coloured
Viennese Hearts*.[3] In them the heart is primary, as it is here, but architectonic structures and symbols, with natural or religious implications, are
employed as well.

*When I first used the heart I didn't know it would
become an abiding theme. Typically, though, I always go where my romance takes me, so it is an
emblem that I return to with a lot of affection.*
Jim Dine, in Beal 1984

1. Shapiro essay in *Dine*, New York
1984, 10.

2. Beal 1984, 36.
3. See *Dine*, New York and London 1990

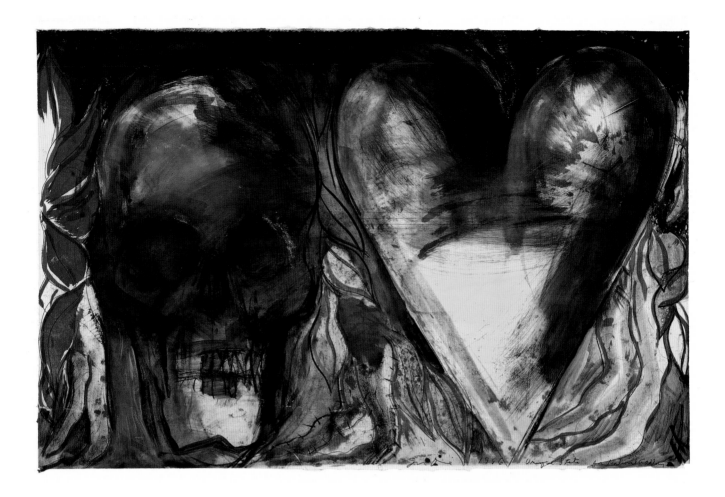

12 Yellowheart and a Devil, 1985–1987

Color direct gravure and softground etching, with painted additions
39¼ x 59½ (99.7 x 151.1)
Collaboration: Greg Burnet, Patrick Foy, Deli Sacilotto, Donald Saff
Edition: unique

In the edition impression of *Yellowheart and a Devil* (fig. 12a),[1] the brilliant yellow pervades the sheet and plays an active role overall, functioning as powerfully in the skull and in the field as in the yellow heart of the title. The red is also vivid, dancing across the sheet in bloodlike strokes apparently drawn directly with the fingers. The green in the leaves varies from highly textured to flat color, suggesting differences in the effects of illumination. The black ranges from soft modeling—on the right side of the yellow heart, for example—to the rather dense form that presses down from the top of the sheet, as if a black cloud were hovering above.

In the National Gallery's unique impression of *Yellowheart and a Devil*, with painted additions, Dine has developed a more somber if less frightening image. The blood-red is less potent. Instead, the red shows through areas of black and yellow paint and white crayon that the artist has added. The yellow skull, too, has been considerably overpainted, starkly differentiating between the skull and the heart. This recalls the relationship between these two elements in the paint and charcoal drawing in black and white on brown-paper-covered board done the previous year in Los Angeles (fig. 12b). Compellingly, the cavities of the skull play an important role in both works.

My color is always subjective. It has only been descriptive a few times in the still lifes of the 1970s. I never really think about painting atmosphere, but what I do think about is sharpening my draftsmanship and about the power of objects.

Jim Dine, in Beal 1984

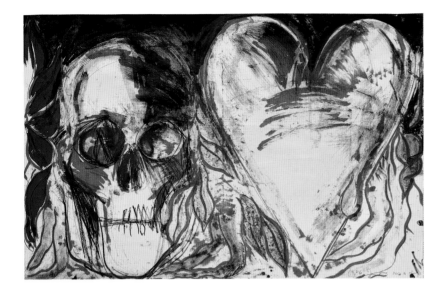

12a. *Yellowheart and a Devil*, 1985–1987 (app. 71)

12b. Drawing for *Yellowheart and a Devil*, c. 1985–1987, charcoal and ink on foam core, in two parts: left: 40¼ x 30¹/₁₆ (102.2 x 76.3), right: 40⁵/₁₆ x 30¼ (102.4 x 76.9), 1986.26.221–222

In working the unique impression, Dine made notable modifications in the field, forcing the ground to recede somewhat and allowing the skull and heart to stand out more freely. The artist has also added leaves and other linear elements, both drawn onto and incised into the surface. The incisions are most evident in the lower left segment of the sheet, moving horizontally across it, strengthening the physical presence of the painted print while suggesting the physicality of the artist at work. In that sense, these incisions parallel the handprints and fingerprints often featured in Dine's softground etchings and seen here along the lower edge, just above the artist's signature.

The sensuousness of this unique print provides a remarkable view of Dine's approach to his drawings as well as his prints. The emotional play of the hand, the sense of its pressure and variations in its speed, the many ways materials can be used—stroked, rubbed, layered, scraped, brushed, washed—all combine to reveal the artist's tensions and to evoke similar concerns in our own approach to viewing.

In all three versions of *Yellowheart and a Devil* seen here, the heart impinges on the skull/devil, pressing into its space and suggesting, perhaps, that love is a more powerful presence than death. Both images are forceful themes in Dine's art: the heart also appears in *The Heart and the Wall* (cat. 11), and the skull in another of the 1986 Graphicstudio prints, *A Side View in Florida* (app. 69). A conjunction of these two elements in Dine's dictionary of images was explored in the two versions of another in this group, *My Nights in Santa Monica* (app. 66, 67). In these, three hearts overlap across the low horizontal format, the central one enframing a skull. Following the bottom edge, staccato strokes (green in the non-bistre version) seem to signify grasses, a reference to nature that may be traced back to Dine's paintings of the 1960s.

All of Dine's 1986 Graphicstudio prints were started from drawings on mylar, which were transferred by gravure to etching plates prior to the artist's arrival in Florida. By the time he came to the workshop, proofs had been pulled and Dine was able to set to work immediately, adding direct markings by various methods to develop the images more fully.

1. The exhibited print is a unique, hand-painted impression. The standard edition consists of eleven impressions plus seven proofs.

13 Untitled Cast Concrete, 1981–1985
Cast concrete, aluminum, spray paint
Head: 19 x 12 x 4½ (48.3 x 30.5 x 11.4)
Stand: 50½ x 15 x 15 (128.3 x 38.1 x 38.1)
Edition: 4, one of which is unpainted
Collaboration: Donald Saff, with Chuck Fager, Lawrence Voytek, Ron Wolfe

Portrayed here is Jim Dine's wife Nancy, who has been a prime model for the artist since he began in the mid-1970s to concentrate on working directly from the figure. Indeed, Nancy Dine's portrait as well as Dine's self-portraits have come to be among his most important themes.

In 1980 Nancy was featured in several sculpture portraits in hand-painted bronze: *Nancy Hand Painted*, *Nancy Hand Painted II*, *Nancy Hand Painted III*. Other bronze portraits of Nancy, dating from the early 1980s, include *Painted Nancy with Cement Base*, *Nancy with Wooden*

13a. Jim Dine spray-painting *Untitled Cast Concrete* outside the observatory studio, December 1985

Base, and *Five Large Heads in London*, all 1983.[2] Don Saff has mentioned that in undertaking this Graphicstudio project he wanted to demonstrate to Dine the fidelity to his original clay model that was possible using concrete, which is far less costly than bronze and would be compatible for large outdoor sculpture.[3] Dine seems not to have been swayed, however, for he has not used the material again but has continued to work in bronze through the 1980s, as sculpture has played an increasingly important role in his art.[4]

The elongated form that functions here as a base may be tracked in Dine's art back to *The Hammer Doorway* of 1965, in which two hammer handles were stretched to a height of more than six feet, their relatively tiny heads perched atop. Another early piece that is even more pertinent to this one is *Angels for Lorca* (1966), in which two hats and a wig, all cast in fiberglass, rest atop three tall aluminum rods on flat circular bases. A precedent for Dine's placement of portrait heads on long, rodlike bases is the work of Alberto Giacometti (whom Dine greatly admires, as apparent in his statement at right), especially his *Head of a Man on a Bed* (1947).[5] The elongation in Dine's work, however, is more radical.

Dine's Graphicstudio head was produced in only four proof copies. From the artist's original clay portrait, Graphicstudio staff made a plaster mold, from which a wax positive was made to facilitate production of a rubber mold that would form the concrete, a mixture of Portland cement, fine silt sand, and a polymer additive. Dine spray-painted three of the proofs (fig. 13a) to produce a bright visage in which the articulation of features is modified by the strong color areas. The fourth was treated with Trewax, which enhances the meticulously rendered surfaces of the head, allowing all aspects of the modeling to be visible. In it, one perceives the artist's manipulation of the details of eyes, nose, mouth, and hair as well as the sense of dimensionality in the neck and chest.

Dine's virtuosity as a sculptor echoes his approach to his prints and his work in other media. The process of forming is always vivid in the final work, and one senses the passion with which the artist embraces both subject and media, searching for an appropriate wedding of the two.

1. See Ackley 1983.
2. The 1980 sculptures are reproduced in Shapiro 1981, pl. 196. The 1983 sculptures are reproduced in *Dine*, New York 1984, with an essay by Michael Edward Shapiro.
3. Saff, conversation with Fine, 20 November 1990.
4. In addition to *Dine*, New York 1984, see *Dine*, New York 1986.
5. This is suggested by the juxtaposition of illustrations in the Shapiro essay in *Dine*, New York 1984.

14 Youth and the Maiden, 1987–1988

Woodcut, heliorelief woodcut, softground and spitbite etching, and drypoint with painted additions
78⅝ x 140⅛ (199.8 x 355.9) in three sections
Edition: 16; 1 BAT; 2 PP; 2 PrP; 1 NGAP; 1 GP; 1 USFP; 1 TP
Collaboration: Greg Burnet, Patrick Foy, Michael Harrigan, Alan Holoubek, George Holzer, Tom Pruitt, Johntimothy Pizzuto, Donald Saff, Eric Vontillius

This powerful mixed-media print is one of eight that Dine completed at Graphicstudio in 1987–1988. In addition to *Youth and the Maiden*, these include *The Foreign Plowman* and *The Oil of Gladness* (cats. 15, 16), *The Mead of Poetry #1*, *The Mead of Poetry #2*, *The Mead of Poetry #3*, *Ravenna in November*, and *Red Dancer on the Western Shore* (app. 73–78, 80, 81).

Youth and the Maiden is Dine's largest print to date, virtually enveloping the viewer in its mysterious presence.[1] Its triptych format conjures memories of altarpieces, and its juxtaposition of images suggests the breadth of the artist's exploration in religion, myth, and art history while developing his own artistic vocabulary. Dine's references to an extensive and varied selection from the art of the past is well documented in his many published interviews and statements.[2] Among the works that played a role in the development of *Youth and the Maiden* were two from the sixteenth century: Andreas Vesalius' anatomical text, *De Humani Corporis Fabrica*, illustrated by skeletal figures that are set off, as are the figures in *Youth and the Maiden*, by vast areas of sky; and Domenico delle Greche's woodcut after Titian's *The Death of Pharaoh and His Army Submerged in the Red Sea*, cut from twelve separate blocks that together measured approximately 46-by-88 inches. The latter was massive among prints of the sixteenth century, just as Dine's is an impressive size among prints of the twentieth.

Trees in foliage, skeletons, a flayed figure, a sheathed woman based on a Hellenistic sculpture: all carry ritualistic overtones. By repeating these elements in his own work, Dine has made them as much his as are the robes and hearts long associated with his art.[3] The braided doll figures, which may give the print its title, are less pervasive in their shared meanings or associations with Dine's art, yet they recall his 1972 etching, *Braid (First State)*, and other works from that period that feature hair.[4] At the same time they suggest German peasant dolls thought to have mystical powers on behalf of fertility as well as curative powers if burned to ashes and swallowed. Portions of *Youth and the Maiden* were used for other prints completed at Graphicstudio during this working session. The tree may be seen in *Ravenna in November*, and the draped figure in *Red Dancer on the Western Shore*, printed in two sections. Several elements were used in *The Foreign Plowman*.

Graphicstudio staff printed *Youth and the Maiden* from Dine's multiple copperplates and woodblocks. The plates were drawn in several of the etching media, including spitbite, softground, and drypoint. The woodblocks were both hand-cut and worked in a heliorelief process recently developed at Graphicstudio (see technical note at the end of the present catalogue). The complex of processes, both overprinted and used adjacent to each other, achieved an atmospheric richness in *Youth and the Maiden*. The silvery gray wood grain behind the skeleton at the left of the central panel establishes a darker ground than is evident in the rest of the print, where a fluid blue field, either aquatint or woodcut, creates an aura of light.

The large central section of the print is actually composed of four sheets of paper joined together. One sheet carries the skeleton, with its somber gray field enhanced by touches of printed blue and black as well as glimpses of the white paper, providing a rich array of visual incident

I let things grow a little more now. . . . I can let a print alone and then come back to it. In fact, I like to do that. It's more of a way I'm working now that I come back to everything—years later.

Jim Dine, conversation with Ruth Fine, 1990

throughout. To the right of the skeleton is a segment bearing the left portion of the Hellenistic figure, the white of the paper showing through her carved dress. She is completed on the adjacent sheet, where the blue of the field modifies the dress as well, joining the figure to the field, as does the undefined area of black to the right of the figure's midsection. Dramatic in texture, the function of this black section is formal rather than narrative. The juxtaposition in this sheet of blue woodcut striations and granular aquatint surface closely related in hue is similarly intriguing. The right segment of this central panel repeats the woodcut tree seen at the far left, but the etched branches here are more forceful than those in the left-hand impression, intensifying their contrast against the flatter gray woodcut field.

Examination of Dine's use of black alone suggests the sophistication with which the artist combines print processes. The wood grain is important in the trees and in the gray field, but it plays a less important role in the draped woman and braided dolls, revealing how printed blacks featuring wood grain differ from blacks where the grain is less visible. Etched blacks have a more velvety quality than either of the woodcut blacks. Light gray etched and/or drypoint marks add another level of delineation in the skull at right.

What is crucial here is the interplay between the distinctive surfaces, which coalesce to establish the drama of the scene. Etched fingerprints add tone and texture; in addition, painted areas—for example, on the head of the flayed figure in the right panel and throughout the blue field—add light and soften edges, enhancing the physicality of the piece. As always, the painted areas play a multiple role: as formal and subject elements and as further references to the forming process. In exploring these various printmaking techniques, Dine also reveals his enormous sensitivity as a draftsman. In his layering of surfaces, repetition of images, atmospheric color, and references to both a cultural and personal history, he invites the viewer to share his own responses to modern experience.

1. Parts of this entry have been published in *Art for the Nation*, the National Gallery's fiftieth-anniversary gifts exhibition catalogue. For a discussion of the print in context with others by Dine of this period, see Saff, "*Youth and the Maiden*: A Morphology of Complex Boundaries in the Art of Jim Dine," in *Dine*, New York 1988, 30–39. This essay as well as a conversation with the artist in New York on 20 September 1990 are the sources for information presented here.

2. See "Conversations" and "Dine on Drawings" in Glenn 1985, 31–51, 196–210; see also Shapiro 1981, 203–211.

3. For Dine's best-known subjects, see Beal 1984; the catalogue includes comments by the artist throughout.

4. Castleman 1991, makes the connection between the braided figures and the title and reports that the source of the figures was a book on the history of dolls.

15a. The studio during the proofing session for
The Foreign Plowman, September 1987

15 The Foreign Plowman, 1987–1988

Woodcut, heliorelief woodcut, spitbite etching, with painted additions
Five panels, each: 70⅝ x 24½ (179.5 x 61.5)
Edition: 10; 1 BAT; 2 PP; 2 PrP; 1 NGAP; 1 GP; 1 USFP; 1 TP
Collaboration: Greg Burnet, Patrick Foy, Alan Holoubek, Tom Pruitt, Donald Saff, with
Marcia Brown, George Holzer, Johntimothy Pizzuto, Eric Vontillius

The Foreign Plowman conflates several elements in Dine's 1987–1988
Graphicstudio prints: moving from left to right, the flayed skull may be
seen in *Youth and the Maiden* (cat. 14), the female head in *The Mead of
Poetry #1* (app. 73, 74), the tree in *Youth and the Maiden* and *Ravenna
in November* (app. 80), the male head in *The Mead of Poetry #2* (app.
75, 76).[1] Combined, they function as a series of emblems laden with the
historical and mythic meanings with which Dine has increasingly imbued
his art in recent years. The central element is the tree, suggesting the
land, everlasting nature. (Is it two trees at once, or one tree at different
stages of life, or a tree and a shadow of another tree, or a tree and a
memory of another tree? Or all of these at once? Such sorts of questions
are applicable to every element in the piece.) The tree is flanked by the
figures of a woman and a man; the woman is clothed whereas the man

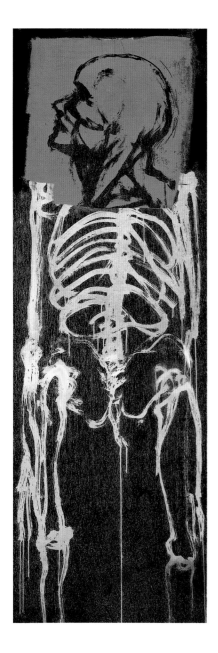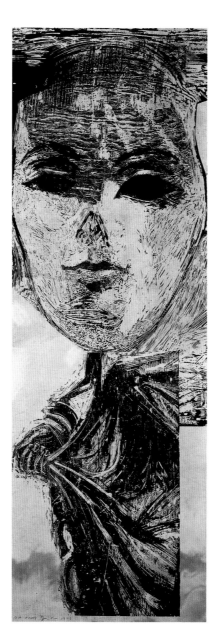

has a skeletal body. Their portrait heads are based on those of Queen
Nefertiti and King Akhenaton—historical personages of mythic stature,
from a civilization of enormous cultural significance. And these figures
are flanked in the two outside panels by a skeletal figure at left (death)
and a female nude at right (sex, love), with a riot of other elements including an outstretched hand reaching across the lower part of the figure's legs.[2] The two end panels have black backgrounds, distinguishing
them from the three central panels with background elements suggestive
of landscape.

Dine's representation of Egyptian royalty may relate to his interest in
Domenico delle Greche's woodcut after Titian, *The Death of Pharaoh
and His Army Submerged in the Red Sea* (see cat. 14). His title, as Don
Saff has pointed out, calls to mind Hans Holbein's 1583 woodcut, *Death
and the Plowman*.[3] How these diverse images interact with other elements within their panels and among the other panels is not readily
defined. Dine's message is not specific and circumscribed, nor is it uni-

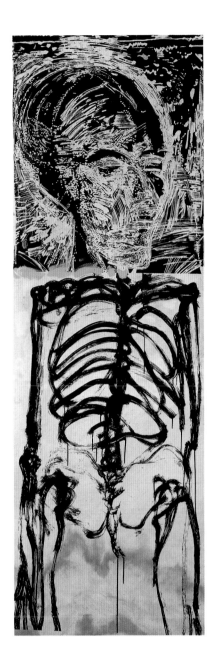

lateral or static. As described by Konrad Oberhuber, director of the Albertina in Vienna where the print was exhibited in 1989, in *The Foreign Plowman*, "Jim Dine has surrounded the tree of life and its shadow—the tree of consciousness and death—with the two aspects of femininity and masculinity, virginity and sensuality, intellectuality and joy of life, introversion and extroversion, dream and consciousness, and ultimately, life and death."[4]

Higher in key and more celebratory in stance than *Youth and the Maiden*, this print displays a similar technical diversity. In *The Foreign Plowman,* however, the hand-painting plays a more immediately visible role: a strong square of blue paint surrounded by strokes of black enframes the flayed head in the left panel, and below it strokes of bright yellow enliven the hip joints. This yellow travels horizontally across the five panels lightening up the region where what may be seen as green grass meets blue sky. Touches of white paint and of blue further modify the three central panels.

Usually [a work] starts with one panel and then it grows. It's another way of correcting. It grows because it's needed. . . . I don't usually start off with more than two.

Jim Dine, conversation with Ruth Fine, 1990

Perhaps as much as any aspect of the richly worked *Youth and the Maiden* and *The Foreign Plowman*, the panel with the nude seen here shows Dine's virtuosity in carving an image in wood. Short broad strokes convey the volume of the figure's breasts and arms, and the several hands meeting at her waist imply another figure, perhaps embracing her from behind. (Or does this suggest the movement of a single figure?) Over the lower part of the legs the diversity of hand-carved marks ranges from the finest striations to wiggly lines and networks of crosshatching, to wide slabs vigorously cut into the wood. These marks provide very different surfaces than compose the central tree, which has been cut into the wood by the heliographic method (see technical note at end of this volume).

1. In *The Mead of Poetry #1* the female head floats freely, with a slight suggestion of her neck at the left, but no body; in *The Mead of Poetry #2* the male head and neck are defined and the distribution of dark and light provides a suggestion of shoulders as well.
2. For Dine's use of the tree, see Beal 1984, 118–133. For a discussion of *The Foreign Plowman* in context with others by Dine of this period, see Saff, in *Dine*, New York 1988, 30–39. This essay and a September 1990 conversation with the artist are the sources for the information given here. This work was at one time planned to be a folding screen and a proof exists in that format.
3. Saff, in *Dine*, New York 1988, 37.
4. Oberhuber, in *Dine*, New York 1988, 13.

16 The Oil of Gladness, 1987–1988

Heliorelief woodcut, softground and spitbite etching, and power tool drypoint on Arches Cover paper
79¹/₈ x 37³/₄ (201.0 x 95.8)
Edition: 50; 1 BAT; 10 AP; 2 PrP; 1 NGAP; 1 GP; 1 USFP
Collaboration: Greg Burnet, Patrick Foy, Alan Holoubek, Donald Saff, Tom Pruitt, with George Holzer, Johntimothy Pizzuto, Eric Vontillius

Dine's art is filled with art historical references. His respect for the art of the past as a dynamic source of inspiration today has been essential in his development since the late 1960s when he left New York to live abroad for several years. *The Oil of Gladness* introduces Dine's Venus image in the Graphicstudio context. The image first appeared in his work more than a decade ago, when he inserted a small plaster cast of the Louvre's Venus de Milo into a still-life painting that also included an Egyptian statuette.[1] Similar sources have made their mark on Dine's other works from this session at Graphicstudio, including a second Hellenistic statue of a woman, the inspiration for both *Red Dancer on the Western Shore* (app. 81) and the central figure in *Youth and the Maiden* (cat. 14).

The Venus functions for Dine as "a link to art history . . . and is about the relationship of art and the history of art to objects."[2] By 1985 Dine had completed twenty-three prints with the Venus image, and through the rest of the decade he has added to that number. He has produced an important body of sculpture as well: of single Venuses, double Venuses, and groups of several figures, ranging from small tabletop versions to heroic figures well over human scale. Several sculptures have faceted areas of color similar to what is seen in this dramatic multimedia print. By now Dine has virtually transformed this icon of Western art history into a symbol widely associated with his own work, along with the heart, the bathrobe, and so forth.[3] In this particular print the juxtaposition of discrete color areas within a black linear structure echoes the scheme seen earlier in *The Woodcut Bathrobe* (cat. 8). The immediate source for

Dine's Venus prints was a photograph of one of his own headless Venus sculptures rather than the plaster cast of the Louvre sculpture. Just as the bathrobe has come to stand as an emblem of maleness, the Venus, even more readily, may stand for universal female sexuality.[4]

The distinctive combination of processes employed in *The Oil of Gladness* offers a clarity and richness that is characteristic not only of Dine's prints but of his drawings as well, which tend to be worked in a similar complex of media. The softly textured grain of the wood here is cut across by incisive contours and modeling drawn into it, made possible by the use of the heliorelief process developed at Graphicstudio, which incorporates a photographic process and sandblasting (see technical note at end of the present catalogue). This woodblock, printed in black, provides the overall configuration of the Venus and establishes its planar divisions. A watery spitbite aquatint, printed in blue, evokes an atmospheric ground (in abstract terms) or the sky (if one wishes to be literal). And the individual panels of color, also achieved through aquatint, all have distinctive qualities that enhance their differences in hue. Using primary colors (red, yellow, and blue) and secondaries (orange and green), Dine also included subtle variants and gradations: red violet, blue green, a brownish brick red. Delicate softground and drypoint lines add rhythmic and textural elements throughout, their rich blackness reinforcing the grayer tonalities of the woodblock. Especially along the edges of the work, direct imprints from Dine's hands and fingers appear, having been pressed into the softground and etched into the plate. They define the artist's identity within the print, establishing an intimate relationship between Dine and his feminine image. They also add further importance to the parallel subject crucial in Dine's art: that of the working process.

The fullness of Dine's approach is evident in any isolated segment of *The Oil of Gladness*. The gestural, hairlike black marks in the background, for example, are combined with wood grain, handprints, and more vigorously established lines, all seen against the fluidity of the aquatint color. This play of masterfully activated surfaces and the use of a variety of means to describe form are increasingly evident in the evocative facture of Dine's art.

I always seem to make references through paint or objects to an older art. It's a link to my past.
Jim Dine, in Beal 1984

1. Jean E. Fineberg, "'Not Marble': Jim Dine Transforms the Venus," in D'Oench and Fineberg 1986, 25. Fineberg's essay provides an overview of Dine's use of the subject to that date. Since then, it has remained an important motif for the artist, especially in his sculpture.

2. Fineberg, in D'Oench and Fineberg 1986, 25.
3. The bathrobe began as a symbolic self-portrait and over time has evolved into less personalized metaphors.
4. The point has been made by Fineberg, in D'Oench and Fineberg 1986, 38.

DIVERSE EARLY YEARS

Theo Wujcik at the lithography press, c. 1970

RICHARD ANUSZKIEWICZ

Born in Erie, Pennsylvania, 1930
Lives and works in Englewood, New Jersey

As a STUDENT at Erie Technical High School, Richard Anuszkiewicz took art classes every day from Joseph Plavcan. He attended the Cleveland Institute of Art on scholarship (B.F.A. 1953) and won a Pulitzer Traveling Fellowship his final year that he used to study with Josef Albers at Yale University's School of Art and Architecture. Attempting at first to reconcile Albers' color and compositional theories with the realism he had been practicing since high school, he eventually focused on abstraction. After Yale (M.F.A. 1955) Anuszkiewicz continued to paint while attending Kent State University (B.S. in education, 1956). He was given his first one-man exhibition at the Butler Institute of American Art in Youngstown, Ohio, in 1955.

In 1957 Anuszkiewicz moved to New York and worked at the Metropolitan Museum of Art for awhile, repairing scale models of classical Greek architecture and sculpture, then at Tiffany & Company (1958–1959), designing miniature silver animals. He also traveled extensively in Europe and North Africa during this period.

Anuszkiewicz' first one-man show in New York was held at the Contemporaries Gallery in 1960, from which Alfred Barr bought a painting for the Museum of Modern Art. By mid-decade Anuszkiewicz' work had been featured in such seminal exhibitions as *Geometric Abstraction in America* (Whitney Museum of American Art, 1962) and *The Responsive Eye* (Museum of Modern Art, 1965). The latter helped secure his reputation as a leading proponent of the American "op art" movement in the 1960s. In keeping with Albers' Bauhaus sensibility, Anuszkiewicz undertook various commercial projects, including the design of playing cards, banners, serving trays, and even a painted fur coat. In 1972 he designed outdoor murals for a YWCA building in New York City and an office building in Jersey City.

Anuszkiewicz' interest in prints, specifically Japanese prints, developed at Yale. The first prints he produced were screenprints—Christmas cards for the Museum of Modern Art from 1963 to 1965. His first lithograph was offset, executed in 1964. In addition to Graphicstudio, Anuszkiewicz has worked in New York at Atelier Editions, Chiron Press, Lassiter-Meisel, New York Institute of Technology Print Workshop (Old Westbury), and Triton Press, and in Stuttgart at Edition Domberger, and Peter Haas. His prints have been featured in one-man exhibitions organized by the Sterling and Francine Clark Art Institute, Williamstown, Massachusetts (1979), and the Fine Arts Gallery, Florida State University, Tallahassee (1981). Other solo exhibitions have included those at the Cleveland Museum of Art (1966), Hopkins Art Center, Dartmouth College (1967), De Cordova Museum, Lincoln, Massachusetts (1972), La Jolla Museum of Contemporary Art (1976), John and Mable Ringling Museum of Art, Sarasota (1978), Carnegie Institute, Pittsburgh (1980), Museum of Fine Arts, St. Petersburg, Florida (1981), Lowe Art Museum, Coral Gables (1981), Butler Institute of American Art, Youngstown (1984), Tampa Museum (1986), Cleveland Institute of Art (1988), and Newark Museum, New Jersey (1990).

Richard Anuszkiewicz working on a construction in his studio, 1988

17 Tampa Winter, 1972–1973

Color lithograph on German etching paper
31 x 22¹/₂ (78.7 x 57.2)
Edition: 70 (I/XX through XX/XX; 1/50 through 50/50); 1 BAT; 1PrP; 3 PP; 5 AP;
1 USFP
Collaboration: Donald Saff, Theo Wujcik

Richard Anuszkiewicz toured Graphicstudio on his first visit to Florida
in 1971 and returned by invitation, completing five color lithographs—
Clearwater, *Largo*, *Tampa Summer*, *Tampa Winter*, and *Sun Coast*
(cat. 18)—between February 1972 and October 1973. Anuszkiewicz had
experimented with lithography on only two prior occasions, both times
using the offset method to create single-color lithographs.[1] He maintains
that the Graphicstudio prints were his "first full experience with
lithography."[2]

At Graphicstudio, Anuszkiewicz worked with Theo Wujcik, who had
left the workshop to become a full-time faculty member at the University
of South Florida but agreed, at Donald Saff's request, to take on this
challenging project. According to Saff, "The project was even more difficult than we anticipated. For instance, each sheet of paper had to be
picked clean of impurities that wouldn't have mattered in other forms of
printing, even other lithographs; Anuszkiewicz' light colors wouldn't obscure any impurities. Matching extremely light wet inks with dry printed
color was also formidable."[3]

The compatibility of Wujcik and Anuszkiewicz was key to the success
of the project. Anuszkiewicz recently recalled:

Theo was great to work with. He was a very dedicated artist in his own
right, so he was a stickler for detail and had tremendous patience. It was a
matter of getting the colors the right shade, because they are so high-keyed.

In order to get them in the sequence I wanted, we had to do a tremendous amount of proofing, requiring a lot of patience and color control. . . . I did make some preliminary studies, but nothing that you would interpret as real working drawings. I would make some calculations of how I wanted to divide up the space and then I would choose the colors and we would color test and proof.[4]

Because they were working with such delicate colors, it was critical that the light be consistent during the mixing and proofing process: "I made mixtures and saw proofs under warm light because it was constant and controlled, and it would more than likely be the kind of light that the final print would be viewed in."[5]

Tampa Winter is a loose color reversal of *Tampa Summer* (app. 8), each reflecting a particular sense of climate.[6] Each print is composed of five different colored sets of sixteen concentric bands that form a rectangle. In *Tampa Winter* a subtle color transition is established from the radiating light and warmth of the shimmering yellow bands at the center to the coolness of the blue tint around the perimeter. The bands widen and narrow consistently in each group, from the thinness of a pen line at the edges of each set to about one-eighth inch in the middle. A steady undulating effect is created by the rhythmic widening and narrowing of the lines. From a short distance away, the thinnest lines visually dissolve and the paper appears to turn gray. The image seems to pulsate, as foreground becomes background becomes foreground again (and figure becomes ground becomes figure again.)

The delicate gradation of hues in *Tampa Winter* represents a contrast to the artist's work of the 1960s in which he juxtaposed pure complementary colors.[7] In an apparent paradox, Anuszkiewicz achieves a soft, ephemeral quality in this print by using a calculated system of rigid lines and hard edges: "My introduction of more [colors] led me to the greater use of line. Always color determines the form. You might say, there was a further coming together of ends and means. The greater complexity or potentiality of the color was matched by the capacity of the linear means to deliver subtler gradations of hue and chromatic nuances among evenly saturated colors."[8]

The interdependency of form and color in *Tampa Winter*, the unabashed symmetry of the composition, and the consistency of the undulation result in a poetic, meditative image that transcends any initial impression of a strictly mathematical or scientific investigation of optical effects.

What I like about printing is that you're working with a new medium, and it's a collaboration because you're working with a printer . . . [who] performs a function that you can't actually perform. And you're working with new colors, as the printer's inks are different from acrylics.
Richard Anuszkiewicz, in Corbino 1980

1. Anuszkiewicz' two offset lithography projects were *Architectural*, 1964 (no edition), and *Yellow Reversed*, 1970 (published by *Art in America* [March–April 1970], insert between pp. 56 and 59). See *Anuszkiewicz*, Tallahassee 1981.
2. Anuszkiewicz, telephone conversation with Corlett, 13 September 1990.
3. Baro 1978, 19.
4. Anuszkiewicz, telephone conversation with Corlett, 1990.
5. Anuszkiewicz, telephone conversation with Corlett, 1990. The artist also uses controlled light conditions when working on his paintings. See *Anuszkiewicz*, New York 1975.
6. For a painting close in spirit to these two Tampa prints, see *Winter Moon–Summer Moon* (1972), reproduced in *Anuszkiewicz*, La Jolla 1976.

7. Anuszkiewicz summarized this change in his work: "By the late sixties and early seventies . . . the introduction of more colors began to dictate changes of image and format to a 'series' involvement by using multiple squares, vertical bands, and bands around a center. The colors of the bands or squares, adhered to a sequential and spectrum-like arrangement. This kind of family grouping had a much softer appearance than the earlier stark complementary two or three color paintings, and I refer to them as 'soft' hard-edge paintings. The sequential arrangment of color also led to works dealing with the reversal of color order." (See the brochure for the *Anuszkiewicz* exhibition, Jerusalem 1976.)
8. *Anuszkiewicz*, New York 1975.

18 Sun Coast (triptych), 1972–1973
Color lithograph on buff Arches Cover paper
Each sheet: 30 x 22½ (76.2 x 57.2)
Edition: 70 (I/XX through XX/XX; 1/50 through 50/50); 1 BAT; 1PrP; 3 PP; 1 CTP;
5 AP; 1 USFP
Collaboration: Donald Saff, Theo Wujcik

As in *Tampa Winter* (cat. 17), color and form interlock in *Sun Coast* to create a whole that is greater and more complex than the sum of its component parts.[1] Each panel of the *Sun Coast* triptych is divided vertically and is exactly symmetrical, with each half of each panel composed of concentric bands printed in two colors: the inner eight bands in one color, and the outer fifteen bands in another. Each panel, while self-contained, is also visually connected to the adjacent one by an internal tension established by the overall interlocking color scheme. The central panel, which serves as the fulcrum, is composed of bands of blue and cool green. On its left half the green bands surround the blue, while on the right half the reverse is true. On the left half of the left panel yellow bands surround pink, while on its other half warm green bands surround purple. This color structure is exactly reversed on the right panel. Thus the yellow-pink combinations are set against the outer edges of both side panels, while the purple-green combinations are adjacent to the central panel.

The dynamics of the color relationships change as the placement of the colors changes across the three panels. The yellow on the far left shim-

mers like a halo around an ethereal pink, while on the far right that same yellow, now surrounded by pink, glows more softly. The structural symmetry of the *Sun Coast* composition is somewhat mitigated by the effects of these color interchanges, creating, as with *Tampa Winter*, a lyrical and meditative image. Similar color scheme reversals can be found in Anuszkiewicz paintings from the period, such as *Spring Warm* and *Spring Cool* (both 1973).[2]

The color of the paper plays an important role here, too. Optical effects generated by the color lines cause the warm buff paper to appear brighter in the center of each panel. Anuszkiewicz asserts that it was in his Graphicstudio prints that he really began to explore the possibilities of ink color against paper color: "In *Yellow Reversed*, the offset lithograph I did for *Art in America*, I worked with yellow on white, using the color of the paper. Very shortly after that I went to work at Graphicstudio, where I expanded upon that, working on five editions. The lithographs produced there are very light, very high-keyed prints, that use my color against the white or buff color of the paper."[3]

It's the color performance that determines the form. Color performance and form are one. It's not a matter of coloring a geometric pattern or scheme. My [work has] a color atmosphere or color climate, a particular feeling, because I work in families or groups of color. You're seeing a gestalt, a totality. You see systems, groups of colors that function to create a total environment. I work for that.

Richard Anuszkiewicz, in New York 1975

1. Anuszkiewicz' interest in Gestalt psychology and the mechanics of visual perception may be gleaned from his master's thesis topic, "A Study in the Creation of Space with Line Drawing," influenced by Rudolf Arnheim's *Art and Visual Perception.* See Gruen 1979, 73.

2. For color reproductions of these paintings, see Lunde 1977, plates 200 and 201.

3. Anuszkiewicz, telephone conversation with Corlett, 1990.

ARAKAWA

Born in Nagoya City, Japan, 1936
Lives and works in New York City

SHUSAKU ARAKAWA was seven years old when the onset of World War II led his family to place him in a Buddhist monastery for two years to protect him. The conditions he endured there produced persistent nightmares, however, and in the hope that his fears could be alleviated, he was sent to live with a neighborhood doctor and his wife for three years after the war. Arakawa became interested in medicine as a teenager and worked as the doctor's assistant while studying drawing, painting, and science in high school.

From 1954 to 1958 Arakawa studied medicine, mathematics, and art in Japan and staged several "happenings." In 1960 he was affiliated with a neo-Dada group in Tokyo and also participated in a demonstration against the continued existence of American military bases in Japan. To escape the controversy in which he then found himself embroiled, Arakawa moved to New York in 1961, where he met John Cage, Marcel Duchamp, and writer/philosopher Madeline Gins, whom he married.

Arakawa and Gins began to collaborate on a prodigious project called *The Mechanism of Meaning,* which melds physics, metaphysics, phenomenology, and epistomology into a visual art form. A part of this series, approximately one hundred panels featuring images, texts, and objects, was first shown at the Venice Biennale in 1970. By this time Arakawa was also involved in filmmaking. He wrote and directed *Why Not: A Serenade of Eschatological Ecology* (1969), and collaborated with Gins on *For Example* (1971). Both films were shown at the Whitney Museum of American Art, New York.

Arakawa working on a lithographic plate for *Untitled 3* (cat. 19C), 1973–1974

In the course of his visual explorations of human thought processes and the structure of meaning, Arakawa has experimented with many printmaking media, including silkscreen, lithography, embossing, etching, and aquatint. In addition to Graphicstudio, Arakawa has worked in New York with Aeropress, Handworks, Maurel Studios, and Styria Studios, and in Minneapolis with Vermillion Editions. Multiples, Inc., New York, has published many of his prints.

In 1986 Arakawa was awarded the Chevalier des arts et des lettres by the French government. Major exhibitions of Arakawa's prints have been held at the Museum of Modern Art, New York (1974), and the Williams College Museum of Art (1979). In addition to *The Mechanism of Meaning*, which traveled in Germany and Switzerland in 1972, one-man exhibitions of his work have been held at the Museum of Modern Art, Tokyo (1958), Württembergischer Kunstverein, Stuttgart (1966), Musée d'art moderne de la ville de Paris (1970), Minneapolis Institute of Arts (1974, 1979), Städtische Kunsthalle, Düsseldorf (1977), Stedelijk Museum, Amsterdam (1978), National Art Museum, Osaka (1979), Lenbachhaus, Munich (1981–1982), Arts Club of Chicago (1981), Seibu Museum, Tokyo (1979, 1987), Padiglione d'arte contemporanea di Milano (1984), Aldrich Museum of Contemporary Art, Ridgefield, Connecticut (1984), Tokyo Museum of Contemporary Art (1989), and the Joseloff Gallery, University of Hartford, Connecticut (1990).

19A-F "No!" Says the Signified, 1973–1974

Six prints plus screenprinted title page and lithographed colophon, housed in a gray, fabric-covered box with screenprinted title; 72 boxes (including proof sets) were issued

In his art Arakawa explores the interior, mental world, rather than providing a window on, or a reflection of, the physical world. His approach has consistently been one of open-ended examination of thought processes, the work functioning as a vehicle for complex investigations that merge the visual arts with linguistic, literary, philosophical, mathematical, and scientific theories to probe epistemological, metaphysical, and ontological issues. Arakawa delves into the abstract nature of thought and the vicissitudes of language and meaning, revealing the artificial and ephemeral nature of knowledge. He celebrates the function of nonsense in expanding the thinking process.

Arakawa's art is about intangibles revealed through intellectual constructs peculiar to the organization of thought and the conceptualization of reality. He challenges the illusion that we are equipped to fully comprehend the reality we occupy by deploying those constructs—especially language systems, but including scientific and mathematical models that use maps, charts and diagrams, arrows and annotations.[1]

The exquisite surfaces of *"No!" Says the Signified* (a title Arakawa had used for a 1972 painting) are characterized by the rich rendering of tactile passages of color, line, and texture. Remarkably, these prints represent Arakawa's first experimentation with lithography.[2] Humor and the potential for confusion are key ingredients of Arakawa's aesthetic. Using the idiosyncracies of language, he employs various word games, including non sequiturs and conundrums, throughout the suite.

Arakawa's epigrams are often the equivalent of "visual koans"—Zen Buddhist meditations that defy traditional reason and thereby, when pondered, act as catalysts for enlightenment.[3] "When 'always and not' signifies something 'the signified or if' belongs to the zero set! have we met before?" is the recurring epigram of the present series. Screenprinted on the fabric cover of the portfolio box, it reappears in *Untitled 2* and is the "subject" of *Untitled 4.*

In *Untitled 1* a yellow stripe vertically divides the composition. The message along the bottom, traversing its entire width, warns: "The two areas separated by the yellow stripe should never be united into one perception." Yet if one reads the message, one has already violated its instruction. The black wash background on the right and the ruler at the top also extend across the stripe, so in either reading the message or studying the composition, the viewer has lost the option of choosing whether or not to comply with the instruction.

Untitled 1 suggests a state of flux and metamorphosis: in the sense of movement conveyed by the fluid handling of the black ink; and in the word "forgotten" and its mirror image on the other side of the yellow stripe, reflecting the shifting nature of reality. If the print were held before a mirror, the right-reading letters would reverse and the reversed letters would read correctly. Mirror reversals also occur in *Untitled 5* and elsewhere in the suite. In both *Untitled 1* and *Untitled 2* Arakawa has expanded his representation of mutually exclusive perceptions by including a small photographic image of the print on the verso of the page (figs. 19a,b). Front and back, like mirror images, can "never be united into one perception."

Arakawa occasionally unites visual and verbal language cues with appeals to the sense of touch. In *Untitled 1* the texture of a sandpaper tri-

When "always and not" signifies something
"the signified or if" belongs to the
zero set.
"No!" says the signified.

(SENTIMENTAL OURNEY)
The Mechanism of Meaning
by Arakawa

19A **Untitled 1**
Color lithograph with collage on buff
Arches Cover paper
Verso: lithograph
22¹/₂ x 30¹/₁₆ (57.2 x 76.4)
Edition: 60 (I/XX through XX/XX;
1/40 through 40/40); 1 BAT; 2 PrP; 2 PP;
6 AP; 2 PuP; 1 USFP; 1 CP
Collaboration: Paul Clinton, Charles
Ringness, Donald Saff

19a. Verso of *Untitled 1*

angle (also used in *Untitled 4*) is set off with red, yellow, and blue acrylic paint. Tactility is further suggested by the image of a thumb being pulled through the wash on the right half of the composition, implying a viscosity and depth of surface that contrasts with the rough and rigid sandpaper.[4]

Untitled 2 relates directly to Arakawa's 1972 painting, *Courbet's Canvas*, and to a panel reproduced in *The Mechanism of Meaning* (1978 edition).[5] Each is inscribed with a similar message: "We are told to forget about gray all right. Then it is non-gray we must forget about to be in accord with this painting. This makes me angry. Of course neither is pos-

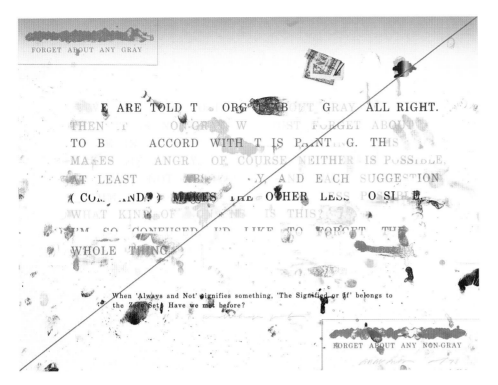

FORGET ABOUT ANY GRAY

E ARE TOLD T ORG B T GRAY ALL RIGHT.
THEN I ON-GR W ST F RGET ABOU
TO B ACCORD WITH T IS P NT G. TH
MA ES ANGR OF COURSE NEITHER IS P SSI LE.
AT LEAST B Y AND EACH SUGGE TION
(CO ND?) MAKES THE O HER LE S PO SI E
WH T KIN OF NE IS THIS?
M SO CONFUSED D LIKE TO F RGET TH
WHOLE TH NG

When 'Always and Not' signifies something, 'The Signified or If' belongs to
the Z Set Have we met before?

FORGET ABOUT ANY NON-GRAY

19ʙ Untitled 2

Color lithograph with screenprint on Rives
BFK paper
Verso: lithograph
22¼ x 30¼ (56.5 x 76.8)
Edition: 60 (I/XX through XX/XX;
1/40 through 40/40); 1 BAT; 2 PrP; 2 PP;
7 AP (one with verso measuring 22 x 30);
2 PuP; 1 USFP; 1 CP
Collaboration: Paul Clinton, Julio Juristo,
Charles Ringness, Donald Saff

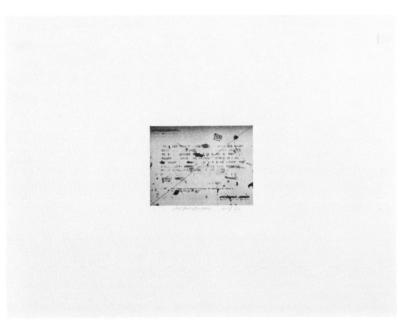

19b. Verso of *Untitled 2*

sible, at least not absolutely, and each suggestion (command?) makes the
other less possible. What kind of nonsense is this? I'm so confused I'd
like to forget the whole thing."[6] At the top left corner of *Untitled 2* the
words "forget about any gray" are paradoxically located below a long
gray daub and printed in gray. At the bottom right, again beneath a gray
daub and printed in gray, the instruction is to "forget about any non-
gray." Arakawa seems here to be working toward "Blank," a concept that
did not solidify in his work until the late 1970s (see cats. 20–21). At the
top right, just above the main text, three images—a photolithograph of a
folded dollar bill, a white screenprinted spatter, and a delicate, self-

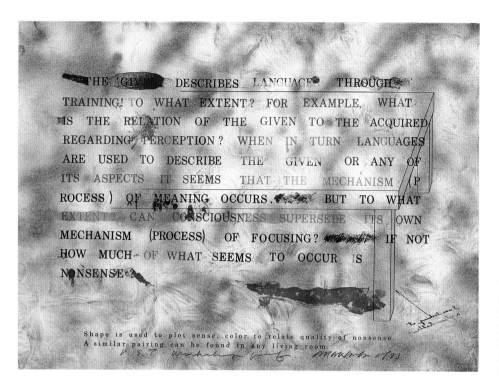

19C **Untitled 3**
Color lithograph on Arches Cover paper
22¹/₂ x 30¹/₈ (57.2 x 76.5)
Edition: 60 (I/XX through XX/XX;
1/40 through 40/40); 1 BAT; 2 PrP; 2 PP;
7 AP; 2 PuP; 1 USFP; 1 CP
Collaboration: Julio Juristo

contained lithographic rainbow roll—function as signifiers, as a cryptic
rubric for the paragraph. The message below, composed of multicolored
letters, is readable, if not readily understandable, although some of the
letters are obscured by smudges, blotches of color, stains, and handprints, all of which are part of the message, evoking a connection between artist and viewer. Such marks appear in every print in the series,
fingerprints appearing in the first five of the six.

Reading the message provides but one level of interpretation. As in
virtually all of Arakawa's work, the letters not only create words but
function visually as form and color. Yet if one can read English, one is
compelled to read the messages, however interrupted by other visual input such as smudges, daubs of color, fingerprints, or diagrams.

The statement of *Untitled 3* cryptically addresses language's role in
the thinking process: "The given describes languages through training!
To what extent? For example, what is the relation of the given to the
acquired regarding perception? When in turn languages are used to
describe the given or any of its aspects it seems that the mechanism (Process) of meaning occurs. But to what extent? Can consciousness super-
sede its own mechanism (process) of focusing? If not how much of what
seems to occur is nonsense?" Arakawa's concept of the "given" is a component of an epistemological inquiry that frequently surfaces in his
work. In 1977 his wife and collaborator Madeline Gins suggested that
"even, if by some quirk, the given turns out to be antithetical to the
modes of the mind, we have no choice but to begin with what we have,
the thinking field, the mechanism of meaning will always until we learn
to change it be our point of departure and that which gives any call of
continuity its sense."[7]

Along the bottom of *Untitled 3* is the cryptic message: "Shape is used
to plot sense, color to relate quality of nonsense. A similar pairing can be
found in any living room." Arakawa has included an incomplete diagram
of a table, highlighted in yellow—a "pairing" of shape and color, and

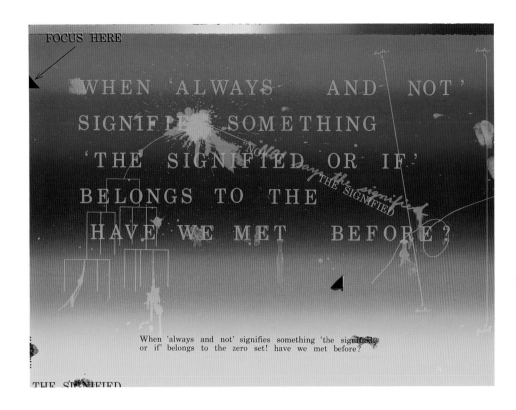

FOCUS HERE

WHEN 'ALWAYS AND NOT' SIGNIFIE SOMETHING 'THE SIGNIFIED OR IF' BELONGS TO THE HAVE WE MET BEFORE?

THE SIGNIFIED

When 'always and not' signifies something 'the signified or if' belongs to the zero set! have we met before?

19D Untitled 4
Color lithograph with collage on Arches
Cover paper
22½ x 30¼ (57.2 x 76.8)
Edition: 60 (I/XX through XX/XX;
1/40 through 40/40); 1 BAT; 2 PrP; 2 PP;
7 AP; 2 PuP; 1 USFP; 1 CP
Collaboration: Paul Clinton, Julio Juristo,
Donald Saff

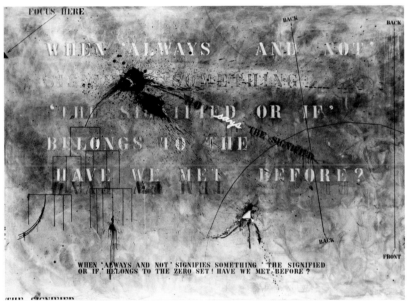

19c. *"No!" Says the Signified II*, 1972–1973, acrylic on canvas, approx. 72 x 108 (182.9 x 274.3), courtesy Ronald Feldman Fine Arts, New York

therefore sense and nonsense. To its right is a note, in mirror reverse: "I was looking at a yellow table."

Signs and symbols commonly used to convey information—such as diagrams with arrows and annotations—are an integral part of Arakawa's iconography. The chartlike structure and diagrammatic lines found in *Untitled 4*, for example, also appear in a related painting, *"No!" Says the Signified II* (fig. 19c). With its own double record of the central epigram,

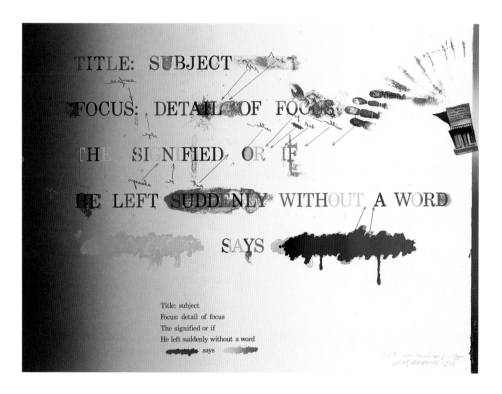

19E **Untitled 5**
Color lithograph with screenprint on
Arches Cover paper
22½ x 30¹/₁₆ (57.2 x 76.4)
Edition: 60 (I/XX through XX/XX;
1/40 through 40/40); 1 BAT; 2 PrP; 2 PP;
6 AP; 2 PuP; 1 WP; 1 CP
Collaboration: Paul Clinton, Julio Juristo,
Charles Ringness, Donald Saff

repeated from the bottom of *Untitled 2* and from the portfolio cover, *Untitled 4* might be seen as the keystone of the portfolio.

In *Untitled 5* color, words, marks, imprints, arrows, notations, and the photographic image of a matchbox all interact to produce the message, a visual support for the artist's comment that "words function like numbers or arrows pointing to something else . . . with the words, colors and shapes, I try to create a sentence."[8] The complex interplay of images and symbols used to produce the message is analogous to the eclectic way Arakawa approaches printmaking. He combines a variety of techniques to produce his prints: tusche washes, lines drawn with lithographic pencil, fingerprint smudges, the blended roll, photographic processes, and screenprint.

The handwritten message along the bottom of *Untitled 6*, printed using the rainbow roll technique, is a modification of the epigram of the portfolio: "Always (and not) the signified (or if) waiting to be *stretched* back into the zero set. Will you remembering?" Arakawa continued his exploration into the structure of language, combining verb endings to create the words "movinged" and "printinged," which occupy the center of the composition.[9] The photographic veracity of selected elements in *Untitled 6* provides a compelling presence that occupies a different perceptual plane than the words or diagrams do. An image of a printer's roller (photolithographically produced) is placed vertically along the left edge of the composition. The handwritten instruction, "do not focus here," with an arrow pointing to the handle of the roller, is readily violated by the viewer. In contrast, at the center of the composition the handwritten words, "focus here," with an arrow extending horizontally toward the right edge of the page, are written over themselves several times and thus appear out of focus and are in fact difficult to focus on. Contradictions among expression, instruction, perception, intention, and possibility are a recurring theme of Arakawa's work.

The series as a whole, printed from aluminum plates as well as traditional limestone, is a splendid example of lithographic surfaces at their

19F Untitled 6
Color lithograph on Arches Cover paper
22¹/₂ x 30¹/₈ (57.2 x 76.5)
Edition: 60 (I/XX through XX/XX;
1/40 through 40/40); 1 BAT; 2 PrP; 2 PP;
2 TP; 8 AP; 2 PuP; 1 USFP; 1 CP
Collaboration: Julio Juristo, Donald Saff

richest and reveals the artist's propensity for experimentation. Arakawa created the smoky black background of *Untitled 3*, for example, with tusche wash and airbrush spray on stone. Don Saff recalls that Arakawa had drawn "four stone washes in an effort to familiarize himself with the media and to gain confidence in the printer's ability to properly etch and print the delicate tonal range he sought. In the final days of the proofing session, Arakawa asked Julio Juristo to prepare another stone and with swift decisiveness produced an extraordinarily rich and delicate wash which was eventually used in the last print."[10]

1. Madeline Gins, in *Arakawa*, Düsseldorf 1977, 24, wrote: "In the thinking field it has not yet been established how much of that which we fail to see the point of is indeed a functional 'blind spot.' The thinker's blind spots might be areas of oversight which make his attention to a subject uneven, off balance. . . . By putting the thinking field in front of us, Arakawa gives us an opportunity to make distinctions between what has until now been only blank and what may be functionally 'blind' about the way we think."
2. See Saff's discussion of this project in Baro 1978, 20.
3. Jean-François Lyotard, in his essay, "Longitude 180 W or E," in *Arakawa*, Milan 1984, used the phrase "visual koan" to describe Arakawa's epigrams.
4. Arakawa's combination of languages—written, verbal, and visual—was noted by Danielle Rice in *Arakawa*, Chicago 1981: "Arakawa unites these various languages and forces them to work together."

5. Arakawa and Gins 1979.
6. The text beneath the related panel in *The Mechanism of Meaning* elaborates on the implications of the message: "A condition of suspended confusion through which 'I' may shift under observation. Or a means for viewing thoughts which might pass between 'I' and 'me.' So, from irregular or parallel intentions, something slowly is forming." See Arakawa and Gins 1979, 90.
7. Gins, in *Arakawa*, Düsseldorf 1977, 29.
8. Arakawa, quoted by Stephen Eisenman and Brian Lukacher, in Williamstown 1979, 8.
9. The purpose of this invention was described by Gins, in *Arakawa*, Düsseldorf 1977, 27, where she referred to "movinged" as "a word image invented by Arakawa in an earlier painting to give a sense of 'continuous past present.'"
10. Saff 1974, 16.

20 The Sharing of Nameless, 1984–1986
Color lithograph and screenprint with embossing on Arches Cover Buff paper
36⅝ x 56¹¹/₁₆ (93.1 x 144)
Edition: 60; 1 BAT; 3 PP; 2 PrP; 1 NGAP; 1 GP; 1 USFP; 11 AP
Collaboration: Julio Juristo, David Yager, with Robbie Evans, George Holzer, Ron Kraver,
Deli Sacilotto, Donald Saff, Steven Sangenario

21 The Sharing of Nameless, 1984–1986
Color aquatint and etching with embossing on Arches Cover paper
31¹³/₁₆ x 47⁷/₁₆ (80.8 x 120.5)
Edition: 60; 1 BAT; 4 PP; 2 PrP; 1 NGAP; 1 GP; 1 USFP; 10 AP
Collaboration: Doris Simmelink, Robert Townsend, Donald Saff, David Yager, with
George Holzer, Derrick Isono, Deli Sacilotto, Chris Sukimoto, Sarah Todd

Arakawa returned to Graphicstudio in 1984 to produce two prints, one
a lithograph with screenprinting, the other an aquatint. These two
works, both entitled *The Sharing of Nameless*, are related to a group of
drawings and canvases that explored themes the artist had begun to investigate in the late 1970s.[1] Many iconographical elements found in the
prints, such as the arrows and the maplike grid structure, appear with
some frequency in the related works as well.

In conjunction with his studies on the "Mechanism of Meaning," Arakawa has been exploring the scientific theory of space-time, in particular
its relationship to what he has defined as the concept of "Blank," an idea
with epistemological overtones: "Blank may be considered the basic gen-
erating level of human capability. . . . It is everything of an individual
aside from the current instant of perception."[2] Arakawa's "spacetime," is
rooted in theoretical physics but takes exception to it as well. In 1986
the artist wrote: "Philosophy, physics, and art all pivot around the essential question of the nature of spacetime. I don't believe that spacetime
exists in any of the ways in which it has so far been represented by
Newton, nor by Einstein. It's not that there is no spacetime, but that
spacetime is by nature so short-lived that it continually eludes us; we
strongly suspect its presence and are forever generalizing about our
suspicions."[3]

*To trap questions, areas, operations, answers;
to make them visible by combining two or more
languages. Draw and name it. . . .*

*My medium is the area of perception created,
located, and demonstrated by the combining
(melting) of languages, systems into each other
in the same moving place.*
Arakawa 1969

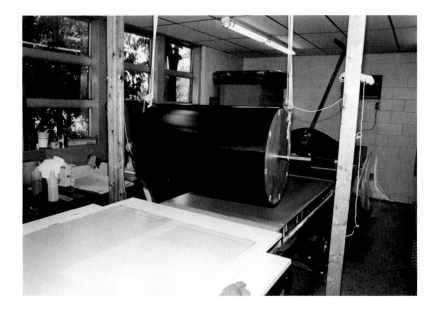

20a. Special system for maneuvering the oversized roller used to print Arakawa's lithograph
The Sharing of Nameless

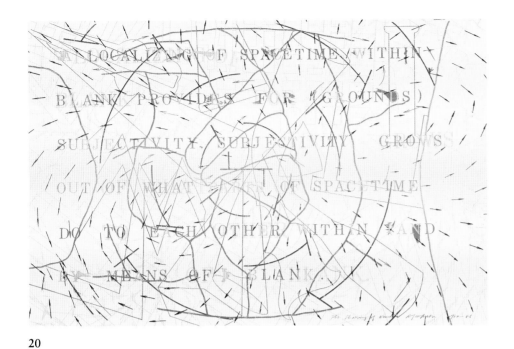

20

The text of *The Sharing of Nameless* refers to both of these concepts: "A localizing of spacetime within Blank provides for (grounds) subjectivity. Subjectivity grows out of what parts of spacetime do to each other within (and by means of) Blank." In an interview with Madeline Gins published in 1987, Arakawa explained the interrelationship of these ideas in his art in somewhat less elusive terms: "Painting Blank: I have used this as a means to investigate what I think may be an entirely different originating process of that which has up until now been thought of as spacetime, and which may conditionally still be called spacetime, and the way in which this affects what we think of as subjectivity."[4] In merging diverse disciplines such as epistemology and theoretical physics into an interlocking web of visual systems, Arakawa probes the human thought process.

Multiple levels of Blank are alluded to in *The Sharing of Nameless* prints: in the complex layering of written language, notations, and corrections, with visual structures that resemble maps, diagrams, and other systems with a cognitive function. In the lithograph (cat. 20) these layers include: a maplike, labyrinthine linear pattern that is somewhat circular in structure superimposed on a grid structure that strongly suggests the layout of city blocks;[5] diagrammatic drawings of self-contained shapes; smears and blotches ("mistakes"); words in gray; words in yellow; selected letters with a peach-tone overlay; embossed words; and a multitude of arrows that simultaneously (and paradoxically) suggest dispersion, rotation, and an intense level of energy that seems somehow to be both random and controlled.

Arakawa often taps the visual lexicon of mathematics and science, and individual shapes sometimes suggest textbook diagrams illustrating scientific principles—human systems for visualizing the nonvisual. The large form in the shape of a bent hourglass that appears near the middle of both the lithograph and the aquatint (cat. 21) resembles a scientific diagram in Stephen Hawking's *A Brief History of Time* that illustrates the configuration of an event in space-time.[6] The arrows, which appear in

21

such multitudes in both of these prints and in the other related works, are a staple of scientific diagrams and also bring to mind Hawking's "arrows of time": "something that distinguishes the past from the future, giving a direction to time."[7]

In the Graphicstudio prints, as in many of the related drawings and paintings, the multiple layers of lines and shapes have a transparent quality, as if executed on tiers of glass. The interaction between the various layers enables the viewer to experience subtle shifts of meaning and interpretation, and new perceptive possibilities are revealed. In the lithograph, for example, Arakawa seems to be engaging in wordplay: the last three letters in "localizing of" read "goof" when two layers of letters are perceived together. A cool intellectual reading of the lithograph is tempered by the dazzlingly rich surface color and texture that results from the combination of lithography and screenprinting. The embossing of certain words—"to," "of," "for," "and"—adds still another dimension, another layer, another texture. The soft, horizontal bands of warm color behind the grids and diagrams contribute to a sense of depth, or of space between the layers. To create the subtle blending of color, a blank (unetched) plate was inked using the rainbow roll technique. The oversized diameter of the roller allowed the entire surface of the plate to be inked with one complete rotation. Unmanageable by hand, this movement was facilitated by a specially designed suspension mechanism (fig. 20a).

In contrast to the suggestion of space between the layers of the lithograph, space relationships in the aquatint seem compressed. The aquatint is smaller, and the surface density of arrows, lines, and tone is greater. The rigidity of the underlying tonal grid structure further restricts the space, especially as compared with the softness of the blended roll in the lithograph. Saff has noted that this was an extremely difficult aquatint to accomplish, due to the subtlety of the tonal gradations: "It was very tough to get the richness and control it, and Arakawa is extremely and appropriately demanding."[8]

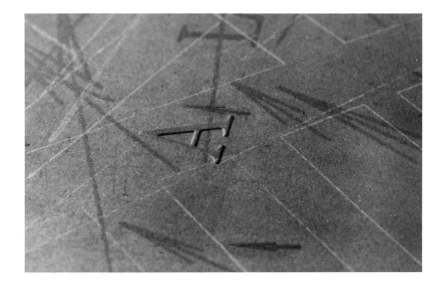

21a. Detail of the embossing of etched version of
The Sharing of Nameless

The aquatint displays an approach to the subject and composition that is similar to that seen in the lithograph (interacting layers of arrows, grids, embossed letters), yet it maintains its own distinct identity. The aquatinted grid of squares that forms the ground is delicately graduated in tone so that a penetrating quality of light is suggested that radiates from the lower right corner toward the upper left. Each square is separated by a fine line of demarcation. The text is the same as in the lithograph, but here Arakawa has maximized the qualities inherent in the aquatint process by interweaving a dense web of line and tone, without introducing the second, overlapping layer of select words. In contrast to the softer edges of the embossed letters in the lithograph, the embossing in the aquatint is sharp enough to cast a slight shadow (fig. 21a), which adds another, temporal, layer.

1. See *Arakawa*, Ridgefield 1984, which reproduces numerous related drawings and paintings, including the acrylic on canvas *The Sharing of Nameless* (1982–1983). In Robert Metzger's essay for the catalogue, "(Not) All About Arakawa," he notes that Arakawa began work on the "Blank" drawings in 1978. See also Gins 1985, 103–104.
2. Arakawa, in Gins 1987, 67.
3. Arakawa 1986, 62.
4. Arakawa, in Gins 1987, 67.

5. Saff, in conversation with Fine, June 1990, identified the grid as a map of Paris.
6. Stephen Hawking, *A Brief History of Time: From the Big Bang to Black Holes* (New York and Toronto, 1988), 26. Illustrations by Ron Miller.
7. Hawking 1988, 145, discusses three arrows of time: thermodynamic, psychological, and cosmological.
8. Saff, conversation with Fine, 1990.

CHARLES HINMAN

Born in Syracuse, New York, 1932
Lives and works in New York City

GROWING UP IN Syracuse, Charles Hinman attended art classes at the Syracuse Museum of Fine Arts. Later he spent a year as a professional baseball player on the farm team for the Milwaukee Braves while working on his degree at Syracuse University (B.F.A. 1955). After graduation, Hinman moved to New York, studying with Morris Kantor at the Art Students League, where he met fellow students James Rosenquist and Lee Bontecou. In 1956 he was drafted into the army and served for two years as a social worker in a military prison in California.

After his stint in the service, Hinman returned to New York, where he shared a loft with Rosenquist for a time on Coenties Slip. He taught mechanical drawing at Staten Island Academy (1960–1962) and woodworking shop at the Woodmere Academy, Long Island (1962–1964). He moved to a studio on 95th Street in 1961, and two years later began to explore the possibilities of the shaped canvas, bringing to his art the drafting techniques and carpentry skills he had been teaching. His shaped canvases debuted in the *Seven New Artists* exhibition at the Sidney Janis Gallery in 1964. That same year Hinman's first one-man show was held at the Richard Feigen Gallery, New York.

In 1966 Hinman was an artist-in-residence at the Aspen Institute in Colorado. He continued teaching in New York throughout the 1960s and 1970s, at Cornell University (New York City program), Syracuse University, Pratt Institute, the School of Visual Arts, and Cooper Union. Hinman's printmaking activities have included screenprinting, lithography, and embossing. During the 1980s he worked at Bummy Huss Paper in New York, producing cast paper reliefs. More recently, he completed an etching project with Dan Stack at Copperplate Editions in New York.

Important one-man exhibitions of Hinman's work have been held at the Tokyo Gallery, Tokyo (1966), Lincoln Center, New York (1969), Galerie Denise René-Hans Mayer, Krefeld, Germany (1970), Galerie Denise René, Paris (1971), Donald Morris Gallery, Detroit (1979), and the North Carolina State University Visual Arts Center, Raleigh (1990). During the 1980s major commissions included paintings for the Grand Hyatt Hotel, New York (1980), the Southeast Bank, Miami (1983), and the Madison Green Building, New York (1984). In 1980 The Everson Museum of Art in Syracuse organized a major exhibition of Hinman's works, which traveled to the Laguna Gloria Art Museum in Austin, and the Museum of Art, Fort Lauderdale.

Charles Hinman, New York City, 1968

22 Untitled, 1969

Color lithograph on Arches Cover paper
22½ x 29⅛ (52.1 x 74)
Edition: 70 (1/60 through 60/60; I/X through X/X); 1 BAT; 2 CTP; 3 AP
Collaboration: Donald Saff, Anthony Stoeveken
Gift of Ruth and Don Saff

Hinman first caught the attention of the art world during the early 1960s, with shaped canvases that dynamically projected color and form directly into the viewer's space while challenging the boundary between reality and illusion. One writer noted in 1965 that "Hinman's actual volumes contradict materiality in their buoyancy; they are shaped air."[1] Like those canvases, this *Untitled* print, Hinman's first experience with lithography,[2] is marked by a kind of buoyancy, richness in color, and spatial interplay.[3] The simplicity of the palette is typical of Hinman's work in this period: blue, red, and yellow, overlayed in sections to produce orange and green. The colors interact with the white of the paper and at the same time seem to hover above its surface, which results in a fluctuating sense of space.

Ruled, diagrammatic blue lines drawn with lithographic pencil define the structure of the image and recall the techniques of mechanical drawing that Hinman taught at the Staten Island Academy in the early 1960s. The image, in fact, looks somewhat like an isometric projection gone awry: edges disappear; boxlike structures within related boxlike structures read almost, but not quite, dimensionally.[4] The shifting spatial relationships and incongruities—interior evolves into exterior, front becomes back—suggest a sense of revolving movement, like a paddle wheel. Hinman has explained that in his work he strives to create "two separate entities that play *against* each other, to make the pieces work with real and illusory space, thus combining two separate realms that come together and play *with* one another."[5]

The surface of the print is surprisingly tactile. The softness of the lithographic pencil mark belies the mechanical nature of the lines, and the borders of the individual colors are fluid. In some cases overlapping colors are visible along the edges of the color bars, further contradicting

Part of the goal is to reduce expression to the most essential terms. The further the reduction, the fewer the decisions to be made, and the fewer the decisions, the more important each one is relative to the other.

Charles Hinman, in *Art in America*, 1966

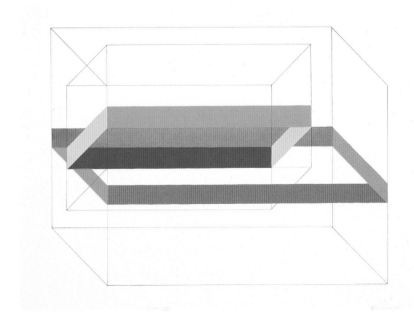

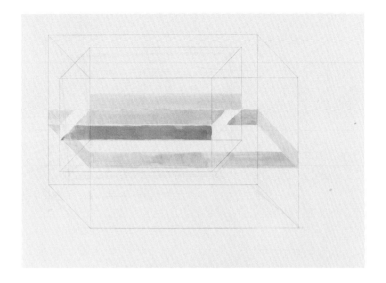

22a. Study for *Untitled*, 1969, watercolor over graphite, 24 x 34¹/₄ (60.9 x 87), 1985.48.18

any initial impression that the work is a precise, hard-edged image. The orange section on the right, for instance, is "off-registration," revealing yellow at the bottom edge and red along top. Because none of the edges is crisply delineated, the color areas seem to vibrate. Hinman noted in 1980 that "from the beginning, my paintings were about movement and color and the sensual achieved through materials."[6] This aesthetic is equally revealed in this Graphicstudio print and in the other lithograph and embossings produced by Hinman at the workshop.

The dialogue of rhythm and movement that is typical of Hinman's graphic work and inherent in the shaped canvases as well has been described by William Katz in the context of Hinman's constructions: "The way he stretches and shapes the canvas so that one plane slides into another, the arc of the shaped air, the feint of a long rectangle appearing to rush back because it is constructed of unequal sides, the sensuously grave push and pull, the motion and speed suddenly suspended are all born in his sportman's instinct and grace."[7]

The supple rendering in the print was foreshadowed by the relaxed quality of Hinman's preparatory drawing (fig. 22a). The looseness of line and apparent casualness in the application of color in the drawing is typical of Hinman's approach to preparatory studies.[8] The image underwent refinement in the transition from the study to the final print: lines in the drawing became more disciplined in the print without becoming rigid or mechanical.

1. Johnson 1965, 62.
2. Hinman, conversation with Corlett, 14 November 1990.
3. Corinne Robins, "Painting as a Three-Dimensional Statement: The Art of Charles Hinman," in *Hinman*, Syracuse 1980, 13–14, draws an analogy between an airborne ball in the game of baseball—which Hinman played professionally for a year—and the floating quality of Hinman's work.
4. Johnson 1965, 64, further notes that "Hinman, who constructs what might be called the malleable solids of modern geometry, says that he starts with geometry and strives toward 'the unknown from the known.' "
5. Quoted by Robins, in *Hinman*, Syracuse 1980, 14.
6. Quoted by Robins, in *Hinman*, Syracuse 1980, 13.
7. Katz, "Between Painting and Sculpture: A Dialogue with Chuck Hinman," in *Hinman*, Syracuse 1980, 28.
8. For examples of Hinman's preparatory studies for his canvases, see *Hinman*, Syracuse 1980, 51–56. William Katz noted in his essay for that catalogue (p. 28): "Chuck begins his constructions with a series of charcoal studies which serve the function of game plans or strategies. Freely and rapidly establishing volumetric relationships, he uses these drawings as a medium through which his 'conscious mind can direct [his] art.' "

NICHOLAS KRUSHENICK

Born in East Bronx, New York, 1929
Lives and works in New York City

ONE OF NICHOLAS KRUSHENICK's childhood memories is of his fascination in watching a colorful mural progress toward completion in the Greek Orthodox church his family attended. By the time he was in the army, he had begun to consider a career as a professional artist, and a month after he was discharged, he entered the Art Students League in New York on the GI Bill, studying there from 1948 to 1950. Krushenick then attended the Hans Hoffman School (1950–1951), studying directly under Hoffman, whom he came to admire greatly.

As a student, and continuing through the 1950s, Krushenick explored abstract expressionism. He also constructed stage sets, created department-store window displays, worked at the Museum of Modern Art in New York as a framer, and managed an antique shop. In 1957 Krushenick cofounded the cooperative Brata Gallery in New York with his brother, John. Until 1962 the Krushenicks exhibited their own work there, along with the work of other artists such as Al Held and George Sugarman. By 1960 Nicholas Krushenick was employing the black outlines and confined areas of flat, brilliant color that characterize his mature style. Krushenick's first important one-man show was held at the Graham Gallery, New York, in 1962. In 1964 he was included in the *Post-Painterly Abstraction* exhibition organized by Clement Greenberg for the Los Angeles County Museum of Art. In August of that year *Art in America* included him in its "New Talent U.S.A." survey.

Krushenick has been a teacher since the mid-1960s, serving as visiting artist at numerous institutions, including the Cooper Union and the School of Visual Arts in New York, as well as Cornell University, Dartmouth College, Minneapolis School of Art, the University of Wisconsin, and Yale University. He currently teaches at the University of Maryland.

Krushenick began to experiment with screenprinting in the late 1950s and became an active printmaker by the mid-1960s. In 1965 he was awarded a fellowship at the Tamarind Lithography Workshop in Los Angeles, where, working with master printers Kenneth Tyler and Clifford

Nicholas Krushenick discussing *Untitled* (cat. 23) with Charles Ringness, 1970

Smith, he completed twenty-two lithographs during his two-month tenure. He has since executed screenprints at Edition Domberger, Stuttgart, and Galerie der Spiegel, Cologne.

A major exhibition of his work was held at the Walker Art Center, Minneapolis, in 1968, at which time Krushenick designed sets and costumes for the adjacent Tyrone Guthrie Theatre's production of Franz Josef Haydn's comic opera, *Man in the Moon*. The Jaffe-Friede Gallery at Dartmouth College exhibited a selection of the paintings and screenprints he produced while he was artist-in-residence there in 1969. Other one-man exhibitions include those held at the University of South Florida (1970), University of Alabama, Birmingham (1973), Portland Center for the Visual Arts, Oregon (1974), California State College, San Bernardino (1975), State University of New York, Alfred (1976), Newport Art Association, Rhode Island (1977), Metropolitan Museum of Miami (1979), Aldrich Museum of Contemporary Art, Ridgefield, Connecticut (1981), Stamford Museum, Connecticut (1988), and the University of West Florida, Pensacola (1988).

23 Untitled, 1970

Color lithograph printed on Rives BFK paper
Diptych: each sheet 22 x 28½ (55.9 x 72.4); overall size 22 x 57¹/₁₆ (55.9 x 144.9)
Edition: 40 (I/X through X/X; 1/30 through 30/30); 1 BAT; 1 PP; 3 TP; 1 AP; 1 WP; 1 PrP; 1 CP
Collaboration: Donald Saff, Charles Ringness

Krushenick's Graphicstudio lithographs are indicative of the gradual shift that occurred in the artist's work beginning in the late 1960s, away from the organic shapes and more fluid lines that had previously characterized his art toward a more architectonic imagery, marked by angular shapes and crisp, straight lines.[1] Dynamic surface patterns and a sense of movement dominate Krushenick's images. The diagonal arrangement of the black crosses in this print sets up a staccato rhythm that flows onto and off the page, activating the overall surface. The implied extension of the image beyond the physical boundaries of the page is a compositional device the artist has frequently employed.

A brilliant red, framed on each side by yellow bands and the whole outlined in black, draws attention to the center of the composition. This area reads simultaneously as a red void behind silver planes or as a flat red shape between them. The suggestion of both revelation and concealment, pushing and pulling, opening and closing, is typical of the deliberate ambiguity and visual play that characterize Krushenick's work, despite the clarity and impact of his forms. Executed as a diptych, the print emphasizes the relationship between the left and right sides of the composition. There is a kind of symmetry in which one half is upside down and mirror reversed in relation to the other.

Krushenick's selective palette and his use of flat areas of clear, vibrant color, primaries and secondaries, outlined in black, recall the standard rendering techniques used in commercial advertising and comic books. This led to his being associated in the early 1960s with the pop art movement.[2] The use of bold lines and flat colors has also been fundamental to the vocabulary of diverse artists such as Matisse and Léger, whose influence Krushenick has acknowledged: "I'm not too conscious of any influences in my work but if I had to name a couple, they would probably be Matisse and Léger."[3]

We are stuck with three basic colors and thirteen basic shapes on this universe. Those sixteen stinking elements are all we have. I think it's unfair, so I am trying to figure out a way to unstick ourselves, to expand out intellect one more time. Scientists say 94 percent of our intellect is dormant. I'm just trying to get that one percent more out of myself while I am here.
Nicholas Krushenick, in Strohl 1978

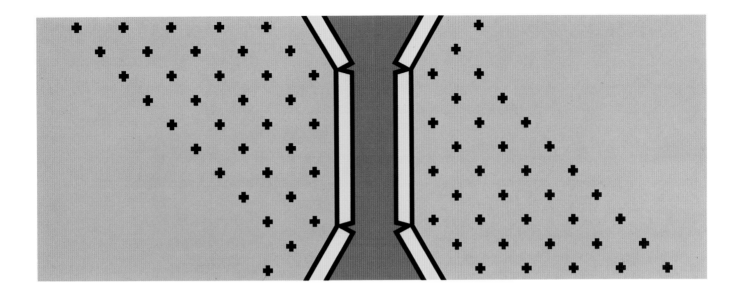

To create this and his other Graphicstudio lithographs, Krushenick worked with ruling pens and rulers, drawing the negative areas on the plates with gum stop-out. When the stop-out dried, lacquer was rubbed into the untouched areas to establish the positive image.[4] The black outlines in each of the images were executed using photographic stencils.[5] The production of Krushenick's seemingly simple, hard-edged, flat-form images using the lithographic medium presented certain challenges to the Graphicstudio shop. As Saff has noted, the images "could have been realized easily as silkscreens. Granted that the artist may have wished the effect of ink absorbed into the surface rather than that of ink riding upon it, this effect could have been achieved and the problem solved by use of a flatbed press. Instead, the printers hand-rolled the plates, trying to make an intimate and individual procedure mechanical and impersonal. The result was an outstanding exhibition of control."[6]

1. Krushenick's work from the early and mid-1960s is reproduced in Robins 1969, 60–65. That from the late 1960s is illustrated in Battcock 1969, 26–27.

2. See, for example, Kenneth Baker, "Abstractions a la Pop," *The Christian Science Monitor*, 16 March 1970.

3. Krushenick, conversation with Don Cyr, New York, 1967, quoted in Hannover 1972, 14. The artist went on to qualify the influence of Matisse: "The strange thing about it is that I think Matisse is the greatest artist of the twentieth century. Yet, when they had [the] big Matisse show at the Museum of Modern Art, I remember going to the show and thinking that [it was a] superb, impeccable, beautiful, gorgeous show. After standing there for two hours looking at these beautiful paintings, I came to a certain conclusion. I said, 'Well, yes, but that's the French way of doing it and I'm an American. I want to paint it like an American.' There was a certain loss that I felt at the time. For him it was beautiful and right but for me it wasn't. So at that moment, whatever real influence Matisse had on me had ended." See also Strohl 1978, 12. Dean Swanson, in *Krushenick*, Minneapolis 1968, quoted the artist's comment that "Léger put black outlines around forms since the year 1, and nobody ever called him a Pop painter." Swanson also discusses the affinity between Krushenick's work and Matisse's cut-paper collages.

4. Charles Ringness, telephone conversation with Fine, 1 October 1990.

5. The entire image of the lithograph listed as no. 130 in the appendix was executed using the photographic process.

6. Saff, in Baro 1978, 19–20. In this interview Saff further commented: "But can the expenditure of time and energy be justified simply because superior skill is exercised in a manual process?" For further discussion of this issue, see Ruth Fine's introduction in the present catalogue.

24 Untitled, 1970
Color lithograph printed on Rives BFK paper
28¹/₂ x 21¹⁵/₁₆ (72.4 x 55.7)
Edition: 40 (I/X through X/X; 1/30 through 30/30); 1 BAT; 1 PP; 1 CTP
(minus yellow run); 2 TP; 2 AP; 1 WP; 1 CP
Collaboration: Donald Saff, Theo Wujcik

Krushenick's imagery is suggestive but never actually representational,
an effect that the artist's statement on the facing page may help to explain. The segmented triangle here, for example, might suggest an
advertising-style rendering of a pencil point, but in no way should it be
taken as a literal representation of one. Krushenick himself seems to support the notion that his images intentionally allude to a material reality,
with the sources always remaining ultimately unidentifiable: "I have a series of forms and shapes that I am in love with. When I want sort of to
refine them, I make a lot of drawings, playing around to see if a new one
is going to work, do what I want it to do. It's very difficult because it has
to have a sort of quality that I'll accept. They have to have a certain kind

of dynamic element. They can't be too literal as a form. They have to have a certain kind of mystery, so you can't identify them, but they suggest many forms."[1]

Unlike cats. 23 and 25, this print incorporates the white of the paper as an additional color and compositional element. Alternating white and silver bars create a syncopated rhythm that fills the upper two-thirds of the composition. The progression is countered by the point of the segmented triangle and by the yellow band that wraps around the bottom corners and extends upward to meet the lowest silver bar. All of these forms are boldly outlined in black. Discussing this type of compositional arrangement, Krushenick commented: "I think the stripes more or less work as an open-space idea, because usually the stripes are almost three-quarters of the painting. And then there's always another element that's agitating the painting."[2]

As already noted, spatial ambiguity is a key ingredient in Krushenick's art, and here the white areas can be seen as flat bands on a surface or as spatial gaps between the silver bands. This silver and white pattern appears simultaneously to overlap the yellow band and to meet it on the same plane.

1. Robins 1969, 62.   2. Robins 1969, 62.

I walk around the city an awful lot. I just walk around the city and get visually stimulated over the way a fire escape is hanging or a neon sign that's blinking someplace. And . . . most of the time its just a slight something of something that will hit me and it will sort of record in my brain. I may never use it but it just sits there, and somehow I suspect that when I sketch, some of these things come back to me in different ways—translated for myself.

Nicholas Krushenick, in Hannover 1972

25 Untitled, 1970
Color lithograph printed on Rives BFK paper
28 1/2 x 21 15/16 (72.4 x 55.7)
Edition: 23 (I/X through X/X; 1/13 through 13/13); 1 BAT; 1 PP; 3 TP (1 minus silver run; 2 minus yellow run); 2 AP; 1 WP (no CP: plate held over for printing second state)
Collaboration: Donald Saff, Theo Wujcik

Krushenick began to incorporate black outlines into his work in 1959. They provided a framework for his compositions while isolating planes of color and thereby minimizing the effect of color afterimages. The outlines also contribute their own visual effect, as here, where their interplay with the electric red-orange and brilliant yellow makes the vibrant forms they define appear to hover over the surface of the page. This sort of percussive imagery prompted one critic to comment: "Krushenick is to contemporary art as Frank Zappa was to the Beatles."[1]

Krushenick used the suggestion of overlapping planes to interlock the color and the compositional structure. The silver sawtooth shapes, for example, may be read either as overlapping triangles or as alternating triangles and diamonds on the same plane. They appear to be either behind the yellow bands or on the same plane, either slicing into the red fields on the same plane or out in front of them. The three red fields surrounded by yellow bands may also be read as either overlapping or on the same plane. The top edge of the composition is not enclosed within a black line, which suggests the continuation of the image beyond its boundaries. Deliberate spatial ambiguity coupled with brilliant color energizes the surface, creating a highly charged composition.

With its suggestion of overlapping planes and partially hidden shapes, this print directly reflects the artist's interest in collage, which began about 1958.[2] In 1960 Krushenick exhibited cut-paper collages at the Brata Gallery. As his Graphicstudio lithographs attest, this additive, layered approach to composition had a major influence on the development of his work in other media.

Krushenick used the plates for this lithograph to produce a second state (app. 129), keeping the same compositional structure to experiment with different color combinations. "It is intriguing as hell to put up a series of prints and look at variants in color. . . . Printmaking allows me to make changes in color or try variations using the same images already affixed to the stone, plate or screen."[3]

1. Strohl 1978, 12.
2. See I. Michael Danoff, "Nicholas Krushenick," unidentified source in vertical file of the library at the National Museum of American Art, Washington, D.C.
3. Krushenick, unpublished interview with Dellinger, 1989.

EDWARD RUSCHA

Born in Omaha, Nebraska, 1937
Lives and works in Los Angeles

EDWARD RUSCHA'S INITIAL interest in art as a child in Oklahoma City,
where his family moved in 1942, was nurtured by a neighbor who was
a cartoonist. Ruscha enrolled in his first painting class with portrait
painter Richard Goetz in 1948 and continued to study art in high school,
simultaneously developing an interest in Dada and in the commercial
printing process. Planning to study commercial art, he drove to Los Angeles the summer after graduation with a friend and occasional collaborator, Mason Williams. He enrolled in the Chouinard Art Institute (later,
California Institute of the Arts), where he studied from 1956 to 1960.

Ruscha worked intermittently in commercial art while attending
Chouinard, including six months at Plantin Press in 1958, learning how
to run the presses and set type. In 1961, after leaving a layout job with
an advertising agency, Ruscha traveled in Europe for seven months. He
worked briefly in commercial advertising after his return but soon decided to devote his full attention to fine art. One last commercial art
position was with *Artforum* magazine, where he did layout from 1965
to 1967 using the pseudonym Eddie Russia.

Ruscha's background in commercial art, his interest in Dada, and the
influence of the work of contemporaries like Jasper Johns and Robert
Rauschenberg began to coalesce in his experiments with collage and
montage. It was during this period that he created his first paintings in
which typographical forms played a major role. His work was included
in the *New Paintings of Common Objects* exhibition held at the Pasadena Art Museum in 1962, the same year he painted *Large Trademark
with Eight Spotlights*, an image of the 20th-Century Fox logo and his
first painting to use three-dimensionally rendered letters. Words and
phrases formed from illusionistically rendered droplets of water or wind-
ing ribbons, and expressing the artist's wry wit, were to become the signature of Ruscha's art.

Ruscha's first prints were lithographs executed in 1962. He has since
explored etching, aquatint, and screenprint (experimenting in the latter

Edward Ruscha, detail of black-and-white Cirkut
photograph of the artist with his books, taken by
Oscar Bailey in Tampa, 1970

with organic dyes instead of printer's ink). He has worked with numerous printers and workshops in addition to Graphicstudio, including Cirrus Editions, Ltd., Gemini G.E.L., and Tamarind Lithography Workshop in Los Angeles, Crown Point Press in San Francisco, Landfall Press in Chicago, Styria Studios in New York, and Editions Alecto, Ltd., in London. In 1974 he was awarded the Skowhegan School of Painting and Sculpture Medal in Graphics. During the 1970s he also experimented with filmmaking. And more recently, his special projects have included the large circular mural and lunette paintings in the Miami Dade Public Library, completed in 1987.

Ruscha's first one-man exhibition was held at the Ferus Gallery in Los Angeles in 1963, his first New York exhibition at the Alexander Iolas Gallery in 1967. Other major exhibitions have been held at the Albright-Knox Art Gallery, Buffalo (1976), InK, Halle für Internationale neue Kunst, Zurich (1979), Portland Center for the Visual Arts, Oregon (1980), San Francisco Museum of Modern Art (1982), Westfälischer Kunstverein, Münster, Germany (1987), Lannan Museum, Florida (1987), Museum of Contemporary Art, Chicago (1988), Institute of Contemporary Art, Nagoya, Japan (1988), Musée national d'art moderne, Centre Georges Pompidou, Paris (1989), Whitney Museum of American Art, New York (1990), and the Museum of Contemporary Art, Los Angeles (1990). Ruscha's graphic work has been featured in shows organized by the Minneapolis Institute of Arts (1972), Arts Council of Great Britain (1975), Auckland City Art Gallery, New Zealand (1978), and the Los Angeles Institute of Contemporary Art (1979).

26 Twentysix Gasoline Stations, 1970–1971

Color lithograph on Arches paper
$16^{1}/_{16}$ x $20^{1}/_{8}$ (40.8 x 51.1)
Edition: 40 (I/X through X/X; 1/30 through 30/30); 1 BAT; 1 PP; 1 working proof,
signed "O.K. to print E.R."; 3 TP; 6 CTP; 3 AP; 1 WP; 1 CP
Collaboration: Donald Saff, Charles Ringness

Edward Ruscha's book *Twentysix Gasoline Stations*, the subject of this
lithograph, documents the road trip between Los Angeles and Ruscha's
hometown of Oklahoma City in a roundabout, casual way, using images
of twenty-six service stations located between the two cities. The gas stations do not appear in the book in the order they would be found on the
road, and Ruscha cautions that the book is not intended to be a travel
guide.[1]

A pioneer in the artists' book movement, Ruscha published *Twentysix
Gasoline Stations*, his first book, in 1963.[2] With the publication of ten
additional books by 1970, the year he came to Graphicstudio, books
had become an important part of his artistic production.[3] Ruscha's
books were mass produced in relatively large editions, printed by a high-
quality commercial printer, and priced inexpensively.[4] Most of them are
small in size.[5] The intimacy of the book as a medium was important to
Ruscha: "I've always been interested in words. And books. Just opening
them up and holding them. I like that."[6]

The same year that Ruscha produced the book *Twentysix Gasoline
Stations*, he created a pencil drawing, *Flipping* (fig. 26a), that featured a
pair of hands cradling a copy of *Twentysix Gasoline Stations* and gently
turning its pages. Ruscha also rendered this book in a triptych executed
in graphite on paper in 1964.[7] When Ruscha came to Graphicstudio in
November 1970, he again chose this book as subject matter, along with
six of his other titles.[8] By producing drawn and printed images of his
books, Ruscha had begun to give the galleries what he later suggested
they seemed to want—books that could be appropriately hung on the
walls: "every year I have at least two shows of my books in galleries and
they put them on the walls, because that's what they want. Though its
OK by me; it's not the same thing. . . . The way they're supposed to be
seen, of course, is when someone hands someone else just one book at a
time and place where they don't expect it."[9]

At the time of his visit to Graphicstudio, Ruscha was focusing his artistic production entirely on graphic work.[10] He has described his work
there as "a venture into the world of 'atmosphere.' Making drawings of
my books in small environments seemed to be fitting and stimulating at
the moment. Also, I felt that the prints from Graphicstudio were biographical and personal and did not venture into the work of popular or
familiar art. This made them enticing but rather obscure since my books
are of an underground nature."[11]

In making the book, Ruscha initially found the title, the phrase
"twentysix gasoline stations," the typography, and the layout more important than the actual content: "The first book came out of a play with
words. The title came before I even thought about the pictures. I like the
word 'gasoline' and I like the specific quality of 'twenty-six.' If you look
at the book you will see how well the typography works—I worked on
all that before I took the photographs."[12] In the Graphicstudio lithograph the artist returned to the book's cover and the individual letters
that compose the title. The lettering at first gives the impression of being
standard machine-generated type, but closer examination reveals that
the precision is that of the artist's hand, with the subtle variations from
letter to letter an integral part of the impact of the print.

*If there is any facet of my work that I feel was
kissed by angels, I'd say it was my books.*
Edward Ruscha, in Failing 1982

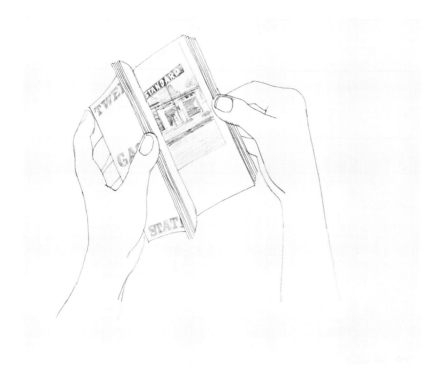

26a. *Flipping*, 1963, pencil, 14 x 17
(35.5 x 43.2), collection of Andrew Bogle,
Auckland, New Zealand

A small pool of liquid is depicted emerging from beneath the book in the print, the moisture beginning to buckle its pages. The typography, too, in the word "stations," is subtly distorted on the undulating cover.[13] David Bourdon has commented that "most of Ruscha's words require some added twist, either a morphological change in the type (as in his liquid letters), or juxtaposition with a trompe-l'oeil conceit, such as his actual-size renderings of flies, pills, olives, and drops of oil, juice, and water."[14] In *Twentysix Gasoline Stations* Ruscha achieves this "morphological change" indirectly, by altering not the typography, but the image of the page on which it is written.

The delicacy and elegance of Ruscha's draftsmanship is further revealed in the soft, modulated, atmospheric gray background. The book seems simultaneously to float in a nebulous space and to rest on a surface in a pool of liquid. Ruscha achieved this deliberately ambiguous background by using a piece of silk fabric to apply rubbing crayon to the stone. Then, as Saff explained, "the printers were challenged to maintain that peculiar softness and suggestion of insubstantiality during their etching and printing procedures."[15] According to printer Charles Ringness, "Rubbing crayon is probably one of the most volatile and dangerous and technically difficult drawing materials to handle because it wants to 'fill in.' "[16] Ruscha used gum mask to achieve the softer lines, such as those along the spine of the book, and he added lithographic pencil to enhance other edges, such as those at the the bottom of the gently warping pages of the book.

1. See Barendse 1981, 10. In Failing 1982, 80, Ruscha is quoted as saying: "I used to drive back four or five times a year and I began to feel that there was so much wasteland between L.A. and Oklahoma that somebody had to bring the news to the city. Then I had this idea for a book title—*Twentysix Gasoline* *Stations*—and it became like a fantasy rule in my mind that I knew I had to follow. Then it was just a matter of being a good little art soldier and going out and finishing it. It was a straightforward case of getting factual information and bringing it back. I thought of it as making a sort of training manual for people who

want to know about things like that."   Amsterdam 1976, cat. 597.

2. The publication date for the book was confirmed by Pat Poncy for Edward Ruscha, in a telephone conversation with Corlett, 9 November 1990.

3. In addition to *Twentysix Gasoline Stations*, the books Ruscha published through 1970 are *Various Small Fires and Milk*, 1964; *Some Los Angeles Apartments*, 1965; *Every Building on the Sunset Strip*, 1966; *Royal Road Test* (collaboration with Mason Williams and Patrick Blackwell), 1967; *Thirtyfour Parking Lots in Los Angeles*, 1967; *Business Cards* (collaboration with Billy Al Bengston), 1968; *Crackers* (collaboration with Mason Williams), 1969; *Nine Swimming Pools*, 1968; *Real Estate Opportunities*, 1970; and *Babycakes*, 1970. For more on Ruscha's books, see Bourdon 1972, 32–36.

4. *Twentysix Gasoline Stations* was produced in three editions: the first was an edition of 400 numbered copies; the second, an edition of 500 copies produced in 1967; and the third, an edition of 3,000 copies, printed in 1969. At the time of publication, it was priced at about $4 (see Armstrong 1989, 46 n. 2).

5. *Various Small Fires*, *Some Los Angeles Apartments*, *Nine Swimming Pools*, and *Real Estate Opportunities* all measure 5$\frac{1}{2}$ x 7 inches.

6. Kangas 1979, 17.

7. The triptych is reproduced in *Ruscha*,

8. The other books Ruscha rendered at Graphicstudio are *Various Small Fires*, *Real Estate Opportunities*, *Crackers*, *Some Los Angeles Apartments*, and *Nine Swimming Pools*. One lithograph—*Royal Road Test*—was abandoned before editioning.

9. Barendse 1981, 10.

10. Between about 1969 and 1972 Ruscha produced only prints and drawings. He told Howardena Pindell (see Pindell 1973, 125): "the [paint]brush is too heavy."

11. Ruscha, unpublished correspondence with Jade Dellinger, 20 October 1987.

12. Coplans 1965, 25.

13. Ruscha had used the device of dripping liquid in a work entitled *Sin, with Dripping Liquid* (1967, gunpowder on paper), reproduced in Bourdon 1971, 27. There, the pool of viscous liquid forms directly beneath the letter *S*, causing the letter itself to wrinkle without the intermediary of warping pages of a book. Larson 1972, 54, observes that Ruscha's liquid word paintings and prints of the late 1960s and 1970s are also brought to mind with the appearance of the liquid in the print of *Twentysix Gasoline Stations*.

14. Bourdon 1971, 26.

15. Baro 1978, 18.

16. Charles Ringness, telephone conversation with Fine, 1 October 1990.

27 Real Estate Opportunities, 1970–1971

Color lithograph on Arches paper
16$\frac{1}{8}$ x 20$\frac{1}{8}$ (40.9 x 51.1)
Edition: 40 (I/X through X/X; 1/30 through 30/30); 1 BAT; 1 PP; 1 working proof, signed "O.K. to print E.R."; 3 TP (2 like the edition; 1 minus yellow run); 3 AP; 1 WP; 1 CP
Collaboration: Charles Ringness, Donald Saff

Ruscha's book *Real Estate Opportunities* was completed the same year he worked at Graphicstudio. A collection of twenty-five snapshots of vacant lots, it was produced by offset lithography in an edition of 4,000. In Ruscha's account: "Sometimes the ugliest things have the most potential. I truly enjoyed the whole afternoon while I shot those pictures. It's a great feeling to be on a self-assignment, out looking for subjects. I went off in the car and I went down to these little towns, to Santa Ana, Downey, places like that. I was exalted at the same time that I was repulsed by the whole thing."[1]

Ruscha produced this lithograph using the same method he used for the other prints in the group (cats. 26–29): gum mask to protect the white areas, followed by rubbing crayon applied with silk to the stone to achieve the special softness of the surface, and lithographic pencil for harder lines. Color areas—the yellow of the pencil here—were drawn onto separate aluminum plates.[2] He depicted the pencil floating above the book in an immaterial space that nevertheless is receptive to cast shadows. The gradual lightening of the background tone from top to

I found that it is important for objects to be their actual size in my paintings. If I do a painting of a pencil or magazine or fly or pills, I feel some sort of responsibility to paint them natural size—I get out the ruler.

Edward Ruscha, in Failing 1982

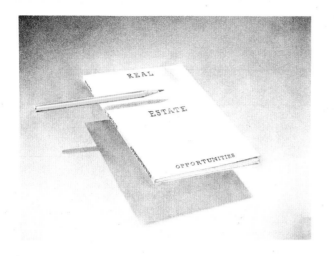

Unikalny proof   E. R.   1970

bottom implies depth, yet the firmness of the shadow edges suggests a flat surface. The intangibility and ambiguity of the surrounding space is similar to that in other prints in this informal series.

Poised over the book as if ready to be used to make notations, the pencil reinforces the "training manual" appearance that Ruscha seeks to project with the use of standard type: "Type always gives it a manual look; it has that factual kind of army-navy data look to it that I like."[3] The pencil, of course, is also a drawing tool, a link between the image of the book and the artist who created it. Pencils have appeared with some frequency in Ruscha's paintings—see *Noise, Pencil, Broken Pencil, Cheap Western* (1963), for example.[4] Words and letters have no prescribed size and therefore can be rendered in any dimension, but Ruscha chooses not to tamper too much with the physical dimensions of the real objects he renders. The scale of the book and the pencil in *Real Estate Opportunities* is nearly actual size.[5]

Here, as in all of Ruscha's Graphicstudio prints, the book is rendered at an oblique angle, rather than frontally as are many of his word images. A strong diagonal, seen both in *Real Estate Opportunities* and in *Some Los Angeles Apartments*, is a compositional device that Ruscha has explored continuously throughout his career. "I do have a thing for diagonals. That's why I think that a lot of the juice in my work has to do with abstraction."[6]

1. Bourdon 1972, 35.
2. See Baro 1978, 79.
3. Bourdon 1972, 33.
4. Reproduced in *Ruscha*, San Francisco 1982, pl. 18. For a discussion of the painting and Ruscha's use of the pencil, see Anne Livet's essay in that catalogue, "Introduction: Collage and Beyond."

Livet tells of Ruscha's Catholic education and a nun who would rap his knuckles with a pencil for misbehaving.
5. The image of the book, rendered in perspective, measures about 4½ x 5 inches, compared to the actual book's 5½ x 7 inches.
6. Ruscha, in Fehlau 1988, 72.

28 Some Los Angeles Apartments, 1970

Lithograph on Arches paper
16¼ x 20⁵/₁₆ (41.3 x 51.3)
Edition: 40 (I/X through X/X; 1/30 through 30/30); 1 BAT; 1 PP; 1 working proof,
signed "O.K. to print E.R."; 3 TP (1 light; 1 dark; 1 like edition); 1 WP; 1 CP
Collaboration: Donald Saff, Theo Wujcik

The book *Some Los Angeles Apartments*, published by Ruscha in 1965
and similar in format to the earlier *Twentysix Gasoline Stations*, features
photographs of thirty-two Southern California apartment complexes,
their addresses printed in the white border beneath each image. The fi-
nesse and precision of Ruscha's draftsmanship can be seen in the lithograph that depicts this volume, especially in the sophisticated rendering
of the background tones and shadows, accented with subtle streaks ema-
nating from the edges of the pages and pointing on a diagonal toward the
bottom left corner of the sheet. The pages of the book separate, as if by
the movement of air, and the streaks seem to imply motion—as if the
book were speeding away at an oblique angle to the picture plane. Such
streaks, rather than literal transcriptions of reality, are reminiscent of
conventions used by animators to indicate movement.

Ruscha often boldly appropriates such devices from the illustrator's
lexicon for his own aesthetic purposes—perhaps in part as a result of his
study at Chouinard, the training ground for Walt Disney animators.[1] In
his playful *Domestic Tranquility* series, for example, published by Multiples in 1974, each of four lithographs features a single item—an alarm
clock, plate, egg, and bowl (fig. 28a)—floating, or sailing, through
space (the ambiguity is surely intended). Although there are no streaks
depicted in the prints from the suite, movement is suggested by the angle
of the items in relation to the picture plane and the rendering of the space

*I've wondered at times whether if I lived in an-
other city, my art would be different, and I suppose it would be. The iconography of this place
does mean something special to me. I love it because it feeds me and it feeds my work.*
Edward Ruscha, in Failing 1982

28a. *Clock*, 1974, from the Domestic Tranquility series, color lithograph, 20 x 26 (50.8 x 66), published by Multiples, Inc. and Castelli Graphics

behind them. The general appearance of these works shares a certain kinship with the animator's art.

Some Los Angeles Apartments, like all of Ruscha's Graphicstudio lithographs, is marked by an extraordinary range of tonality, the gentle modulations of light contrasted and masterfully juxtaposed with deep, silvery grays, displaying the great subtlety that can be achieved in lithography.

1. This point was made in Kay Larson, "Billboards against the Sunset," *New York*, 26 July 1982, 60.

29 Nine Swimming Pools, 1970
Lithograph on Arches paper
16¹/₈ x 20¹/₁₆ (40.9 x 51)
Edition: 40 (I/X through X/X; 1/30 through 30/30); 1 BAT; 1 PP; 1 working proof, signed "O.K. to print E.R."; 3 TP; 3 AP; 1 WP; 1 CP
Collaboration: Donald Saff, Theo Wujcik

In his book *Nine Swimming Pools* Ruscha interspersed among numerous blank pages reproductions of nine color snapshots of swimming pools followed by a photograph of a broken glass.[1] That publication is pictured in this lithograph. Ruscha depicted the book receding into space at an angle similar to that in the print *Twentysix Gasoline Stations*, but instead of showing a liquid curling the pages, Ruscha showed the first few pages of *Nine Swimming Pools* gently bent back as if caught by a light breeze. In a nuance that further reveals the artist's powers of observation, the breeze lifts not only the corner but the entire edge of these pages.

The smoky, atmospheric effects achieved in the Graphicstudio prints are similar in appearance to the subtle tonalities possible using the rather unusual medium of gunpowder, with which Ruscha began to experiment in 1967.[2] Ruscha's working method with the gunpowder parallels the process of producing the Graphicstudio lithographs, and it is likely that his work in both print and drawing media exerted a mutual influence on each other.[3] Ruscha used cotton to apply the gunpowder to the paper for

the drawings, silk to apply the rubbing crayon to the stone for the prints. He created firm edges in the drawings by temporarily masking certain areas with tape, paralleling the use of the gum mask in the lithographs.[4] To further define certain lines in the prints—along the edges of the individual pages of *Nine Swimming Pools*, for instance—Ruscha would work back into the drawing on stone with lithographic pencil. In gunpowder and pastel drawings such as *Three Hanging Books* and *Nine Swimming Pools* (both 1972) Ruscha also continued to explore the imagery of the floating book.[5]

Ruscha executed his first word paintings in the late 1950s.[6] Typographical forms floating in an atmospheric, ambiguous space have continued to play an important role in his work since the early 1960s. Ruscha, however, has never limited himself to typography. Many works in his oeuvre contain no words at all.[7] The Graphicstudio lithographs explore typography, but they also retain the context of the lettering as the title on a realistically rendered book. In this way Ruscha exploits the delicate balance between sign / symbol and illusion.

When I work I like to get into the area of head scratching. The best place for me to operate is this little free-for-all zone where I don't have any real restriction and I can say what I want. If I [can] hit upon something that puzzles and attracts me at the same time, then I've entered that area. A lot of my work is actually met with real head scratching.

Edward Ruscha, in Mitchum 1979

1. The first edition, published in 1968, was 2,500 copies; the second edition, published in 1976, was 1,900 copies.
2. Gunpowder is mostly charcoal, combined with sulfur and potassium nitrate.
3. Charles Ringness, in a telephone conversation with Fine, 1 October 1990, pointed out that Ruscha had previously worked with rubbing crayon at the Tamarind Lithography Workshop. See, for example, Ruscha's *Annie* (1969), reproduced in Antreasian and Adams 1971, 182.
4. See Bourdon 1971, 27.
5. For a reproduction of Ruscha's gunpowder drawing of *Nine Swimming Pools*, see *Ruscha*, Auckland 1978. For a discussion of Ruscha's gunpowder drawings, see Bourdon 1971, 26–27:

"Ruscha's involvement with gunpowder came about one day, when he spread some on the floor, watered it, and then watched the granular material break down into a fine dust." Ruscha's first exhibition of gunpowder drawings was held at Alexander Iolas Gallery, New York, in 1967, the same year he began to experiment with the medium.
6. The painting *Su* (1958) was one of Ruscha's first. See Failing 1982, 77.
7. Paintings such as *The Los Angeles County Museum on Fire* (1965–1968) or *It's a Small World* (1980) do not use typographical forms and are further testament to the depth and diversity of Ruscha's oeuvre. Both are reproduced in *Ruscha*, San Francisco 1982, plates 67 and 121.

RICHARD SMITH

Born in Letchworth, Hertfordshire, England, 1931
Lives and works in New York City and Telluride, Colorado

RICHARD SMITH BEGAN his formal art education in 1948 at the Luton
School of Art in England. His studies were interrupted in 1950 for service in the Royal Air Force, but after two years in Hong Kong, he received his discharge and resumed his art studies at St. Albans School of
Art in Hertfordshire. He was enrolled at the Royal College of Art in London from 1954 to 1957, where he became intrigued with popular culture
and the mass media. He later published articles on these subjects in the
Royal College publication, *Ark*. Also attending the college during this
period was Peter Blake, with whom Smith had shared a studio.

In 1956 Smith traveled to Paris, where he was impressed by the "allover" style of American abstract expressionist Sam Francis, whose work
was being exhibited there at the time. That same year he saw Rothko's
work exhibited in London. In 1957 Smith was awarded a Royal College
of Art scholarship for travel in Italy, then returned to England and
taught mural painting for a year at Hammersmith College of Art. In
1959 he received the Harkness Fellowship of the Commonwealth Fund
to travel in the United States. On his arrival in New York, he contacted
Ellsworth Kelly, who introduced him to New York artists Robert Indiana, Jack Youngerman, and Agnes Martin. Smith made the acquaintance
of Franz Kline and Mark Rothko at the Cedar Tavern.

Smith's work had been included in group exhibitions in England during the 1950s, but he had his first one-man show in New York at the
Green Gallery in 1961. After his New York debut he returned to England
and taught still-life painting at St. Martin's School of Art until 1963.
During this period he also experimented with filmmaking, producing
Trailer in 1962 with Robert Freeman. At the height of the pop art movement Smith could count among the visitors to his Bath Street Studio such
notables as the Beatles, fashion designer Ossie Clark, and filmmaker Ken
Russell. After a showing of his work in his Bath Street Studio in 1962,
followed by an exhibition at the Institute of Contemporary Arts in London, Smith returned to New York in 1963. He taught in Aspen, Colorado, in 1965, at the University of Virginia in 1967, and at the University of California at Irvine in 1968. He then returned again to England,
to East Tytherton, Wiltshire, and in 1971 was honored with the award
of Commander of the British Empire. Smith moved back to New York
City in the late 1970s and established a second studio in Colorado in
1988.

Smith had been producing print editions for less than a decade when
he was awarded the Bradford Print Biennial's first prize in 1976. In addition to his work at Graphicstudio, Smith has worked with numerous
printers and workshops, including Aeropress and Tyler Graphics in New
York, White Ink, Ltd., Ian Lawson, Alan Cox at Sky Editions, Advanced
Graphics, and J.C. Editions, all in London, and Duerreci in Rome.

Retrospective exhibitions of Smith's graphic works have been orga-
nized by the Arnolfini Gallery, Bristol (1970), and by the Arts Council of
Great Britain, London (1975). Other important solo exhibitions have
been held at the Whitechapel Art Gallery, London (1966), Museum of
Modern Art, Oxford (1972), Museo de arte contemporaneo de Caracas,
Venezuela (1975), Tate Gallery, London (1975), Hayden Gallery, Massa-
chusetts Institute of Technology (1978), and Stadtsmuseum, Ulm,
Germany (1980).

Richard Smith, Chicago, 1988

30 Evergloom, 1969

Color lithograph on Arches Cover paper
Sheet dimensions as folded: 15¹/₈ x 22¹/₂ (38.4 x 57.2)
Edition: 70 (I/X through X/X; 1/60 through 60/60); 1 BAT; 4 TP; 1 USFP
Collaboration: Donald Saff, Anthony Stoeveken
Gift of Ruth and Don Saff

During the 1960s Richard Smith's images—which included as subject matter the ubiquitous, aggressively marketed cigarette pack—caused him to be identified with the British pop art movement. But his primary concern was the role of popular culture—especially the impact of the burgeoning mass media and advertising industries—in transforming human communication and perception. He was especially interested in the work of Marshall McLuhan, whose *Mechanical Bride* was widely read at the time.[1]

The son of a printer, Smith began his work in printmaking in the late 1960s: "When I actually began to make editions of prints in '67/68, . . . the processes of printing as well as the idea of the image bore on the concept of the print. This has been a constant through my printmaking. Image/Process."[2] During this time Smith was also exploring the compositional possibilities of cut and folded paper in his drawings: "I was making some drawings and it occurred to me that the simplest way of altering something was either to cut it or fold it. Just to fold the corner up was enough—it changed the look of it, the quality of the flat surface, and so it developed out of that, folding in sequences."[3]

Executed in 1969, Smith's Graphicstudio print projects were a continuation of that investigation.[4] *Evergloom* is composed of interlocking layers of a single sheet of paper—strategically folded and cut.[5] A 22-by-30-inch sheet of paper was printed on both sides, then folded in half. The image on the top side of the sheet was united with that on the underside by making right-angled incisions in both halves of the sheet, folding back the corners formed by the cuts both underneath and on top, then

The sources, the references I make, the things I think about in the studio, or think about when I'm starting a picture might have a whole range of references for me. I might think of thighs and hills, buildings, ways of structure. Some could be very definite, but they're mostly very tangential to what I'm doing. It's part of one's mental make-up to think in outside images.

Richard Smith, in Smith 1970

drawing the bottom sheet through the opening in the top and allowing the folds to relax. Color, line, and paper are interwoven in this way.

Both of Smith's Graphicstudio lithographs (see also cat. 31) involve manipulation of the materials to create an ongoing dialogue between the two-dimensional (surface) and the three-dimensional (space/structure). The slits in the page function simultaneously as structure (to move the image into three-dimensional space) and as line, interacting with the line and color of the composition. In the same way, the paper protruding from the underside of the fold functions both as an area of color and as a part of the three-dimensional structure.

The variety of marks Smith used further contributes to the layered effect in *Evergloom* and accounts for the rich tonality of the print. Ink and tusche washes of varying fluidity and opacity are integrated with rhythmic, insistent linear strokes executed with various lithographic pencils. The inseparable nature of the artist's draftsmanship and his color sensibility is clearly evident in the multiple, subtle layering of tone and mark. Smith has offered the following analogy to explain his approach to his art: "I tend to think of colour ripening, or colour shimmering, and I think of hedges of colour, because there is a density in my colour like the density of a hedge. You can see through the colour, but it's still solid, a wall, though you can penetrate it and see the different parts of the hedge on various levels. Think of a blossoming hedge with colour varying within that area, varying in light as well as density."[6] The illusion of depth is evoked through these interwoven layers of color and line, described by the artist as "space, the way that fur is a space: You can sink your fingers into it. It is still a surface fabric, but it has hidden depths."[7]

Smith's active lithographic line had a counterpart in the active surfaces of his paintings of the same period.[8] This interconnectedness can also be seen in the relationship of his Graphicstudio prints to drawings and paintings executed at this time. The apparent "folds" and overlapping layers of the canvases suggest, as Barbara Rose has pointed out, the aesthetic characteristics of paper.[9] Smith himself noted:

> With the kind of paintings that are concerned with folded corners there has
> been a change from corners folded through more than ninety degrees, like
> *Kodak* or *Clairol Wall*, to those where the fold is just a corner of the canvas

30a. Study for *Evergloom*, c. 1969, pastel with graphite and watercolor on paper, 15 x 22 (38.1 x 55.9), 1985.48.54

tipped forward slightly, where one is really back to the rectangular stretcher again. It's complicated to make that kind of structure in wood and canvas where it's the simplest thing to do with paper. They get heavy and rather unwieldy. To get, like in the drawings, several layers of paper—to do that with a canvas structure is very difficult. It never works the same, it has to make its own laws. The paintings I have done like that I am very happy with. I am especially happy with *Malaya* which has gone so far that its relationship to the drawings is like a body to an X-ray.[10]

1. Denvir 1970, 80, asserts that "*Mechanical Bride* had a great influence on Smith at this time."
2. Smith 1976, 156.
3. See Rose 1975, 167.
4. Other prints related to the Graphicstudio lithographs in their cut/folded structure include the six prints in the *Horizon 70* portfolio, and *Bramble* (1970) (see *PCN* 1, nos. 4, 5 [Sept./Oct. 1970], 88, and [Nov./Dec. 1970], 109); as well as *Sixteen Pieces of Paper* (1969) (see Smith 1969, 242). The artist discusses the interrelationship of these prints (excluding the Graphicstudio work) in Smith 1976, 156.
5. Although the Graphicstudio documentation sheets identify this work as *Untitled*, Smith later called it *Evergloom* (confirmed with artist by Feigen, Inc., Chicago, January 1991). The work is recorded in Baro 1978 as *Untitled*, following the documentation sheets.
6. Denvir 1970, 78.
7. Rose 1975, 166.
8. This observation was made in Gilmour 1970, 23. See, for example, the painting *Riverfall* (1969), reproduced in *Smith*, London 1975, 83. See also Barbara Rose's essay in that catalogue.
9. *Smith*, London 1975, 30.
10. Smith 1970, 20. For reproductions of *Clairol Wall* (1967) and *Malaya* (1969), see *Smith*, London 1975, cats. 31 and 42.

31 Everglad, 1969

Color lithograph on Arches Cover paper
Sheet dimensions as folded: 15$\frac{1}{8}$ x 22$\frac{1}{2}$ (38.4 x 57.2)
Edition: 70 (I/X through X/X; 1/60 through 60/60); 1 BAT; 1 USFP
Collaboration: Donald Saff, Anthony Stoeveken
Gift of Ruth and Don Saff

This print, *Everglad*, is a structural correlate to *Evergloom* (cat. 30).[1] But in contrast to *Evergloom*, with its single imposing cut and folded section, this lithograph has three smaller cuts with upturned corners, arranged side by side at the bottom of three vertical subdivisions of the composition. A staccato rhythm is suggested by the slightly staggered alignment of the bottom edges of the folds.

In these cut and folded images Smith explored the simultaneous splitting apart and joining together of the sheet. As in cat. 30, the slicing and folding becomes part of the image—and part of the mystery. The viewer is aware that these techniques have been used to accomplish the interleaving and complete the image. But the images have an intricate, meditative quality not unlike the configurations produced by the Japanese art of paper folding. Indeed, Smith has characterized his work in this manner as "large-scale origami."[2]

The strokes that activate the surface of the print are kept under control here by the underlying geometry of the compositional structure, thus an elegant balance is achieved between mechanical and free-flowing line. This is characteristic of much of Smith's work of the period. In addition, the combination of energetic line and turned-back corners lends a certain lightness to the image, and the folded corners suggest the idea that significance often lies beneath the surface—as in the turning of a page, the pulling back of a curtain, the removal of a cover. Both revelation and concealment are implied, reflecting Smith's interest during the 1960s in

31a. Study for *Everglad*, c. 1969, pastel with graphite and watercolor on paper, 15 x 22¹/₁₆ (38.1 x 56), 1985.48.55

the effects of commercial packaging. In 1967 he noted that "everything comes in boxes. You buy boxes when you are shopping, you do not buy visible goods; you don't buy cigarettes, only cartons. The box is your image of the product."[3]

The curtainlike quality of the composition—the "fabric" of lithographic strokes bordered by three-dimensional edges lifting away from the picture plane—might also suggest Smith's interest in the theater, about which he had written in 1969 in conjunction with another series of prints, entitled *Sixteen Pieces of Paper*:

> The images in the prints are proscenium images or doorways with the curtain drawn, the door closed. The four prints have titles which are vaguely theatrical, *Interval*, *Exit*, *Prop*, etc. . . . These were single sheet prints cut and folded. You set up a doorway as something to go through, but in the prints the space enclosed may actually project forward. I think the theatre is an interesting format; I am thinking of making a paper theatre—a flexible proscenium-based area to "perform" the drawing. The proscenium idea has cropped up quite often in the paintings. I'm interested in theatre as a kind of "directed space": it relates technically to my activity as a painter. The dialogue between the illusion of space and real space has been a constant theme with the paintings.[4]

This dialogue between "the illusion of space and real space," between surface and structure, between the two-dimensional and the three-dimensional is, not surprisingly, an integral part of Smith's printmaking aesthetic as well and is clearly evident in the artist's work at Graphicstudio.

The preparatory drawings for these prints (figs. 30a, 31a) were executed in pencil, pastel, and watercolor. The structure of the drawings is somewhat different from that of the prints. Rather than being composed of a single sheet folded in half, the drawings consist of three individual sheets layered one on top of the other. The top white sheet of each drawing, which has an opening that functions somewhat like a mat, contains the edges of the image, which remain uncovered in the final print. The apparent spontaneity of the line and the freshness of color in the drawing for this lithograph is elegantly translated in the print.

1. Although the Graphicstudio documentation sheets identify this work as *Untitled*, Smith later changed the title to *Everglad* (confirmed with the artist by Feigen, Inc., Chicago, January 1991). The work is recorded in Baro 1978 as *Untitled*, following the documentation sheets.
2. See Seymour 1970, 261.
3. From an interview with Bryan Robertson, in *Smith*, London 1966; quoted in Barrett 1967, 36.

4. Smith 1969, 242. *Sixteen Pieces of Paper* was created by layering separate sheets of paper rather than folding a single sheet. In Smith 1976, 156–157, the artist described this print: "With *Sixteen Pieces of Paper*, I printed four different colored pieces of paper which were then used in different ways to make four images, the paper being cut and interleaved to form the image. The drawing was made with a knife, the printing was purely color and surface."

Painting, drawing, and printmaking are all equally capable of incepting ideas which can transfer to other mediums, so though not necessarily as direct as painting prints or printing paintings the processes are closely bound.
Richard Smith, in Smith 1976

NEW DIRECTIONS

Patrick Foy (left) and Greg Burnet proofing Mapplethorpe's *Irises* (cat. 46), 1987

VITO ACCONCI

Born in the Bronx, New York, 1940
Lives and works in Brooklyn

VITO ACCONCI'S PARENTS were Italian immigrants. Though relatively poor, they provided an environment that was rich in art and music, and Acconci thought from the time he was five years old that he wanted to be a writer. He studied at Holy Cross College in Worcester, Massachusetts (B.A. 1962), and did graduate work at the University of Iowa Writers' Workshop (M.F.A. 1964). After graduate school Acconci returned to New York and taught English composition at several colleges. Shifting from writing prose to writing poetry, he also began to frequent art galleries. Jasper Johns' work interested him, and during the late 1960s Acconci and Bernadette Mayer coedited the Xerox magazine *0 to 9* (a very Johnsian title).

In 1969 Acconci turned from poetry to the visual arts and began to produce the performance pieces, bodyworks, installations, and videos, for which he is best known. In recent years his installations have increasingly employed architectural elements and he has created works for public places, including the Palladium in New York (1986) and the Coca-Cola Company in Atlanta (1987).

Acconci first combined print and performance in his 1970 piece *Trademarks,* applying printer's ink to bite marks he made on his body and transferring their impressions to other surfaces. In 1971 he used this procedure for an edition of fifty lithographs at the Nova Scotia College of Art and Design (NSCAD) lithography workshop. In addition to the NSCAD workshop and Graphicstudio, Acconci has made prints at Crown Point Press in San Francisco and Landfall Press in Chicago, as well as several college- and university-based workshops, including the Minneapolis College of Art and Design, the University of Nebraska at Omaha, and the Print Workshop, State University of New York, Albany.

From 1968 to 1971 Acconci taught at the School of Visual Arts in New York, and he has participated in numerous visiting artist programs, including those of NSCAD, Cooper Union in New York, Minneapolis College of Art and Design, University of North Carolina at Chapel Hill, Yale University, and the Parsons School of Design, New York.

Acconci's important one-person exhibitions include those held at the Sonnabend Gallery, New York (1971), San Francisco Museum of Modern Art (1978), Kunstmuseum, Lucerne (1978), Stedelijk Museum, Amsterdam (1978), Centre d'arts plastiques contemporains, Bordeaux (1979), Museum of Contemporary Art, Chicago (1980), Kölnischer Kunstverein, Cologne, and Kunsthaus Zürich (1981), Institute of Contemporary Art at the Virginia Museum of Fine Arts, Richmond (1982), Whitney Museum of American Art, New York (1983), Ackland Art Museum, University of North Carolina, Chapel Hill (1985), U.S.F. Art Galleries (1986), La Jolla Museum of Contemporary Art (1987), Museum of Modern Art, New York (1988), Gray Art Gallery, East Carolina University, Greenville (1989), and Landfall Press, New York (1990).

Vito Acconci discusses working proof for
Building-Blocks for a Doorway, 1984

32 Building-Blocks for a Doorway, 1983–1985

Color hardground, softground, photoetching, and aquatint on Arches Cover paper
Two panels (each composed of two joined sheets): 93⁷/₈ x 47¹/₄ (238.4 x 120) each
Edition: 8; 1 BAT; 1 PP; 1 PrP; 1 NGAP; 1 GP; 1 USFP; 2 CTP
Collaboration: Michael Harrigan, Susie Hennessy, George Holzer, Susan McDonough,
Deli Sacilotto, Donald Saff, John Slivon, David Yager

Work on *Building-Blocks for a Doorway* began in the spring of 1983,
was set aside, then taken up again and completed in 1985. During this
period Acconci also executed three other prints at Graphicstudio, a
trilogy of photoetchings addressing sociopolitical themes, *End Mask,
People Mask, Red Mask* (app. 1–3).

The concept of etching plates as structural units combined to create
a single work—an idea that Acconci had previously explored in works
such as the Crown Point Press *20-Ft Ladder for Any Size Wall* (fig.
32a)¹—is fully realized in *Building-Blocks for a Doorway*, where each
plate functions as a separate "brick" in the wall. Acconci noted: "When I
first made etchings at Crown Point Press in 1977, I . . . [focused] on
things that maybe people who do prints take for granted. I focused on
that notion of embossing. Here you have something that looks like a
brick, a building block. . . . What interested me was the notion that

*The thing that's really interested me about
Graphicstudio (and also the Crown Point Press
time) [is] here's someone who's really an outsider
to prints coming into contact with people who
know something about prints [in] almost a kind
of collision. . . . I think I want certain kinds of
things, but I'm not even sure what I want until
you, [the] print people, can show me. So that notion of being shown availabilities, being shown
possibilities, is something that I've liked a lot.*

Vito Acconci, interview with David Yager, 19 May 1983

142

here is this embossed image; here is this kind of building block. Can you use this building block to literally build a wall? In [*Building-Blocks for a Doorway*] it's almost literally like building a wall. Can you make this paper into a kind of architecture?"[2]

Because of the size limitations of the etching press, four separate templates were needed to hold the sixty-two plates in place during printing, one for each quadrant of the image. Small but important details, such as matching the direction of the grain of the paper for each quarter section, added to the complexity of the project. According to Deli Sacilotto, who was closely involved with the final stages of the project, often working with student assistants: "It was always tricky because we had so many people [wiping the plates]. And one time we did the whole thing—set it up, ran it through—and realized that one plate hadn't been inked. Here we were looking at this entire section beautifully printed and one plate was just blank. [It] was a very unusual project."[3]

The archway of *Building-Blocks for a Doorway*, composed from individual plates bearing single aquatinted letters of the alphabet, is suggestive of children's building blocks. Moving left to right around the inside of the arch, the alphabet metamorphoses into the word "hippopotamus." Acconci recently wrote: "I wanted to get to a point in the alphabet where two successive letters would be at the beginning of a word—the word, then, could continue where the alphabet left off. But of course there could have been other words beginning with 'h-i.' I liked 'hippopotamus' because it announced itself as Latin, it announced a classical arch; I liked 'hippopotamus' because the animal seemed unnecessary, too bulbous, too much between forms instead of being a form in itself. I liked 'hippopotamus' because the animal seems archaic, a throw-back, a reminder of a pre-historic time—something, in other words, like this . . . print."[4]

In a progression that parallels the movement of the letters around the arch, the blocks of seemingly random patterns and lines on the bottom left side of the wall also give way gradually to the more structured images on the right, the lines metamorphosing into words, then text fragments. Many of the patterned blocks on the left recall the appearance of marbleized endpapers in books, an idea reinforced by their presentation across from blocks of text on the right.

Language and literature have been central themes of Acconci's oeuvre dating from his earliest work as a poet and his audiovideo and performance pieces of the 1960s and 1970s. To execute this Graphicstudio print, Acconci brought books from his extensive personal library to the workshop, for use both as references and as sources in the creation of the imagery.[5] The texts he chose to excerpt included theoretical writings on architecture, literature, and social structure. But intermixed with these are passages from his own writings and a litany of vernacular expressions—"WOW! GOODY! PHEW! WOWIE! GROOVY!. . ."—printed in boldface in the corner of a block in the top right quadrant of the wall. As Acconci has explained: "There were three kinds of text: the handwritten—first-person narratives, either fictional or autobiographical, like prison diaries (the idea of a person trapped in his/her self, the body as prison, as structure); literary criticism—the act of writing as the act of building, words as bricks; architecture texts—the simulated building, a building in the mind, a building of the mind. . . . the process in general went from tenuous, fragile building—handwriting—to permanent building, print, down in black and white for all time."[6]

A disparate amalgamation of sources, messages, and meanings, *Building-Blocks for a Doorway* evokes the function of the wall as a place

32a. *20-Foot Ladder for Any Size Wall*, 1980, photoetching in eight parts, 244 x 43 (619.8 x 109.2), published by Crown Point Press

for graffiti, posters, and messages, as an intellectual meeting ground, a center of communication, "a kind of presentation device," in Acconci's words. Acconci has further stated: "When I started this print . . . I was probably thinking . . . that because it's a wall, it's a place where I could bring together, summarize, or introduce for myself a lot of elements that I didn't quite know how to handle in a sculptural space. . . . I could make it like architectural literature, or bring together these architectural notions, these literature notions, all in one. . . . I could deal with notions of history. I could deal with notions of past."[7]

The desire to read, to decipher *Building-Blocks for a Doorway*, is compelling. Yet in his use of text fragments, Acconci both taps and frustrates this desire. Rarely does he use a complete sentence or a full paragraph. His appreciation of Faulkner is revealing: "My earliest writing hero was Faulkner. It had nothing to do with plots or characters. I loved the way he could never make a sentence end. There was constant comma, constant parenthesis. He refused to make a sentence end, almost as though ending the sentence was a drastic moment. You keep something going from one page to the next, the page as sea, rolling from one page to another."[8]

In *Building-Blocks for a Doorway* Acconci creates a wall that functions as both barrier and passageway.[9] The title, in fact, suggests the paradox of erecting a wall in order to frame an opening. With its fragments of text, the print is a "passage-way" in more than one respect. The artist has also noted: "What is important to me is that the bottom of the print be at ground level: sort of like beating your head against the wall."[10] Thus the archway's relatively small interior dimensions (about 6-by-2½ feet) are consistent with Acconci's claustrophobic treatment of space in other constructions of the mid-1980s in which he explored the psychological implications of the cramped passageway or confinement in a tight space.[11]

1. See also *3 Flags for 1 Space and 6 Regions*, and *2 Wings for Wall and Person*, photoetchings published by Crown Point Press in 1981. All three works are illustrated in Cohen 1984, 87.

2. Acconci, videotaped interview with David Yager, 1983.

3. Sacilotto, conversation with Fine, 25 September 1990.

4. Acconci, correspondence with Corlett, 7 December 1990.

5. Some of the books brought by Acconci to the workshop include: Harold Bloom's, *The Anxiety of Influence: A Theory of Poetry*, Michel Foucault's, *Power/Knowledge: Selected Interviews and Other Writings 1972–1977*, Erving Goffman's, *Relations in Public: Microstudies of the Public Order*, Frank Ching's, *Architectural Graphics*, and William Faulkner's, *As I Lay Dying*. In an interview with Yager in May 1983, Acconci stated: "I'm feverish about having books around. I have to carefully categorize my books. I have a real structural system. My library starts with 'body' and ends with 'critical theory and revolution' and there are about 64 categories in between. . . . When I am about to do a piece I have to pull out a certain number of books to have around me even if I don't necessarily read them or even look at them—they're sort of there like pets, they're sort of coddled—table of contents to skim over, book titles to skim over. I guess basically what keeps me going is constantly trying to figure out what's in the air."

6. Correspondence with Corlett, 1990.

7. Interview with Yager, 1983.

8. Quoted in Avgikos 1981, 5.

9. Walker 1986, 29, makes a similar observation: "Passage is indeed the key concept, as the arch defines the boundary and connection of two distinct spaces, embodying both the positive and negative aspects of a wall."

10. Correspondence with Corlett, 1990.

11. See, for example, *People's Wall* (1985), and *Storage Unit (For Things and People)* (1984), illustrated in Onorato 1987, 47, 51. See also Walker and Feinberg 1987, 8.

ALICE AYCOCK

Born in Harrisburg, Pennsylvania, 1946
Lives and works in New York City

Alice Aycock

FROM CHILDHOOD, ALICE AYCOCK aspired to an artistic life. Inspired by stories told by her grandmother, which she later learned had their source in *Gulliver's Travels*, Aycock thought at first she would like to be a writer, but her interests shifted to the visual arts before she was twenty. Her sculptural-architectural sensibility was undoubtedly encouraged by her father, a construction engineer. As a child she watched him design and construct a scale model of a house he then built. Aycock's mother was especially supportive of her daughter's career, and one of the artist's first site pieces, *Low Building with Dirt Roof (for Mary)* (1973), was built with her mother's help on family property near New Kingston, Pennsylvania.

Aycock went to Douglass College in New Brunswick, New Jersey (B.A. 1968), then moved to New York and attended Hunter College (M.A. 1971), where Robert Morris was her teacher and adviser. She traveled intermittently, visiting sites in the American Southwest (Great Kivas), Greece and Turkey (Knossos, Epidaurus, Mycenae), England, and Mexico (Aztec temple at Malinaleo). Her master's thesis, "An Incomplete Examination of the Highway Network/User/Perceiver Systems," was inspired in part by the underground passageways of the Mycenaean tholos tombs and the labyrinthine corridors of the ancient ruins at Knossos.

Aycock's early works were site-specific structures, constructed of wood, stone, and earth, that drew heavily on childhood memories but were also rich with allusions to ancient history and architecture. In the late 1970s her sources expanded to include literary references, often accompanied by cryptic, elusive texts. During the 1980s the work incorporated steel and other components evoking industry, which reflected her investigations into the power and poetry of the machine and the mystery of metaphysical forces.

In addition to her work at Graphicstudio, Aycock has also worked at Tandem Press at the University of Wisconsin–Madison. She has produced screenprints in Chicago with John W. Roberts, and at Ohio University. A sculpture edition, *Celestial Alphabet* (1983), was published by Multiples, Inc., New York. She has been visiting artist at various institutions, including the University of South Florida, Hunter College, Williams College, Rhode Island School of Design, Princeton University, and the San Francisco Art Institute.

Aycock has created installations throughout the world, including Israel, Germany, the Netherlands, Italy, Switzerland, and Japan, and at numerous locations in the United States, including the Museum of Modern Art, New York (1977), San Francisco Art Institute (1979), Museum of Contemporary Art, Chicago (1983), Sheldon Memorial Art Gallery, Lincoln, Nebraska (1985), State University of New York, Buffalo (1988), Atlantic Arts Center, New Smyrna Beach, Florida (1989), and the Storm King Art Center, Mountainville, New York (1990). In 1983 a retrospective exhibition was organized by the Württembergischer Kunstverein and traveled in Germany, the Netherlands, and Switzerland.

33 How To Catch and Manufacture Ghosts: Collected Ghost Stories from the Workhouse, 1981

Photoetching with pastel additions on Pearl Grey Stonehenge paper
29 x 38¹³/₁₆ (73.7 x 98.5)
Edition: 60 (I/XXX through XXX/XXX; 1/30 through 30/30); 1 BAT; 1 PP; 1 PrP;
1 USFP; 15 AP (1/14 through 14/14; 1 unnumbered)
Collaboration: Susie Hennessy, Carol Todaro, with Joseph Alexander, Stan Gregory,
Betty Ann Lenahan, Margaret Miller, George Pappas, Donald Saff, Jeffrey Whipple,
David Yager

Alice Aycock first came to the campus of the University of South Florida to participate in the university's visiting artist program. Ensuing discussions between Aycock and the U.S.F. art department resulted in a proposal to build a large-scale, outdoor, partly motorized structure composed of glass, steel, galvanized metal, and wood, entitled *Collected Ghost Stories from the Workhouse* (see Introduction, fig. 19). It was to be located behind the art department building on the U.S.F. campus.[1] That particular location appealed to Aycock because within view of the site was the university's physical plant, a technical-looking structure that provided a visual counterpart to Aycock's design.[2]

Aycock, her assistants, and U.S.F. professor Thomas McLaughlin, the project's director, worked with approximately thirty U.S.F. graduate and undergraduate students on the construction of the sculpture, which took about a year and a half to complete. McLaughlin recalls: "There were a lot of really hectic times with Alice because of her extravagances, but that is what made that piece special—her ability to just dream and let us figure out the physicality of how things would work."

The drawing used by the construction team during the fabrication of the sculpture was similar, but not identical, to the rendering in the Graphicstudio print.[3] Aycock's print, her first photoetching, was the pilot project of the reactivated Graphicstudio, and full facilities had not yet been assembled.[4] The making of the plate was completed at the private studio of two former U.S.F. students, Susie Hennessy and Carol Todaro; proofing was done using the U.S.F. art department's press; and the edition was completed at Palm Press in Tampa. Hennessy traveled to Aycock's New York studio to work out the details of the hand-coloring, which was completed by Hennessy and Todaro under Aycock's instruction.[5] The hand-coloring imparts an ephemeral, floating quality to those elements.

Aycock used isometric projection to diagram her elaborate, mysterious mechanism. The components are labeled on the print with a letter that corresponds to a cryptic description at the right of the image that identifies the purpose of that component. For example, the two spheres at the top are marked with the letter *N*, which, according to the legend, is "a climbing indicator (also called an apparatus for determining the specific heat of gases)." The letter *J* beneath the two spheres identifies "another of Wauksbee's electrical machines. . . ." Aycock has explained: "For this piece I was inspired by devices and apparatus that I found in various history books on technology. The devices were archaic 18th and 19th c[entury] objects that are no longer relevant. Some of the elements are derived from experiments with electrostatic machines. . . . Wauksbee was an inventor who probably made electrostatic machines. The piece is [in] large part my interpretation of the history of invention and that is how Wauksbee figures into the iconography."[6]

Drawing on a complex array of sources for her imagery, Aycock sees art as "a method of acquiring knowledge in a very broad interdisciplin-

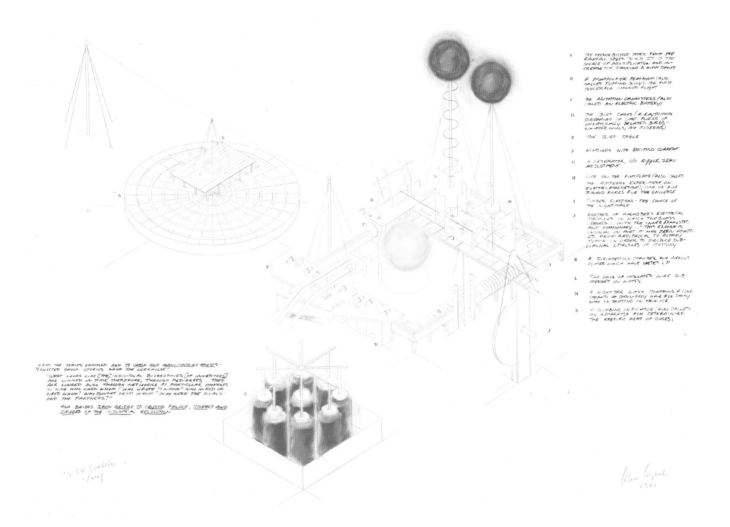

ary way, so that I realized that if I read a philosophy book, I could use that in my art."[7] McLaughlin noted that when he would pick the artist up at the Tampa airport, "both of her arms would be stacked with books about inventors, scientific dreamers, mechanical mechanisms, things she would look at, use as sources for her pieces." Aycock's particular conflation of fantasy and references to conceptual systems—alchemy, chemistry, eighteenth-century physics, modern industrial architecture—defies simple interpretation and offers an aesthetic vision that transcends the linear thought process: "A friend recently pointed out that I seem to relate everything to everthing else."[8] In *Collected Ghost Stories from the Workhouse*, she created a machine that is a metaphorical extension of the intellectual constructs developed over the centuries in an attempt to explain, and even control, the universe.

Aycock's fascination with the industrial machine has precedents in the aesthetic of such artists as Francis Picabia, Jean Tinguely, and Marcel Duchamp. Her U.S.F. project had "to do with an obsession or interest I have at the moment in dead industrial landscapes."[9] The sculpture, in fact, includes a specific reference to one particular such landscape, as McLaughlin has explained: "The tubes that go from the center section over to the agitation devices are drawn from the Standard Oil refinery in New Jersey. . . . It's almost a direct image taken from outside New York."

On the New Jersey Turnpike there is a Standard Oil refinery that I've looked at for years and always loved—especially at night with all the lights and smoke. It's like a giant chemistry lab, almost like a city.

Alice Aycock, in Poirier 1986

Exploring unseen physical forces, Aycock combined references to the history of experimentation with electricity—including Leyden jarlike elements, spheres that recall the Van de Graaff electrostatic generator, and a horizontal panel reminiscent of a transistor circuitry board—with other associations to eighteenth-century science and invention. The component labeled *B* on the print, for example, is based on an antique rendering of the Montgolfier balloon-launching platform.[10] The device labeled *A* is "the french bicycle track," the rings of which which rotated on the sculpture at different speeds and in opposite directions, recalling eighteenth-century mechanical models of the solar system.[11] McLaughlin noted that Aycock "found the glass jars somewhere in SoHo, I think on Canal Street, in one of those flea markets, and those came down on the plane. . . . She was really attached to them; they were important metaphysical parts for her."

Meeting Aycock at the airport often brought surprises, and on one occasion, taking her to her plane was also an adventure. McLaughlin recalls that "she had a channel-tuning device from a TV set in her purse, so when that goes through the detector, obviously they're going to get excited about it. This guard had it in her hand, and we're late for the plane, and obviously we're trying to hurry, so I reached for the thing to [try to explain] to the woman what it actually was, and as soon as I reached, things got real serious. I think Alice did make it to her plane, but just barely. But we caused a big stir in the Tampa airport over this little channel operator because they couldn't understand why anybody would be carrying that around."

1. The sculpture was dedicated in February 1981 and remained in place for about four years. It was dismantled in 1985. The title of the sculpture series—How to Catch and Manufacture Ghosts—was taken from an eighteenth-century book on magnetism and electricity (see Poirier 1986, 81–82). Another work in the series, bearing the same name as the series, was installed at John Weber Gallery, New York, in 1979. Other works in the series were installed at University of California at Irvine and at Plattsburg College, New York (see Mary Ann Marger, "Viewers Spin Their Wheels over Mechanical Sculpture," *St. Petersburg Times*, Graphicstudio workshop files, no date).
2. Unless otherwise noted, information about the sculpture project was provided by Thomas McLaughlin in a conversation with Corlett, 25 October 1990.
3. The drawing is reproduced in *Aycock*,

Tampa 1981, 19.
4. See the introduction to the present catalogue for the history of Graphicstudio.
5. Susie Hennessy, conversation with Fine, 11 July 1989.
6. Aycock, correspondence with Corlett, 13 December 1990.
7. Poirier 1986, 80.
8. Aycock, "Work 1972–1974," in Sondheim 1977, 105.
9. Benbow 1980, 8B.
10. McLaughlin indicated that the source for this particular element was such a drawing.
11. Edward Fry, in *Aycock*, Tampa 1981, identifies and discusses the specific iconography of the work (see also Fry 1981, 63–64). The other motorized components on the sculpture were the "agitation cannisters," labeled *C* on the print, which agitated, according to McLaughlin, just like a washing machine.

OSCAR BAILEY

Born in Barnesville, Ohio, 1925
Lives and works in Burnsville, North Carolina

OSCAR BAILEY EARNED A B.A. in art from Wilmington College in Ohio in 1951 and shortly thereafter went to work for a commercial printer in Delaware, Ohio. When the shop obtained a copy camera, Bailey asked to work with it. His interest in photography grew, and soon he bought his own camera—the best he could get for a full week's pay. Bailey taught himself how to use it, and after three or four years, he decided to make photography his career. He enrolled in the M.F.A. program at Ohio University, graduating in 1958 with a degree in photography.

Bailey was professor of photography at State University College in Buffalo, New York, from 1958 until 1969. He left to start the photography program at the University of South Florida, where he was a professor until he retired in 1985. Bailey came to U.S.F. when the first phase of Graphicstudio was just beginning, and he became an active participant in the program, contributing his photographic expertise to a number of projects, including those of James Rosenquist and Robert Rauschenberg.

In 1962 Bailey became a founding member of the Society for Photographic Education. In addition to his tenure at U.S.F., his teaching activities have included visiting artist appointments at the Penland School of Crafts in North Carolina (1971, 1973, 1979) and a period as artist-in-residence at Artpark in Lewiston, New York (1977). In 1972 Bailey supervised the publication of the book, *Silver Bullets*, a collection of photographs by U.S.F. art students.

One-man exhibitions of his work have been organized by Indiana University (1960), Kalamazoo Institute of Arts, Michigan (1963), Ohio Wesleyan University (1964), International Museum of Photography, George Eastman House, Rochester, New York (1964), University of Oregon, Eugene (1969), University of South Florida, Tampa (1972, 1974), University of Colorado, Boulder (1976), Southern Illinois University, Carbondale (1977), University of North Florida, Jacksonville (1978), and the Lynch Gallery, St. Petersburg, Florida (1981).

Oscar Bailey signing the edition of one of his Cirkut photographs, *Asheville, North Carolina* (app. 20), with Liz Jordan (left) and Michelle Juristo

USF PROOF

34

USF PROOF

35

34 Tampa X 2, 1982–1983
Color Cirkut photograph on Kodak Ektacolor 78F surface paper
10 x 68¹¹/₁₆ (25.4 x 174.5)
Edition: 45 (1/15 through 15/15; I/XXX through XXX/XXX); 1 PP; 1 PrP; 1 WP; 1 GP;
1 USFP; 5 AP
Collaboration: Doug Brown, George Holzer, Judith Sasso, David Yager

35 Woods, North Carolina, 1982–1983
Color Cirkut photograph on Kodak Ektacolor 78F surface paper
10 x 66¹/₄ (25.4 x 168.3)
Edition: 50 (1/20 through 20/20; I/XXX through XXX/XXX); 1 PP; 1 PrP; 1 WP; 1 GP;
1 USFP; 5 AP
Collaboration: Doug Brown, George Holzer, Judith Sasso, David Yager

The undulating lines of the expressway in *Tampa X 2* and the rolling
hills in *Woods, North Carolina*, with its interwoven pattern of trees and
shadows, are the product both of Oscar Bailey's vision and of the unique
effects of the antique Cirkut camera: "The Cirkut camera (developed just
before the turn of the century) was designed to photograph vast pan-
oramas and large groups of people. It is mounted upon a circular-topped
tripod, and a spring-driven motor causes it to rotate from left to right,

exposing a long roll of film as it moves. The film for my camera is eight inches wide and sixty inches long. As the camera rotates the film is pulled from its roll—past a shutter—onto a take-up drum. A series of gears sync the rotation of the camera and the speed the film [as it] moves past the shutter. When everything works right we can have a photograph that covers a little more than 360 degrees."[1]

Bailey's Cirkut photographs are actually contact prints. The eight-inch-wide film used in the camera is no longer made, so it must be specially ordered from Kodak. Development requires specialized equipment, so the film is sent to a commercial lab for processing. Once the negative had been produced for the Graphicstudio prints, the edition was carried out by George Holzer using U.S.F. art department equipment. Bailey has produced both black-and-white and color images using the Cirkut camera. His four Graphicstudio editions are color.

In *Tampa X 2* the buildings on the far left of the image reappear on the far right. The rhythmic interplay of the bowing freeway overpass in the background with the sinuous shadows under the bridge in the foreground (the bridge appears at either side of the image) combines with the syncopations of the vertical support columns of the highway architecture to create the visual poetry of the composition. The print features the

The Cirkut camera obviously does not present the world as the eye sees it. I like that.
Oscar Bailey, correspondence with Corlett, 1990

Crosstown Expressway in Tampa, which was still under construction at the time the photograph was taken.

Bailey notes that "if you would set the photograph on edge and pull the two ends around until the buildings on each end [the same buildings] line up, you could see how the world actually looked. But when you lay it out flat, then you get the distortion."[2] Presenting a circular view as a flat image, the Cirkut photograph confuses our notion of end and beginning, front and back, left and right. (By contrast, the camera can also be used to create "flat," linear images with very little distortion if the subjects being photographed are arranged in an arc around the camera so that they are always the same distance from the camera lens.)

Woods, North Carolina, a late fall/early winter landscape photographed on the artist's property in North Carolina, reveals Bailey's wit. It is punctuated at both ends by a small but brightly dressed figure, apparently hanging in the air among the trees. The suspended figure is Bailey's son, also a photographer and filmmaker—"he and I help each other out occasionally"[3]—who marks the passage of time by changing his pose. Bailey has noted: "As a photographer I have thought of the 'time' needed to record an image in terms of fractions of a second. The 'time' to record an image with the Cirkut camera can be as short as 10 and as long as 40 seconds."[4]

The camera used to photograph these images was made in 1915 and is the second one Bailey has owned. He acquired his first Cirkut camera in the late 1960s: "[My uncle] was an amateur photographer. And when he died, his widow had an auction. I was there helping, and she just gave me a lot of his photographic equipment. That would have been about 1968. That was my first one. He had stored it in a room that was damp, and it was moldy and everything. But I did clean-up and got it to working. Then about 1973 or '74 I bought one from a fellow out in Wyoming. It had been stored in a dry climate out there and it was in real good shape. That's the one I'm currently using."[5]

1. Bailey, correspondence with Corlett, 26 September 1990.
2. Bailey, telephone conversation with Corlett, 16 November 1990.
3. Telephone conversation with Corlett, 1990.
4. Correspondence with Corlett, 1990.
5. Telephone conversation with Corlett, 1990.

CHUCK CLOSE

Born in Monroe, Washington, 1940
Lives and works in New York City

CHUCK CLOSE HAD A childhood marked by a medical problem that made it difficult for him to engage in strenuous activities. One alternative he found was the production of backyard magic and puppet shows. He also spent many hours drawing, wholeheartedly supported by his parents, who sent him to art classes as well. When Close was eleven, his father suffered a fatal stroke; his mother continued to encourage him to pursue an artistic career.

Close attended community college in Everett, Washington (1958–1960), where his career goals changed from commercial to fine arts. In 1960 he transferred to the University of Washington (B.A. 1962). His success there led to an invitation to the Yale Summer School of Music and Art in Norfolk, Connecticut (1961), and graduate work at Yale's School of Art and Architecture in New Haven (B.F.A. 1963, M.F.A. 1964). Fellow students included Jennifer Bartlett, Rackstraw Downes, Nancy Graves, Robert Mangold, Sylvia Plimack Mangold, and Brice Marden. Close studied at the Akademie der Bildenen Künste in Vienna on a Fulbright Fellowship in 1964–1965. He accepted his first teaching position in 1965 at the University of Massachusetts, where he began to shift from the organic forms, arbitrary color, and abstraction of his student years to the photographic vocabulary and large-scale compositions of his mature style. He has also taught at the School of Visual Arts, New York University, and Yale Summer School of Music and Art.

In 1967 Close moved to New York and executed his first black and white painting: a large-scale nude based on photographs he had made in Massachusetts. Between 1968 and 1970 he painted several black and white portraits based on photographic images of friends. At the end of that period he reintroduced color into his paintings by applying the principles of the photomechanical color process. With photographic portraits as a constant, Close has explored a wide variety of media, including colored pencils, watercolors, pastels, oil paint, photography and film, and various print-related media including paper pulp.

Close first experimented with etching at Yale, where he served for a time as Gabor Peterdi's assistant. At the urging of Bob Feldman of Parasol Press, he created his first professional print in 1972: working with Kathan Brown at Crown Point Press, San Francisco, he produced *Keith*, the first work in which he revealed the grid system he had been using to translate his photographic images. In addition to Graphicstudio and Crown Point Press, Close's printmaking activities have included making lithographs at Landfall Press in Chicago and Vermillion Editions in Minneapolis as well as handmade paper editions with Joe Wilfer, published by Pace Editions, Inc., New York.

Important one-man exhibitions include those organized by the Los Angeles County Museum of Art (1971), Museum of Contemporary Art, Chicago (1972), Laguna Gloria Art Museum, Austin (1975–1976), Musée national d'art moderne, Centre Georges Pompidou, Paris (1979), Walker Art Center, Minneapolis (1980–1981), Aldrich Museum of Contemporary Art, Ridgefield, Connecticut (1987), and the Art Institute of Chicago (1989). Exhibitions featuring his works on paper include those held at the Edwin A. Ulrich Museum, Wichita State University, Kansas (1975), the Contemporary Arts Museum, Houston (1985), and the Butler Institute of American Art, Youngstown, Ohio (1989).

Chuck Close buffing the plate for *Leslie/ Fingerprint* (cat. 37), February 1986

36 Marta/Fingerprint/Silk Collé, 1986

Direct gravure on silk collé (China silk on 1114 lb. cold-pressed d'Arches Aquarelle paper)
54¹/₈ x 40¹/₂ (137.5 x 102.9)
Edition: 10; 1 BAT; 1 PP; 2 PrP; 1 NGAP; 1 GP; 1 USFP; 3 SP
Collaboration: Greg Burnet, Patrick Foy, George Holzer, Deli Sacilotto, Donald Saff

Close's sitters have always been personal friends or family. He prefers
subjects who are relatively unknown to the public (as opposed to
celebrities)—although some of his sitters, such as composer Philip Glass
or artist Nancy Graves, have achieved considerable public recognition
since Close first photographed them. The Graphicstudio fingerprint series features images of his wife, Leslie (cat. 37), and daughter, Georgia
(fig. 38a), representative of the subjects he was portraying most often at
that time: "The one thing that I realized about this body of work is that
almost all of them are women and children, mostly people who are either
relatives or people who are very close to me. Most of the women are
mothers, grandmothers, daughters, with whom I have a personal relationship, rather than art-world friends. It's funny that I would find myself, it's not by accident but without realizing it, making such a large
body of works of mothers and children and grandmothers."[1]

As with the other gravures in the series, Close created *Marta* by pressing his thumb in lithographic ink and transferring a succession of fingerprints directly onto a sheet of translucent mylar. With the selective use of
an eraser once the fingerprints had been made on the mylar, Close was
able to refine the marks.[2] This drawing was then placed in contact with
sensitized carbon tissue and exposed to light. The carbon-tissue emulsion hardens in varying degrees where light passes through the mylar to
the carbon tissue underneath, the amount of light determined by the
various tones of gray and black of the fingerprints. The carbon-tissue
emulsion remains softest where the image on the mylar is darkest. Once
exposed, the carbon tissue is adhered face down to the copperplate. The
plate is then washed in warm water, removing any soft (unexposed)
emulsion and leaving on the plate a residue of varying thickness that corresponds to the varying shades of gray in the original drawing. The remaining emulsion slowly dissolves when the plate is immersed in ferric
chloride. Areas of the plate covered with the thinnest residue are etched
the deepest and therefore print the darkest; those with the thickest layers
of residue are etched the least and print the lightest.[3]

Comparing the individual prints in the series, one can see the range of
effects possible using this method. Close greatly varied the size and shape
of the fingerprints to achieve delicate tonal modulations that enabled
him to suggest such subtleties as the different fabric textures in the
clothing of each sitter. Emily's fair skin is even differentiated from Leslie's ruddier complexion. In *Marta* Close has rendered such amazing detail as lashes, pupils, and individual wisps of hair.

Marta, *Leslie*, and *Emily* were each printed in two editions, one directly on paper, the other on silk collé, as in this image of *Marta*. Close
had earlier executed fingerprint drawings directly on silk, but his work
at Graphicstudio represented his first experience with silk collé in etching. To print the silk collé editions, the first for Graphicstudio as well,
Patrick Foy devised a method of fixing the Chinese silk to the paper
without bubbles or distortion. A piece of silk was placed on top of an
unetched copperplate the same size as the printing plate, then sprayed
with water, squeegeed, and blotted, causing the fabric to cling to the surface of the plate. Adhesive was brushed over the entire surface of the

*My friends loan me their images—no strings
attached—to do whatever I will with them and,
in many cases, I might use those images ten years
later.*

Chuck Close, in Cottingham 1983

154

fabric, and the excess fabric around the edges of the plate was carefully trimmed. The plate with the silk and adhesive were placed on the press bed into a registration device that matched the position of the printing plate and run through the press with a sheet of dampened paper so that the silk would transfer from the plate to the paper. The unetched plate was then removed from the press bed, and the paper to which the silk was adhered was run through the press with the etched and inked plate to produce the final silk collé image.[4]

1. Close, interview with Arnold Glimcher, in New York 1986.
2. Confirmed by Deli Sacilotto, telephone conversation with Corlett, 28 February 1991.
3. See "Prints and Photographs Published," *PCN* 17, no. 2 (May/June 1986), 59. The drawings on mylar were made during the summer of 1985. Close had previously executed a fingerprint lithograph by pressing ink directly onto the plate. See *Phil/Fingerprint*, 1981, in "Prints and Photographs Published," *PCN* 12, no. 4 (Sept./Oct. 1981), 111.
4. Information about the silk collé process is from Deli Sacilotto, in conversation with Fine, 25 September 1990.

37 Leslie/Fingerprint, 1986
Direct gravure on 1114 lb. cold-pressed d'Arches Aquarelle paper
54¼ x 40¾ (137.8 x 103.5)
Edition: 45; 1 BAT; 2 PP; 2 PrP; 1 NGAP; 1 GP; 1 USFP; 1 TP; 7 AP
Collaboration: Patrick Foy, George Holzer, Deli Sacilotto, Donald Saff

Since the late 1960s Chuck Close has focused almost exclusively on portraiture as the vehicle for his art.[1] His monumental portrait heads have
invited comparison with the early fourth-century colossal Roman head
of *Constantine the Great* and the huge seventeenth-century stone heads
on Easter Island.[2] Close's work at Graphicstudio exemplifies his approach to his subject: isolating a head that is rendered considerably
larger than life on a neutral ground without any reference to setting, the
artist willfully exploits the impact of enormous scale on the viewer's
perception.[3]

In works such as *Leslie* the commanding presence of the subject's head
forcefully engages the viewer with a directness of gaze and often a remarkably neutral expression. Indeed, Close's portraits have occasionally
been likened to mugshots or passport photographs—images whose sole

37a. *Keith/Square Fingerprint*, 1979, stamp-pad ink on paper, 29¹/₂ x 22 (74.9 x 55.9), Collection of the Reynolda House, Museum of American Art, Winston-Salem

purpose is identification.[4] The artist has also explored the possibilities of more revealing facial expressions, however, as seen in the Graphicstudio print *Georgia* (fig. 38a).[5]

Close uses photographs as a point of departure the way other artists might use preliminary sketches: "For years I've taken photographs that do not have an object status of their own. They are simply a notation system for information to be used later in any number of ways. To me they are not 'photographs,' but my work could not have existed without photography."[6] For Close, a photograph "represents a frozen, poem-like moment in time. It remains constant, and the painting, however long it takes to make, is always about that quintessential moment."[7]

Close's meticulously detailed, continuous tone paintings of the 1960s and 1970s, for which he first became known, were executed with an airbrush, creating a smooth, anonymous surface analogous to the surface of the photographs on which the paintings were based. Throughout his career, however, the artist has explored numerous methods for rendering images. Among his richest and most varied surfaces are those realized using fingerprints, as in the Graphicstudio prints and in paintings similarly developed. The fingerprint images do not emulate the photographic surface or maximize characteristics of a photographic image such as depth of field, as do Close's earlier continuous tone works.[8] Instead, their tactile surface, no longer anonymous, irrevocably asserts the presence of the maker.

Close began to explore the aesthetic possibilities of his own fingerprints in 1978, creating a series of drawings with stamp-pad ink on paper. In his first fingerprint images Close inserted the impression of his finger into the regular boxes of a grid (fig. 37a).[9] After a year, however, he stopped using the grid with his fingerprints, possibly because using a fingerprint, a self-contained unit, allowed him to build his compositions incrementally without the imposition of the additional grid structure.[10]

I've always worked large. I've always wanted to make large works so that it would rip it loose from the way we normally see images of each other—to make it so big that it's hard to see as a whole. . . . I wanted to make big, aggressive, confrontational images that you couldn't ignore—that you had to have feelings about either one way or the other—you love them or hate them. . . . The bigger they are the longer they take to walk by—so the harder they are to ignore!

Chuck Close, interview with Jade Dellinger, 1987

Since the late 1970s Close has employed his fingerprint technique in a variety of media, including lithography, ink, and oils (see fig. 37b, a portrait of his wife's grandmother): "A finger is a blunt and kind of a dumb tool, but if you're drawing with a pencil you have to feel through it, or a brush, or whatever you try to have be an extension of your hand. In this case it actually is my hand, so I can feel how much ink I am picking up, and I can also feel how much ink I am putting down."[11]

37b. *Fanny/Fingerpainting*, 1985, oil on canvas, 102 x 84 x 2½ (259.1 x 213.4 x 6.3), National Gallery of Art, Washington, Gift of Lila Acheson Wallace, 1987.2.1

1. In some of his recent works Close has returned to the nude and to other subjects such as flowers. See Westerbeck 1989.
2. For an analogy to *Constantine the Great,* see Levin 1978, 149 n. 5; for a comparison with the Easter Island heads, see Finch 1989, 114.
3. Close's paintings as a rule are larger in scale than his prints.
4. See Levin 1978, 148. In Gerrit Henry, "The Artist and the Face: A Modern American Sampling," *Art in America* 63 (Jan.–Feb. 1975), 41, Close acknowledged his interest in this particular characteristic: "I'm not really that interested in photography, but one thing I like about photographs is the snapshot or mugshot quality of a California driver's license. It's got such an immediacy and a strong reason to exist in terms of nailing down what a certain driver looks like. It doesn't have anything to do with vanity, it doesn't have anything to do with the ego of the sitter or whatever. I've never done commissioned portraits because I've never wanted to get involved with those ego problems."
5. Finch 1989, 115, 119, 161, reproduces and discusses recent works such as *Alex* (1987) and *Lucas* (1986–1987), suggesting that they are "powerful and satisfying character studies in a very nearly traditional sense. As in portraits of the 16th and 17th centuries, the subjects of the paintings are made known to us with remarkable fidelity, even as they remain enigmas." Close has also recently deviated slightly from the frontal pose, as in his painting *Cindy* (1988), also reproduced in Finch 1989, 118.
6. Close, in Sandback and Sischy 1984, 50.
7. Close, in Lyons and Storr 1987, 30. Close produces his own photographs in collaboration with a professional photographer (see Cottingham 1983, 103).
8. Close's fingerprinted images can be compared to his pulp paper pieces of the 1980s and to his work of the 1970s and 1980s in which the underlying grid structure is exposed. See Curtis 1984 for a discussion of the development of Close's pulp paper pieces.
9. Much has been written about Close's use of the grid, first as a substructure for his compositions, and later as an overt and integral part of the composition. During the 1970s and 1980s Close actively pursued the creation of his imagery within the context of the overt matrix of the grid. The fingerprint works and the pulp pieces, while not relying exclusively on the grid, do not abandon the module/unit as building block of a composition.
10. See Simon 1980, 83. Close, in conversation with Arnold Glimcher (New York 1986), remarked: "The fingerprint is a very personal mark; even though it's more personal and physical, the way I'm working is still similar in the way the paintings are constructed or 'built.' I still work incrementally. The increments are now fingerprints."
11. Sandback and Sischy 1984, 50.

38 Emily/Fingerprint, 1986

Direct gravure on 1114 lb. cold-pressed d'Arches Aquarelle paper
54¹/₁₆ x 40⁷/₈ (137.3 x 103.8)
Edition: 45; 1 BAT; 2 PP; 2 PrP; 1 NGAP; 1 GP; 1 USFP; 1 TP; 7 AP
Collaboration: Patrick Foy, George Holzer, Deli Sacilotto, Donald Saff

Close's desire to "build a powerful image without using powerful gestures"[1] has fueled his drive for alternative methods of expression. In
1984 the artist noted that only fifteen to twenty photographs had formed
the basis of his work over the previous eighteen years, each of them serving as a point of departure for numerous works.[2] He "kept the image
constant and manipulated the process of developing that image."[3] Close
executed fingerprint drawings in 1984, for example, using the same photographs of Emily, Marta, Leslie, and Georgia that are the sources for
the Graphicstudio prints.[4] The same photographs used for the gravures
of *Marta* and *Georgia* (cat. 36, fig. 38a) also served as the source for
paintings of these subjects in 1986, both executed on a black ground
using white oil-based ink.[5]

Close has always shown concern for the effect a method of rendering
has on the impact of a work. Comparison of *Emily* with *Georgia* (fig.
38a) illustrates how the size of the individual fingerprint relative to the

38a. *Georgia*, 1984–1986 (app. 39)

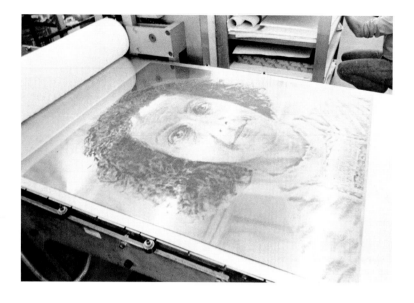

38b. Plate for *Emily/Fingerprint* on the press, 1986

overall scale of the composition significantly alters the appearance of the image. The bigger the module of tone (i.e., the fingerprint) in relation to the overall composition, the more abstract the image. The nuances created with individual fingerprints in *Emily* result in an image that is far more illusionistic than was possible in the small-scale portrait of *Georgia*, in which marks the same size appear larger in relation to the image and form more abstract patterns.

Close has always exploited the inherent tension of a three-dimensional object rendered illusionistically in two dimensions. Compelling surface detail functions as an integral component of his work, regardless of medium. As with his monumental continuous tone paintings—where each hair and pore serves simultaneously to animate the surface of the painting and to provide a meticulously detailed description of the individual face—the fingerprint works oscillate between surface pattern and representational description: "You can alternate between what is physically, actually there and then slip into the image and back and forth. I think how you do it influences the way it looks and what it means. So, I'm interested in changing how I do it all the time—to try to orchestrate as many experiences for the viewer as possible. . . . I wouldn't spend 14 months standing in front of a painting if I thought that the image was the [only] thing. Otherwise, I would just snap a picture, and that would be that!"[6]

In *Emily* Close manipulated the marks to achieve a high degree of subtlety, differentiating between the glassy moistness of eyes and the various textures of hair, clothing, and skin. The fingerprint, on one level, functions as a literal representation of the skin's pores. Indeed, Close complicates the meaning of identity through the interplay of the photographic record and the fingerprint, merging his own identity, in the fingerprint, with that of his sitter.

I don't think it's generally understood the degree to which intuition and invention actually exists in work like mine, which seems so matter-of-fact.
Chuck Close, in New York 1986

1. Close, in Lyons and Friedman 1980, 16.
2. See Sandback and Sischy 1984, 50.
3. Close, in DeLoach 1982, 2.
4. These drawings are lithographic ink on silk paper. See Lyons and Storr 1987, 148–150, where all four are reproduced.
5. Lyons and Storr 1987, 146–147. In addition, there are parallel images based on photographs obviously taken at the same time. Diamonstein 1980, 115, quotes Close as saying: "The problem is to see how many times I can keep going back to the well and still come up with something different."
6. Close, unpublished interview with Dellinger, 1987.

ROBERT W. FICHTER

Born in Fort Myers, Florida, 1939
Lives and works in Tallahassee

Robert Fichter, digitized self-portrait produced
on an Apple Macintosh computer

WHILE GROWING UP in Sarasota, Florida, Robert Fichter was intrigued
by the landscape of sculptural ruins that remained on Long Boat Key
from John Ringling's pre-Depression era attempt to recreate the Italian
Renaissance. Surveying the deterioration of civilization has since become
a leitmotif of Fichter's art. His interest in photography began in high
school, where he was a yearbook editor. But he was well on his way to
completing the requirements for a degree in anthropology at the University
of Florida, Gainesville (B.F.A. 1963), when he decided to switch to
the fine arts, studying painting, printmaking, and photography. During
his undergraduate years Fichter's political and social consciousness was
revealed in the iconoclastic student literary magazine, *Scope*, that he
helped to found.

After graduation from Gainesville, Fichter took the advice of photographer
Jerry Uelsmann, his professor and mentor, and enrolled at Indiana
University, Bloomington (M.F.A. 1966), studying with Henry
Holmes Smith. Both Uelsmann and Smith played central roles in Fichter's
development as a photographer. Through Uelsmann, Fichter also
met Nathan Lyons, who hired him as assistant curator of exhibitions at
the International Museum of Photography at George Eastman House,
Rochester, New York (1966–1968). Having access to the museum's rich
troves on the history of photography and its ambitious exhibition program,
designed to reveal the expressive possibilities of the medium, gave
Fichter fertile ground for his photographic explorations.

In 1968 Fichter moved to Los Angeles, taking a teaching position at
UCLA, where he was an assistant professor for two years. He moved back
to Florida in 1971, joining the faculty of Florida State University, where
he is currently a professor in the art department. Fichter returned to
UCLA once during the 1970s, as a visiting associate professor of art
(1976). He was also visiting artist at the School of the Art Institute of
Chicago in 1977.

In addition to his work at Graphicstudio, Fichter has produced etchings,
lithographs, and photographs at the Visual Arts Research Institute,
Arizona State University, Tempe (1984), and lithographs at the Tamarind
Institute, Albuquerque (1987). He has also produced two artist's
books featuring computer-generated imagery: *After Eden*, published by
the U.S.F. Art Galleries (1984); and *A-X Cavation* (text by James
Hugunin), published by University of Colorado, department of fine
arts (1988).

Fichter's first one-man exhibition was held at the George Eastman
House in 1968. Other important exhibitions of his work have been
shown at the School of the Art Institute of Chicago (1974), Los Angeles
Center for Photographic Studies (1981), U.S.F. Art Galleries (1984),
Southeastern Center for Contemporary Art, Winston-Salem, North
Carolina (1986), and the Gallery of Art, University of Northern Iowa,
Cedar Falls (1990). In 1982 a major retrospective of his work was
organized by the International Museum of Photography at George
Eastman House and traveled to the Fine Arts Gallery, Florida State University,
Tallahassee; Frederick White Gallery, UCLA; Museum of Contemporary
Photography, Columbia College, Chicago; San Francisco
Museum of Modern Art; Art Museum, University of New Mexico; and
the Brooklyn Museum.

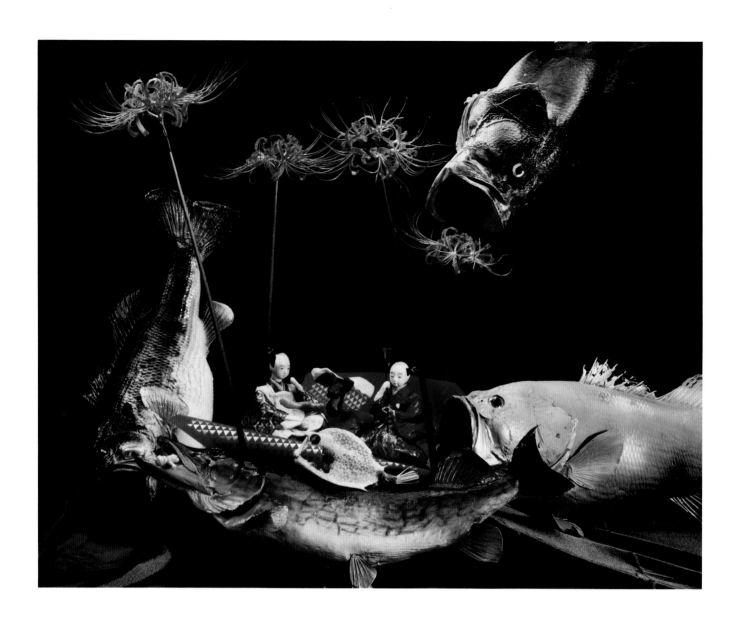

39 Hurricane Signal, 1984
Cibachrome print
20 x 24 (50.8 x 61)
Edition: 33; 1 GP; 1 USFP; 2 AP
Collaboration: David Yager

Robert Fichter worked at Graphicstudio in 1984, producing two etchings (one that incorporates an offset lithograph) and one lithograph (app. 83, 87, and 93).[1] During this period eight cibachrome prints, including this one, were editioned at Photographic Specialties in Minneapolis under Graphicstudio supervision (see also cats. 40, 41, and app. 88–92).

A statement from an undergraduate essay the artist wrote in the early 1960s (see facing page), charts an aesthetic course that Fichter continues to explore in his art. He addresses political, cultural, and environmental themes using a highly personal and eccentric troupe of fantastic creatures he has dubbed his "Cast-O-Characters."[2] Many of them have a role in his Graphicstudio works: Baby Gene Pool in *Mutant Magic #1: Baby Gene Pool Takes the Stage*; Bones in *Nature Returns*; Zen Monk teaching the flow of the universe in *Space Heater*; and Mr. Roboto Techno-Observer in *Total Readymade*. *Hurricane Signal* features incarnations of the Kimono Clad Person (Baby Gene Pool's muse) and the omnipresent Fish-Out-Oh-Water, a character that appears frequently among Fichter's repertoire of images, taking on an array of roles in the artist's bizarre allegories. Fichter's biting imagery and his penchant for satirical, even cynical, social commentary has invited comparison to the nineteenth-century cartoonist Thomas Nast, whose work Fichter has even incorporated into his own on occasion.[3]

Fichter has explored a wide variety of techniques, media, and processes, with an insatiable interest that inspired one photographer to comment, "he goes through them like Kleenex."[4] In the catalogue *A X Cavation* that Fichter produced in conjunction with James Hugunin, the artist listed nearly two dozen processes he has employed.[5] In the late 1970s he began to fabricate three-dimensional scenes specifically for the camera: "I don't think of them as that much different from the assembly work that goes on in gum printing and blueprinting; it seemed natural when I started putting these things together."[6] Fichter "doesn't take pictures, he makes 'em. He's a printmaker."[7]

For *Hurricane Signal* Fichter fabricated a three-dimensional tableau and then transformed it through photography, using the cibachrome process to achieve the rich colors and textures. The brilliant hues are amplified by the deep black field against which they are set: "I think about it as a way of making collages, except it's the ultimate healing process for making a collage. . . . It binds it all together, putting together lots of different diverse sources and making them one thing. . . . When I'm setting it up, it looks entirely different than it does through the camera; the camera becomes the picture plane."[8]

Featured are four fish preserved by a taxidermist—Fichter's perennial Fish-Out-Oh-Water. As Robert Sobieszek has explained: "Mr. Bass is . . . complex. He is a familar Florida animal, he can be the mythical carp of the orient invested with magical powers, or he can be the product of a befouled nature while escaping his polluted waters to gain oxygen. Mr. Bass can be aggressive if he wills, swallowing little Jonah or the fleshless remains of Everyman prostrated before big business; or he can be vulnerable, as in his guise as the 'Fish-Out-of-Water,' to such things as lectures on what death is all about. He is the symbol of survival in the face of adversity, telling us in one drawing that 'the one that lives is the one that gets to tell the tale!'"[9]

In *Hurricane Signal* allusions to the Jonah story and to the mythical Orient—with the Kimono Clad persons, the carp, and the red spider lily (*Lycoris radiata*), an exotic flower whose dramatic blooms are native to China and Japan—combine to create a multilayered, if elusive and unsettling, dramatic scene. The cibachrome is visually seductive: in the decorative use of brilliant reds and lush greens; and in the rich textures of the fish scales, fabric, and the gold brocade of the figurines' costumes. Yet there are ominous, even sinister, overtones. One fish descends from above and appears about to devour a bloom. Another is about to swallow a child. All of the fish seem to be closing in on the seated figures, who are oblivious to the danger. Only the dog between them, with its front legs outstretched and mouth agape, seems to be aware of impending doom. Fichter artfully elicits a foreboding quality, with the swarming, circular arrangement of fish evoking the eye of a hurricane—that insidious, threatening, absolute stillness in the center of a raging storm—something with which Fichter, as a native Floridian, would be familiar.

The task of the modern photographer working with the contrived image is to see symbols that offer meaning and meanings over a greater span of aesthetic so that the image gets to the viewer's gut before he can turn away.

Robert Fichter, in Sobieszek 1983

Sobieszek remarked on the dark nature of Fichter's work: "The 'gothic' element in Southern art and culture is important in approaching Fichter. It is the image of the peaceable kingdom infiltrated by death and violence, the vernal pastoral sullied by deterioration and meanness."[10]

In an exhibition catalogue that included *Dürer with Red Flower* (cat. 41) and *Hurricane Signal* as well as three other Graphicstudio prints, Fichter stated: "The cibachrome photographs presented here are attempts to create visual statements about mankind's relationship to the rest of the universe. Mankind at one time existed in an unbroken circle with the rest of the universe. That circle has been broken. We will reap the benefits of that brokenness. One thing leads to another and so on and so forth."[11]

1. During this period Fichter also produced several proofs of another etching entitled *Pyramid Enigma*, but no edition was produced.
2. See *After Eden*, Tampa 1984.
3. See, for example, *Veteran Recruit #2* (1980), which features the Nast cartoon of the same name, reproduced in Jenkins 1983, 7. Jenkins (p. 12) notes the affinity between these two artists.
4. Evon Streetman, Florida photographer, as quoted in Sobieszek 1983, 6.
5. The list, in Fichter and Hugunin 1988, included: gelatin silver print, Polacolor, chromogenic development print, gum-bichromate, Verifax transfer, photo-

silkscreen, Inko dye lacquer transfer, graphite, watercolor, acrylic, colored pencil, decals, offset lithography, stone lithography, paint, intaglio etching, color xerox, cyanotype, photolithography, computer graphics.
6. Fichter, videotaped interview with David Yager, c. 1983.
7. Fichter and Hugunin 1988.
8. Fichter, speaking generally about the process of photographing three-dimensional tableaux, in the interview with Yager, c. 1983.
9. Sobieszek 1983, 9.
10. Sobieszek 1983, 3.
11. Fichter, in Tallahassee 1985, 37.

40 Frog Biology, 1984

Cibachrome print
34⁷/₈ x 27¹/₄ (88.6 x 69.2)
Edition: 5; 1 WP; 1 USFP; 5 AP
Collaboration: David Yager

As an undergraduate at the University of Florida, Fichter studied biology and anthropology until his fourth year. Then, seeing the work of professor of photography Jerry Uelsmann and being overwhelmed by the expressive potential of the medium, he adopted new career plans.[1] But the relationship of the human species to the natural world and the ecological fate of that world at the hands of industrialized nations that do not respect it have remained a continuing theme in Fichter's art. In his own words: "I am vastly interested in the biological world in an ecological sense, and . . . interested in the themes and subthemes that it suggests to me: the place of man in the physical world as an interacting species with the most highly developed apprehension system."[2] Thus nature and humanity's relationship to it are underlying themes in *Frog Biology*.

This print shows a vase of red spider lilies standing in front of a biological chart that illustrates a dissected Leopard Frog (*Rana Pipiens*), clearly identified on the chart. The feathery bursts of the brilliant red blooms suggest a visual rhyme with the intricate network of blood vessels and capillaries meticulously detailed on the chart. The bulbous seed pods, with their withered blooms, also provide an analogue for the frog's organs and veins. The interconnectedness of the natural world, the poetic interplay of the manifestations of natural forms—as in the resonance between the frog and the flower—becomes unsettled by the realization that the flowers have been cut, the fish preserved through taxidermy, and

The implication of a Biological Garden is that of a place where specimens are prepared for later study, and by extension, that too would be the function of the Psychological Garden. Thus, imagery is drawn from a biological world and is developed only when I feel that the image has psychological relevance to my current feeling. . . . The forms that I select from the biological world create the reality of my work and become, through their melodramatic presentation, the psychological side of my work.

Robert Fichter, in Sobieszek 1983

the frog dissected, all for the benefit of humanity's intellectual and aesthetic pursuits. Sketchy white chalk lines on the chart locate the major organs and bisect the muscle of the leg, further suggesting the cold, clinical way people often investigate the world through science.

The antique frog diagram—a Webers' Biological Chart copyrighted in 1926[3]—with its tattered edges and discolored paper, lends an aura of timelessness to the image. This association would not have been suggested if the chart had been crisp and new, the epitome of the state-of-the-art in scientific investigation. Because the chart is "outdated," yet still reflects the intrusive methodology behind much past and present scientific inquiry, it expresses something unchanging about the nature of human thought.

1. As Fichter has explained in *After Eden,* Tampa 1984, 8: "Four years into a degree in Anthropology at the University of Florida, I was simultaneously shown the photographic work of Jerry Uelsmann and confronted by the fact that I would never pass Spanish I and receive a B.A. degree. I took one look at the possibilities of photography as a creative means of expression and began working twenty-four hours a day at making art."

2. Fichter, "Notes from a Biological and Psychological Garden," M.F.A. thesis statement, Indiana University, 1966.
3. The following phrases are readable on the chart featured in this cibachrome: "Webers' Biological Charts / Dissections and Text by [I.M.?] Valentine / Department of Biology, Yale University / Latham Litho. & Ptg. Co. Long Island City, N.Y. / Copyright 1926 by R. Weber / Leopard Frog—Rana Pipiens."

41 Dürer with Red Flower, 1984

Cibachrome print
35 x 27¼ (88.9 x 69.2)
Edition: 5; 1 GP; 1 USFP; 4 AP
Collaboration: David Yager

The Garden of Eden just before the Fall is one of the themes interwoven in the complex iconography of Fichter's *Dürer with Red Flower*. Created explicitly for the camera, the two Plasticine figures in the vignette—particularly the blue one on the left, with hand extended—and the apple-bearing snake on the tree in the center suggest the well-known 1504 engraving *Adam and Eve* by the Northern Renaissance artist Albrecht Dürer (fig. 41a),[1] whose self-portrait of 1498 Fichter has also added to the iconographic mix. Superimposed over the Dürer self-portrait is one of Dürer's sheets of studies in physiognomy.[2]

Dürer produced many self-portraits, but the one from which Fichter chose to reproduce a detail was painted the same year Dürer produced his remarkable folio of fourteen woodcuts of the Apocalypse.[3] The scorched edges of Fichter's detail of the portrait suggest an abstruse reference to this fiery prophecy.[4] The multiple meanings that can be drawn from these art historical references—interwoven as they are with biblical allusions and the suggestion of the natural world altered by human ac-

We are throwing ourselves out of the garden. Our grandchildren will really understand the Garden of Eden story.

Robert Fichter, in Fichter 1984

tion (the cut flowers and the stuffed bird)—include the implication, as in *Frog Biology* (cat. 40), of a dark underside to humanity's study both of itself and of the world traditionally associated with the Renaissance period in Western civilization.

Another possible reading of the imagery suggests a rather macabre cycle of life: beginning with Adam and Eve (the Fall) and ending with the Apocalypse, as if humanity were doomed from the start. This is the ultimate continuum: people and the world they temporarily occupy, as inextricably intertwined with an inevitable, dark destiny that is a consistent presence in Fichter's art.[5] In *Dürer with Red Flower* Fichter seems also to be expressing an intellectual and psychological kinship with the Northern Renaissance artist. They share an affection for the natural world, revealed by Dürer in his exquisite renderings of animals and plants. Thus, in its references to Dürer, Fichter's photograph also may be a self-portrait of sorts.

As with *Hurricane Signal* (cat. 39), *Dürer with Red Flower* is rich in color and texture, inviting close study of the characteristics of individual subjects: the weave of the green fabric; the malleable, pinched substance of the Plasticine; the velvety surface of the flower petals; and the softness of the bird feathers.

41a. Albrecht Dürer, *Adam and Eve*, 1504, engraving, 9¹³/₁₆ x 7⁹/₁₆ (24.9 x 19.3), National Gallery of Art, Washington, Rosenwald Collection, 1943.3.3491

1. Dürer adopted Adam's gesture from the Apollo Belvedere.

2. See Walter L. Strauss, *The Complete Drawings of Albrecht Dürer*, vol. 5, *Human Proportions* (New York, 1974), p. 2498, fig. HP: 1513/41, for a reproduction.

3. According to Heinrich Wölfflin, *The Art of Albrecht Dürer* (London, 1971), 59: "The book of the *Apocalypse*, dark and depressing as it is, was the first important subject on which Dürer tried his strength. The book had immense significance at that time. There was a general feeling that the end of the world was near. Everyone was prepared to see mysterious omens in natural occurrences and there was a general nervous watchfulness for portents and miracles. . . . And now, people possessed, in the *Apocalypse*, a description of the terrible things which were awaiting mankind."

4. Fichter 1984, 7, described his own apocalyptic vision: "While on a trip to Colorado, . . . I drew a calendar called 'Seven Days to the End of the World.' It was designed to be used when you felt you had only seven more days until the end of the world. The first characters were Bones and Ms. Bones who danced the apoc-oh-lyp-tic tango. I added Baby Gene Pool as their mutant child. Baby Gene Pool (he/she/it), represents for me all the unborn biological life forms that are being transformed by our chemical-electrical-mechanical pollutions of our environment. I had finally gotten close to what I had wanted to create; a popular form of narration that could bear a message and be interesting to look at simultaneously. In 1983, CNN Cable News reported that a couple was seeing a video display manufacturer because they believed that their child, who was born with a single eye, was deformed because the mother had worked at a video display terminal."

5. Similar metaphors are explored in the artist's book, *After Eden*, Tampa 1984, published in conjunction with an exhibition of Fichter's work held at the U.S.F. Art Galleries.

LEE FRIEDLANDER

Born in Aberdeen, Washington, 1934
Lives and works in suburban New York

LEE FRIEDLANDER TOOK his first photograph when he was fourteen, and he built a darkroom soon thereafter. Following high school he enrolled in the Los Angeles Art Center School, but he was dissatisfied with the program and attended only briefly in 1953. Instead, he continued his education independently, working with one of the school's instructors, Edward Kaminski.

Friedlander began photographing jazz musicians when he was in Los Angeles. His passion for their music led to his meeting Nesuhi Ertegun, a founder of Atlantic Records. Soon after moving to New York in 1956, Friedlander was hired by Atlantic to photograph recording artists such as John Coltrane and Ray Charles for album covers. During the 1950s and early 1960s he also freelanced for Columbia and RCA and for popular periodicals including *Esquire* and *Sports Illustrated*. About this time Friedlander purchased his first Leica camera, the brand he uses still.

Friedlander had also been doing some noncommercial work, and in 1963 he had his first one-man show at George Eastman House, Rochester, New York. His inclusion in New York's Museum of Modern Art exhibition, *New Documents* (1967), firmly established his reputation. In the early 1960s Friedlander discovered the work of E. J. Bellocq, a turn-of-the-century New Orleans photographer whose place in the history of photography he helped to establish by printing his glass-plate negatives.

In 1959 Friedlander moved out of New York City to one of its northern suburbs. In 1969 Petersburg Press published *Photographs by Lee Friedlander and Etchings by Jim Dine*, which included sixteen works by each artist. The following year Friedlander produced *Self Portrait*, his first book of photographs, issued by his own publishing company, Haywire Press, which has since published many of his books and portfolios: among them *Lee Friedlander: Photographs* (1979), *Flowers and Trees* (1981), and *Cherry Blossom Time in Japan* (1986). Other Friedlander portfolios that have been published as books are *The American Monument* (Eakins Press, 1976), *Factory Valleys* (Callaway Editions, 1982), and *Like a One-Eyed Cat* (Harry N. Abrams, Inc., 1989).

Lee Friedlander trimming *Kerria Japonica Shrub/ New City, New York, 1974* (cat. 421), 1975

Friedlander was the first photographer to receive the MacDowell Medal for Lifetime Achievement in the Arts (1986), and in 1990 he received a John D. and Catherine T. MacArthur Foundation Award. His numerous one-man exhibitions have included those held at the Museum of Modern Art (1972, 1974), Corcoran Gallery of Art, Washington, D.C. (1976), Institute of Contemporary Art, Boston (1977), National Gallery of Victoria, Melbourne, Australia (1977, 1981), Hudson River Museum, Yonkers (1978), Museum of Fine Arts, Boston (1978), Musée d'art contemporaine, Montreal (1979), Akron Art Institute (1982), San Francisco Museum of Modern Art (1982), Baltimore Museum of Art (1983), Tel Aviv Museum (1985), and the Institute of Contemporary Arts, London (1986). A retrospective entitled *Like a One-Eyed Cat* was organized by the Seattle Art Museum (1989) to travel in the United States and abroad.

42A–O Photographs of Flowers, 1974–1975

Fifteen photographs mounted on 16 x 20 (40.6 x 50.8) Harumi paper plus title page and colophon page, housed in a blue fabric-covered box
Each edition: 90 (I/XX through XX/XX; 1/70 through 70/70); 10 AP; 2 production proofs
Collaboration: Oscar Bailey, Donald Saff; printed by Lee Friedlander with the assistance of Larry Miller and Peter Foe. Debossing of the Harumi paper by Tom Kettner; mounting by Peter Foe, supervised by Michelle Juristo; colophon page and box label printed by Mark Stock. The calligraphy of the colophon page, title page, and box labels was executed by Virginia Team. Blue fabric-covered boxes by Cantelmo Bookbinding Company, New York

Throughout his career Lee Friedlander has approached his subject matter somewhat thematically, exploring and re-exploring subjects that continue to interest him, including flowers and trees, landscapes, gardens, the figure, monuments, the workplace, and street scenes. To create the *Photographs of Flowers* portfolio, Friedlander selected images he had photographed between 1972 and 1974 in Europe and America.[1] A special darkroom was set up for this project, the first photographs to be published by Graphicstudio.

As the images in the suite reveal, Friedlander takes advantage both of the camera's propensity for flattening space and distorting scale and of other photographic effects such as tilted camera angles, seemingly arbitrary cropping, and unedited detail. Yet the allover compositions of abstract expressionist painting are evoked in the structured interplay of light and dark, horizontal and vertical, that can be seen in *Hollyhocks* (cat. 42E), or in the sprawling forms and interlocking tones of gray that constitute *Cactus* (cat. 42G). This formalist approach to composition is interpreted through, and defined by, the idiosyncrasies of the photographic process, as Friedlander constructs images from fragments that reflect contemporary life while at the same time emphasizing the artificiality of the image in relation to the world.[2]

Friedlander's photographs underscore the fact that the camera does not correct, adjust, and interpret the way the human eye does. In the print *Kerria Japonica Shrub* (cat. 42I), for example, the photographer capitalized on the profusion of visual detail, unedited by the camera, to create a composition that weaves the patterns of leaves—interlocking those that had fallen and those still on the bush—into a complex matrix that can be read simultaneously as a two-dimensional design or as a representation of a three-dimensional situation. Similarly, in *Wall of Potted Plants and Trees* (cat. 42A) the camera angle flattens the corner, and the

Once I heard Charlie Parker, I was sure anything was possible. Everyone probably has a touchstone like that. It was an emancipating experience for me. The imagination and technique! I was dumbfounded. And he was still within a tradition.

Lee Friedlander, in Woodward 1989

42A **Wall of Potted Plants and Trees/Putney, Vermont, 1972**
Image: 6⅞ x 10¼ (17.5 x 26)

42B **Roses in Vase/New York City, 1974**
Image: 12¹⁵/₁₆ x 8½ (32.9 x 21.6)

glass windows dissolve, to create an interwoven collage of indoor and
outdoor image fragments in which the horizontal rows of potted plants
offer a counterpoint to the verticality of the window frames and trees.
Near the bottom of the composition, the distinction between the interior
and exterior space is further confused by the way that delicate paper-
whites in full bloom are superimposed on the wintry landscape.[3]

Throughout his career Friedlander has explored compositions structured around a foreground barrier, and in most every image in this portfolio an object looms in the immediate foreground. This can provide "a cognitive, not a formal, tension like the annoyance you feel when your theater seat is behind a pole or your view out the car window is blocked by a passing truck."[4] Perhaps the most dramatic example here is *Chry-*

42C **Rosebush with Leafy Background / Fort Lee, New Jersey, 1972**
Image: 9⅝ x 6½ (24.5 x 16.5)

42D **Chrysanthemums at Flower Market / Paris, 1972**
Image: 6¹³/₁₆ x 10¼ (17.3 x 26)

santhemums in Garden Pot (cat. 42H), which reveals only a glimpse of the landscape behind a garden pot so dominating in its presence that even the flowers planted in it are cut off by the top edge of the image. In other works the barrier is more subtle. The landscape in *Evergreen Tree* (cat. 42J) is blocked by an evergreen at the center of the composition, while in the extreme foreground a deciduous sapling, barren except for three pairs of elegantly transparent leaves, forms a delicate tracery that screens the sky. Likewise, in *Rosebush with Leafy Background* (cat. 42C) the tangle of foreground and background foliage and the extension of the rosebush branches to all four sides of the image make the picture plane impenetrable. Friedlander uses obstruction aggressively, but

42E **Hollyhocks/Taos, New Mexico, 1972**
Image: 6^{15}/$_{16}$ x 10^{7}/$_{16}$ (17.6 x 26.5)

42F **Roses with Eaten Leaves/Parc St. Cloud, France, 1973**
Image: 6^{11}/$_{16}$ x 10 (17 x 25.4)

172

gracefully. *Potted Rose* (cat. 42O), with its roses in full bloom silhouetted against a pale gray sky and darkened landscape, reveals a lyricism that is characteristic of the artist's flower images: "You have to be responsible to the subject. A flower can't look like concrete."[5]

Friedlander's flowers and trees sometimes suggest parodies of the garden and floral pictures that were abundant in the photographic journals of the 1930s and 1940s.[6] His wit is evident in *Roses in Vase* (cat. 42B), for example, where he has cropped all but two of the blooms, focusing instead on the severed stems and the profusion of ferns that are standard in florist shop arrangements. He tilts the photographic frame slightly, threatening the stability of the vase on the tabletop. In *Petunias* (cat. 42M), he establishes a similar tension with an immense-looking tree

42G Cactus/Brooklyn Botanical Gardens, 1973
Image: 8 x 12 (20.3 x 30.5)

42H Chrysanthemums in Garden Pot/ Luxembourg Gardens, Paris, 1972
Image: 4³⁄₄ x 7¹⁄₂ (12.1 x 19.1)

42I **Kerria Japonica Shrub/New City, New York, 1974**
Image: $7^{3}/_8$ x $11^{1}/_{16}$ (18.7 x 28.1)

42J **Evergreen Tree/Northern France, 1972**
Image: $6^{1}/_2$ x $9^{7}/_8$ (16.5 x 25.1)

branch—its size exaggerated by its proximity to the camera—that seems to hover just above a cluster of delicate flowers.

Friedlander is expert at maximizing the effect of odd juxtapositions. In *Single Rose Bloom in Formal Garden* (cat. 42κ) he structured the composition around the vertical alignment of the rose, a precisely pruned, cone-shaped tree in the garden, and a towering, naturally growing pine behind it. Friedlander recently noted: "One of the reasons you photograph is that you're curious about what things are going to look like as a photograph. . . . But in a way, you're also not surprised. You have an inkling of what things might look like because you work all the time and you kind of recognize what happens in the transformation. A photograph is not reality. It's really something else. It's a photograph."[7]

Humanity's penchant for controlling nature—formal gardens, cultivated flower beds, pruned lawns, potted plants—could be considered a leitmotif in these images. Many of the photographs suggest tension between artificial environments and the natural world: the regular horizontal pattern of a wire fence against a wild, unstructured thicket (*Climbing Rose Vines*, cat. 42N), potted plants placed in a natural setting (*Potted*

42K Single Rose Bloom in Formal Garden/ Bagatelle Gardens, Paris, 1973
Image: 10 x 6⅝ (25.4 x 16.8)

42L Potted Fern/Mariposa, California, 1972
Image: 7¹⁄₁₆ x 10⅝ (17.9 x 27)

42M **Petunias/Salinas, California, 1972**
Image: 9¹³/₁₆ x 6⁹/₁₆ (24.9 x 16.7)

42N **Climbing Rose Vines/Saratoga Springs, New York, 1973**
Image: 7¹/₈ x 10³/₄ (18.1 x 27.3)

Fern, cat. 42L), cultivated plants in a constructed environment (*Chrysanthemums at Flower Market*, cat. 42D), cut flowers brought indoors (*Roses in Vase*, cat. 42B). Friedlander has continued to explore this imagery, and in 1981 he published a selection of his work in a book entitled *Flowers and Trees*, which featured photographs taken between 1972 and 1978.

43C **Necking,** 1984–1985
Direct gravure with drypoint and roulette on Arches
Cover paper
35¹⁵/₁₆ x 24¹⁵/₁₆ (91.3 x 63.3)

43D **Grooming,** 1984–1985
Direct gravure with aquatint, drypoint, and roulette on
Arches Cover paper
36 x 24⁷/₈ (91.4 x 63.3)

43E **Mopping,** 1984–1985
Direct gravure with aquatint, drypoint, and roulette on
Arches Cover paper
35¹³/₁₆ x 24¹³/₁₆ (91 x 63.1)

man's forearm. Glier's drawing style, with its quick, lively, energetic strokes and often cursory treatment of details—such as the arm and hand holding the blow-dryer in the reflected figure of *Grooming* or the lamp in *Sitting*—seems to merge the illustrator's art (as might have been seen, for example, in the pages of *Vanity Fair* during the first decades of this century) with the look of commercial advertising: "Most often, drawing is less illusionistic than painting—its colors more limited, its techniques harder to disguise. It tends to present itself as an artifice more than as a window onto the world; it is more clearly an abstraction of life."[4] Something of Alice Neel and Jonathan Borofsky, whose influence Glier acknowledges, can also be seen in Glier's style.[5] Combining the directness and accessibility of commercial techniques with formal compositional concerns and the fluid draftsmanship of swift animated line and broad washes, Glier blends popular culture with high art. In his social consciousness he might also be seen as extending the tradition of earlier American social realists such as John Sloan.

Mopping borrows directly from the illustrator's lexicon, with the sweeping action of the mop indicated by the circular stroke that surrounds the midsection of the figure. The blur of the man's left arm and the vigorous zigzag strokes to the left and right of his torso reinforce the sense of movement. Broad brushstroke washes mark the path of the wet mop on the floor, and behind the figure the floor shines brightly, reflecting the light from the windows. In contrast to the movement in *Mop-*

ping, the solitude and calm of a leisure moment is evoked in *Sitting*. The handling here also suggests a commercial art style, although the insistent chiaroscuro, the richness of the blacks against the brightness of the white areas, might also be seen as Caravaggesque.

The drawings for all of these works were executed on mylar using oil crayon. Deli Sacilotto has described the collaboration with Glier: "He did the drawings in his studio on the Lower East Side, and I came up once or twice. Once I brought him the mylar, we worked out the format, we tried some tests using different materials, and then he made the drawings. I came up to see them. After he made the drawings, I made the plates. Then he came down [to Tampa], we proofed them up, and he worked on them. In some cases he changed a few things, adding some straight aquatint, perhaps a little drypoint, a little roulette work. One or two of the plates I think he left exactly as they were."[6] Many of the tones in *Necking* were accomplished with aquatint, while what appears to be a converging flock of birds outside the windows in *Mopping* were drypoint additions to the plate. The image for *Sitting*, once transferred to the plate, was printed with little, if any, reworking.

1. Glier, in Damsker 1984, 90.
2. Glier, in Damsker 1984, 90.
3. Glier, in Damsker 1984, 90.
4. Glier 1988, 100.
5. See Damsker 1984, 90.
6. Sacilotto, conversation with Fine, 25 September 1990.

ALFRED LESLIE

Born in the Bronx, New York, 1927
Lives and works in New York

IN HIGH SCHOOL ALFRED LESLIE was interested in body building and
won an annual competition when he was eighteen, earning the title "Mr.
Bronx." He also had a precocious talent for drawing, and he planned on
being a professional artist. After serving in the United States Coast
Guard in 1945–1946, Leslie studied briefly at the Art Students League,
where he was also a model. Between 1947 and 1949 he enrolled at New
York University—for one year, nine months, and sixteen days, the maximum provided for by his GI Bill—studying with Tony Smith.

To support himself during the early years of his career, Leslie worked
as a house painter, carpenter, truck driver, and in light manufacturing.
During these same years he experimented with filmmaking: *The Eagle
and the Foetus* (1945–1947); *Directions: A Walk after the War Games*
(1946–1949); *Pull My Daisy*, in collaboration with Robert Frank, Jack
Kerouac, and others (1959); and *The Last Clean Shirt*, a collaboration
with Frank O'Hara (1963). Leslie also wrote songs, designed stage sets
for several theater groups, and in 1959 edited and published the literary
magazine, *The Hasty Papers*.

In the 1950s Leslie explored abstract expressionism and—having captured the attention of critic Clement Greenberg, who had included him
in his *New Talent* exhibition at the Kootz Gallery (1949)—rapidly
earned a place among the best of the second generation abstract
expressionist painters. Leslie never completely abandoned realism, however, and during the early 1960s he turned away from abstraction to create a narrative art, depicting everyday people, places, and events in a
heroic manner, with dramatic lighting that has been likened to stage
lighting and to the paintings of Caravaggio. In 1966 Leslie's studio in
New York was destroyed in a fire that tragically claimed the lives of
twelve fire fighters. Most of his work of the previous years was lost.

Prior to his work in etching at Graphicstudio, Leslie had worked in
lithography at Landfall Press, Chicago. He has been a visiting artist at

Alfred Leslie making the drawing for *Folded
Constance Pregnant*, October 1985 (above him
the observatory roof is rolled back)

Amherst College and Youngstown State University in Ohio. He has received numerous grants for both painting and filmmaking, including a grant from the Guttman Foundation for Avant-Garde Film (1962).

Important one-man exhibitions of Leslie's work have been held at the Museum of Fine Arts, Boston, Hirshhorn Museum and Sculpture Garden in Washington, D.C., and Museum of Contemporary Art in Chicago (1976–1977), Kilcawley Center Art Gallery, Youngstown State University (1977), Worcester Museum of Fine Art, Butler Institute of American Art in Youngstown (1984), Newport Harbor Art Museum in Newport Beach, California, and Philbrook Art Center, Tulsa (1985), College of Saint Rose, Albany (1988), Boca Raton Museum of Art (1988), and the Saint Louis Art Museum (1991).

44 Folded Constance Pregnant, 1985–1986

Color softground etching printed on T. H. Saunders hot-pressed drawing paper
106⁷/₈ x 73¹/₂ (271.5 x 186.7)
Edition: 30; 1 BAT; 2 PP; 2 PrP; 1 NGAP; 1 GP; 1 USFP; 2 AP
Collaboration: Patrick Foy, Susie Hennessy, George Holzer, Deli Sacilotto, Donald Saff

Cycle-of-life themes—pregnancy, birth, old age, death—have played a significant role in Alfred Leslie's art: "It was a matter of my trying to find subjects that are generally discredited—subjects that have, perhaps, been treated falsely by a lot of other painters, subjects that were part and parcel of the literature of painting—to take them and try to find truth in those subjects. I think there are truths in old people, truths to be seen in babies, nursing mothers, children and family life."[1] Leslie's wife, Constance, seen here, has been an important model for the artist, and the celebration of her pregnancies may be seen in many of his paintings and drawings.[2] Folded Constance Pregnant is based on a painting executed in 1975. Leslie's first published etching, it is a heroic initial undertaking.

Constance's larger-than-life figure is keenly observed. A single masterfully drawn contour line defines the swollen shape of the belly while communicating the tautness of stretched skin. The subtlety and expressiveness of Leslie's draftsmanship is equally apparent in the description of the bumps and hollows of the kneecap, or the simplicity of the line that defines the curve of both the back and the edge of the arm. The artist's concentration on isolated figural elements results at times in unclassical proportions, as apparent in this figure's oversized hands and feet.

The elegance of the overall contour, a simple yet richly revealing line, recalls the sinuous figure studies of Matisse, whose drawings Leslie acknowledges as being among those that have influenced him: "Well, the drawings of Da Vinci—particularly his drawings of drapery—Holbein, Ingres, David, the so-called old masters. Those were the artists that made a great impression on me in terms of handling. . . . When it comes to the present, Matisse's drawings impressed me a great deal, and the drawings of Arshile Gorky. I think those are the two that I joined together."[3]

The directness and intensity in the treatment of the figure is characteristic of Leslie's style. Strong light limits the shadows to the shoulders, chest, and feet, emphasizing the contour line. In the print, as in the painting, the artist does not incorporate references to a specific environment; only the slight shadows beneath the feet anchor the figure on solid ground. By isolating Constance's towering form, Leslie established a

I look to make a fusion between the mind, the eye and passion.
Alfred Leslie, in Leslie 1983

NGA–Folded Constance Pregnant–1 1985–86

bold spatial and compositional presence for the figure while suggesting her inner strength and dignity.

Scale serves an important function in Leslie's art. In 1975 he wrote that he had intentionally "increased the size of [his] paintings so that there could be no question but that they were meant for public viewing and an institutional life and service."[4] As Leslie explained in a talk to U.S.F. students in the fall of 1985, the initial dimensions of the painting *Constance Pregnant* were nine by six feet, the width of which he reduced to four and a half feet in the completed work. In the etching, then, Leslie returned to the original proportions.[5]

In preparation for the execution of the print, a photomontage, scaled to the size of the 1975 painting, was produced at Graphicstudio and served as Leslie's model for the preparatory drawing. After the full-sized preparatory drawing was complete, the artist made a tracing on mylar of its contour, without modeling. The mylar tracing was placed over the

prepared softground plates, which had been secured to an upright ply-wood mount in the observatory studio. Newsprint was sandwiched between the plate and the mylar drawing to facilitate the lifting of the soft-ground.

The unique solution of folding the paper twice horizontally and using three plates with three runs to print the full image was developed especially for this project. The folding of the paper into thirds meant that the first side printed would have to be put through the press a second and third time, its inked surface protected by a cover sheet that, when removed, would pull away some of the color. To compensate for the progressive lightening of the color of the first and second runs as they passed through the press again, three different shades of the same reddish brown ink were used, one for each run. The first run was the darkest, the last one the lightest (see also cat. 62).

44a. Patrick Foy (left) and George Holzer at the etching press, lifting the printed sheet from the top plate of *Folded Constance Pregnant,* 1986

1. Arthur 1979, 85. Leslie made these comments in the context of a discussion of *A Birthday for Ethel Moore*, another work exploring the cycle-of-life theme.
2. Other works depicting pregnancy and birth include the painting *Coming to Term* (1968–1970), from the *Act and Portrait* triptych (reproduced in Frank H. Goodyear, Jr., *Contemporary American Realism since 1960* [exh. cat., Pennsylvania Academy of the Fine Arts] [Philadelphia, 1981], 115, figs. 57–59), and related drawings such as the eleven ren-

derings in the Coming to Term series (1970–1971) and the five studies in The Nursing Couple series (1972–1973), shown along with the painting *Constance Pregnant* at the Oil and Steel Gallery, New York (5 May through 16 June 1984). The group was called "The Course of Birth."
3. Arthur 1979, 84.
4. "Artist's Statement," in *Leslie,* New York 1975; reprinted in *Leslie,* Boston 1976.
5. Graphicstudio videotape 2.

ROBERT MAPPLETHORPE
Floral Park, New York, 1946–New York City, 1989

ROBERT MAPPLETHORPE WAS raised in Queens, a middle child in a Catholic family from which he was later somewhat estranged. He attended Pratt Institute in Brooklyn from 1963 to 1970, taking courses in painting, drawing, and sculpture, with no intention at that time of becoming a photographer. During the 1960s he and poet/musician Patti Smith became close friends, living together for several years, part of that time at the Chelsea Hotel in Manhattan. Mapplethorpe produced collages, and his jewelry designs had attracted a potential financial backer, but he chose not to continue in that direction. During this period he had also developed an interest in experimental film, exemplified by his feature role in Sandy Daley's *Robert Having His Nipple Pierced* (1970).

Mapplethorpe had discovered the shops and bookstores on 42nd Street as a teenage art student, and they had a profound effect on his work. His initial interest in photography was, in part, an outgrowth of the collages he had been constructing with images from pornographic magazines. With his first camera, a Polaroid SX-70 provided by the late curator of prints and photographs at the Metropolitan Museum of Art, John McKendry, Mapplethorpe was able to produce photographic images of his own. Later he would acquire a 4-by-5-inch view camera, and finally a Hasselblad. Throughout his career, Mapplethorpe used a variety of photographic processes, including photogravure, Polaroid, platinum prints on paper and linen, cibachrome, and dye transfer. He did not have a strong interest in darkroom processes, so he worked closely with his technician to obtain the look he wanted in his work.

Mapplethorpe produced photographs for liquor advertisements as well as for fashion and interior design publications, and he was known for his portraits of entertainment and art world celebrities. During the 1970s he was the staff photographer for Andy Warhol's *Interview* magazine, and his photographs appeared in journals such as *Vogue* and *Esquire*. His last commissioned portrait was of U.S. Surgeon General C. Everett Koop for *Time* magazine, taken less than two months before the artist's death. Mapplethorpe was an avid collector of photography, arts and crafts pottery, and furniture (which he also designed). Books featur-

Robert Mapplethorpe signing the edition of *Irises* (cat. 46) in his New York studio, July 1987

ing his photographs include *Certain People: A Book of Portraits* (Pasadena, Twelvetrees Press, 1985), and *50 New York Artists* by Richard Marshall (San Francisco, Chronicle Books, 1986).

Mapplethorpe's first one-man exhibition was held in 1976 at the Light Gallery, New York. Major exhibitions of his work have been held at the Chrysler Museum, Norfolk, Virginia (1978), Los Angeles Institute of Contemporary Art (1978), International Center of Photography, New York (1979), Van Reekum Museum, Apeldoorn, the Netherlands (1980), Kunstverein, Frankfurt am Main (1981), Contemporary Art Center, New Orleans (1982), Musée national d'art moderne, Centre Georges Pompidou, Paris (1983), Institute of Contemporary Art, London (1983), Centro di Documentazione di Palazzo Fortuny, Venice (1983), Hara Museum of Contemporary Art, Tokyo (1984), Australian Center for Contemporary Art, South Yarra, Victoria, and Melbourne (1986), Stedelijk Museum, Amsterdam (1988), National Portrait Gallery, London (1988), Institute of Contemporary Art, University of Pennsylvania (1988), and the Whitney Museum of American Art, New York (1988). In 1988 the artist established the Robert Mapplethorpe Foundation with the dual purpose of providing funds for AIDS research and for the visual arts.

45 Untitled #1, 1985

Color photogravure and screenprint on Arches Cover paper
30¼ x 24⅞ (76.9 x 63.2)
Edition: 60; 1 BAT; 2 PP; 1 PrP; 1 GP; 1 USFP; 12 AP
Collaboration: Deli Sacilotto with Nick Conroy, George Holzer, Patrick Lindhardt, Donald Saff, David Yager

Robert Mapplethorpe's photography can be grouped in three broad categories: portraits, still life (particularly images of cut flowers, as in cats. 46–48), and the figure (including homoerotic and sadomasochistic themes). Particularly in his later images the quality of light, his investigation of texture and sculptural form, and his interest in culturally charged subject matter all bind his work in these genres into a cohesive artistic whole. As Patti Smith expressed it, "each photograph a still from life. each photograph a select and subversive work shot from a beautifully corrupt agent of god."[1]

Untitled #1 is one of five images of black men Mapplethorpe produced as photogravures at Graphicstudio in 1985, the first prints in this medium published by the workshop. The project was undertaken by Deli Sacilotto, with whom Mapplethorpe had worked previously in gravure; the plates were executed in New York and the editions printed in Tampa. Four of the five prints in the series (*Untitled #2* through *Untitled #5*) were single-color photogravures. Sacilotto stated recently, however, that Mapplethorpe "wanted each one to be slightly different—not the usual techniques. He suggested hand watercolor. We got to talking about flocking in the background, which we ended up using in one of the prints [*Untitled #5*]."[2] The hand-coloring was executed according to the artist's specifications by a U.S.F. graduate student.

According to Sacilotto, *Untitled #1*, printed in three colors, is "one of the few, if not the only, full-color hand-printed photogravure in existence. I don't know if anybody else has done that. It involves process color—red, yellow, blue, printed in that order. Of course, the registration problem was extremely difficult. We worked with dampened paper

The work is very direct. I try not to have anything in the picture that is questionable. I don't want anything to come in at an angle that isn't supposed to come in at an angle.
Robert Mapplethorpe, in Kardon 1988

and tremendous pressure, so if you get slight expansion or slight mis-registration it would throw it out entirely. We ended up printing at least 140 [impressions] in order to get 80 good prints."

During the late 1970s and early 1980s Mapplethorpe produced a number of studies of the black male nude, leading to the 1986 book, *Black Book*.[3] Asked why he chose the black nude as a subject, he responded: "I was attracted visually. That's the only reason I photographed them. But once I started, I realized there's a whole gap of visual things. There have been great photographs of naked black men in the history of photography, but they are very rare. Some of my favorite pictures happen to be the pictures of black men."[4] Mapplethorpe's traditional art background at Pratt Institute is evident in his classical treatment of the nude. Though he is quoted as having described the instruction he received there as "old-fashioned and extremely academic," he also acknowledged the importance of his study of the figure: "The best education for a photographer is art school and drawing from the figure. . . . Drawing from a live model has helped me envision what I have envisioned."[5]

In *Untitled #1* Mapplethorpe isolated the black male figure, against a vibrant red ground that darkens in tone toward the edges. A silver border, screenprinted around the perimeter of the composition inside the plate line, confines the color and reflects the artist's long-standing interest in framing and the formal structure of his images as objects. The mannered pose and use of the backdrop celebrates the artifice of the studio environment. Space is indeterminate. The distance between subject and ethereal red background is unclear. The figure's back twists gracefully, as his arms, bent at the elbow and raised above his head, each outline a triangle of red. The spareness of the highly structured composition and the asymmetrical yet exactly balanced form of the model underscore the strength and solidity of the figure.

The corporeality of the figure, a hallmark of Mapplethorpe's nudes, is defined through the interplay of light and shadow, emphasizing the musculature of the arms and back. Mapplethorpe suggested in fact that if he "had been born one hundred or two hundred years ago, [he] might have been a sculptor, but photography is a very quick way to see, to make sculpture."[6] Shimmering highlights reveal the texture of the skin as well as the form of the figure at the thigh, the buttocks, the small of the back, along the backbone and shoulder blades, at the back of the head, and culminating with the right thumb. The luminescent glow of the saturated red surrounding the upper torso and head further enriches the deep skin tones of the model.

Stemming from the Western academic tradition of the nude in art, *Untitled #1* is nonetheless an uncommon rendering of the subject. The print reflects Mapplethorpe's ability to create images that are loaded with cultural overtones and elicit multiple, intense, and conflicting responses from the viewer. Depending on one's point of view, the black man so rendered may be seen either as elevated (vital and empowered), or as exploited (as an object, a stereotype of a sexual creature, and/or a noble savage). In apparent paradox, his imagery may be thought objectionable either because it threatens the status quo or because it seems to be a product of it. Mapplethorpe's images demand an emotional response from the viewer that reflects back on our culture, suggesting that the ambiguity is not inherent in the subject itself but rooted in society's biases and preconceptions.[7]

1. Smith 1977, 33.
2. Sacilotto, conversation with Fine, 25 September 1990. The following quotation is also from this discussion.
3. Published in New York, at St. Martin's Press, with a foreword by Ntozake Shange.
4. Mapplethorpe, in Kardon 1988, 29.
5. Mapplethorpe, in Larson 1983, 87.
6. Mapplethorpe, in Kardon 1988, 27.
7. Morgan 1987, 121–122, discusses the audience response to Mapplethorpe's work.

46 Irises, 1986–1987

Photogravure on White Somerset Satin paper
45^{1}/₁₆ x 38³/₈ (114.5 x 97.5)
Edition: 30; 1 BAT; 2 PP; 2 PrP; 1 GP; 1 NGAP; 1 USFP; 15 AP
Collaboration: Deli Sacilotto with Greg Burnet, Patrick Foy, George Holzer, Donald Saff

Mapplethorpe's passion for twentieth-century art glass and pottery has been well publicized, but if one had not heard of it, one could deduce it from his photographs of flowers. Many of his images, including two of the Graphicstudio photogravures, feature the pure, elegant forms of vases that were in the artist's own collection. In *Irises* Mapplethorpe has captured the iridescent surface of an Aurene glass vase crisply silhouetted against a background flooded with light. *Hyacinth* (cat. 47) features a ceramic pot.[1] As is characteristic of Mapplethorpe's compositions, *Irises* is organized around a subtle geometry. The square format is bisected by the vertical edge of the light pattern on the wall. The shelf provides a horizontal counterbalance. The symmetricality of the vase is echoed in the balanced, fanlike arrangement of the irises. The interplay of the triangular shapes that define the vase, the flowers, and the pattern of light is anchored by the merging of the shadowed silhouette of the vase with the darkened edge of the shelf. Even the shadows of the irises on the wall supply a visual weight critical to the composition's stability: "with flowers, I can always juggle things around. It can take two hours to just set up the lights. . . . If I click when I'm doing a day of flowers, I can get three or four pictures in one day. . . . I get flowers sent to me, and I have

Maybe I experiment a little more with flowers and inanimate objects because you don't have to worry about the subject being sensitive or worry about the personality. I don't think I see differently just because the subject changes.
Robert Mapplethorpe, in Kardon 1988

to shoot them that day. Sometimes I bring a friend who's an art director to make it easier."[2]

Constructed of light and shadow, the forms in *Irises* manifest a sculptural solidity that is typical of Mapplethorpe's work. The masterful manipulation of light yields a pristine clarity and stillness that has also become a signature of his style. Here he captures the luminosity of glass, as distinct from the light-absorbing quality of the pottery in *Hyacinth*. Light defines the individual petals of the flowers and creates a multitude of delicate gray undertones. These are beautifully achieved through the photogravure process, which is capable of imparting a gauzy atmospheric quality through the subtle grain of the aquatint ground.

The shallow pictorial space, only as wide as the shelf, is animated by light; and Mapplethorpe's use of sidelighting, which has been compared to Vermeer's, imparts an almost mystical aura.[3] Mapplethorpe's attention to light was eloquently described by his friend Patti Smith as early as 1977, ten years before *Irises* was produced: "Light too is tenderly manipulated. nothing is left to chance. like Jackson Pollock he believes there are no such things as accidents. and like Cocteau he believes that light has no licence of escape when summoned for a work of promise. light as imposing as granite. braids tapestry a trapezoid of light. the pale bronze planes of Brancusi or silvers and shadows lacing a textured wall. light which falls on the art not the artist. light as the subject itself."[4]

1. See Christie's, New York, sale 6930, 31 October 1989, lot nos. 103, 104, and 105 (ill. p. 59), for examples of Aurene glass that had been in Mapplethorpe's collection; and lot 347, for examples of ceramic ware in his collection (ill. p. 137). For further discussion of Mapplethorpe's collection, see "The Perfect Pot: A Celebrated Photographer Brings His Ceramic Collection into Focus" (photographs by Robert Mapplethorpe) *Art & Antiques* (Sept. 1986), 86–89.
2. Mapplethorpe, in Kardon 1988, 25.
3. Bourdon 1977, 7, makes reference to Vermeer in the context of Mapplethorpe's use of light.
4. Smith 1977, 13.

46a. Film positives for Robert Mapplethorpe's photographs (cats. 46, 47) hanging to dry in the Nebraska Avenue darkroom, October 1986

47 Hyacinth, 1986–1987

Photogravure on silk collé (China silk on 638 g/m² cold-pressed Saunders
Waterford paper)
45¼ x 38⅜ (114.9 x 97.5)
Edition: 27; 1 BAT; 1 PP; 1 NGAP; 1 GP; 1 USFP; 2 AP
Collaboration: Deli Sacilotto with Greg Burnet, Patrick Foy, George Holzer, Donald Saff

In *Hyacinth*, as in *Irises* (cat. 46), Mapplethorpe achieves a Mondrian-like balance of compositional forces. The rigid horizontal line of the shelf is counterbalanced by the strict verticality of the band of light on the wall. The consistent diagonal patterning within the shaft of light, as it strikes the surfaces of the plant, pot, and wall, acts as a unifying force, and the pot—located off-center—is visually balanced by the hyacinth bloom that leans to the left in the opposite direction of the diagonal streaks of light. A bright highlight on the rim of the pot finds a counter-point in the sliver of light that strikes the front edge of the shelf to the left of the pot.

In *Hyacinth* Mapplethorpe manipulates light to achieve a subtler effect than the frozen quality of the light in *Irises*. The top surface of the shelf is not as reflective. The light pattern on the wall is subdued. The light striking the hyacinth blooms is much softer than that on the irises; individual petals are not as sharply defined. The softness of the illumination is further enhanced by the warmth of the creamy undertone of the silk on which the image has been printed. The sheen of the fabric im-

Perfection means you don't question anything about the photograph. There are certain pictures I've taken in which you really can't move that leaf or that hand. It's where it should be, and you can't say it could have been there. . . . In the best of my pictures, there's nothing to question—it's just there. And that's what I try to do.
Robert Mapplethorpe, in Kardon 1988

parts a richness to the surface that is not attainable on paper. Light reflects off the textured surface of the fabric through the ink so that even the blackest areas glisten.

Mapplethorpe was fascinated by the effects possible with silk collé, a process described in cat. 36, and he had each of the three Graphicstudio flower photogravures produced in a silk collé edition as well as in an edition on paper. The interrelationship of fabric with pictorial imagery had been a particular and abiding concern of Mapplethorpe's, as may be seen in numerous works of the late 1970s.[1] His silk collé prints may be viewed as an extension of his interest in integrating photographic images with fabric panels, mirrors, and frames. In 1987, the same year the Graphicstudio prints were completed, Mapplethorpe executed a number of platinum prints on linen.[2]

1. Marshall 1988, 13, discusses Mapplethorpe's use of fabrics in his works of the 1970s.

2. Marshall 1988, 15, discusses the platinum prints on linen, some of which are reproduced in that catalogue.

48 Orchid, 1986–1987

Photogravure on Arches Cover paper
45⅛ x 38⅛ (114.7 x 96.8)
Edition: 30; 1 BAT; 2 PP; 2 PrP; 1 GP; 1 NGAP; 1 USFP; 11 AP
Collaboration: Deli Sacilotto with Greg Burnet, Patrick Foy, George Holzer, Donald Saff

The space in which Mapplethorpe's *Orchid* exists is at once airless and yet heavy with atmosphere, tranquil and yet unsettling. When compared with the style of the other two flower images produced as photogravures at Graphicstudio (cats. 46, 47), the iconic quality of *Orchid* is underscored. Mapplethorpe has eliminated the vase and any sense of spatial orientation. The flower looms large, willfully projecting itself into the picture plane. Mapplethorpe maximizes the natural symmetry of the plant, yet the slight bend in the stem, disrupting that symmetry and suggesting both delicacy and dignity, is the mainstay of the composition. The soft, grainy texture created by the aquatint ground evokes the velvety, tactile, palpable, fleshlike quality of actual petals.

Prior to his experience at Graphicstudio, Mapplethorpe had worked with Deli Sacilotto on a portfolio of ten photogravures, also of flowers.[1] His photographs of flowers are often well suited to the photogravure process, because, as Sacilotto has explained: "The ideal photographic positive for photogravure has a carefully graduated range of tonalities with good shadow detail. The middle and dark tones should be well defined and not too dense or a single continuous tone will result in these areas."[2]

It is frequently noted that Mapplethorpe's flower images can be interpreted as sexual metaphors, and indeed his flowers, like his nudes (see cat. 45), are both provocative and benign. Mapplethorpe himself explained that his flowers "don't look like anyone else's flowers. They have a certain archness to them, a certain edge that flowers generally do not have."[3] Although there is some suggestion of that archness in the erect posture of *Orchid*, it is perhaps better seen in the phallic stalks of *Hyacinth* (cat. 47). Flowers, which have often been associated with female sexuality (most often in the work of Georgia O'Keeffe), here evoke male sexuality, confronting cultural stereotypes regarding the definition of feminine and masculine. Mapplethorpe's sadomasochistic and homo-

It's funny, but I don't even like flowers very much. They're something to photograph, and I'd rather have the photograph than the flowers. When I've photographed them, I'll take them out of the studio and put them in my living environment, and feel they're not right—there's not enough space around them.

Robert Mapplethorpe, in Evans 1984

erotic imagery has received far more publicity than his flowers, but the flowers have attracted considerable attention from photography aficionados.[4]

1. The portfolio was copublished by the Barbara Gladstone Gallery and Sacilotto's Iris Editions in 1983, and the following appeared in *PCN* 14, no. 5 (Nov.-Dec. 1983), 175: "Many of his favorites are here—tulips, of course, lilies, and baby's breath—each a formal study of light, shadow, and shape. As always, Mapplethorpe's understanding of photographic history tells in his own work, and the series projects not the aggressive sexuality of his photographs of flowers but the quiet grace and tonal delicacy possible in photogravure."

2. Sacilotto 1982, 108.

3. Mapplethorpe, in Kardon 1988, 25.

4. See Tully 1989, C1 and C6, in which the following was noted regarding the Sotheby Parke Bernet, New York, sale 5921, 1 Nov. 1989, lot 748: "The most expensive single lot, 'Floral Still Life'—a trio of photogravures sold for $60,500. The stunning and dramatically lit close-ups of an orchid, a hyacinth and a vase of irises were purchased by an unidentified American collector. . . . According to [Paris-based dealer Harry] Lunn, the edition of floral still lifes that sold today for approximately $20,000 per image was originally offered for $3,500 in 1987." The images were the silk collé versions of the Graphicstudio gravures: *Orchid, Irises,* and *Hyacinth.*

MIRIAM SCHAPIRO

Born in Toronto, Ontario, 1923
Lives and works in New York City

MIRIAM SCHAPIRO, AN ONLY CHILD, was born into a creative family of
Russian-Jewish heritage that supported her desire at a young age to become an artist. Her father was an artist and industrial designer, who began teaching her art when she was six. At fourteen, she enrolled in WPA
evening classes to study the nude model, and while in high school she attended Saturday classes at the Museum of Modern Art. Schapiro continued her studies at Hunter College, majoring in art, but transferred to
the University of Iowa (B.A. 1945; M.A. in printmaking, 1946; M.F.A.
in painting, 1949). At Iowa she studied with Argentine printmaker
Mauricio Lasansky and became his first assistant. She also helped to
establish the Iowa Print Group.

Schapiro lived in Missouri from 1950 to 1952, then returned to New
York, where she and her husband, Paul Brach, would often socialize
with other artists at the Cedar Tavern or The Club. In 1967 she and her
family moved to California, staying there until 1975. In 1971 she and artist Judy Chicago founded the Feminist Art Program at the California Institute of the Arts in Valencia, the best-known product of which is the
collaborative project, *Womanhouse*. Schapiro and Sherry Brody created
The Dollhouse for that project. Schapiro's investigations into women's
traditional art inspired her "femmages" (see cat. 49 n. 1), and her exhibition of the monumental *Anatomy of a Kimono* at the Andre Emmerich
Gallery, New York (1976), helped reestablish the decorative as a respect-
able force in the visual arts. Her diverse accomplishments include a
large-scale "femmage" for the Orlando Airport, stained-glass windows
for Temple Shalom in Chicago, a thirty-five-foot-tall pair of dancers,
Anna and David, in brightly painted aluminum and stainless steel, installed in Rosslyn, Virginia, and *Rondo*, a book of original dance and
personal images published by Bedford Arts.

Schapiro has traveled extensively as a visiting artist, delivering lectures
and helping to promote a strong women's art movement. She was a
founder of the feminist periodical *Heresies*. In addition to her work at
Graphicstudio, she has produced editions at Bummy Huss Paper, Inc., in

Miriam Schapiro (right), assisted by Liz Jordan,
applies collage elements to *Children of Paradise*
(cat. 49), 1984

New York, Fabric Workshop in Philadelphia, Minneapolis College of Art and Design, Rutgers Center for Innovative Printmaking, Smith Anderson in Palo Alto, and the Tamarind Lithography Workshop in Los Angeles. Among her honors have been the prestigious Skowhegan Award; honorary doctorates from the College of Wooster, Ohio, and the California College of Arts and Crafts; and the Honors Award from the Women's Caucus for Art.

One-person exhibitions of Schapiro's work include one at the Lyman Allen Museum, New London, Connecticut (1966), *The Shrine, The Computer and the Dollhouse* at Mandeville Art Gallery, University of California at San Diego, Mills College in Oakland, California, and the University of Wisconsin at La Crosse (1975–1976), *Femmages* at Oberlin College, Ohio (1977), shows at the College of Wooster Museum, Ohio (1980), Kent State University, Ohio (1983), Atlanta Center for the Arts, New Smyrna Beach, Florida (1984), and Artlink Contemporary Artspace, Fort Wayne, Indiana (1986), *I'm Dancin' as Fast as I Can* at Guilford College, Greensboro, North Carolina (1986), and an exhibition at the Phyllis Rothman Gallery, Fairleigh Dickinson University (1990).

49 Children of Paradise, 1983–1984

Color lithograph and collage on Arches Cover paper (collage elements on Rives BFK "light-weight" paper)
31⁷/₈ x 48 (80.9 x 121.9)
Edition: 60; 3 PP; 2 PrP; 1 GP; 1 USFP; 15 AP; 1 WP
Collaboration: Susie Hennessy, George Holzer, Julio Juristo, Margaret Miller, Deli Sacilotto, David Yager, U.S.F. art students

In *Children of Paradise* Miriam Schapiro applied to the art of printmaking the collage principles she has called "femmage."[1] Schapiro has been creating femmages since the early 1970s, initially inspired by her use of found materials in her exploration of autobiographical and woman-centered themes for her contribution to *Womanhouse,* a feminist installation project at the California Institute of Arts.[2] Combining scraps of fabric, lace, quilting, and other handwork with paint and, here, printer's ink, Schapiro's femmages intentionally recall traditional handwork techniques such as appliqué and quilting.[3]

In the forefront of the feminist movement, Schapiro invented femmage as a means of bringing together the disconnected public and private aspects of her life: "The change came when I applied fabric to canvas. I always felt my life had been separated, that I walked out on my intimate life, my domestic life, as a wife, a mother, a child of my parents, when I went to the studio. My real life was one thing, my art another."[4]

Schapiro's strength as a colorist is clearly revealed in her bold use of vibrant and competing hues in both *Children of Paradise* and its preliminary study *Together* (fig. 49a). Two articles of children's clothing, a girl's dress and a boy's suit, serve as the core elements around which Schapiro has built the composition. Layering color and texture in the form of hearts and teacups cut from fabrics and houses cut from patterned paper—all familiar in Schapiro's repertoire of images—she creates a highly structured composition that nevertheless appears unstructured, reminiscent of the haphazard arrangements of some crazy quilts.[5] The large, patterned bandanna in *Together* has been turned on end in *Chil-*

The collagists who came before me were men, who lived in cities, and often roamed the streets at night scavenging, collecting material, their junk, from urban spaces. My world, my mother's and grandmother's world, was a different one. The fabrics I used would be beautiful if sewed into clothes or draped against windows, made into pillows, or slipped over chairs. My "junk," my fabrics, allude to a particular universe, which I wish to make real, to represent.

Miriam Schapiro, in Ruddick and Daniels 1977

dren of Paradise to form a diamond but serves the same unifying purpose in both compositions. The centered rectangle/square is a compositional device often used by Schapiro.[6]

Schapiro worked from fabrics she brought with her to the Graphic-studio workshop—"pieces from woman's culture"[7]—as well as material she collected in Tampa, to create about a dozen preliminary femmages before executing the edition print. In the print Schapiro's layering of transparent inks with fabrics, possibly suggesting "levels of the past,"[8] locks the cutout shapes into a compositional whole. The fabric heart in the bottom left corner, for example, is echoed in the background lithography, connecting the layers of the image.

Julio Juristo printed *Children of Paradise* for Graphicstudio at Topaz Editions. The background of the print was printed from three plates hand-drawn by Schapiro in tusche and crayons. Approximately sixteen collage elements were added to each print. The clothing elements, along with the lace in the upper right corner, were created using photolithography, then razor-cut and drymounted to the lithographic background. A template ensured that the placement of the collage elements in each print was identical to the next.[9] Yet the fabrics used in the edition vary greatly in color and pattern from print to print, making each print unique. Schapiro completed the collage work with the assistance of U.S.F. art students. As the artist recalls, "They worked on the 15 preliminary works and they bought fabric with me when I went on my fabric searches. We talked about their work, their plans. They were constantly involved in my process as enablers."[10]

Schapiro's work is informed by a unique blend of modernism, auto-biography, women's history, and a feminist world view. In both *Children of Paradise* and *Together* the artist evokes the nurturing environment of people's private lives—childhood, homes, capacity for love. In describing her world view, Schapiro has said: "The 'intimate point of view,' a woman's point of view, begins in her kitchen. 'What does a kitchen have to do with the people of Bangladesh?' men will say. Well, but we say it has everything to do with it; the kitchen is where values are formed. The hearth is in the home. Nurturance means caring—caring for one's family, for the poor, for the oppressed of the world."[11]

The cutout figures carry multiple associations, reminiscent of cutout cookies and paper dolls as well as the traditional techniques of appliqué practiced by generations of women. The heart and the house are recurring elements in Schapiro's artistic vocabulary. The domestic associations of the house are but one layer of its importance. In fact, Schapiro has "come to see feminist art as a house, an ideological house, under whose roof each woman has her own individual room. She no longer has to be isolated; she can have community and she can work out her ideas collectively."[12] The heart, too, has multiple meanings:

> The heart shape is often considered a woman's shape. Candy boxes in the shape of hearts are frequently gifts from men to women. Heart shaped pillows are seen on women's beds. Hearts masquerade as potholders, pin cushions and hooked rugs. Outside of their functional nature, what do these objects symbolize?
>
> From the lexicon of quilt imagery, the hearts blend in with flowers, cups and houses, baskets, trees, stars and bars, squares and birds—all things domestic and rural.
>
> Hearts stand for feelings.[13]

In her description of *Together*, written in 1984 for a U.S.F. exhibition catalogue, Schapiro stated: "'Femmage' artist that I am, I have brought together 'something old, something new, something borrowed, something blue.' In other words, I have allowed myself to be stirred by sentimental values in my effort to make my point about a sentient surface laden with memory and history. 'Being' is represented in the two clothing

49a. *Together*, 1983, collage with fabric, patterned paper (wallpaper/shelfpaper), and lithographed elements, 31½ x 48¼ (80 x 122.5), 1985.48.52

people, the little boy in his suit and the little girl by her dress. Here once again, the culture of women as differentiated from the culture at large has provided me with the role models for what I hope is a more universal statement about us as children, when we were very young."[14]

1. Schapiro and Melissa Meyer coined the term "femmages" to describe Schapiro's approach to collage. See Shapiro 1985; originally published in *Heresies*, no. 4 (1978): "We feel that several criteria determine whether a work can be called femmage. Not all of them appear in a single object. However, the presence of at least half of them should allow the work to be appreciated as *femmage*. 1. It is a work by a woman. 2. The activities of saving and collecting are important ingredients. 3. Scraps are essential to the process and are recycled in the work. 4. The theme has a woman-life context. 5. The work has elements of covert imagery. 6. The theme of the work addresses itself to an audience of intimates. 7. It celebrates a private or public event. 8. A diarist's point of view is reflected in the work. 9. There is drawing and/or handwriting sewn in the work. 10. It contains silhouetted images which are fixed on other material. 11. Recognizable images appear in narrative sequence. 12. Abstract forms create a pattern. 13. The work contains photographs or other printed matter. 14. The work has a functional as well as an aesthetic life."

2. The *Womanhouse* project involved the refurbishing of a house by Schapiro, Judy Chicago, and a group of twenty-one of their women students in the Feminist Art Program at the California Institute of the Arts. Once repaired, the rooms of the house were designed not for habitation but as aesthetic constructions following feminist themes. See Schapiro 1987, 25–30.

3. An earlier print in which Schapiro combined femmage with printmaking techniques is *Female Concerns* (1976), executed at the Minneapolis College of Art and Design.

4. Schapiro, in Degener 1985.

5. Schapiro discusses the history of the quilt and its relationship to her art in her essay, "Geometry and Flowers," in Robinson 1983, also describing the construction of her femmage compositions: "I attached fabrics to my painted surfaces. After painting a simple geometric structure, which served as a container for a burst of fabrics, I often glued sheer materials like printed chiffon over my acrylic scaffold. They appeared to flutter against the structure like a bird seeking freedom from the cage."

6. See, for example, *American Dreams* (1977–1980); *Wonderland* (1983); and *Invitation* (1982), all reproduced in *Schapiro*, St. Louis 1985.

7. Schapiro, correspondence with Corlett, 1990.

8. The concept of "levels of the past" was set forth by Schapiro with regard to *American Dreams*, in *Schapiro*, St. Louis 1985.

9. Schapiro, correspondence with Corlett, 1990.

10. Schapiro, correspondence with Corlett, 1990.

11. Quoted in Paula Bradley and Ruth A. Appelhof, "Excerpts from Interviews with Miriam Schapiro," in Gouma-Peterson 1980, 44.

12. Schapiro, quoted in Lyons 1977, 43.

13. From Schapiro's description of the femmage, *An Amethyst Remembrance* (1982), published in *Schapiro*, St. Louis 1985.

14. *Humanism*, Tampa 1984, 19.

JOEL-PETER WITKIN

Born in Brooklyn, New York, 1939
Lives and works in Albuquerque

JOEL-PETER WITKIN WAS one of triplets, but his sister died before birth, leaving only two boys. The dissimilar religious backgrounds of his parents—his father was Jewish and his mother a devout Catholic—led to their divorce when Witkin and his brother were still very young. The boys were raised in a deeply religious atmosphere by their mother. Witkin's agglomeration of unusual memories from childhood—including his having seen the decapitated head of a little girl roll out from under a car after a terrible automobile accident—has played an important role in shaping his artistic vision.

Witkin obtained his first camera while still a teenager in the mid-1950s: a twin-lens reflex Rolleicord that he bought used. He read manuals and taught himself the fundamentals of the camera's use. His earliest camera assignments were unusual, consistent with the unsettling experiences Witkin recounts from his childhood. His first photograph was of a rabbi who claimed to have spoken with God. Later he took his camera to the freak show at Coney Island at the request of his brother, who wanted the images for his paintings.

Witkin attended sculpture classes at night at the Cooper Union School of Fine Art in New York, and between 1958 and 1967 he worked for various commercial photographers, interrupted for a time by military service. Witkin had been drafted into the army, but in the hope of of retaining some control over how he would be used, he enlisted for three years and worked as a combat photographer. His assignments included recording on film the bodies of soldiers who had committed suicide or died in training accidents. Witkin has said that it was not death itself that he found so disturbing but rather the human capacity for institutionalizing violence. In 1967 Witkin worked as photographer for City Walls, Inc., an organization that produced murals in the five boroughs of New York.

Witkin returned to Cooper Union after the army (B.F.A. 1974). That same year he was awarded a fellowship in poetry at Columbia University. It was during this period that Witkin began his personal exploration of Eastern religions. He traveled to India to study yoga, photographing sacred sites as a means of financing the trip. In 1975 Witkin began graduate studies in photography and art history at the University of New Mexico, Albuquerque (M.A. 1976, M.F.A. 1981).

Witkin's first solo exhibition was held in 1969 at the Moore College of Art in Philadelphia. Additional one-man exhibitions of his photographs have been held at the Cooper Union School of Fine Art (1972), Projects Studio One, New York (1980), San Francisco Camerawork (1982), Kansas City Art Institute (1983), Stedelijk Museum, Amsterdam (1983), Institute Franco-American, Paris (1985), Aspen Museum, Colorado (1985), University of New Mexico (1986), Hochschule der Künste, Berlin (1986), Museum of Fine Arts, Santa Fe (1986), Centro de Arte Reina Sofia Museum, Madrid (1988), the Berert Gallery, Rotterdam (1989), and the Palais de Tokyo, Paris (1990). In 1985 a major exhibition of Witkin's photographs was organized by the San Francisco Museum of Modern Art and traveled to the Museum of Contemporary Photography, Columbia College, Chicago (1986), Brooklyn Museum (1986), Milwaukee Art Center (1986–1987), and La Jolla Museum of Contemporary Art (1987).

Joel-Peter Witkin (left) and Deli Sacilotto examining a proof for *Helena Fourment* (app. 248), 1985

50 Ragazzo con quattro bracci, 1985

Photogravure on Arches Cover paper
22⁹/₁₆ x 19¾ (57.3 x 50.2)
Edition (proofs only): 1 BAT; 1 PP; 1 PrP; 1 GP; 1 USFP; 1 NGAP ["NAT"]; 4 AP
Collaboration: George Holzer, Deli Sacilotto, David Yager

Joel-Peter Witkin's approach to his subject matter led one critic to comment: "Witkin descends into circles of Hell, Dante with a camera, and returns with living nightmares that nice people like you and I may wish not to have seen."[1] *Ragazzo con quattro bracci (The Boy with Four Arms)*, is much subtler in its impact than other images by Witkin.[2] The four arms of the standing figure recall the multiple heads and arms of ancient Hindu dieties, so they are in that sense familiar and even acceptable. Other perversions of this vision, however, seep into the viewer's consciousness more slowly.

This image, like many of Witkin's photographs, evokes the nineteenth-century studio portrait—in the use of drapery, in the even, natural lighting, and in the carefully posed, formal stance of the full-length figure, his knee artfully turned outward, his arm gracefully poised, holding what might be a glove. Further study of the image reveals that the face appears to be eerily masked and the glovelike object held by the figure could be a disembodied hand or hoof. With these revelations, the unidentifiable object on the cloth-covered pedestal to the figure's right becomes suspect. But by far the most disconcerting detail in the scene is the haunting, ghostly image of what seems to be a detached head on the floor among the folds of the drapery. Often in Witkin's world the horror of his vision is immediately repellent, but occasionally, as here, what at first appears to be a visual curiosity reveals itself, in a terrible moment of realization, to be a grisly spectacle.

For Witkin the photograph is only half formed once the film has been exposed. The negative—only a stage in the creation of the image—becomes the matrix on which the final image is constructed. Witkin employs techniques such as scratching the negatives on the emulsion side and/or the base side, which result in black and/or white additions, respectively. In this way he is able to eliminate, obliterate, or obscure certain details and at the same time augment the image by adding specific marks and lines: "I scratch to make the photograph more mysterious and produce physical changes that I can't obtain in the model. Sometimes I scratch the surface with a skin. I'm not changing the body, I'm creating a set of formal events that make the image more powerful aesthetically."[3]

In addition to altering the negative, Witkin also manipulates his images in the darkroom during the enlargement process. By placing tissue paper over the photographic paper to diffuse the light during exposure, for example, he imparts an atmospheric quality to the resulting image. Altering the photographic image through scratching or otherwise marking the negative or print is probably as old as photography itself and is not uncommonly found on nineteenth-century ambrotypes and tintypes.[4] Using these techniques, along with sepia and selenium toning, Witkin creates images that in general appear more antique than modern, recalling the imperfect look of the nineteenth-century photograph. The photogravures, too, printed in warm black tonalities, have the appearance of nineteenth-century photographic images and in this way imbue the work with the authority of a historical record.

Because Witkin's images are created in part through darkroom manipulation, the usual techniques for producing a photogravure could not be used to produce these Graphicstudio prints. As Sacilotto has explained:

If something visual is made strong enough, and resonates deeply enough with the viewer—it becomes fact.

Joel-Peter Witkin, telephone conversation with Mary Lee Corlett, 1991

"Because Witkin manipulates images during the printing process, he ends up with a print that doesn't exist in a negative."[5] So in order to produce the photogravures, a continuous tone, contact negative was made from the print, from which a continuous tone positive could then be made for use in the gravure process.[6]

1. Edwards 1983, 28.
2. The photographs for all three of Witkin's photogravures (cats. 50–52) were produced in 1984.
3. Witkin, in Lotringer 1987, 49.
4. For a history of the altered photograph and a discussion of other photographers who have employed these techniques, see *The Markers* [exh. cat., San Francisco Museum of Modern Art] (San Francisco, 1981).
5. Sacilotto, conversation with Fine, 25 September 1990.
6. In a telephone conversation with Corlett, 7 March 1991, Witkin noted that his decision not to produce an edition of these photogravures was made because he was not fully satisfied with the tonalities. This being his first experience with gravure, he was, however, satisfied with the proofs that had been pulled and agreed to have them stand as part of the Graphicstudio Archive at the National Gallery.

51 Portrait of Nan, 1985

Photogravure on Arches Cover paper
22⅝ x 19¾ (57.4 x 50.2)
Edition (proofs only): 1 BAT; 1 PP; 1 PrP; 1 GP; 1 USFP; 1 NGAP ["NAT"]; 4 AP
Collaboration: George Holzer, Deli Sacilotto, David Yager

Witkin's *Portrait of Nan* is a disturbing interpretation of the painting of
the same name executed by Grant Wood in 1933 (fig. 51a). Witkin's
photograph is replete with macabre references to the Wood painting, a
portrait of that artist's younger sister. Nan had been the model for what
is certainly Wood's most famous painting, *American Gothic* (1930). In
that painting Wood had manipulated his sister's appearance through her
priggish costume and hairstyle and her sternly rendered features to meet
his iconographic needs. In his *Portrait of Nan*, however, Wood created a
more tender portrait, and the iconographic elements in that composition, such as the fruit, the chick, and the heavy drape in the background,
deliberately recall the conventions of colonial American portraiture.[1]

Witkin's *Portrait of Nan* includes a T-shaped section from Wood's
painting that shows Nan's face, neck, and blouse, so the connection between the two works is unmistakable. The Miró-like drawing across the

*I am interested in historic references, social refer-
ences, and aesthetic references. A photographic
reality has a connection through a painting—a
painting to a photograph again—that's a double
value to me.*

Joel-Peter Witkin, in San Francisco 1985

model's chest in Witkin's photograph echoes the pattern on Nan's dress in the Wood portrait, and the strange objects on the shoulders of Witkin's Nan, who is naked except for her gloves, echo the bows on her counterpart's dress. Witkin has twisted his model's hair in sections and pinned it to the wall in a sinister parody of the gracefully marcelled hair of Wood's Nan. By scratching the negative, he has obscured the method used to attach the hair to the wall, but the black and white marks produced by the scratching intensify the menacing appearance of the image. Witkin has replaced the small chick in Wood's portrait—a pet that Nan had just acquired at the time of the sitting[2]—with an antelope fetus. Witkin thus transforms the wholesome image of Nan into a gruesome caricature, suggesting in the process humanity's sordid underside. Confrontation with the dark side of the human condition has a long and varied past in the history of art—from Michelangelo to the surrealists, Bosch to Goya.

The beauty of the surface of this photogravure and the other six that Witkin produced at Graphicstudio, with the paper shimmering through the satiny inks and the elegant gradations of tone, provides a sharp contrast to the disquieting images.

1. References to antique styles are common in the work of both Wood and Witkin. See Wood's *Victorian Survival* (1931), which imitates the look of a daguerreotype, reproduced in Wanda M. Corn, *Grant Wood: The Regionalist Vision* [exh. cat., Minneapolis Institute of Arts] (Minneapolis, 1983), pl. 13.
2. See Corn 1983, 102.

51a. Grant Wood, *Portrait of Nan*, 1933, oil on masonite, 34½ x 28½ (87.6 x 72.4), Elvehjem Museum of Art, University of Wisconsin–Madison: Collection of Helen B. Boley

52 Harvest, 1985

Photogravure on Arches Cover paper
22⁵/₈ x 19³/₄ (57.4 x 50.2)
Edition (proofs only): 1 BAT; 1 PP; 1 PrP; 1 GP; 1 USFP; 1 NGAP ["NAT"]; 4 AP
Collaboration: George Holzer, Deli Sacilotto, David Yager

Witkin's subjects have included cadavers, disembodied heads, and de-
caying corpses. Recording these subjects on film, then manipulating the
photographic images to create horrifying visions that shock and repel,
Witkin confronts the viewer with the discomforting realization that one
is fascinated as well as repulsed by the dark side of life.

In *Harvest* Witkin incorporates a scientific specimen of a human head
in a grisly composition that directly confronts the reality of death and the
conflicting, highly charged emotions of curiosity, fear, avoidance, and
even acceptance that accompany the knowledge of its inevitability: "I
saw the head in a collection of medical oddities. It is a dry specimen
made of wax around the turn of the century. I admired it the first time I
saw it and asked the curator to ship it to me in New Mexico. Because of
it's delicacy and rareness, my request was refused. I therefore traveled to

it. I felt I was on a pilgrimage, not to bring death back to life, but to show death's face as a witness to the supernatural."[1]

Harvest is a grim reinterpretation of the compositions by the sixteenth-century Italian painter Giuseppe Arcimboldo in which vegetables, fruit, flowers, and other elements from the natural world are arranged and rendered in such a way as to represent human faces.[2] Arcimboldo's compositions address life and death themes—the seasons, the cycle of life. Witkin's *Harvest* suggests a similar interpretation, but the inclusion of the form of a disembodied head is shockingly explicit and elicits a gut-level response from the viewer rather than a purely intellectual one. Like Arcimboldo, Witkin incorporates vegetables in his composition, but he composes a macabre visual poetry with them, using their root structures to create a visual analogue with the nerves of the head:

> My wife and I spent six hours in selecting and placing the vegetables before the image was recorded on film. In addition to being about death, this image also relates to the body's connection with food. The head, a very strange, quiet thing, doesn't show violence, although parts of the face and neck are exposed to show nerve endings and muscles where there had been connections to the rest of the body. . . . I often travel with things to be used in my images, on this occasion a piece of tree from the Southwest. For reasons I cannot quite explain, it was important to use this in the arrangement. It turned out to be a good idea for it helped to hold the entire thing together.[3]

1. Witkin, in Coke 1985, 16–17.
2. See *The Arcimboldo Effect*, New York 1987.
3. Coke 1985, 16–17.

I want to create something as powerful as the last thing a person sees before death.

Joel-Peter Witkin, in *Photo Metro* 1988

INNER SPACE AND OUTER SPACE

James Rosenquist working on copperplate for *Welcome to the Water Planet* (cat. 62), 1987

JAMES ROSENQUIST

Born in Grand Forks, North Dakota, 1933
Lives and works in Aripeka, Florida, and New York City

JIM ROSENQUIST HAD AN itinerant childhood. An only child, he moved
with his family frequently throughout the Midwest. His parents shared
with him their interest in airplanes and things mechanical. In junior high
school Rosenquist took art classes, and he later won a scholarship to attend Saturday classes at the Minneapolis School of Art. After high school
he enrolled in the University of Minnesota's art program, studying with
Cameron Booth. During the summer he worked for a contractor in Iowa,
Wisconsin, and North Dakota, painting signs and bulk storage tanks.

In 1954 Rosenquist painted his first billboard for General Outdoor
Advertising in Minneapolis. A year later, on scholarship to the Art Stu-
dents League in New York, Rosenquist studied with Edwin Dickinson,
Will Barnet, Morris Kantor, George Grosz, and Vaclav Vytacil. In 1957
Rosenquist joined the sign painters union and in 1958 went to work for
ArtKraft Strauss Company painting billboards. He also worked on win-
dow displays for Bonwit Teller and Tiffany & Company.

By 1960 Rosenquist had set aside enough of his commercial earnings
to allow him to spend a year painting in his studio. He moved to
Coenties Slip, where he shared a loft with Charles Hinman. Rosenquist
had tentatively explored the use of commercial methods and materials in
his studio work of the late 1950s, but after his move to the Slip, he left
behind both the abstract expressionist and figurative modes he had employed in his early work and developed the montagelike arrangement of
deliberately fragmented images from popular culture—inconsistently
scaled and enigmatically juxtaposed—that characterized the monumental paintings of his mature style.

Rosenquist had his first one-man exhibition at the Green Gallery in
New York in 1962, and every painting was sold. In 1963 he completed a
mural for the New York World's Fair, and *Art in America* selected him as
"Young Talent Painter" of the year. Two years later the artist finished
painting the monumental, highly publicized *F-111*, which toured Europe
during the 1960s and has been considered an important expression of
the anti-Vietnam War movement. During the 1970s he became active in
issues of artists' rights legislation. In 1976 Rosenquist built his house and
studio in Aripeka, Florida.

Since the early 1960s Rosenquist has worked extensively at numerous
printmaking workshops in addition to Graphicstudio, including Aeropress, Gemini G.E.L., Petersburg Press, Styria Studios, Tyler Graphics,
Ltd., and Universal Limited Art Editions. Among Rosenquist's honors is
the World Print Award, which he received in 1983 from the World Print
Council at the San Francisco Museum of Modern Art.

A retrospective of Rosenquist's graphic work was held at the John and
Mable Ringling Museum of Art, Sarasota, Florida, in 1979. Additional
exhibitions of his prints have been held at Stedelijk Museum, Amsterdam (1975), Smith College Museum of Art (1985), and the U.S.F. Art
Galleries (1988). Important one-man exhibitions of Rosenquist's work
have been held at the Museo d'arte moderna, Turin, Italy (1965), National Gallery of Canada, Ottawa (1968), Wallraf-Richartz Museum,
Cologne (1972), Whitney Museum of American Art, New York (1972),
National Gallery of Victoria, Australia (1977), Albright-Knox Art Gallery, Buffalo (1979), Denver Art Museum (1985), and Florida State University, Fine Art Gallery, Tallahassee (1988).

53 Cold Light, 1971

Color lithograph on Arches Cover paper
22⁹/₁₆ x 30¹/₈ (57.3 x 76.5)
Edition: 100 (I through XXX; 1/70 through 70/70); 1 BAT; 1 PrP; 1 PP; 1 TP; 2 CTP;
1 AP; 1 WP; 1 CP; 2 CoP
Collaboration: Oscar Bailey, Charles Ringness, Donald Saff

The first successful moon landing in 1969, certainly one of the most mo-
mentous events of human history, forever altered the framework of humanity's relationship to the universe. When James Rosenquist came to
work at Graphicstudio for the first time in 1971, the space program was
already woven into the fabric of American life. And as Donald Saff has
noted: "We had not yet tired of watching television images of men walk-
ing on the moon. The excitement generated by visions of space exploration, the moon, the cosmos and all that is implied by humankind's
adventure into space was still at the forefront of the imagination of
thoughtful people around the world."[1]

Cold Light is the title print in a suite of eleven lithographs produced by
Rosenquist during this period, seven of which feature an image of the
moon. The prints range in approach from seemingly traditional lithographs such as the delicate and intimate Fedora (app. 213), which combines Rosenquist's elegant tusche washes with a photographically
rendered flag, to the technically inventive and animate three-dimensional
work, Mastaba (cat. 54).

Compositionally, the Cold Light print relates most directly to Moon
Box (app. 217), with its raised American flag platform, low verdant horizon, and cool blue sky pierced with a brilliant full moon. It shares with
Moon Beam Mistaken for the News (app. 216) the conflation of the
moon with the newspaper, calling attention to events on earth while perhaps suggesting that the exploration of space might provide a new context in which man would henceforth experience the spectrum of world
events.

The design of the Tampa Tribune masthead featured in Cold Light includes two suns, each with faces and glasses, offering an ironic foil for

210

the moon centered in the sky above the black newspaper template. The headlines and texts of the articles are clearly readable for the most part and pertain to some of society's most sobering preoccupations during the period, particularly events in China and Laos. Direct reference to specific world events, while not unique to the Cold Light series, are not especially common in Rosenquist's oeuvre. Neither are the symmetry and the depictions of space in traditional perspective, both of which contribute to a mood of poetic, meditative stillness. The cool blues and greens of the sky and landscape also offer a serene counterpoint to the color-activated surface of the newspaper, which was achieved with the process known as a "rainbow roll," whereby several colors of ink are rolled onto the stone at once. The newspaper was photographed by Oscar Bailey in his studio using a view camera, which made it possible to capture the entire image in sharp focus without blurring on either side.[2]

The personal, provocative, complex associations on which Rosenquist drew for this series are suggested by his comparison of the newspaper template with "the platforms on which some American Indians used to place their dead out on the plains."[3] The newspaper is raised on the platform as if it were a sacred artifact. But it also serves as a filter that "colors" public perceptions of human events, perhaps implying that society has used mass media to separate itself from its own reality. Thus the themes suggested by the imagery of *Cold Light* range from the role of the mass media in modern society to the significance of humanity's exploration of space. The latter continues to be a major force in shaping Rosenquist's own world view as reflected in his art, influencing such works as the controversial mural *Star Thief*[4] and his most recent projects at Graphicstudio (see cat. 62).

Things I cannot figure out intrigue me and that is my work. The various questions become my work. I want to reinforce the question before I forget. It is like taking a risk to find new feelings. That's the opportunity; to discover things.

James Rosenquist, in Multiples, Inc., press release, 1973

1. Donald Saff. "Rosenquist at Graphicstudio . . . A Personal View," in *Rosenquist*, Tampa 1988, 7.
2. Oscar Bailey, telephone conversation with Corlett, 30 August 1990.
3. Bernstein 1973, 7.
4. *Star Thief* became the subject of controversy when it was scheduled, and then ultimately rejected, for installation at the Miami International Airport. Former Astronaut Frank Borman, then president of Eastern Airlines, stated: "I have had some exposure to space flight and I can tell you without equivocation that there is no correlation . . . between the artist's depiction and the real thing." See Heartney 1986, 101.

54 **Mastaba**, 1971
Color lithograph on Rives BFK paper with Plexiglas face and styrene beads
32¼ x 24¼ x ⅛ (81.9 x 61.6 x .9)
Edition: 100 (I through XXX; 1/70 through 70/70); 1 BAT; 1 PrP; 1 PP; 3 TP; 1 CTP; 3 AP; 1 WP; 1CP; 2 CoP
Collaboration: Oscar Bailey, Alan Eaker, Donald Saff, Theo Wujcik

Part of the Cold Light suite, *Mastaba* is composed of a lithograph on which is superimposed a three-dimensional Plexiglas hourglass form that allows plastic beads to spill from top to bottom (and back again) if the piece is rotated from end to end, as was part of the original concept. (The work was to have been mounted on a hand-operated turntable on the wall.) *Mastaba* was among the earliest Graphicstudio projects to involve collaboration between an artist and the faculty of the University of South Florida. In the creation of the hourglass face Rosenquist worked with sculptor Alan Eaker, newly hired by the university's art department. Eaker had worked with plastics on the West Coast before coming to Tampa, so was familiar with the nature and limitations of the material.

Eaker built the template molds to Rosenquist's specifications at Faulkner & Plastics in Tampa, where the piece was also editioned. The hourglass face was formed through press molding, in which a sheet of Plexiglas was heated and pressed between an inner and an outer mold. The face mold was then glued to a flat sheet of Plexiglas to create a hollow sandwich into which the beads were inserted. Various materials were tested for the beads before styrene was finally selected: "everything from salt in the hourglass, to styrene beads, to urethane beads, to sand . . . all types of materials, to create the shapes that would be appropriate for the image."[1] In addition, the flow of the beads through the channel generates a quiet, mesmerizing sound. With the incorporation of the hourglass in *Mastaba*, Rosenquist activated the surface of the lithograph not only visually but also physically, introducing three-dimensional depth and movement.

Rosenquist also evoked the concept of time, not only because the hourglass is an instrument that measures time but because a kind of metamorphosis occurs as the beads move from one chamber to the other, revealing once-hidden images and obscuring others that were previously exposed. New patterns of residual plastic dust form in the emptying chamber with each new run of the beads. Thus the overall image is continuously transformed by a process that can only occur in time, merging the third and fourth dimensions (space and time) with the more traditional two-dimensional art of the print.

The images that are alternately obscured and revealed behind the hourglass at the top of the composition include a coffee can and the sole of an old shoe. At the bottom a fragment of a detergent box—"BOLD!" additionally marked "NEW!" and "ENZYME" in strident colors—is alternately exposed and hidden. In fact, the flow of beads in the hourglass on one level mimics the appearance of powdered detergent being poured. Detergent boxes have reappeared in several of Rosenquist's paintings, and in a 1972 interview Rosenquist related an experience that offers one possible association for their appearance in his work: "I saw soap boxes being designed in advertizing agencies and they used to pin the soap boxes on the walls to see who would look at them the most and I thought there's more visual things worked out there than there is in an artist's studio working singularly, so I thought of imagery spilling from my billboard experience—imagery spilling off the picture plane—and then after you see that imagery, what's behind it. It's like a thought or a feeling."[2]

To create the photographic imagery for *Mastaba*, Rosenquist worked with photographer Oscar Bailey, who was, like Eaker, a U.S.F. art department faculty member. Bailey explained the collaboration: "He and I would go out [on photography expeditions] together. He wanted a garbage dump. I knew of an area so I took him there. He would find an area [of garbage] and I would photograph it."[3] Rosenquist has commented that the imagery of *Mastaba* suggested "unfinished garbage."[4] Indeed, in addition to the images directly behind the hourglass, other "throwaway" items such as cans of motor oil or soup and a turkey dinner box appear to tumble forward, pushing against the picture plane and creating a sense of agitation that is given added urgency by the movement of the beads through the hourglass. The entire composition is precariously stabilized by the symmetry of the hourglass.

The physical characteristics of an actual mastaba—an Egyptian tomb with a rectangular base and sloping sides—reverberates in this rectangular-shaped print with the "sloping sides" of the hourglass. The reference to a tomb and the superimposition of an hourglass over a pile of "unfinished garbage" seem to warn of time running out and the impending death of the planet.[5]

I decided to make pictures of fragments, images that would spill off the canvas instead of recede into it, like a medicine cabinet. I thought each fragment would be identified at a different rate of speed, and that I would paint them as realistically as possible.

James Rosenquist, in Goldman 1985

1. Alan Eaker, interview with Fine, 13 July 1989.
2. Siegel 1972, 32. Examples of other Rosenquist works that feature a detergent box include *Midnight Sun* (1975), and *Spring Cheer* (1975), both reproduced in
Goldman 1985, 59.
3. Oscar Bailey, telephone conversation with Corlett, 30 August 1990.
4. Bernstein 1973, 8.
5. Saff, in *Rosenquist*, Tampa 1988, 8.

55 **Rails**, 1976
Color lithograph and screenprint on Arches paper
34³/₄ x 71³/₁₆ (88.3 x 180.8)
Edition: 60 (I/XX through XX/XX; 1/40 through 40/40); 1 BAT; 1 PrP; 3 PP; 3 AP; 1 USFP; 1 CP
Collaboration: Oscar Bailey, Julio Juristo, Patrick Lindhardt, Donald Saff

In *Rails* Rosenquist used the image of a lightning bolt to slice the composition boldly in half, then created a balance that depends not on exact symmetry, but on the delicate counterbalancing of the visual force of the imagery on either side. The composition has a light left and dark right side that, given Rosenquist's study of Eastern philosophy, is intriguingly analogous to the Chinese symbol for yin and yang. The artist balances the visual interest inherent in the subtle textures of the railroad track and its gravel bed (for which visual identification comes slowly) against the easily recognizable images of the sunglasses and rocking horse. The left

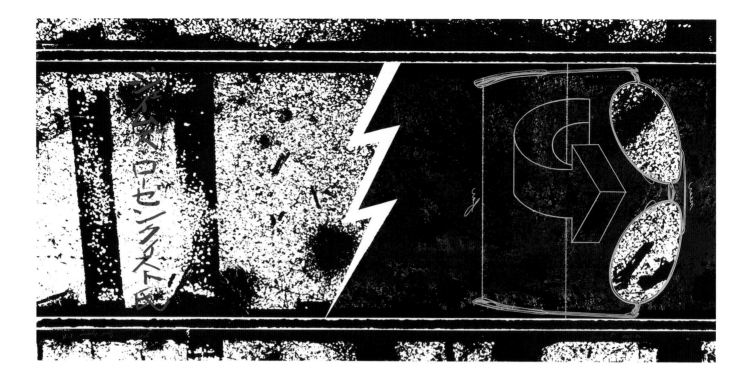

side of the composition is given additional visual weight by the insertion of the artist's name, written in Chinese characters, in blue, the only color among the neutral tones of black, white, and silver.

Implied movement is integral to *Rails*, just as actual movement is a component of both *Mastaba* and *Mirage Morning* (cats. 54, 56). The railroad track, a facilitator of movement, alludes to "locomotion," while the split of the lightning bolt, the rocking of the winged horse (on "rails"), and the pair of sunglasses—whose rotation on an axis is suggested by the large arrow indicating movement around the central snapline—are all additional metaphors for motion and energy. Ironically, a winged horse attached to rockers may also conjure the notion of thwarted motion.

The screenprinted image of the winged horse, related to the Mobil Oil Company logo based on the mythological Pegasus, recalls Rosenquist's childhood and the many hours he spent at his father's Mobil station in Atwater, Minnesota.[1] It is a motif that reappears often in Rosenquist's work of the period and can be found in another Graphicstudio print, the screenprint *Miles II* (app. 225). In other prints from the period, such as *Fast Feast* (1976) or *Tin Roof* (1977), the horse and rocking chair are halved vertically and then merged.[2]

Sunglass variations recurred with some frequency in Rosenquist's repertoire during the mid-1970s. Reference here to the rotation of the sunglasses is further indicated in the notations "near" and "far" on the right and left sides of the image. The words are reversed, suggesting that viewers are seeing the "back side" of the glasses as they revolve, while also serving as a reminder of the reversal that is a key by-product of the printmaking process. Rosenquist incorporated these terms in later prints such as *Star, Towel, Weathervane* (1977), in which the revolving sunglasses become analogous to the rotation of a weathervane.

Rosenquist's vocabulary—typified by his reuse of the sunglasses and the rocking horse—is in a perpetual state of metamorphosis, as the imag-

There are things put together that are mysteries.
I like to collect those mysteries.
James Rosenquist, in Battcock 1972

214

ery, interrelationships, and attendant layers of meaning continue to evolve with each use.

1. This point is made in Goldman 1985, 17–18, 57.

2. Reproductions of these works can be found in *Rosenquist*, Tampa 1988, 20, 29.

56 Mirage Morning, 1975

Color lithograph on Arches paper, with window shades, string, stones, and Plexiglas
36¼ x 74¼ x 2¾ (92.1 x 188.6 x 7)
Edition: 60 (I/XX through XX/XX; 1/40 through 40/40); 1 BAT; 1PrP; 2 PP; 3 AP; 1 USFP; 1 CP
Collaboration: Julio Juristo, Patrick Lindhardt, Charles Ringness, Donald Saff

The complexity of Rosenquist's iconography lies in his constant reordering of elements to yield wholly different visual results each time—like combining notes on a musical scale. Layers of meaning are dependent on reading these combinations, but ultimately the context remains mysterious and undefinable. Nowhere is this more evident than in the prints executed at Graphicstudio during the mid-1970s—including *Rails*, *Mirage Morning*, and *Pale Cradle* (cats. 55–57).

In *Mirage Morning*, a print with three-dimensional elements, Rosenquist used motifs found in many of his paintings and prints of the 1970s—tire tracks, the carpenter's snapline (which had been standard equipment for Rosenquist as a billboard painter), and perhaps most important, the combination of the circle, triangle, and square.[1] To create the circle in *Mirage Morning*, the rim of a galvanized metal tub was coated with liquid tusche and pressed against the lithograph plate. The carpenter's snaplines used to form the square and triangle were made by dipping a string into the tusche and snapping it against the plate to recreate the look of a chalk line. Tire track impressions generate horizontal

When I was working for ArtKraft Strauss on walls there were experiences that are nothing, but I think about them. There were a lot of devices used. We would take a gallon can and tie a string on it to form a chalk line, and drop it down about four stories and snap a vertical line that went out of sight. You know there's a line down there somewhere but you couldn't see it.

James Rosenquist, in Siegel 1972

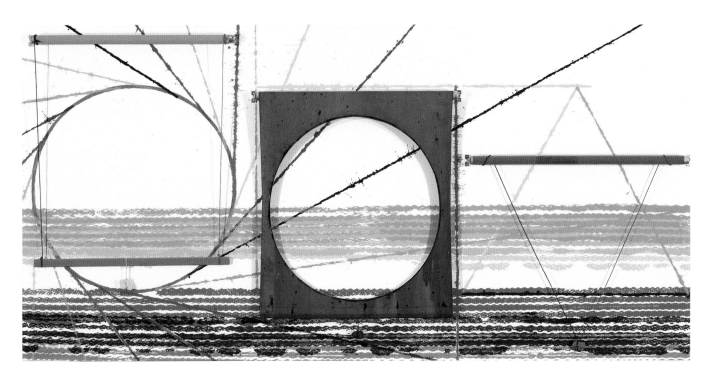

waves of brilliant color across the surface of the print. The cool blues
and greens at the bottom edge topped by warm red, yellow, and hot pink
above suggest the shimmering appearance of heat rising from a sun-
baked surface. The radiating spokes emitted from the printed circle—
also created by the carpenter's snapline—simultaneously suggest rotation
and light.

Donald Saff has suggested that *Mirage Morning* may be linked to
Rosenquist's appreciation for the nineteenth-century Japanese
philosopher-artist Gibon Sengai, whose "picture of the universe is reduced to a circle-triangle-square image in which the Zen master uses the
circle to represent infinity as the formless basis of all beings; the triangle
as the beginning of all forms; and the square as the triangle doubled in a
doubling process whose infinite unfolding gives us the multiplicity of the
forms that comprise the universe."[2] In *Mirage Morning* the circle, rectangle, and triangle are laid out across the print in a linear fashion. The
window-shade attachments form alternate shapes: the printed circle is
overlaid by a square-shaped window shade, the printed rectangle lies beneath the window-shade circle, and the triangular-shaped shade is
"doubled in a doubling process"—it is pointed downward in the opposite
direction of the printed triangular form beneath. Each window shade is
weighted with a rock painted with one of the three primary colors—
yellow, blue, or red. The shades are permanently mounted to the surface
of the Plexiglas, but their heights are not fixed. Saff has noted that "the
viewer can alter and modify the images even as the universe itself
changes in its natural evolution."[3] Yet if the viewer were to alter the image (i.e., the universe) by raising or lowering any of the shades, the delicate balance created by the carefully opposed shapes would be upset.
The composition thus radiates an inner geometry and symmetry—the
ultimate balancing of forces.

The circle, square, and triangle appeared together in Rosenquist's
work for the first time in 1973 in the print *Off the Continental Divide*
(fig. 56b) and a related painting, *Slipping Off the Continental Divide*. In
the painting the artist included Chinese characters for each of the shapes,
but deliberately paired each shape with a symbol that represents another.
Judith Goldman has suggested that in *Slipping Off the Continental Divide* Rosenquist's use of the trilogy of shapes reflects the personal up-
heaval in his life and his "attempt to regain his equilibrium" and that in
the intentional confusion of the symbols he "attempts to obscure mean-

56a. Charles Ringness preparing window-shade
elements for *Mirage Morning*, 1975

56b. *Off the Continental Divide*, 1973, lithograph, 42 x 78 (106.7 x 198.1), published by
Universal Limited Art Editions

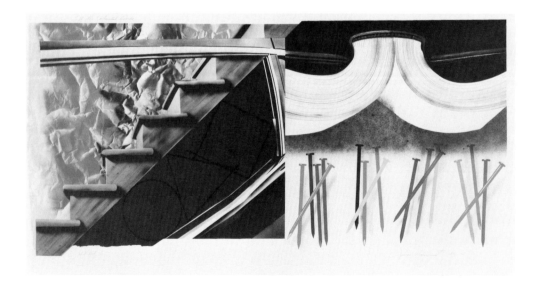

ing."[4] Yet when Rosenquist reinvents these forms in *Mirage Morning*, also overlaying each shape with an alternate, the effect is one of consummate balance.

In contrast to the dark, obscured forms in *Off The Continental Divide*, the circle, square, and triangle in *Mirage Morning* are out in the open, exposed to the bright light of day, as the title and vibrant colors imply. Rosenquist was to return to these three forms again and again throughout the decade, reshaping their significance each time.

1. During this period Rosenquist produced myriad prints using these elements. Other Graphicstudio works that feature tire tracks include *Miles, Miles II,* and *Tampa–New York 1188* (app. 221, 225, 226). The use of the snapline can be seen in *Tampa–New York 1188* and *Rails* (cat. 55). *Earth and Moon* (app. 212) and *Tampa–New York 1188* also combine the triangle, circle, and square.
2. Saff, in *Rosenquist*, Tampa 1988, 9. In 1965 Rosenquist had studied Eastern phi-

losophy and history at the Institute of Humanist Studies in Aspen, Colorado. In 1966 he spent a month in Japan, having traveled there initially to participate in the Tokyo opening of the exhibition, *Two Decades of American Painting.*
3. Saff, in *Rosenquist*, Tampa 1988, 9.
4. Goldman 1985, 54–56, also points out Rosenquist's first combination of the circle, square, and triangle and reproduces both print and painting on p. 55.

57 Pale Cradle, 1975–1976

Color lithograph and screenprint with collage on Arches Cover paper
41³/₄ x 29¹¹/₁₆ (106 x 75.4)
Edition: 60 (I/XX through XX/XX; 1/40 through 40/40); 1 BAT; 1 PrP; 2 PP; 3 AP; 1 USFP; 1 CP
Collaboration: Julio Juristo, Donald Saff

As in *Mirage Morning* and *Rails*, Rosenquist conflated familiar elements in *Pale Cradle* in an unfamiliar way to create a work with new, yet still elusive layers of meaning. The print investigates themes common to his work of the 1970s—including associations from childhood and references to the passage of time—using images central to his visual vocabulary during this period, including nails, pails, and the carpenter's snapline.

Five screenprinted nails, four horizontal and one placed on a diagonal over the top, float on a field of spattered red printed in lithography. The nails appear to be loosely tangled amid the threads of an actual yarn pentagram. The title of the print suggests that the yarn refers, on one level, to the childhood game of cat's cradle, which Rosenquist would later render explicitly in a painting entitled *Bow String* (1979).[1] The pattern of the yarn might also suggest a pinwheel, another image Rosenquist often depicted in this period.

The nails recall the pattern of slashes commonly used when counting, keeping track, or marking time. They appear in numerous works from around this time, including the lithographs *Off the Continental Divide* (fig. 56b) and *Short Schedule* (1973). Concerning the latter work, Rosenquist remarked: "When a person is waiting for something and marking off time, juxtapositions of images race through one's mind. The joke is that the thread of one's intuition is usually found in a threadbare spot."[2] Cryptic though this comment may be, its reference to "marking time" and "the thread of one's intuition" seem to be ideas subsequently explored in *Pale Cradle*. Varying nuances of meaning are attached to recurring images like the nails, somehow rendering them simultaneously interrelated and unrelated from picture to picture.

For me, juxtapositions become a flash that are important because they reveal a new way of feeling or seeing, which I have not felt before. I do my painting to remind myself that I felt like that. I am not trying to make an abstraction, but to put down things that remain questions or are mysterious. This is important to me.

James Rosenquist, in Multiples, Inc., press release, 1973

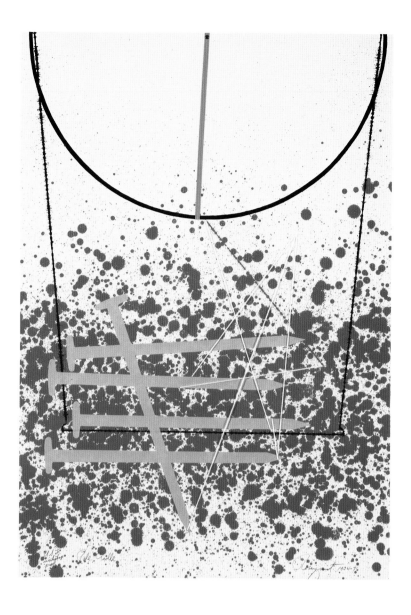

The red pendulum at the top of the print further implies timekeeping and offers a complement to the record-keeping associations of the arrangement of nails. When read in conjunction with the snaplines as part of a single image, the blue arc that traces the pendulum's trajectory is transformed into the wire handle resting alongside a pail. This relationship becomes clearer when *Pale Cradle* is compared to an earlier lithograph and screenprint, *Pale Angel* (1973),[3] in which the image of a pail and the "pale/pail" wordplay suggested by the title are obvious.[4]

Pale Cradle is a flat image, with no illusion of depth and no modeling of form. Rosenquist's interest in varying textures is apparent in the smoothness of the screenprinted nails juxtaposed with the stipple of the red spatter, or the woolly texture of the yarn collage with its printed snapline counterpart. Rosenquist, in fact, completes the final edge of the yarn pentagram with a printed snapline.

1. Reproduced in Goldman 1985, 162.
2. Quoted in Multiples, Inc., press release, 1973. *Short Schedule* is reproduced in *Rosenquist*, Amsterdam 1973, cat. 43.
3. Reproduced in *Rosenquist*, Amsterdam 1973, cat. 42.
4. See also *A Pale Angel's Halo* (1973), reproduced in Goldman 1985, 56. *Pale Tent* π (1976, published by Pyramid Arts and reproduced in *Rosenquist*, Tampa 1988, 21), combines a pail (aerial view) with nails.

58 Shriek, 1986

Color monoprint and lithograph collage
42¹/₄ x 71⁵/₈ (107 x 181.9)
Edition: 29; 2 BAT; 1 PP; 2 PrP; 1 GP; 1 NGAP; 1 USFP; 1 AP
Collaboration: Alan Holoubek, Donald Saff

59 Sister Shrieks, 1987–1989

Color monoprint and lithograph collage
48 x 80 (122 x 203.3)
Edition: 39; 2 BAT; 2 PP; 2 PrP; 1 NGAP; 1 GP; 1 USFP; 3 AP
Collaboration: Marcia Brown, Michael Harrigan, Alan Holoubek, Johntimothy Pizzuto,
Tom Pruitt, Donald Saff

Shriek and *Sister Shrieks* accent Rosenquist's mastery as a colorist.[1] In them the artist created a highly charged dialogue between competing colors, with streaks of fuchsia accented with lime green and tempered with silver gray, deep green, and rich ochers set against a vibrating red orange background, all working in such a way as to activate the surface without dissonance. In both of these prints Rosenquist capitalized on the interaction of textures, pitting the smooth, satiny surface of the lithographic elements against the lush monoprinted background.

The splintered female "advertising" smiles in *Shriek* collide with the natural flower forms, evoking the classic nature/culture dichotomy. Rosenquist explored this theme in numerous prints during the 1980s, including other Graphicstudio prints such as *The Kabuki Blushes*, *Crosshatch and Mutation*, and *Flowers and Females* (cats. 60, 61, and Introduction, fig. 32), as well as in many paintings. Indeed, women's faces have been a constant image in Rosenquist's art.[2] The razor-sharp points of the lithographic elements seen in *Shriek* have been softened in *Sister Shrieks* with more fluid forms. The splintered imagery electrifies the surface wherever Rosenquist uses it, but even in *Shriek* these slivers appear relatively passive when compared, for example, with the intercutting diagonals streaking across the canvas in various directions in paintings such as *Persistence of Electrical Nymphs in Space* (1985).[3]

Rosenquist executed the monoprinted areas of these prints by applying acrylic paint on a Plexiglas surface. He placed preparatory drawings (figs. 58a, 59a) under the Plexiglas as a guide and referred to a small col-

I'm interested in contemporary vision—the flicker of chrome, reflections, rapid associations, quick flashes of light. Bing—Bang! I don't do anecdotes. I accumulate experiences.

James Rosenquist, in Goldman 1985

58a. James Rosenquist in his Aripeka studio preparing the mylar for the monoprint portion of *Shriek*, January 1986

58

lage that he taped to his chest and viewed in a mirror, the mirror reflection corresponding to the reversed image on the monoprint template. Dampened paper was then pressed against the painted image and rubbed by hand to transfer paint to the paper. Two or three sheets could be printed before fresh paint had to be added to the Plexiglas, with the first impression lifting the most paint, and subsequent pulls taking progressively less. After paint had been reapplied several times to the Plexiglas, and a number of monoprints had been made, the Plexiglas was cleaned and an entirely new surface of paint was applied, using the same

58b. Alan Holoubek placing lithography element for *Shriek* on the drying rack, 1986

59

preparatory drawing under the Plexiglas as a guide. Slight variations among the prints are thus integral to the edition.[4]

    The lithographic elements were printed from aluminum plates, using gum stop-out to achieve the hard edges and airbrushing Rhind's stop-out to create the image. After printing, the elements were trimmed by hand and mounted on the monoprint background. This combination of the

59a. Drawing for *Sister Shrieks*, c. 1987–1989, acrylic paint and pencil on mylar, 48³/₄ x 83¹/₄ (123.8 x 211.4), 1991.75.167

splintered lithographic images with monoprint backgrounds was, in part, the artist's solution to the problem of achieving greater scale: "Given the limitations of the presses, I thought if we could . . . print pieces of things and adhere them to this big [painted] paper, then we'd have a big print. . . . So we did [monoprint] images, and they're all different backgrounds. Yet the printed lithography was the same, and we collaged the surface so there was a big print [created] on . . . small presses."[5]

Shriek and *Sister Shrieks* were worked at Rosenquist's studio at Aripeka, with Graphicstudio staff traveling there to complete the project. Rosenquist's facility for combining seemingly disparate image fragments into a compositional whole has its analogue in his working method: "Jim does six hundred things at one time—literally, I mean. . . . He'll be drawing a plate and ten minutes later—and this is no exaggeration—tearing apart an engine, you know [laughing]. And you're helping him . . . and you don't know how that happened!"[6]

1. *Sister Shrieks* is related to a painting of the same name executed in 1987. Both *Shriek* and *Sister Shrieks* are from Rosenquist's Graphicstudio series Secrets in Carnations. Other prints in this series are *The Kabuki Blushes*, *Crosshatch and Mutation*, and *Flowers and Females*.
2. Goldman 1985, 50, has suggested that the subject of woman is as central to

Rosenquist's art as to de Kooning's.
3. Reproduced in Ratcliff 1985, 93.
4. Information provided by printer Alan Holoubek, in a taped conversation with Fine, 13 July 1989.
5. Rosenquist, in conversation with Fine, 8 October 1990.
6. Holoubek, taped conversation with Fine, 1989.

60 The Kabuki Blushes, 1986

Color lithograph on Chiri Kozo paper and monoprinted collage on White Somerset Satin paper
39³/₈ x 41⁵/₈ (100 x 105.7)
Edition: 59; 2 BAT; 2 PP; 2 PrP; 1 GP; 1 USFP; 1 NGAP
Collaboration: Alan Holoubek, Tom Pruitt, Donald Saff

The richness of the paper surface selected by Rosenquist for *The Kabuki Blushes* sets this print apart from any other produced by the artist at Graphicstudio. The dynamics of the print are defined by the interplay of the active surface of the paper—and the randomly scattered specks embedded in the sheet—with the softness of the lithographic inks and the thick, lush paint of the monoprint. The paper's particles animate even the printed portions of the image, as the transparent inks allow numerous flecks to show through.[1]

In reverse of the combination monoprint/lithograph of *Shriek* and *Sister Shrieks* (cats. 58, 59), *The Kabuki Blushes* has monoprinted elements collaged to a lithographed ground. The splintered, lithographic images were created for all three prints using Rhind's stop-out varnish and airbrush. There is an airiness and openness to the composition of *The Kabuki Blushes* that is very different from the crowded, kinetic picture plane of *Crosshatch and Mutations* (cat. 61). The fractured, porcelain, masklike female face, with its dark eye and ruby lips, is the only "identifiable" image. The black calligraphic line that loops across the page, the wet, blush red form that looks like a tomato at the top of the composition, and the seemingly floral patterns of the monotype slivers are all highly abstracted. Rosenquist had combined the tomato and the porcelain-faced woman in the lithograph, *Terrarium* (fig. 60b), pro-

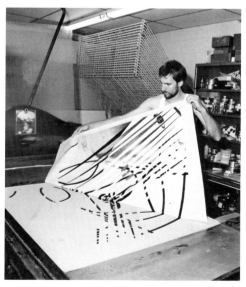

60a. Tom Pruitt printing the lithograph for *The Kabuki Blushes*, 1986

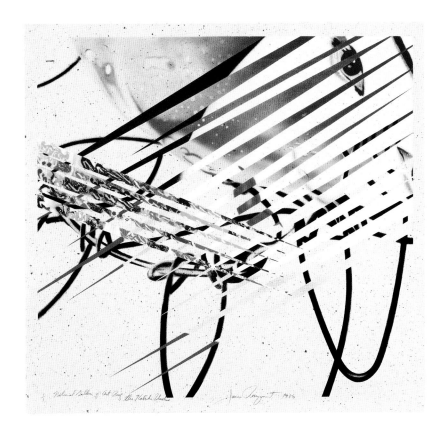

I really wonder what the vestigial feelings of being an animal are in a human being nowadays. Or are people becoming brittle, inhuman, un-animal-like, and more rigid?
James Rosenquist, conversation with Ruth Fine, 1990

60b. *Terrarium*, 1978, lithograph, 29³/₈ x 44⁷/₈ (74.7 x 114), printed by Erickson/Davis/Delaney/Sanchez

duced almost a decade earlier. These forms, contained within hard edges of separate glass bottles and isolated from each other in the earlier work, are shattered in the Graphicstudio print, overlapping and merging in a particled, ethereal space. The painted, artificial appearance of the female face evokes the highly stylized Japanese Kabuki theater referenced in the print's title.

1. The print is related to the painting, *The Kabuki Blushes* (1984), reproduced in Goldman 1985, 182. The impact of the activated surface of the speckled paper is especially evident when the print is compared with the painting.

61 Crosshatch and Mutation, 1986

Color monoprint and lithograph collage
42¼ x 51⁷/₁₆ (107.3 x 130.7)
Edition: 29; 2 BAT; 2 PP; 2 PrP; 1 GP; 1 USFP; 1 NGAP
Collaboration: Alan Holoubek, Tom Pruitt, Donald Saff

Splintered, overlapping, and interwoven image fragments, as seen in *Crosshatch and Mutation*, first appeared as pictorial devices in Rosenquist's work about 1980. Precedents for this sliced imagery, however, can be traced in his work at least as far back as the late 1960s when the artist completed several paintings on mylar sheets that he then cut into vertical strips. In one such painting, *Forest Ranger* (fig. 61a),[1] Rosenquist further obfuscated the picture plane by hanging two sliced mylar panels so that they overlapped and intersected at right angles to each other. The fractured imagery was also foreshadowed in two Graphic-studio prints, *Miles* and *Miles II* (app. 221, 225).

Rosenquist's splintered images call to mind shafts of light, or kaleidoscopic patterns, or even the electronic weave used as a transition between video frames or between functions on computer screens. As Saff has pointed out, they can also be compared to "the visual experience that comes from looking at a distant world through the leaves of the Palmetto Palm, which is so common to the Florida landscape."[2] Indeed, palmetto palms surround Rosenquist's house and studio in Aripeka (fig. 61b). Rosenquist commented recently, "I keep thinking about the metamorphosis between flora and fauna. I also wonder what hides behind the façade of a person's face. And I [think about] images of people running through the jungle or running through the bush—seeing glimpses of them in that kind of environment."[3]

The splintered forms order the pictorial space. In an annotation on a charcoal study related to *Crosshatch and Mutation*, executed in 1984 as a drawing for *Digits from the Wildwood*, Rosenquist described his use of fractured imagery in the following way: "The priority is pictorial invention. Crosshatching filled with imagery leaves space for more. Forms I thought I knew have to be re-examined."[4] In her discussion of the compositional arrangement of this charcoal drawing, Bernice Rose observed that Rosenquist's "intention is to intersperse two or more completely dissimilar motifs or textures in such a way as to provoke a sparkle at their point of intersection—to provoke a new pictorial idea, a new invention in the picture plane."[5]

Rosenquist's spiky compositional arrangements have been viewed as inherently violent by some critics, characterized as "assaultive depictions of women . . . literally ripped to shreds"[6] and "paintings that slice up their images and send them across the canvas in narrow strips. . . . [Rosenquist's] patterns are needle-sharp, with edges like razors. Points and edges together suggest claws or fangs. Sometimes one set of image-fangs overlays another. . . . Maybe the artist opposes the stabbing violence of his zig-zags to the blandness of those faces. Maybe he equates them."[7] Whether or not one sees violence in Rosenquist's forms (are Georgia O'Keeffe's flowers sexual?), it is clear that sharp, angular shapes have always played an important role in his compositions. Edges, too, have always been important, both as compositional devices and as a method for amplifying meaning: "I'm not trying to present just cut up slivers of women alone; they're usually very lush with a lot of other [suggestions]. . . . I hope someone will see a whole other image."[8] With the slivers as a vehicle, Rosenquist achieves a lively dialogue between the brightly colored, swirling, abstracted floral imagery of the monoprinted

So, if you take an image and you fragment it— let's say you take a beautiful straight-on photograph of somebody's face and you cut out a section of this face, you could change the character of the feeling of part of that person by the edge of the shape so that if you take two ideas and you connect them and you identify a part of the two ideas, you might unleash what the other part of it is instead of disguising something. . . . It has to do with the edges of what you're seeing.

James Rosenquist, in Siegel 1972

61a. *Forest Ranger*, 1967, oil on mylar, height: 114 (289.6), Ludwig Collection, Wallraf-Richartz Museum, Cologne

elements and the volumetric modeling and "velvety" softness of the female faces of the lithographic elements, resulting in a rich and varied surface.

The interwoven crosshatches in *Crosshatch and Mutation*, with its evolving (dissolving?), overlapping and merging (separating?) images, evoke a sense of transformation: "the ability to put layers of feeling in a picture plane and then have those feelings seep out as slowly as possible."[9]

61b. Trees surrounding Rosenquist's Aripeka studio, 1990

1. See also the *Sketch for Forest Ranger* (1967), screenprint on two vinyl sheets and die cut, reproduced in Tucker 1972, cat. 17.
2. Saff, in *Rosenquist*, Tampa 1988, 9.
3. Rosenquist, conversation with Fine, 8 October 1990.
4. Bernice Rose, *New Work on Paper* [exh. cat., The Museum of Modern Art] (New York, 1985). The drawing is reproduced. This print is also related to the painting *Crosshatching and Mutations* (1984).
5. Rose 1985, 12.
6. Cotter 1987, 88.
7. Ratcliff 1985, 93–94. See also Heartney 1986, 100: "In the 1980's, Rosenquist has been experimenting with new ways of organizing space, and the paintings have taken on an increasingly aggressive tone. Canvases are filled with knife-edge slivers of images—flowers, fish, women and machines—woven together."
8. Rosenquist, conversation with Fine, 1990.
9. *Rosenquist*, in Goldman 1985, 16.

62 Welcome to the Water Planet, 1987–1989

Aquatint on hot-pressed T. H. Saunders drawing paper
75^{13}/₁₆ x 59⁷/₈ (192.6 x 152.1)
Edition: 55; 1 BAT; 2 PP; 2 PrP; 1 NGAP; 1 GP; 1 USFP; 7 AP
Collaboration: Greg Burnet, Patrick Foy, Donald Saff
Gift of Graphicstudio/University of South Florida and the Artist in Honor of the Fiftieth
Anniversary of the National Gallery of Art

Welcome to the Water Planet, with its rich surface and multitudinous shades of gray, is both a tour de force of aquatint etching and a master-work in grisaille. Images familiar from Rosenquist's lexicon—painted fingernails, eyes, flower forms, fish—are set in a more ethereal world than seen in *Shriek* or *Crosshatch and Mutation*, an effect that is height-ened by the monochromatic presentation. The detachment from present reality implied in the use of black and white was something that Rosen-quist appreciated and capitalized on early in his career in works such as *Zone* (1961).[1]

In *Welcome to the Water Planet* Rosenquist merged a dynamic natural world, abundant in aquatic and plant life, with interstellar space.[2] The surface is animated by swirling forms, piercing streaks of image frag-ments, and an effusion of star particles. In the print, galaxies materialize

You really have to physically and mentally re-hearse with a printer. When you get to know a printer . . . after a while you hardly ever speak. In your relationship with a printer you have to have great faith and great trust.
James Rosenquist, Graphicstudio videotape, 1987

from cosmic dust set in motion by solar winds. Each star is meticulously drawn, so that individual orbs are visible around the edges of the largest star clusters. At the center of the composition is an exquisitely depicted, monolithic water lily, overlapped by a bending, curling, plantlike form out of which a face—two eyes, part of a nose, and three fingers of the hand over the mouth area—emerges. The eyes are so delicately rendered that they appear moist.

Coming full circle from his earliest work at Graphicstudio and prints such as *Cold Light* (cat. 53), which also dealt with humanity's relationship to the universe, *Welcome to the Water Planet* suggests a personal cosmology characterized by the merging of time and space, past and present, beginning and end, macrocosm and microcosm. Rosenquist has explored the ideas of *Welcome to the Water Planet* in a series of works of the same title in various media:

> Sometimes I think about a major question or a major theme and then I think about imagery in regards to that. So, currently one of the themes is called "Water Planet." We live on a water planet. And it was an idea of people putting to bed, or putting under their pillow, the fear of the atomic holocaust, a nuclear war. So the idea, the division of the ideas in this series of paintings, came from early settlers in America hiding in lakes or streams while a forest fire went by. The imagery that occurred to me seemed like a water nymph hiding in a water lily while some star nova or nuclear thing went by far away. And also the idea, welcome to the water planet, was a "welcome." It was sort of against chauvinism.[3]

To create the Graphicstudio print, Rosenquist worked from both a mylar drawing and a small collage, the latter of which he taped to the front of his shirt (or, in the case of Florida's hot summers, directly to his bare chest) and viewed in a small hand-held mirror, enabling him to see the image in reverse so that it corresponded to its appearance on the plate.

Due to the size limitations imposed by the dimensions of the standard etching presses, two copperplates were used to produce the image in the scale desired by Rosenquist. Both halves of the plate were worked simultaneously. Creating the expansive tonal range required meticulous working of the two plates, refining the tones through numerous successive bites in the acid. Rosenquist has described the process:

> I'd block everything out with asphaltum and then work specifically on, say, the flower, maybe drop it in the acid once or twice—boom—and then I left that alone. Then I blocked everything out [again] and worked on the sky, and I wanted to get a lot of depth there, so I dropped that in the acid maybe three or four times—boom—then I blocked all that out and worked on the face and I probably dropped that in the acid maybe once or twice; and then I did the other part [of the face] at the bottom and dropped that in a few times before I ever proofed it. I'm getting so I know where I'm at without proofing it a million times and wearing the plate out. And hey, it's fun to see a big picture after you've been moving like little ants and working on all of this stuff and all of the sudden it blossoms.[4]

Airbrush was used to apply the Rhinds varnish stop-out, a fast-drying varnish that sprays easily, imparting the soft, swirling tonalities of the star field. The painterliness of the aquatint process, with the spraying of successive stops-outs to produce the tones, is well suited to Rosenquist's sensibility. In a talk given to U.S.F. students, the artist remarked: "I am mainly a painter."[5]

Saff has called the work on this particular project "the best of collaborations," stating further: "Jim and Patrick [Foy] knew exactly what they were doing every inch of the way. It was straight ahead from beginning

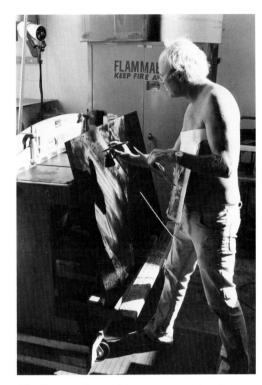

62a. Rosenquist working on copperplate for *Welcome to the Water Planet*, 1987

to end. That plate just kept going back in that acid and there were some 50 or 60 separate bites. It was really like one of these magic things— voilà! Jim just went from an empty plate to a full plate without a hesitation."[6]

1. Reproduced in Cologne 1972, 16, fig. 12. Responding to Jeanne Siegel's question regarding his use of gray, Rosenquist explained: "Yes, I started painting really in grays. Occasionally adding a color but usually in gray because I didn't want my paintings to be gorgeous. It had to do, like my choice of imagery, with not wanting to look contemporary." See Siegel 1972, 33.
2. Cosmic particles occur with some frequency in Rosenquist's oeuvre, appearing in works such as *Star Thief* (1980) and suggesting a different context, as in the color aquatint produced at Gemini G.E.L., *Paper Head on a Nuclear Pillow* (1982). In addition, Rosenquist's *Tallahassee Murals* (1978), executed for the new State Capitol Building, seem to combine aquatic and stellar seas. For reproductions of *Tallahassee Murals* and *Star Thief*, see Craig Adcock, "Interface and Overlay in the Art of James Rosenquist," in Tallahassee 1988, 27–28, 30–31.
3. Rosenquist, interview with Mary Anne Staniszewski, 1987, quoted by Adcock,

in Tallahassee 1988, 38. Other related works include *Welcome to the Water Planet III* (1988), a seventeen-foot mural in the McDonald's International Headquarters, Stockholm; *Welcome to the Water Planet* (1987), a sixteen-foot mural in the Lenox Building, Atlanta; and the color, pressed paper pulp series produced at Tyler Graphics Ltd., 1988–1989.
4. Rosenquist, conversation with Fine, 1990.
5. Rosenquist, Graphicstudio videotape 10, 1987. Airbrush has played an important role in Rosenquist's printmaking almost from the first. He used it with Tatyana Grosman at ULAE in the mid-1960s for lithography: see works such as *Campaign* (1965), *Spaghetti and Grass* (1964–1965), *Dusting Off Roses* (1965), and *Roll Down* (1964–1966), all reproduced in Sparks 1989, figs. 199, 200, 206, and 207. He also used it for aquatints at Gemini G.E.L. at least as early as 1982: see *Plume*, in The Glass Wishes Series, in Fine 1984, cat. 104.
6. Saff, interview with Fine, 1990.

63 The Prickly Dark, 1987–1989

Aquatint on 410 g/m² hot-pressed T. H. Saunders drawing paper
66³/₈ x 67 (168.6 x 170.2)
Edition: 55; 1 BAT; 2 PP; 2 PrP; 1 NGAP; 1 GP; 1 USFP; 7 AP
Collaboration: Greg Burnet, Patrick Foy, Donald Saff

Rosenquist is a superb colorist, yet working in monochrome has been an important part of his aesthetic since the early 1960s. Applying the techniques he learned as a billboard painter, Rosenquist developed a consummate skill with black and white early in his career.[1] His first paintings in his "new" ("billboard") style in 1960–1961, works such as *Zone*, were done in grisaille; and many of his paintings since then have been monochromatic or have contained monochromatic elements.[2]

The Prickly Dark is an elegant composition in black and white, striking in its abstract simplicity.[3] Palpable, fleshy plant forms interact with sharp-edged jags on a dense, smoky black background. An upside-down fragment of a face—part of one eye, a nose, and lips—is contained in the fractured element at the top of the composition, while another large eye is discernible amid the zig-zag pattern that overlaps and obscures the underlying plant form. This again establishes a dynamic tension between natural and artificial forms.

The print was executed in a manner similar to *Welcome to the Water Planet* (cat. 62), with the airbrush enabling the artist to achieve the wide range of subtle tonalities. On *The Prickly Dark* some areas of the plate were also burnished. Meticulous care is fundamental to Rosenquist's working method: "A little more quality, a little hand-schmutzing. Otherwise you see so many prints that are cold and automatic."[4]

Rosenquist has continually explored the power of scale in his work. The overall impact of prints such as *Welcome to the Water Planet* and

The reason for bigness isn't largeness, it's to be engulfed by peripheral vision; it questions the self and questions self-consciousness.

James Rosenquist, quoted by Judith Goldman in Mount Kisco 1989

The Prickly Dark would have been significantly altered if rendered on a smaller scale. In fact, as Patrick Foy has explained, "They were supposed to have been small prints. . . . [But Rosenquist] was down and I was telling him about this printing on folded paper, how we could make these big prints on the small press, talking about something in the future. When he showed up [to do the prints], he showed up with these big drawings, and said that's what he wanted to do."[5]

To achieve the desired scale, the paper for both of these works was folded during the printing process in a way similar to Leslie's *Folded Constance Pregnant* (cat. 44), except that Rosenquist's prints were folded in half instead of thirds. Foy explained further: "We had to do elaborate measures to pre-stretch the paper after it was dampened and folded. We would dampen it and fold it, then we would take it out and blot it, and then we'd put it in the press and bring the pressure down in the middle of the sheet of paper, and then roll it back and forth, tightening the pressure [with each pass] trying to take all of the stretch out of it." Flipping the folded sheet to print the second press run also presented special problems. The printers, in Foy's words, "had to compensate for the fact that when you flipped it over, . . . the first run was then up, facing the blankets, and had to have sheeting put over it, which would then strip some of the ink off, so we had to compensate with the darkness of the ink, typically making the second run lighter, so that it didn't end up [looking] a lot darker."

1. For a brief discussion of Rosenquist's billboard painting and his grisaille works, see Lucy Lippard, "James Rosenquist: Aspects of a Multiple Art," in *Changing: Essays in Art Criticism* (New York, 1971), 94–95.
2. For an example of a work that combines grisaille and color elements, see *Silver Skies* (1962), reproduced in *Rosenquist*, Cologne 1972, 21, fig. 14. For a more recent example, see *Stars and Algae* (1985), reproduced by Adcock, in Tallahassee 1988, 35.
3. A related painting, *Prickly Dark* (1987), is reproduced in *American Masters*, New York, 1990, 35.
4. Rosenquist, Graphicstudio videotape 9, 1987.
5. Foy, telephone conversation with Corlett, 1990. All other Foy quotations are from this conversation.

PLACES AND THINGS

Robert Rauschenberg in his Captiva studio discussing *Araucan Mastaba/ROCI Chile* (cat. 77) with curator Michael Harrigan, April 1987

ROBERT RAUSCHENBERG

Born in Port Arthur, Texas, 1925
Lives and works in New York City and Captiva, Florida

DRAFTED INTO THE United States Navy, Robert Rauschenberg trained as a neuropsychiatric technician. His first exposure to original art came on a visit to the Henry E. Huntington Library in San Marino, California, while he was stationed in San Diego. When he was discharged from the navy, he enrolled at the Kansas City Art Institute (1947), but believing that a serious artist should study in Paris, he traveled there in 1948 and attended the Académie Julien and Académie de la Grand Chaumière. He returned to the United States in the fall of 1948 to attend Black Mountain College in North Carolina, where he studied with Josef Albers. Rauschenberg then moved to New York and studied at the Art Students League with Vaclav Vytlacil and Morris Kantor (1949–1951). He returned intermittently to Black Mountain, developing close friendships there with John Cage, Merce Cunningham, and Jack Tworkov.

During this period Rauschenberg designed window displays for department stores in New York, and in 1951 he had his first one-man show at the Betty Parsons Gallery. In 1952 he traveled extensively in Europe and North Africa, where he created constructions out of wood, rope, and stones. His White Paintings and Black Paintings were shown at the Stable Gallery in New York in 1953. By the late 1950s his "combines" (so called because they were neither painting nor sculpture, but both) secured his reputation as the "enfant terrible" of American art.

Collaboration and experimentation have been constants in Rauschenberg's art, and the list of his collaborators is long and varied—including pianist David Tudor, and dancers Merce Cunningham and Trisha Brown. In 1966 he established Experiments in Art and Technology (E.A.T.) with scientist Billy Kluver to promote interaction between artists and scientists. Rauschenberg has also been active in matters of artists' rights. During the early 1970s he established Change, Inc., to provide quick access to funds for artists in need. In addition to Graphicstudio, his print projects include work with Universal Limited Art Editions, Gemini G.E.L., and many others. He continues to explore the possibilities of print processes in nontraditional ways in all aspects of his art.

Rauschenberg's honors include the Skowhegan Medal for Painting (1982), the Jerusalem Prize for Arts and Letters from the Friends of Bezalel Academy of Jerusalem (1984), and honorary degrees from Grinnell College, Iowa, the University of South Florida, and New York University. He was elected to the American Academy of Arts and Science (1978). Honors have also been bestowed on him by the Royal Academy of Fine Arts, Stockholm (1980), and the Ministry of Culture and Communication, France (1981). In 1986 he received the World Print Council's Award for Excellence in International Cultural Interchange.

Rauschenberg's first retrospective was at the Jewish Museum in New York (1963). Major exhibitions include those organized by the Whitechapel Art Gallery, London (1964), Walker Art Center, Minneapolis (1965), National Collection of Fine Arts, Smithsonian Institution, Washington, D.C. (1976), Staatliche Kunsthalle, Berlin (1980), Musée national d'arte moderne, Centre Georges Pompidou, Paris (1981), Contemporary Art Museum, Houston (1984), and the Whitney Museum of American Art, New York (1990). In 1984 Rauschenberg Overseas Culture Interchange (ROCI) was established, with exhibitions traveling to Mexico, Chile, Venezuela, China, Tibet, Japan, Cuba, the Soviet Union, Germany, Malaysia, and the United States.

64 Made in Tampa: Tampa 2, 1972–1973

Color lithograph and blueprint on Rives BFK paper
29¹⁵/₁₆ x 74¹/₂ (76 x 189.2)
Edition: 40 (I/XX through XX/XX; 1/20 through 20/20); 1 BAT; 1 PrP; 1 PP; 1 TP;
5 AP; 1 Change, Inc., proof; 1 WP; 1 CP
Collaboration: Oscar Bailey, Paul Clinton, Donald Saff

The use of nontraditional materials is one of the most obvious ways in
which Robert Rauschenberg "acts in the gap" between art and life.[1] Essential to the artist's vision, as has often been noted, is his ability to unite
diverse fragments taken from his surroundings into an aesthetic whole.[2]
It is not surprising, then, that Rauschenberg's earliest Graphicstudio
projects—executed between January and March 1972 and including the
twelve prints of the Made in Tampa series—incorporated an array of
found materials, including cardboard boxes collected from area stores,
waterproof paper used by the workshop to wrap prints for shipping (see
cat. 65), and paper trash bags used by the University of South Florida
(the Seasonbags suite; see app. 173–176).

The complexity of Rauschenberg's selection process for the materials
incorporated in his work is described by Andrew Forge, who tells of the
artist's experience in Amsterdam: given free reign there to rummage
through a junkyard in search of materials, Rauschenberg found that deliberately foraging for materials in this way sidestepped a part of the creative process that was essential to his aesthetic.[3] He needed to come
upon his materials naturally. This suggests that there are deep-seated, if
not always obvious, reasons for the choices he makes, reasons that go
beyond the formal qualities of an object.

Rauschenberg had used cardboard as early as the 1950s as the ground
for his collages and as elements in his combine paintings.[4] In 1970–1971
he produced the Cardbird series at Gemini G.E.L.[5] His Made in Tampa
project took an unplanned turn when the boxes and cardboard fragments carefully selected by the artist were removed from the Graphicstudio workshop by the university cleaning staff, who mistook them for
refuse. Printer Charles Ringness has described how they tracked the
boxes to a dump about seven miles outside of town and discovered ap-

*All material has its own history built into it.
There's no such thing as "better" material. It's just
as unnatural for people to use oil paint as it is to
use anything else. An artist manufactures his material out of his own existence—his own ignorance, familiarity or confidence.*

Robert Rauschenberg, in Rose 1987

proximately where the truck driver had dropped them: "There was a big caterpillar driving back and forth in that area, crush[ing] and pack[ing things] down, so we got him to stop and we all got out and started looking."[6] Rauschenberg recalls: "We had a crew of the most elite of Graphicstudio, and then some, going through the city garbage to recognize and find these boxes. We even embarrassed the sanitation department by showing them photographs of their garbage [taken by Oscar Bailey] and asking them if they'd seen it lately." Ringness also noted that "out of fifty boxes or so, we found, I think, ten of them in pretty good shape and . . . one or two that we salvaged [some portion of], but the rest had been buried." They brought back what they could and carried on with the project. Rauschenberg has since suggested that "the most powerful man on the campus was the janitor."[7]

Tampa 2 is marked by a regular, staccato rhythm, set up by the orderly queue of five different views of a box, alternately arranged by size. An aerial view of the box is repeated at the beginning and end of the line, with a solid area of green in the shape of an *X* replacing the box's interior at the right end, serving as a sort of punctuation, and mitigating any sense of visual depth in that image. A certain tension results from the isolation of the box elements on the white field, because the images are conceptually connected to each other as different views of the same box. By isolating each component of the box, Rauschenberg also called attention to the surfaces—the wrinkles, creases, and abrasions of the taped and crumpled cardboard.[8]

1. Rauschenberg once said, "Painting relates to both art and life. Neither can be made. (I try to act in the gap between the two.)" Quoted in Dorothy C. Miller, ed., *Sixteen Americans* (New York, 1959), 58 (cited in Ormond 1985, 5 n. 2).
2. See, for example, Ginsburg 1976, 152–155, which discusses Rauschenberg's work at Universal Limited Art Editions during the mid-1970s when the artist collected paper bags from alongside the railroad track for use in a project.
3. Forge 1969, 17.
4. For an example of Rauschenberg's collages on cardboard, see Berlin 1980, cats. 74–87. For an example of one of his combine paintings with a cardboard element, see Berlin 1980, cat. 13.
5. See Fine 1984, 109.
6. Ringness, telephone conversation with Fine, 1 October 1990.
7. Rauschenberg, conversation with Fine, 7 October 1990.
8. In several works in the Made in Tampa suite, Rauschenberg explored the blueprinting and sepiaprinting processes in conjunction with lithography. *Tampa 2*, for example, combines lithography with blueprinting. For further discussion of these processes, see cat. 67.

65 Made in Tampa: Tampa 3, 1972

Color lithograph with collage and graphite additions on waterproof "tar" paper
43⅞ x 47 x ¼ (111.5 x 119.4 x .6)
Edition: 40 (I/XX through XX/XX; 1/20 through 20/20); 1 BAT; 1 PrP; 1 PP; 4 AP; 1 Change, Inc., proof; 1 WP
Collaboration: Charles Ringness, Donald Saff

A direct connection between the inspiration for a work of art and the materials from which it is made—a concept at the center of Rauschenberg's creative vision—was realized in *Tampa 3*. Without sacrificing the integrity of either, Rauschenberg was able to strike a balance between the character of the objects, the paper bags that became his artistic materials, and his own aesthetic ends. *Tampa 3* is one of five prints from the Made in Tampa series that feature bags rather than boxes. The other four, *Tampa 4* through *Tampa 7*, Rauschenberg collected into a portfolio entitled Seasonbags.

Rauschenberg collaged an actual bag, the standard trash bag used by campus custodians, to the left side of the composition and combined it with its printed counterpart on the right. The pencil lines around the "real" bag vary somewhat in every impression. To produce the printed image, lithographic ink was applied with a roller to the surface of the bag, and the ink was transferred to an aluminum plate by running both bag and plate through the press. Additional plates were made, using a mixture of tusche and water applied to the bag and then run through the press to transfer the marks, for the printing of additional tones of black. The printed bag retains the serrated top edge, the folded-over bottom flap, the overlap of paper at the center joint, while still providing the vehicle for Rauschenberg to explore the spatters, smears, streaks, and patterns that reflect his interest in the quality of the mark on a page.

Rauschenberg's exploration of direct image-making techniques, exemplified in the printed bag produced here, has led him to a variety of nontraditional forms of printmaking, such as his well-known solvent transfers (see cats. 70–72), the light transfer of the image of Tatyana Grosman's scarf in *Veils* (1974), the impression of an automobile tire in the monotype *Automobile Tire Print* (1951), and the light-generated image of a female form in *Female Figure (Blueprint)* (c. 1949).[1] For Rauschenberg the inspiration, the material, and the work of art itself are inseparably intertwined.

Having used boxes and bags as sources throughout the Made in Tampa series, Rauschenberg went one step further in *Tampa 3* and used found material for the printing surface as well.[2] The waterproof "tar" paper, which had been found by Saff in a state surplus properties room,

When an object you're using does not stand out but yields its presence to what you're doing, it collaborates, so to speak—it implies a kind of harmony.

Robert Rauschenberg, in Swenson 1963

234

came in rolls and had the dramatic quality of revealing its black core along the edges when torn. It was certainly not archival quality, and it seemed impervious to most materials that were applied to it—enough of a problem alone to make it attractive to Rauschenberg.

1. For a reproduction of *Veils*, see Sparks 1989, cats. 46. For reproductions of *Automobile Tire Print* and *Female Figure*

(Blueprint), see Berlin 1980, cats. 72, 73.
2. This paper was also used for *Tampa 1*.

66 Made in Tampa: Tampa 9, 1972–1973
Color lithograph and blueprint on Rives BFK (roll) paper
68 x 12⅞ (172.7 × 32.7)
Edition: 40 (I/XX through XX/XX; 1/20 through 20/20); 1 BAT; 1 PrP; 1 PP; 4 AP;
1 Change, Inc., proof; 1 WP; 1 CP
Collaboration: Oscar Bailey, Paul Clinton, Donald Saff

One of the challenges faced by master printer Paul Clinton with Rauschenberg's Made in Tampa suite was the artist's desire to use the commercial printing processes of blueprint and sepiaprint, both of which yield penetrating color. Rauschenberg had first experimented with blueprinting about 1949 when he and Susan Weil exposed the sensitized paper to light to produce full-size images of human figures. He used the process again in *Tampa 9*, in addition to *Tampa 2* and *Tampa 11* (cats. 64, 67). According to Clinton, "Rauschenberg wanted to isolate the cardboard forms in large sheets of Rives BFK paper, and the roll paper was unsized so the sensitizer would bleed out around the forms. We had to figure out a way to process the large prints and keep the white negative spaces clean. . . . So we sat down and developed a way of getting what we wanted."[1] After researching the blueprint process with a local company and with Gainesville artist Todd Walker, Clinton was able to perfect a procedure for working in a large format that achieved both the desired tones and permanence of the color.

In *Tampa 2* the process began with the making of a photographic Kodalith of the image to be printed. A mylar stencil was made to protect the white areas, and the printing paper was then sensitized (the sensitizer is mixed fresh daily to control color and consistency) and left to cure in the darkroom for twelve hours. The stencil later served as an aid to registration. The Kodalith transparency and the sensitized paper were then placed in a vacuum table and exposed to light. The exposed paper was placed in a developer bath, rinsed with water, and allowed to soak. The washing time is critical to achieve proper color intensity and evenness of tone. Finally, the print was dried very slowly, between blotters, for about a week. The slow drying time ensures the permanence of the color.[2]

If there is a leitmotif in Rauschenberg's work in Tampa during this period, it might be in his use of multiple views or incarnations of the same object, often suggesting sequence and therefore the passage of time. In *Tampa 9* Rauschenberg presents the top and side views of a "grit box," arranged one above the other in totemic fashion in an elongated vertical composition that reinforces the cylindrical shape of the box. The blueprinted image at the top provides not only deep color but a distinctive textural appearance that contrasts with the sharper, photolithographed image of the lid below it. The process for creating the softer, blueprinted image here differs from that used in *Tampa 2* in that no Kodalith was used. Instead, clear contact paper was tightly adhered to the top surface of the actual lid by running them through the press to-

66a. Inking the lithography plate for *Tampa 9*, 1972

gether. This assemblage was then soaked in warm water to soften the cardboard fibers of the lid so that they could be removed, leaving only a thin skin of fiber and dyes still attached to the contact paper. A second sheet of contact paper was then fixed to the first, tacky sides together. This sandwich became the "transparency" that functioned in the same way as the Kodalith described above.[3]

The grit box that served as the subject in *Tampa 9* contained carborundum for grinding lithographic stones and was included in the donation of materials to Graphicstudio by Syracuse China Corporation—as is indicated by the inscription "Syr. China" that appears on the top of the canister. This image thus documents an important association in Graphicstudio's history.

As part of its content, my work has always had to include and utilize actual elements from everyday life which were not necessarily considered artists' materials. (In many cases this way of working physically converted a painting into a construction.) My lithography is the realization and execution of the fact that anything that creates an image on stone is potential material.

Robert Rauschenberg, in Ashton 1968

1. Clinton, telephone conversation with Fine, 2 October 1990. Saff has further noted, in Baro 1978, 22: "Transferring a sheet of paper from one bath to another demanded great skill. The prints were wrapped around a thick PVC pipe so that they would not be damaged, and the rinse had to be done with special care to insure a good fix of the chemicals."
2. A description of this process can be found in Saff and Sacilotto 1978, 367–369.
3. This process was described by Clinton in a telephone conversation with Corlett, 21 March 1991.

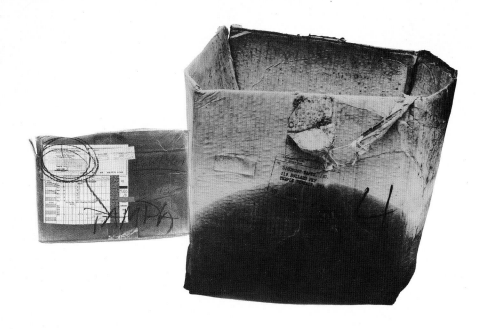

67 Made in Tampa: Tampa 11, 1972–1973

Blueprint and sepiaprint on Rives BFK paper
29⁵/₁₆ x 41³/₁₆ (74.5 x 104.6)
Edition: 40 (I/XX through XX/XX; 1/20 through 20/20); 1 BAT; 1 PrP; 1 PP; 1 TP;
4 AP; 1 Change, Inc., proof; 1 WP
Collaboration: Oscar Bailey, Paul Clinton, Donald Saff

The dull, penetrating brown and blue tones produced by the sepiaprint
and the blueprint processes evoke the greasy, soiled, worn appearance of
the spent cardboard boxes that are the subjects of *Tampa 11*. The labels,
order forms, markings, handwritten notations, and numbers—as well as
the stained and battered appearance of the cardboard itself—all reveal
the depth of information available on the surface of an object.

The use of both the blueprint and the sepiaprint techniques in a single
work created particular challenges for Graphicstudio, due to what Saff
has described as "chemical antipathy."[1] The chemicals used to develop a
blueprint are incompatible with those used to develop a sepiaprint, so incorporating both on the same sheet required that the sepiaprint be executed separately and allowed to dry thoroughly. When the blueprinted
area was produced, it could not be immersed in the developer bath but
had to be carefully hand-brushed with the solution.[2]

Only a few prints—"five, six, no more than ten"—could be completed
in a day. This was also the case for the other images in the Made in
Tampa series that used blueprint or sepiaprint. Clinton has said: "I spent
the year on five prints; it was slow, and interesting. . . . We saw where
we were and then we all went together somewhere else, where we hadn't
been. . . . We had everybody stretching."[3]

*I like the experience that says that a shirt changes
when it gets in the sun a little, or when you go
swimming in it, or when the dog sleeps on it. I
like the history of objects. I like the humanitarian
reportage.*

Robert Rauschenberg, in Rose 1987

1. Saff, in Baro 1978, 22.
2. Clinton, telephone conversation with
Fine, 1990; see also Baro 1978, 22.

3. Clinton, telephone conversation with
Fine, 1990.

68A–D Made in Tampa Clay Pieces

Collaboration: Alan Eaker, Donald Saff, with Julio Juristo

Clay, Rauschenberg has said, was among the materials he most enjoyed working with as a student.[1] The idea for the Made in Tampa Clay Pieces evolved after the Made in Tampa print project was already underway. The artist had previously discussed the possibility of working in clay with Alan Eaker, who, once the print project had begun, brought a variety of clay pieces—slabs, lumps, etc.—to the workshop. As Eaker recalls:

> They sat around the studio for about a week, and nothing happened. [Rauschenberg] didn't mark them, or touch them, or do anything. One day I was in the studio and he was working. He had been doing these cardboard images and had this piece of cardboard, and he said, "You know, this is a really beautiful thing, could you make this in clay?" . . . We made a mold of the cardboard piece; we made the piece in clay; we fired it; we made decals—same size. And where he had pinned up the cardboard piece on the wall to look at it, we nailed up the ceramic piece. He came back to the studio and was working for about half of the day before he realized that it was the clay piece on the wall and not the cardboard. . . . That was when he really got excited about the possibilities. And that became *Tampa Clay Piece 1*. From there, it became a challenge to see how much more complicated the images could be.[2]

The Made in Tampa Clay Pieces provided Rauschenberg with the opportunity to expand on the trompe-l'oeil effects explored in the Cardbirds series produced at Gemini G.E.L. the previous year. He manipulated cardboard boxes and fragments into four prototypes, each presenting a unique combination of creases, crumpled corners, and tears, as well as smudges, marks, labels, tape, and staples. Achieving the

My attitude is that if I am in a working situation, I just look around and see what's around me. If I've picked up something, touched something or moved somewhere, then something starts happening.

Robert Rauschenberg, in Rose 1987

68a. Julio Juristo (right) and Dan Stack emptying a mold for the Made in Tampa Clay Pieces

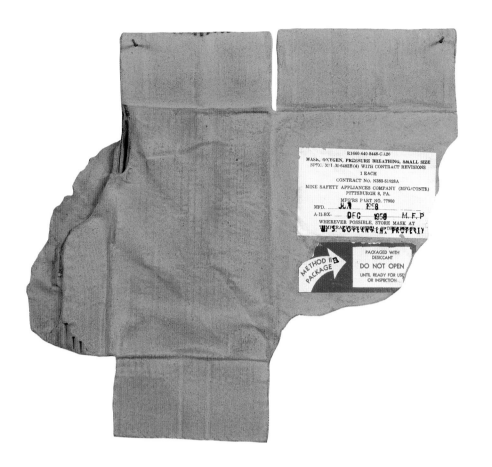

68A Tampa Clay Piece 1, 1972
Clay with screenprinted lacquer decals
14¹/₂ x 15¹/₂ x ³/₄ (36.8 x 39.4 x 1.9)
Edition: 20 (I/X through X/X; 1/10
through 10/10); 1 BAT; 2 PrP; 1 WP;
5 AP; 1 Change, Inc., proof; 3 TP

68B Tampa Clay Piece 2, 1972
Clay with screenprinted ceramic decal
15¹/₂ x 23¹/₂ x ³/₄ (39.4 x 59.7 x 1.9)
Edition: 20 (I/X through X/X; 1/10
through 10/10); 1 BAT; 2 PrP; 1 WP;
5 AP; 1 Change, Inc., proof

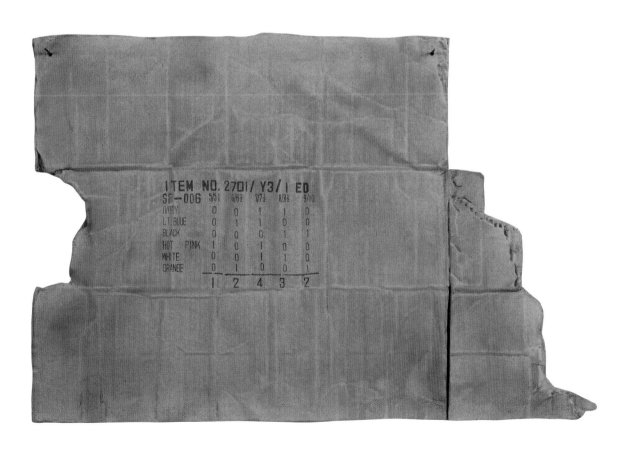

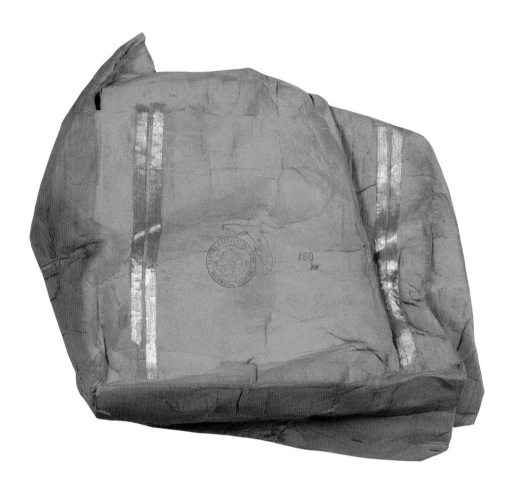

68C Tampa Clay Piece 3,
1972–1973
Clay with screenprinted ceramic decal
and collage (fiberglass and epoxy)
19½ x 24 x 5½ (49.5 x 61 x 14)
Edition: 20 (I/X through X/X; 1/10
through 10/10); 1 BAT; 2 PrP; 1 WP;
6 AP; 1 Change, Inc., proof

68D Tampa Clay Piece 4, 1972
Clay with screenprinted ceramic and
lacquer decals
9½ x 17 x 1½ (24.1 x 43.2 x 3.8)
Edition: 20 (I/X through X/X; 1/10
through 10/10); 1 BAT; 2 PrP; 1 WP;
5 AP; 1 Change, Inc., proof; 1 experimental proof; 3 TP

veracity of the appearance of the soiled cardboard of a collapsed box, with its worn, abraded, distorted labels, was essential to the preservation of the integrity of the prototype and the artist's aesthetic vision in the Made in Tampa Clay Pieces.

Using Ocamulgee clay, a Georgia red terra cotta, and mixing it with a certain amount of stoneware, a clay body was developed that would simulate the color and texture of cardboard when fired. The moist clay was rolled out and pressed into plaster molds of the prototypes. Because of the weight of the clay, a special system had to be devised to release the piece from the mold (fig. 68a): "We had to build a huge structure with the mold mounted on a two-inch steel pipe with fiberglass holding it in place. The mold could then be filled, a plywood sheet put on top, and the whole thing flipped over so that the piece [would] drop out. . . . You couldn't turn the mold [otherwise]. It weighed about 150 pounds."[3] At this point, the piece was allowed to dry, then fired.

Two types of decals were incorporated. Screenprinted ceramic decals were made by using ceramic glaze (in place of printers' ink) to screen images directly onto the fired clay, which was then refired. The ceramic decals simulate labels printed or stamped directly on the cardboard box, as seen in *Tampa Clay Piece 2*. The screenprinted lacquer transfer decals, which simulate "stick-on" labels as seen in *Tampa Clay Piece 1*, were more complicated to produce. First, the entire surface of a piece of decal paper was coated with underglaze varnish. The image of the label was then screenprinted onto the coated paper using a mixture of color glazing oxides and underglaze varnish. Once the screenprinted image had dried, the decal paper was immersed in water to separate the paper backing from the varnished decal. Then the decal was placed in the appropriate area on the clay piece, which had been treated with cellulose gum adhesive.[4] After air drying, the piece was refired to permanently fuse the decal image and the clay.

Packing tape as seen in *Tampa Clay Piece 3* was simulated by taking actual fiberglass tape, removing the adhesive with acetone, and coating the back with epoxy. The tape was then secured in position on the surface of the clay piece and left to dry. Once dry, the top layer of cellophane was removed, leaving the fiberglass fibers and the epoxy for a permanent representation of packing tape.

The last step was to apply a patina so that the new clay would take on the greasy, dirty appearance of old, worn cardboard. Eaker found that the desired effect could be achieved by rubbing the clay with a combination of the natural oils from his face and dirt from outside the studio. For the edition, a little vaseline was substituted for the facial oil.

1. Rauschenberg, interview with Fine, 1990.
2. Eaker, conversation with Fine, 13 July 1989. Further information about the clay body was also taken from this interview.
3. Eaker, conversation with Fine, 1989.
4. Saff, in Baro 1978, 23, noted that this was Julio Juristo's "first project at Graphicstudio. It amused him that he worked so long on a project so foreign to his training. But he did devise processes to make oxide decals adhere properly to the clay and was an inventive contributor to the success of the whole project." See also Saff and Sacilotto 1978, 366, for a description of the process for producing the screenprint lacquer transfer decal.

69 Made in Tampa Clay Pieces: Tampa Clay Piece 5, 1972

Clay and fiberglass with collage
34 x 18 x 3 (86.4 x 45.7 x 7.6)
Edition: 20 (I/X through X/X; 1/10 through 10/10); 1 BAT; 2 PrP; 1WP; 5 AP;
1 Change, Inc., proof
Collaboration: Alan Eaker, Donald Saff, with Michelle Juristo

During the production of the first four Made in Tampa Clay Pieces, Rauschenberg became interested in the burlap sacks that the raw clay was packaged in. According to Eaker, "He kept looking at these bags, . . . and he said, 'It would be nice if we could sort of put those together [with the clay] in some way. . . . What about doing a clay bag?' "[1] The burlap was too flimsy for a mold to be made of it, however, and Eaker found that if the bag itself was coated with clay slip and used as the matrix, the burlap would burn out when fired, leaving a fragile, structurally unstable, clay object. But as suggested in the artist's statement to the right, it is in the nature of Rauschenberg's interaction with his materials that the character of those materials is often discovered through indirect means. Rauschenberg asked if a more suitable fabric could be substituted for the

In one painting I have a brick. It was a painter's problem even though it was a brick instead of a particular color that I was having to deal with. A brick is heavy, and it most comfortably would lie down, but when it was down, fixed or unfixed, on something that clearly would support it, it tended to look less like a brick because it looked like an architectural form of this particular material, and the only way I was able to let it look as BRICK as possible was to suspend it.

Robert Rauschenberg, in Forge 1969

burlap, and Eaker suggested fiberglass cloth, which melts at low temperatures and would actually fuse with the clay when fired, making the piece stronger structurally. Each of the clay bags in this edition is therefore made from a different fiberglass bag fused with clay. As Saff has noted, "The only parameter was the distance between the nails on which the bags are mounted—that was a fixed distance. The bag then patterned itself, and once it took its shape, it was not altered."[2] Each bag is unique, hanging with its own distinctive character. Identification tags supplied by the Burns Brick Company, producers of the clay used for the project, were attached to each bag with wire formed from soldering lead, which, as Eaker has explained, "is much more flexible" than regular wire and could be wrapped around a section of the piece without risk of damaging the fragile ceramic.[3]

69a. Michelle Juristo, dressed in protective clothing, sewing a fiberglass bag for *Tampa Clay Piece 5*, 1972

1. Eaker, conversation with Fine, 1989.
2. Saff, conversation with Fine, December 1990.
3. Kelder 1973, 85, also discusses these projects.

70 Crops: Cactus, 1973

Solvent transfer and color screenprint
60 x 38 (152.4 x 96.5)
Edition: 40 (I/XX through XX/XX; 1/20 through 20/20); 1 BAT; 1 PrP; 2 PP;
1 experimental proof; 3 AP; 1 WP; 1 Change, Inc., proof
Collaboration: Paul Clinton, Donald Saff

Rauschenberg returned to Graphicstudio in the spring of 1973 and executed five solvent transfer and screenprint works collectively called the Crops suite. The title of the series suggests multiple meanings. It refers not only to the plant life for which the individual prints in the series are named—*Cactus, Coconut, Mangrove, Peanuts,* and *Watermelon* (cats.

70–72, and app. 191, 192)—but also to the process of "cropping"—cutting or trimming—an image, as is often done in preparation for publication. "Crops" may also suggest the maxim that one reaps what one sows, as it applies to the world events recorded in the newspaper fragments that make up the composition. And like the individual prints in each edition in this suite, a crop of any given species of plants will share many characteristics, but each individual plant remains unique.

Rauschenberg began to experiment with the solvent transfer technique as a drawing method during the late 1950s.[1] At that time the solvent he used was lighter fluid, and by rubbing the back of a solvent-dampened image with a ballpoint pen, he was able to transfer the image to paper beneath it. His first major project using this technique was the drawings of Dante's *Inferno*, executed in 1959–1960. Use of a printing press to make the transfer, as in the Crops suite, results in a uniform impression that differs markedly from the scratchy, textural transfer achieved by hand with a blunt instrument such as a ballpoint pen.[2]

Images from newspapers and magazines have been an integral part of Rauschenberg's artistic vocabulary since the 1950s. A collage of torn newspaper fragments served as the ground for his Black Paintings of 1951–1952. Said Rauschenberg in 1959: "I began using newsprint in my work to activate a ground so that even the first strokes in a painting had their unique position in a gray map of words. As the paintings changed, the printed material became as much of a subject as the paint, causing changes of focus and providing multiplicity and duplication of images. A third palette with infinite possibilities of color, shape, content, and scale was then added to the palettes of objects and paint."[3] Fragments from newspapers and magazines assert themselves more forcefully in his work of the 1960s. In works such as *Barge* (1963) Rauschenberg expanded his collage technique by screenprinting image fragments from mass media sources directly onto the canvas. In 1970 he produced the monumental *Currents*, a sixty-foot-long composition constructed of pieces torn from eight newspapers published in six cities.[4]

In *Cactus* Rauschenberg manipulated the newspaper to introduce a great variety of forms, combining tangles of shredded newspaper and layers of larger strips, half sheets, and a full sheet, cropped. He also exploited the internal pattern of the newspaper page: the columns of text on the full page of the newspaper at the top of the print, for example, punctuated intermittently by solid circles randomly scattered across the page, are an integral part of the composition. Rauschenberg's reproduction of whole pages of print in reverse is disconcerting. One struggles to recognize a familiar image, word, or phrase—here, the headline "Skylab: America's Cabin in the Sky."

Rauschenberg worked at the press with printers Charles Ringness, Paul Clinton, and Julio Juristo to produce the editions for this and the other images in the Crops series, using the *bon à tirer* he created for each work in the series as a reference for placing newspaper and magazine fragments in the same approximate location on each print. After the fragments were arranged face down on the paper, solvent was liberally sprayed over the images. Glassine, a cover sheet, and the plastic tympan were placed on top, and the whole assemblage was run through the lithograph press. There are, therefore, slight variations between each print in each edition.[5] In 1976 Saff commented to Gene Baro: "One of the printers questioned whether this was an edition. Rauschenberg was irritated, stating that the idea was consistent and that this was sufficient to consider the resulting group of prints an edition. Later, he said that he had, in effect, substituted himself for the stone."[6]

What's really nice about printmaking is working with other people. I like that. . . . If you are working with people, even if there are just two people, you don't get the flat results of one on one. Not only do you get it one to five, but you get a constant exchange that's absolutely limitless, like echoes.
Robert Rauschenberg, in Perry 1978

1. See Calvin Tomkins, *The Bride & The Bachelors* (New York, 1965), 223.
2. Rauschenberg had used the press to produce solvent transfer drawings as early as 1971, but the Crops suite was his first print edition produced in this way. The authors thank David White, Rauschenberg's curator, for confirming this information in a telephone conversation,
29 January 1991.
3. Quoted in Feinstein 1986, 36. Solomon 1963, n. 3, cites an abbreviated version of this quotation.
4. See McCullagh 1985, 85.
5. For a description of this process, see Saff and Sacilotto 1978, 360.
6. Saff, in Baro 1978, 23.

71 Crops: Coconut, 1973

Solvent transfer and color screenprint
60¼ x 38 (153 x 96.5)
Edition: 40 (I/XX through XX/XX; 1/20 through 20/20); 1 BAT; 1 PrP; 2 PP; 1 TP;
3 experimental proofs; 3 AP; 1 WP; 1 Change, Inc., proof
Collaboration: Paul Clinton, Donald Saff

In contrast to the full newspaper pages in *Cactus*, it is the shreds and
strips of newspaper that dominate in *Coconut*, which is further characterized by delicate hues—predominately blue and green in this
impression—and multiple layers of imagery. Screenprinted areas of two
different tones of white (warm and cool), over which the solvent transfers have been executed, add to the complexity of the layers. Rauschenberg arranged the newspaper images so that they are not all turned in the
same direction, underscoring the presence of layers that, in fact, do not
exist in the third dimension. Because the prints are not collages, the fragments have no real edges, and it is more difficult to determine where one
section begins and another ends, particularly where the overlapping is
the most dense. The disorienting arrangement of fragments in *Coconut*,
and in varying degrees in all of the prints of the Crops suite, is perhaps
suggestive of the multiple levels of explanation, incomplete bits of information, and differing perspectives that fashion our interpretation of contemporary events and constitute our vision of reality.

In all of the prints in the Crops series Rauschenberg has combined the
solvent transfer process with screenprint to amplify the multiplicity of
and impart a density to the layers, and to enhance the subtle textures of
the image.

*My images come from everywhere. I support the
post office. Subscribe to everything: magazines,
newspapers, catalogues, ads. I pick up everything
I can get my hands on.*

Robert Rauschenberg, in Kotz 1983

72 Crops: Mangrove, 1973

Solvent transfer and color screenprint
60 x 38 (152.4 x 96.5)
Edition: 40 (I/XX through XX/XX; 1/20 through 20/20); 1 BAT; 1 PrP; 2 PP; 1 TP;
1 experimental proof; 3 AP; 1 WP; 1 Change, Inc., proof
Collaboration: Charles Ringness, Donald Saff

An elegance of line and form and an extreme delicacy of color—the soft grays and touches of pastel pinks, greens, and yellows, primarily confined to the lower third of the composition—characterize this impression of *Mangrove*. The dictionary defines "mangrove" as "any of a genus of tropical maritime trees or shrubs that throw out many prop roots and form dense masses important in coastal land building." The tangled, undecipherable thicket of shredded, reversed newspaper clippings in Rauschenberg's *Mangrove* is reminiscent of this evergreen so important to the Florida coast. It may also be a metaphor for the complexity and interconnectedness of world events and the political, social, and economic forces, represented in the newspaper fragments, on which the future is continually reshaped, as coastal lands can be shaped by the dense roots of the mangrove. But if *Mangrove* looks to the future, it also alludes to the past, its newspaper fragments almost instantaneously out of date. Their scattered arrangement suggests the difficulty faced by those who assemble remnants of information in an attempt to reconstruct and understand the past. *Mangrove* is quintessential Rauschenberg in that its meaning is not predetermined by the artist but remains open to the viewer's interpretation.

Ideally I would like to make a picture [such] that no two people would see the same thing, not only because [the people] are different but because the picture is different.

Robert Rauschenberg, in Forge 1969

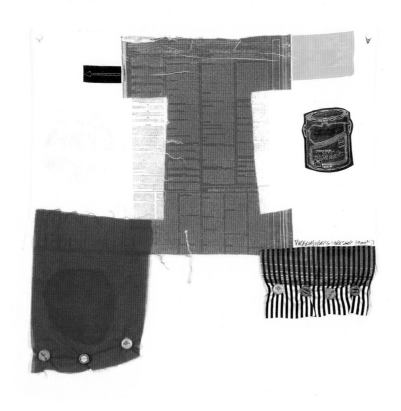

73 Airport: Cat Paws, 1974
Color relief and intaglio printed from newspaper matrices on fabric with collage
Framed: 42⁵/₁₆ x 44⁵/₁₆ x 1¹/₂ (107.5 x 112.6 x 3.8)
Edition: 40 (I/XX through XX/XX; 1/20 through 20/20); 1 BAT; 1 PrP; 1 PP; 10 AP;
1 WP; 1 Change, Inc., proof
Collaboration: Paul Clinton, Tom Kettner, Donald Saff

Rauschenberg's Airport series (see also cats. 74–75, and app. 194, 197)
was the first Graphicstudio project to be realized off-site. The etching
press, and everything else needed to execute the project, was shipped
from Graphicstudio to Rauschenberg's studio in Captiva, because the
artist, having recently returned from a lengthy trip abroad, preferred to
work at home.[1] These prints were also Rauschenberg's first intaglios.

Saff has explained the birth of the project: "Rauschenberg and I
had lengthy discussions concerning this project before sending down
printers, press, and materials. I recall one morning when he came out after shaving with blood on his cheek, saying that he loved the color and
wanted to do a colorful print project. I gathered newspaper matrices—
primarily because I've never seen a successful print made with one of
these, and students try to work with them all the time. I also got some
beautiful heavy-toothed stiff paper. Bob had a great deal of difficulty
with these elements. He said I was thinking 'hard,' while he was thinking
'soft.' So he switched to fabric as a printing base."[2]

Rauschenberg had freely used fabric since the 1950s as a part of the
working vocabulary of his combine paintings and was well aware of its
varied potential.[3] The Airport suite, his first editions on fabric,[4] extended his printing vocabulary in several ways, among them a further
exploration of his interest in the layering of imagery as expressed in the

248

Crops suite. This use of fabric again reveals the rich and unconventional combination of processes and materials that is the linchpin of Rauschenberg's aesthetic. Produced earlier in the same year his unique *Hoarfrost* pieces and the Hoarfrost Editions were executed at Gemini G.E.L., the Airport series represents his earliest interest in the transparent and semi-transparent layers of imagery that can be achieved by printing on fabric.[5]

Rauschenberg used a page from *The Wall Street Journal* (Monday, 18 March 1974) as the basis for the print *Cat Paws*. The newspaper matrix was inked and printed in intaglio and in relief to achieve the orange-on-red tonality. Two pieces of fabric—red muslin and black-and-white satin—were placed over the white cotton for the successful printing of the plate. After the printing, these pieces were lifted away and sewn to the bottom edge of the cotton. Frayed threads along the edges of the muslin were caught between the plate and the cotton during the printing, leaving unprinted hairline impressions that evoke their woven source. These white silhouettes, which weave delicately in and out among the letters of the text at the center of the composition, appear to be accidental, yet they are central to the very look and feel of the work. The creases at the top of the newspaper page, too, were the product of "free collaboration" with the material, created as the fabric rolled through the press.

A collaboration of another sort determined the print's title. While several impressions were laid out to dry, a cat walked across one, leaving on it a bright red imprint of its paw.[6]

I don't believe in chance any more than I believe in anything else. With me, it's much more a matter of just accepting whatever happens, accepting all these elements from the outside and then trying to work with them in a sort of free collaboration.

Robert Rauschenberg, in Tomkins 1965

1. Information obtained from a conversation between Rauschenberg and Fine, 7 October 1990.
2. Saff, in Baro 1978, 23.
3. See, for example, *Hymnal* (1955), reproduced in Berlin 1980, cat. 7. For an example of an early drawing on fabric, see *Lawn Combed* (1954), reproduced in

Berlin 1980, cat. 89.
4. Confirmed in conversation between Rauschenberg and Fine, 1990.
5. For information on the Hoarfrost Editions, see Fine 1984, 112–113.
6. From conversation between Rauschenberg and Fine, 1990.

74 Airport: Platter, 1974

Color relief and intaglio printed from newspaper matrices on fabric
Framed: 52¼ x 35⁵/₁₆ x 1½ (132.7 x 89.7 x 3.8)
Edition: 40 (I/XX through XX/XX; 1/20 through 20/20); 1 BAT; 1 PrP; 1 PP; 11 AP; 1 WP; 1 Change, Inc., proof
Collaboration: Paul Clinton, Tom Kettner, Donald Saff

As in *Cat Paws*, a *Wall Street Journal* page was used for *Platter*, printed onto layered fabrics: blue satin, white cotton, and cheesecloth. The overlapping fabrics, the newspaper page—right-reading and reversed—and the use of both intaglio and relief printing processes, all combined here, characterize the entire Airport suite. The permeability and flexibility of fabric allowed Rauschenberg to establish relationships not otherwise possible between printed images. In *Platter*, for example, the cheesecloth could be flipped over after printing so that the text would read correctly on the backside of the cheesecloth while remaining reversed on the cotton fabric underneath. An interplay between the printed image and patterned fabric is maximized in the upper right quadrant of the composition, where the red and blue floral print fabric is transformed with the overprinting of red and blue images from the newspaper matrices. The

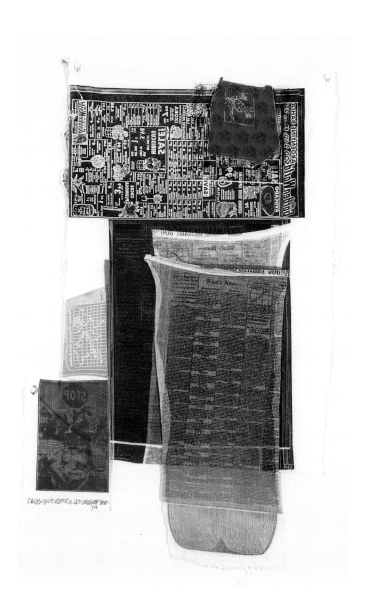

metamorphosis of the patterned fabric overprinted with text results in typical Rauschenberg multiplicity.

Throughout the Airport series Rauschenberg juxtaposed references to sobering world events with bits of popular culture, creating a dialogue between otherwise unrelated images and evoking the sometimes discordant layers that form the fabric of modern life. *Platter* combines the *Wall Street Journal* page with an ad for *Garden World*. *Sheephead* (cat. 75) juxtaposes advertisements for numerous consumer goods—from tires to toothpaste, Lysol to airplane kits—with television listings and somber newspaper headlines such as "'Massive Power Abuse' Cited as Staff Urges Impeachment." *Cat Paws* shows the headline, in reverse, "Islamic Summit Declaration," along with images that might be found in a Sears catalogue—a stack of mattresses, a can of housepaint.

The title of the series as a whole reflects the fast-moving pace of Rauschenberg's life. By the time the pieces, printed in Captiva, assembled in Tampa, were ready to be signed, Rauschenberg was about to leave on another trip. To accommodate his schedule, the editions were packed up and delivered for signing to a room at a Tampa airport hotel.[1]

1. Paul Clinton, telephone conversation with Fine, 2 October 1990.

If you are dealing with multiplicity, variation and inclusion as your content, then any feeling of complete consistency or sameness is a violation of that attitude. I had to try consciously to do a work that would imply the kind of richness and complexity I saw around me.

Robert Rauschenberg, in Seckler 1966

75 Airport: Sheephead, 1974

Relief and intaglio printed from newspaper matrices on fabric with collage
Framed: 45³/₈ x 60⁵/₁₆ x 1¹/₂ (115.3 x 153.2 x 3.8)
Edition: 40 (I/XX through XX/XX; 1/20 through 20/20); 1 BAT; 1 PrP; 1 PP; 14 AP;
1 WP; 1 Change, Inc., proof
Collaboration: Paul Clinton, Tom Kettner, Donald Saff

Techniques used in *Sheephead* to print a composite of newspaper fragments are similar to those that created the other prints in the Airport series, allowing for upside-down images to be printed adjacent to images
that are right-side up and sideways in both intaglio and relief. *Sheephead*, named after a fish found in the waters surrounding Florida, is
unique in the series in that it is printed in black on white, the only color
provided by a blue ruler that has been stitched to the top edge of the
composition.

Rauschenberg's interest in surface, texture, and the interaction of diverse materials is revealed in all the prints of the Airport suite. In *Cat
Paws*, for example, bottle caps are attached so that the muslin and satin
beneath them puckers. This emphasizes the distinctly different textures
of each fabric and increases the overall textural effect, while simultaneously suggesting the grip that is the function of both a cap and a cat's
paw. In *Switchboard* (app. 197), the cheesecloth is allowed to hang free,
supported by an IBM electrographic pencil collage element that pro-
trudes at a perpendicular angle to the picture plane; this adds still another dimension with the gentle movement of the fabric in the
surrounding air.[1] In *Room Service* (app. 194) Rauschenberg included his
own necktie. All of the prints in this series—in their stitched-together
collage of fabrics of various textures, sporting wrinkles and creases, often joined with readymade materials such as bottle caps, pencils, neckties, rulers—have the raw, unpolished look of Rauschenberg's earlier
combine paintings.[2]

*When I was a student at the Art Students League
in New York City, I was surrounded by groups
of artists all investigating the comparable sim-
ilarities and likenesses between things. It was not
until I realized that it is the celebration of the differences between things that I became an artist
who could see.*

Robert Rauschenberg, in Washington 1991

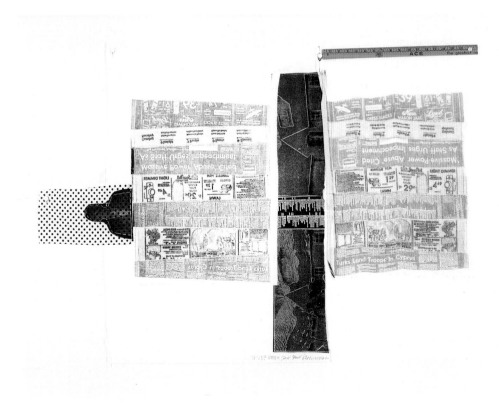

One contribution of the university setting to the character of the Graphicstudio workshop was operative in this project: after the printing was accomplished at Captiva, and a prototype *bon à tirer* completed for each print, the individual elements were brought back to Tampa, where sewing and other assembly was undertaken with the assistance of the U.S.F. theater department.

1. Saff, in a conversation with Fine in 1990, noted that the IBM electrographic pencil is Rauschenberg's favorite tool for drawing and for signing his prints.
2. The addition of the necktie recalls Rauschenberg's combine paintings from the 1950s. See, *Rhyme* (1956), reproduced in *Rauschenberg*, London 1964, cat. 10. More recently, Rauschenberg's neckties were featured in a 1988 sculpture entitled *Uptown Pig Pox*.

76 Chinese Summerhall, 1982–1983

C-print color photograph
29⅞ x 1248¼ (75.9 x 3170.6)
Edition: 5 (unnumbered)
Collaboration: George Holzer, Donald Saff, David Yager, with Doug Brown, Wayne Bryan

Chinese Summerhall, the hundred-foot-long photograph produced from photographs taken by Rauschenberg during a trip to China in 1982, was the artist's first use of color photography in an edition.[1] Its compelling hundred-foot length demands that the viewer move along its full span to absorb its imagery—one cannot remain stationary in front of the composition.

Rauschenberg's work in photography dates back to his studies at Black Mountain College, and his first work acquired by the Museum of Modern Art in New York was, in fact, a photograph brought to the collection by Edward Steichen in 1952.[2] At Black Mountain, Rauschenberg found himself torn between photography and painting, settling on painting when he recognized that the project he would most like to fulfill as a photographer—a colossal "survey" of the United States composed of photographs of every square inch of ground—was unrealizable.[3] In 1979 he began to use his own photographs in his work, allowing them to suggest their own possibilities: "I think of the camera as my permission to walk into every shadow or watch while any light changes. Mine is the need to be where it will always never be the same again; a kind of archeology in time only, forcing one to see whatever the light or the darkness touches, and care. My concern is to move at a speed within which to act."[4]

In June 1982 Rauschenberg traveled to China on a trip arranged by Stanley Grinstein of Gemini G.E.L. for the purpose of collaborating with Xuan papermakers at the Jingxian paper mill in Anhui Province.[5] During this time he took over five hundred photographs, fifty-two of which were incorporated in the monumental *Chinese Summerhall*.[6] After returning to the United States, Rauschenberg began the process of selecting images for possible inclusion in *Chinese Summerhall*. George Holzer recalls that there were approximately fifty rolls of film, twelve exposures each. Holzer printed 11-by-14-inch color photographs of each negative and sent them to Rauschenberg for review. Rauschenberg made his choices, marking each photograph with the size to which it was to be enlarged—ranging from about 20-by-24 to 30-by-40 inches. From these enlargements, images were then cut and pasted to make the full-scale, hundred-foot mock-up.

I mostly sleep on the beach side in my place in Captiva, and it's just the roll, constantly the roll, of the waves. But my hide-away is on the Bay side, where each fish jumps separately, and each bird calls from a different place. China is more like the Bay side.

Robert Rauschenberg, Graphicstudio videotape, 1983

With the mock-up complete, actual production of the photograph still could not begin until individual prints were made of certain images that Rauschenberg had selected for editioning as studies. The finality of the imminent destruction of the negatives, which needed to be cut or trimmed in order to duplicate the images as Rauschenberg had collaged them in the mock-up, prompted the artist to rethink his original intention to edition only six studies as individual photographs. In the end, twenty-eight photographs were editioned individually. Five additional sections, approximately eight feet in length, were later taken, with slight variations, from the full image and were editioned as studies at Graphicstudio and copublished by Graphicstudio and Gemini G.E.L.

Details, cat. 76

Detail, cat. 76

Once production of the hundred-foot photograph began, a small-scale mock-up was made from the contact prints of the negatives so that the cumbersome, and somewhat fragile, full-scale mock-up would not have to be repeatedly rolled out. The fifty-two individual negatives were trimmed, masked, and carefully sealed into glass carriers. Each of the carriers could then be proofed separately, and adjustments made for color balance and exposure. Proofing of the photograph itself was carried out one fifteen-foot section at a time in Saff's studio, using up to five enlargers. Exposing the full one hundred feet took an average of eight to nine hours, and like the proofing, this was accomplished in sections. A dispenser was designed to hold the unexposed roll of photographic paper; after the exposure of a section, the paper would be rolled onto a core as the next section of paper moved into position. All of the actual development was done at the University of South Florida, with the entire photograph taking about two hours to process. The first of the five prints in the edition was finished one day before it was needed at the Castelli Gallery for the Rauschenberg exhibition scheduled to open there on New Year's Eve, 1982.[7]

A composite of vignettes from daily life in China, Rauschenberg's hundred-foot photograph reflects the vicissitudes of life—the protean, unsettled, kaleidoscopic mélange of thoughts, opinions, tasks, goals, and events that characterize human experience in modern society. As Rauschenberg explained, the country "was very rich texturally. In China, images seemed to isolate themselves."[8] As a visual montage, *Chinese Summerhall* reflects in part the perception of the reality of modern life as seen through the lens of the mass media (in the age of thirty-second commercials and ten-second sound bites). Images—cropped, trimmed, soft-focused, sharp-focused, close-up, panoramic, sideways, dissolved into other images—fill one's vision as one traverses the hundred-foot expanse. New connections resonate among the images as they interact in new ways with one another. There are incongruities: a blindfolded bull juxtaposed with a row of glass bottles;[9] the Great Wall dwarfed by a set of wheels—an immovable barrier versus the freedom of movement. There are also analogies: chickens scratch for their dinner, while nearby passengers commute on mass transit.

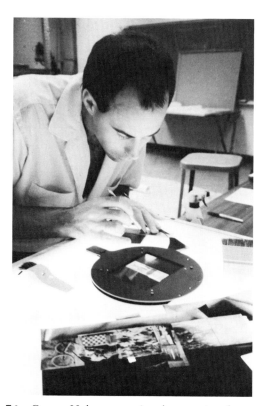

76a. George Holzer preparing the negatives for *Chinese Summerhall*, 1982

Rauschenberg views the scroll as a "compositional tale": "Colors and materials are the characters, and the piece unfolds according to its own appetite—what is already there dictates what goes next. I had no particular program about executing my feelings about China. I let the camera be my witness, as opposed to editorializing."[10] Rauschenberg's art has always charted unexplored territory, reached beyond the known limits. Monumental scale has frequently been integral to this process.[11] About his *Quarter Mile Piece*,[12] a work that was in progress at approximately the same time as *Chinese Summerhall*, Rauschenberg offers this insight: "You can never measure the effect scale has, but it does seem to be something permanent. If I had been born in Connecticut, I wouldn't have had the idea of doing a painting that is a quarter of a mile long."[13]

76b. Production studio for *Chinese Summerhall*, 1982

1. Confirmed in a telephone conversation with David White, Rauschenberg's curator, 29 January 1991.
2. See Smith 1983, 183, for a review of *Rauschenberg: Photographs*, New York 1981; *Photos In and Out City Limits: Boston* (West Islip, NY, 1981); and *Photos In and Out City Limits: New York C.* (West Islip, NY, 1982).
3. See Alain Sayag, "Interview with Robert Rauschenberg," in New York 1981.
4. Rauschenberg, in New York 1981. See Clifford Ackley, introduction to West Islip 1981, for discussion of Rauschenberg's involvement with photography.
5. For an account of the trip, see Donald Saff's essay in Los Angeles 1983. See also Fine 1984, 123–125.
6. George Holzer, conversation with Corlett, 23 August 1990.
7. Information concerning the progression of this project is taken from conversations between Holzer and Corlett, 23 August 1990 and 1 November 1990.

8. Rauschenberg, Graphicstudio videotape, January 1983.
9. Saff explained, in a conversation with Fine, 21 March 1991, that the blindfolded bull may be seen as a metaphor for Rauschenberg in China.
10. Herrera 1983, 57.
11. Early in his career Rauschenberg produced such large-scale works as *Autobiography* (1968), seventeen feet long; *Automobile Tire Print* (1951), around twenty-two feet long; and *Barge* (1963), thirty-two feet long. See also *Booster* (1967), "largest lithograph ever made on a hand-operated press" (Young 1974, 26); *Sky Garden* (1969), "largest, hand-rolled print in existence—a color lithograph and silkscreen on paper" (Greun 1977, 45); and *Currents* (1970), a fifty-four-foot screenprint.
12. A segment of *Quarter Mile Piece* was shown at Edison Community College in Fort Myers in 1982.
13. Rauschenberg 1986, 60.

77 Araucan Mastaba/ROCI Chile, 1985–1986

Sterling silver, lapis lazuli, screenprinted enamel, and hand-applied acrylic on polished
natural aluminum with plywood substructure
Overall dimensions: 20⁵/₈ x 22 x 22 (52.4 x 55.9 x 55.9); base: 14¹/₈ x 22 x 22
(36.3 x 55.9 x 55.9); envelope: 6¹/₂ x 4¹/₂ x ³/₁₆ (16.5 x 11.4 x .4);
lapis lazuli: 3 x 4 x 5 (7.6 x 10.2 x 12.7)
Proposed edition: 25; 2 BAT; 2 PrP; 1 GP; 1 USFP; 1 NGAP; 10 AP
Collaboration: Nick Conroy, Ken Elliott, Donald Saff, with Michael Harrigan, Susie
Hennessy, Darryl Pottorf, Deli Sacilotto, Lawrence Voytek, and Joel Meisner and Co.,
Inc., Bronze Aglow

78 Tibetan Garden Song/ROCI Tibet, 1985–1986

Commercially manufactured cello, chrome-plated #0 wash tub, glycerine, Chinese scroll-
maker's brush, mirrored Plexiglas
43 x 18¹/₄ (109.2 x 46.4) diameter
Proposed edition: 25; 2 BAT; 1 PrP; 1 GP; 1 USFP; 1 NGAP; 10 AP
Collaboration: Nick Conroy, Ken Elliott, Donald Saff, with Robert Calvo, Michael
Harrigan, Susie Hennessy

These sculpture projects are part of the body of work produced in conjunction with the Rauschenberg Overseas Culture Interchange (ROCI).[1]
Both were intended as editions of twenty-five; at this writing, twelve of
the *Araucan Mastaba* works and twenty of the *Tibetan Garden Song*
have been completed.

Perhaps it was inevitable that ROCI should be born, given Rauschenberg's career-long commitment to art as a singular means of communication and a force for social change. As he explained in 1983, "For about
three years, I've had this idea—to get involved in places which haven't
had contemporary American art to look at, countries such as China,
Russia, Sri Lanka, Egypt. Not only to show the work there, but to *make*
work in their setting, to use their materials, to deal with students, to collaborate with the major artist, poet or writer in each country, touching
on every aspect of art."[2]

ROCI was named for the artist's pet turtle, "Rocky," adopted in 1965
after the animal's stage debut with twenty-nine other turtles in a performance piece entitled *Spring Training*, a collaboration between Rauschenberg, Trisha Brown, and others at the First New York Theater Rally. At

77a. Ken Elliott (left) and Nick Conroy constructing the wooden substructures for the edition
of *Araucan Mastaba*, 1987

77

the appropriate moment, Rauschenberg's thirteen-year-old son Christopher released the turtles onto the stage, each with a flashlight strapped to its back. In oriental mythology the turtle is the bearer of the world.

Inspired in part by the richness of his interaction with artisans in China and Japan in 1982, Rauschenberg announced his goals for the ROCI project at the United Nations in December 1984. His stated mission was to promote the cause of world peace by facilitating intercultural understanding through artistic exchange. Since its inauguration at the Rufino Tamayo Museum in Mexico in April 1985, ROCI has toured Ieleven countries, closing with a major exhibition at the National Gallery of Art in Washington in the spring of 1991.

For each venue, using indigenous sources and materials whenever possible, Rauschenberg created new works to celebrate the distinctive life and art of that culture. The new works would be highlighted in that country's exhibition, then would travel to the next stop on the itinerary. After the exhibition moved on, the host country received a gift of Rauschenberg's work, and each progressive venue displayed a selection of works produced by Rauschenberg for all of the previous host countries. The exhibition thus grew organically, offering an eclectic mix of Rauschenberg's paintings, sculpture, photographs, and prints in order to "bring disparate philosophies or attitudes together through art."[3]

Araucan Mastaba was created in conjunction with ROCI's visit to Chile. The title of the piece refers to the Araucan Indian tribe native to Chile, whereas the silver of the envelope and the lapis lazuli pieces that support it were imported from that country for the execution of the edition. The mastaba, a flat-roofed structure with sloping sides found in ancient Egyptian architecture, is constructed of mirrored aluminum fitted over a wooden frame (fig. 77a). The images on each side of the pyramid were screened after the form was assembled, and a special table had to be built to cradle the piece for the screenprinting process.[4] Rauschenberg

I've given up on the politicians. Now it's up to the artists to wage peace.

Robert Rauschenberg, in Kotz 1989

selected the photographs for screening from the many he took while in Chile. The surface on one side, for example, is an image of dried, cracked mud that he photographed while exploring the copper mines in the north of the country.

Like many elements in Rauschenberg's works, the envelope in this piece has a particular history. Saff explains:

> Bob gave me an envelope that he had kept, a small manila envelope that had a string. I don't know whether they still exist. I never see those envelopes with string anymore, not in that size. He gave it to me, and I sent it to [the foundry], and the envelope was lost. So I had the job of calling Bob and asking, "Do you have another one of those envelopes?" He said he didn't, so I went all around looking for another one, and all I could find were the envelopes with the metal clasps. . . . So I called him back and told him I couldn't find that size envelope with a string. . . . His reaction was, "Well, that's O.K., no problem, I'll make one myself." So he got some fabric and from memory in terms of size, sewed up the fabric into an envelope, attached fabric buttons, wrapped string around them and sent me this little fabric envelope.[5]

Tibetan Garden Song is a variation on a sculpture produced for ROCI's Tibetan venue in which Rauschenberg combined an old washtub and a battered cello from which he hung a brick (fig. 78a). As one workshop collaborator explained, "The Graphicstudio work was not supposed to be a copy of that one, but that was the impetus for this variation."[6] The well-worn patina of the original washtub was transformed into a highly reflective surface in the edition through the process of chrome-plating. Three-quarter cellos (child-size) were imported from China, along with the scrollmakers' brushes that replaced the brick. Glycerine was used inside the tub, replacing the water that had led to the original work's eventual deterioration. A mirror at the bottom of the tub in the Graphicstudio piece further enhances the reflective quality of the chrome-plating and the glycerine.

In the shimmering surfaces of *Tibetan Garden Song*, enriched as they are with the suggestion of the resonant musical tones of the cello and the simple cadences that can be elicited from a washtub, Rauschenberg unites the pleasures of the eye and the ear. By alluding to the musical use of the washtub, he also suggests the alternative life of what is otherwise a common object with a mundane purpose. In 1985 he made the following observation, anticipating his work in Tibet: "It's going to be the most difficult country for me to paint for, or do any kind of collaboration, because I've always sort of secretly felt that my work was quite Tibetan already. Seeing some spiritual life in the most common object is very close to what they are all about and they also are not shy about colors. And they have a rich sense of extremes."[7]

78a. *Song for Tibetan Saga/ROCI Tibet*, 1985, assembled construction with glycerine, 47½ x 22 [diameter] (120.6 x 55.9), collection of the artist

1. Two other Rauschenberg projects were editioned at Graphicstudio in conjunction with ROCI: *Bamhue* (app. 208) was inspired by Japan, and *Fifth Force* (app. 206) anticipated an Italian venue, which ultimately did not make the tour. The ROCI exhibition was held at the Museo Nacional de Bellas Artes in Santiago, Chile, from 17 July to 18 August 1985, and at the Tibet Exhibition Hall in Lhasa, Tibet, from 2 December through 23 December 1985.

2. Rauschenberg, quoted in Kotz 1983, 57.

3. Rauschenberg, quoted in Jane Addams Allen, "Rauschenberg's Worldwide Art Exchange," *Washington Times*, 31 May 1985, B5.

4. Ken Elliot and Nick Conroy, taped interview with Fine, 23 August 1990.

5. Saff, taped interview with Fine, June 1990.

6. Elliot, interview with Fine, 1990.

7. Rauschenberg, quoted in Mary Battiata, "Rauschenberg, the Art Explorer: The Avant Garde Master's Plans for a Worldwide Creation," *Washington Post*, 1 June 1985, D1.

78

RECENT EXPERIMENTS

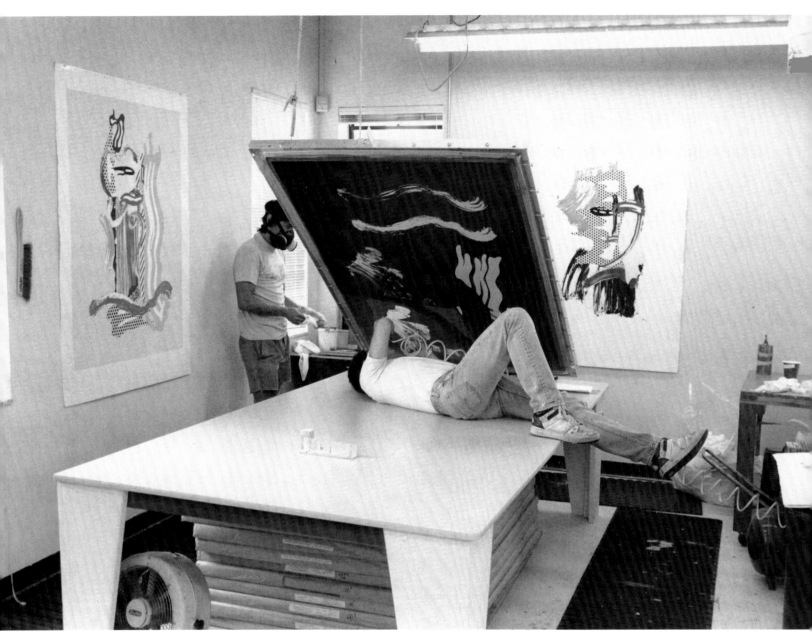

Tim Amory (left) and Richard Karnatz clean the stainless steel screen between runs for Roy Lichtenstein's *The Mask* (app. 138), October 1988

SANDRO CHIA

Born in Florence, Italy, 1946
Lives and works in New York

AS A BOY, SANDRO CHIA played soccer in the Piazza Santo Spirito, after which he would stray into nearby cathedrals where he found himself captivated by the work of Filippino Lippi or Masaccio. Chia's father encouraged this interest by promoting family excursions on Sunday afternoons to the Uffizi Gallery, and by the time Chia was a teenager, he had decided to be an artist.

In 1962 Chia began studies at the Istituto d'Arte in Florence, which offered a traditional program that gave him a solid grounding in conventional methods and materials. He studied etching there with Rodolfo Margheri. His education took an abrupt turn in 1967, when he enrolled at the Accademia di Belle Arti, where for the next few years he was exposed to a progressive philosophy of making art that was intellectual and political in orientation.

After graduating from the Accademia in 1969, Chia traveled to India, and on his return he took an apartment in Rome. During the early 1970s he was involved with installations and process-oriented art, his first one-man show being an installation at the Galleria La Salita, Rome, in 1971. Increasingly dissatisfied with this approach, Chia took up painting again in the mid-1970s. His work was first shown in the United States in 1980, in a three-person exhibition with Francesco Clemente and Enzo Cucci at the Sperone-Westwater-Fischer Gallery in New York. That same year he established a studio in New York City.

In addition to Graphicstudio, Chia has worked with such workshops and printers as Stamperia d'Arte Grafica/Studio S. Reparata in Florence, as well as Patricia Branstead at Aeropress, and Francesco Copello, Felix Harlan, and Carol Weaver in New York. In 1980 Chia was awarded a fellowship to work in Mönchengladbach, Germany. In 1985 he completed a major sculpture commission installed in the public square in Bielefeld, Germany.

Chia has had numerous exhibitions in Europe, the United States, and Japan, including those at the Stedelijk Museum, Amsterdam (1983), Kestner Gesellschaft, Hannover (1983), Städtisches Museum Abteiberg, Mönchengladbach, Germany (1983), Staatliche Kunsthalle, Berlin (1984), Musée d'art modern de la ville de Paris (1984), Kunstverein für die Rheinlande und Westfalen, Düsseldorf (1984), Akira Ikeda Gallery, Tokyo (1984, 1986, 1990), Kunsthalle Bielefeld (1986), and Museum Modernerkunst, Salzburg (1989). An exhibition of Chia's prints was held at the Metropolitan Museum of Art, New York in 1984.

Sandro Chia positioning frame elements for *Father and Son Song* (cat. 79), May 1987

79 Father and Son Song, 1987–1989

Color heliorelief and hand-carved color woodcut on hot-pressed T. H. Saunders drawing
paper, with painted oak and gum plywood frame and assemblage
With frame: 85³/₄ x 75⁵/₈ x 4¹/₄ (217.8 x 192.1 x 10.8)
Edition: 12; 1 BAT (print only); 1 BAT; 1 PP; 2 PrP; 1 NGAP; 1 GP; 1 USFP; 4 AP
Collaboration: Greg Burnet, Nick Conroy, George Holzer, Alan Holoubek, Johntimothy
Pizzuto, Tom Pruitt, Donald Saff, Eric Vontillius
Frame fabricated by Art Techtonics, Tampa
Gift of Graphicstudio/University of South Florida and the Artist in Honor of the Fiftieth
Anniversary of the National Gallery of Art

Sandro Chia's art has been consciously forged from the vast and varied
traditions that form the art historical legacy of Western civilization. He
freely draws on the work of Michelangelo, Tintoretto, de Chirico,
Umberto Boccioni, and Ottone Rosai, all Italians, as well as the Span-
iard Picasso, to name only a few.[1] Conflating stylistic and iconographic
elements to create new relationships, new metaphors, new symbols,
Chia alludes to these sources without quoting them directly. The pensive
posture of the large, seated figure in *Father and Son Song* has roots that
extend to medieval depictions of Adam contemplating his fate. Centuries
later Rodin adapted the pose for his statue *The Thinker*. These references add richness to Chia's image and allow a broader, multifaceted interpretation of the father-and-son theme.

Chia frequently uses shifts in scale to establish the dynamics of his figural relationships. The scheme found in *Father and Son Song* is also evident in such works as *Son Sun Pun* (1985).[2] Both depict the diminutive,
if agile, youth attempting to climb over the looming, heroic, Michelan-
gelesque man, which suggests not only Chia's art historical parentage
but also the dilemma the contemporary artist faces in dealing with this
legacy. Chia has commented:

> As an artist, I can only be a link in a long chain. It is love-hate yes. Tradi-
> tion, this tradition of art, it is the voices of the dead fathers in a way. All the
> dead artists—the dead fathers. On the one hand, this history is fascinating,

79a. Drawing for *Father and Son Song*, c. 1987–
1989, marker on mylar, in two parts, left: 87¹/₈ x
42 (221.3 x 106.7); right: 91¹/₄ x 42 (231.8 x
106.7), 1991.75.74–75

it attracts you. The tradition shows you all the possibilities, the changes to approximate truth, the depth of things. So I love painting. But then there is the tradition also telling you always, you can't be an artist, there is no room for you. So today, you have not only to make the work—some expression of the artist's self—but you have to make the necessity of the work, to create a reason for it. How can I make a painting? That is the existential problem. But then how do I connect with everything that has been done?[3]

Father and Son Song thus suggests a complex personal metaphor that explores the parallel themes of paternity, ancestry, inheritance, and the ongoing give-and-take between generations. These are recurring themes in Chia's oeuvre, as evident from such titles as *Fisher and His Son* (1984) and *Pharmacist's Son* (1981). A corresponding theme, alluded to in the undaunted efforts of the climbing boy in *Father and Son Song*, is that of the fearlessness of youth: "Art and the world are at once united and divided by a profound chasm and any bridges thrown up between the two in order to facilitate reciprocal comprehension and commerce are contrived and inadequate. The only way I know to make the connection is to leap without fear like a courageous boy."[4]

Chia occasionally combines art historical references with allusions to popular culture.[5] In *Father and Son Song* the bold, flat areas of printed color textured by the woodblock invite comparison with a child's

79b. The pattern for placement of the frame elements of *Father and Son Song*, March 1988

wooden puzzle. The association becomes even more compelling with the addition of the assemblage of colorful wooden shapes—each of which can be matched to a shape in the woodcut composition—swirling around the outer perimeter of the image, forming both a visual and physical frame. The floating quality of the wooden forms is echoed within the composition by two black-and-white forms: above the head and across the chest and thigh of the large figure, they appear to be simultaneously in front of and behind the overall composition. Their lack of color might suggest that they are spaces behind missing puzzle pieces. This doubling of the imagery—here the echo of the two-dimensional woodcut with its three-dimensional surroundings—has played a continuous role in Chia's art, dating at least to 1971 when he produced the installation piece *L'Ombra e il suo doppio* (*The Shadow and Its Double*).[6]

There is a special harmony between the general appearance of Chia's images and the technique in which they are executed. Chia has always reveled in the process of making art, maximizing the inherent properties of his medium, whether it be the thick, succulent strokes of oil paint or the delicacy and variety of the etched line.[7] In *Father and Son Song* the sharp lines and bold forms reveal the vigor possible in the woodcut medium, while the beauty of the texture of the woodblock is optimized, as the direction of the wood grain varies from vertical to horizontal to diagonal in the composition. Chia employed both the heliorelief process and hand-carving to execute this woodcut. The energy characteristic of Chia's images can be seen in the sense of movement generated by the lyrical flow of the wood assemblage around the edges of the piece. Furthermore, the use of these wooden shapes is a lighthearted play on the nature of the "woodcut."

Printmaking has long been important to Chia, who at various times has set up his own etching studios in Ronciglione, Italy, and in Manhattan: "Sometimes something from my painting transfers to prints, and sometimes it is the opposite. . . . I like to pass between the two disciplines. This makes the work grow, which can manifest itself in prints, painting, or drawing."[8]

The print shop is a little mysterious, with all those machines and devices. It's like an alchemist's laboratory, a place where transformations occur. And art and alchemy are the same, and unlike science, because they're both looking for something that's impossible to find.
Sandro Chia, in Hawthorne 1986

1. For a discussion of Chia's sources, with mention of Ottone Rosai (1895–1957), see Hughes 1983, 79. See also Ratcliff 1982, 152–159.
2. *Son Sun Pun* is reproduced in *Chia*, Spoleto 1988, pl. 38. Henry Geldzahler discusses Chia's scale shifts in relation to his small etching, *Lesson in Geometry* (1979), in "Sandro Chia Etchings 1972–84," *Chia*, New York 1984, 6.
3. Chia, in Marzorati 1983, 60. In Weisner 1986, 28, Chia also referred to his art works as his sons: "My loved ones, tender sons, I have not abandoned you, but the fact is that the King of France is more capricious than the Pope, and the ferocious attacks of those who do not understand, from London, from Amsterdam, from Basel, always more blind, always more unjust, detain me somewhere else at the moment." Chia often recycles images from within his own oeuvre to create new relationships, suggest new meanings. The reclining colossal figure in *Father and Son Song* is recreated, for example, in the color drawing, *Golden Thoughts* (reproduced in Weisner 1986, colorplate 12). The climbing youth in *Fa-ther and Son Song* can be seen, in reverse, in the painting *Figures at Nightfall* (1986), and in *Revolution Destitution Execution* (1986), where Chia rendered him climbing over the knee of a colossal seated figure (both of these works are reproduced in *Chia*, Spoleto 1988, plates 34, 33).
4. Sandro Chia in a letter to Edy de Wilde, 20 February 1983, published in *Chia*, Amsterdam 1983.
5. One obvious example would be the painting, *Padre, Figlio e Babar*, reproduced in *Chia*, Spoleto 1988, no. 28, where Chia combined the iconography of the Christ Child with a rendering of the elephant Babar, the storybook character created by Jean de Brunhoff.
6. This work was installed at the Galleria La Salita in 1971. Waldman 1982, 10, points out that since that time, double images have continued to resurface in Chia's work.
7. Waldman 1982, 10, notes that in Chia's painting he "celebrates the physical properties of the medium."
8. Chia, quoted in Berger 1982, 169.

ROY LICHTENSTEIN

Born in New York City, 1923
Lives and works in New York City and Southampton, New York

AS A CHILD, ROY LICHTENSTEIN was interested in science, but in high school he began to draw and paint. He also developed a passion for jazz, making frequent visits to jazz clubs, which inspired him to make paintings of the musicians. He studied with Reginald Marsh in summer classes at the Art Students League. After graduation from high school he attended Ohio State University in Columbus, where he was influenced by Hoyt L. Sherman's explorations into the nature of human vision and perception. He was drafted into the army in 1943 and served in Europe until his discharge in 1946, at which point he resumed his studies at Ohio State under the GI Bill (B.F.A. 1946; M.F.A. 1949). He was an instructor at Ohio State from 1946 to 1951 and later taught at the State University of New York in Oswego, and Douglass College, Rutgers University, where he developed a friendship with Allan Kaprow.

Among Lichtenstein's earliest subjects was the American West, rendered in a style influenced by cubism. In the late 1950s his nonfigurative art reflected an interest in abstract expressionism. He was also exploring comic strip imagery in his drawings, and a turning point came in 1961 when he painted *Look Mickey*, the first of his paintings to use comic strip characters and conventions and deliberately imitate commercial printing processes with the benday dot. He quickly emerged as a leading practitioner of pop art and was included in the *New Paintings of Common Objects* show at the Pasadena Art Museum (1962), the first museum exhibition to examine the new style. He has since used his signature style to explore a variety of subjects, including still life, explosions, brushstrokes, and art movements including cubism, surrealism, and expressionism.

Lichtenstein has completed several large-scale public sculptures as well as a number of major murals. He experimented with printmaking as early as the 1950s and has collaborated with Gemini G.E.L. in Los Angeles, Mourlot in Paris, Styria Studios in New York, Tyler Graphics, Ltd., in Mount Kisco, New York, in addition to Graphicstudio. Lichtenstein has been elected to the American Institute of Arts and Letters, New York. Additional honors include the Skowhegan Award for Painting and honorary doctorates from the California Institute of Arts in Valencia and Ohio State University.

Lichtenstein's first museum exhibition was held at the Cleveland Museum of Art in 1966. Other important exhibitions have been organized by the Pasadena Art Museum (1967), Stedelijk Museum, Amsterdam (1967), Solomon R. Guggenheim Museum, New York (1969), Contemporary Arts Museum, Houston (1972), Centre national d'art contemporain, Paris (1975), Staatliche Museen Preussischer Kulturbesitz, Berlin (1975), Saint Louis Art Museum (1981), Columbus Museum of Art, Ohio (1985), and the Museum of Modern Art, New York (1987). His prints were featured in exhibitions at the Fogg Art Museum, Cambridge, Massachusetts (1975), and the Whitney Museum of American Art, New York (1981).

Roy Lichtenstein enjoying his *Brushstroke Chair, Bronze*, and *Brushstroke Ottoman, Bronze* (fig. 80c), July 1987

80 Brushstroke Chair, Wood, and Brushstroke Ottoman, Wood, 1986–1988

White birch veneer, paint, and varnish
Chair: 70¹¹/₁₆ x 18 x 27¹/₄ (179.5 x 45.7 x 69.2)
Ottoman: 20³/₄ x 17³/₄ x 24 (52.7 x 45.1 x 61.0)
Edition: 12 (1/12 through 8/12 without ottomans; 9/12 through 12/12 with ottomans);
1 BAT; 1 NGAP; 1 USFP; 3 AP
Collaboration: Donald Saff and Beeken/Parsons (Bruce Beeken and Jeff Parsons, with Jesse Metcalf)

Brushstroke Chair, Wood, and *Brushstroke Ottoman, Wood*, were an outgrowth of the preliminary research and experimentation conducted at Graphicstudio prior to Roy Lichtenstein's Brushstroke Figures project (see cats. 81–83). Saff explains: "As good fortune would have it, our experiments at Graphicstudio with the Brushstroke form from Mr. Lichtenstein's studio floor included rendering the sample shape in virtually every sculpture medium but bronze. These forms, along with the other experiments in waxtype and various other print media, were presented to Mr. Lichtenstein for this review. He would later relate to me that, upon seeing the samples, his mind immediately grasped the idea for a sculpture project and that the concept of a furniture motif would not leave his thoughts."[1]

80a. Woodworker Jesse Metcalf of Beeken/
Parsons with laminations for *Brushstroke Chair,
Wood*, pressed inside the fabrication mold, 1987

After nine months of research into the structural characteristics as well as the visual aesthetics of the surfaces of various veneers, a satisfactory wood prototype was built at the furniture-making shop of Beeken/ Parsons in Shelburne, Vermont. Drawings on mylar, including side elevations, were made from the artist's cardboard mock-up. The mold in which to press the veneers (fig. 80a) was then fabricated. As Jeff Parsons explained: "We made patterns from those [drawings]. From the patterns we made the parts of the forms, then bolted all the parts of the forms together, and *then* we made the prototype."[2]

The creation of an undulating brushstroke form that was structurally sound enough to function as a chair presented a challenge even to experienced woodworkers: "There was more involved than we thought there probably would be at the onset. Fairly quickly we realized that the amount of pressure that was going to be required to meet the glue specifications was going to be significant. With some primitive calculations we realized the best thing we could do was get some engineering help. A couple of engineers [from] the University of Vermont sat down with us and in about two hours of calculations came up with a shopping list of the steel that we needed to distribute the pressure evenly and deliver the amount of pressure that was going to be required [see fig. 80b]."[3]

Beeken and Parsons discovered that more pressure was needed to close the form than was required simply to shape and adhere the veneers:

The engineers told us that this form needed 462,000 pounds of pressure— about 200 pounds a square inch—and that if we used a torque wrench, 50 foot-pounds of torque on each bolt would do it. We got the torque wrench on there and realized that that amount of pressure was not going to close the form. The form was resisting closing, and it does that because of the veneers. When you run a straight veneer piece across an indentation [in the form], when the indentations come closed, they trap the veneers. It takes a lot of pressure to cause the veneers to slide against the form such that the form can actually close. So, we went with an extension [to torque the bolts down], and we probably have three times the pressure. We think there's between a million and a million and a half cumulative pounds of pressure on this one.[4]

80b. Veneers for *Brushstroke Ottoman, Wood*, being placed in the mold for initial pressing

80c. *Brushstroke Chair, Bronze*, and *Brushstroke Ottoman, Bronze*, 1986–1988 (see app. 133), Collection of Boris and Sophie Leavitt

The final wood edition of the chair was assembled from two major components: the front leg, seat, and back of the chair are one part, while the back leg and underside are another. The ottoman combines two sections in similar fashion. Each component was constructed of twenty-seven sheets of white birch veneer, glued together in three individual layers: seven veneer sheets were pressed and glued for the top layer, while seven additional veneers were laminated for the bottom layer, and thirteen sheets formed the inner core. The cut-out areas of the two exterior layers were accomplished with a jigsaw, following a template developed from the full-scale drawing. The corresponding areas on the central core were hand-painted in blue, and all three layers were placed into the mold for the final gluing. The jigsaw was also used to finish shaping the outer edges. A bronze version of the chair and ottoman was later cast at the Walla Walla Foundry (formerly Bronze Aglow) in Washington state.

Sculpture has had continuing importance in Lichtenstein's oeuvre. The brushstroke furniture is, in one respect, an extension of an idea the artist explored in the 1960s. In a discussion about his painted ceramic sculpture heads of the mid-1960s, Lichtenstein commented that he was intrigued with "putting two-dimensional symbols on a three-dimensional object."[5] The *Brushstroke Chair* and *Ottoman*, like the Ceramic Heads and Stacks of Dishes created two decades earlier, are two-dimensional images interpreted as three-dimensional forms. Lichtenstein mines the vocabulary of the two-dimensional in creating his sculpture, often suggesting how objects depicted on a flat surface might look if they existed in three dimensions as they appear when rendered in two dimensions. In forcing the realization that what appears to be realistically depicted is actually nothing more than an intellectual construct, Lichtenstein calls into question the viewer's understanding of reality and its many possible interpretations.

The idea of an incorporeal entity—the brushstroke—rendered as a solid three-dimensional form was of interest to Lichtenstein throughout the 1980s. His monumental *Brushstrokes in Flight* was installed at the Columbus International Airport in 1982. His twenty-five-foot sculpture, *Salute to Painting*, was unveiled at the Walker Art Center in 1986. That same year, shortly before he began work with Graphicstudio, Lichtenstein completed work with Tyler Graphics, Ltd., on a series of six painted brushstroke wall reliefs. In works such as *Brushstrokes in Flight* Lichtenstein's undulating "strokes" appear to be "painted" over the environment they are set against (reminiscent of the hand with the paintbrush that enters the picture screen in animated features to brush out—or brush in—a change of scene). In a similar way, the *Brushstroke Chair* and *Brushstroke Ottoman*, with their sinuous curves, seem to fold over the surrounding space as if clinging to an invisible surface. Their undulating waves simultaneously suggest motion and, conversely, movement that has somehow been frozen in time.

You see, I think that sculpture, from Egyptian reliefs to Brancusi, is to a large extent the same kind of problem. Volume does enter your experience, of course, but the significance of the volume created is that it forms contrasts. I don't want to argue that sculpture is really two-dimensional. I am just saying that the thing that is significant about this organization is that it is unified in the same way as a drawing. I think it is not important that the artist understand this physiologically or psychologically. If his instincts lead him to this kind of order, it's not important that it be formalized in any way.

Roy Lichtenstein, in Glenn 1977

1. Saff, "Roy Lichtenstein: Waxtype and Other Media in *Brushstroke Figures*," in *Lichtenstein*, Gothenburg 1989.
2. Jeff Parsons, videotape made by Terry Van Brunt at Shelburne Farms, Vermont, summer 1988.
3. Parsons, videotape, 1988.
4. Parsons, videotape, 1988.
5. Lichtenstein, quoted in Coplans 1967 (reprinted in New York 1972, 91).

81 Roads Collar, 1987–1989

Color lithograph, woodcut, screenprint, and waxtype on 638 g/m² cold-pressed Saunders Waterford paper
52⅝ x 28¾ (133.7 x 73)
Edition: 30; 1 BAT; 2 PP; 2 PrP; 1 NGAP; 1 GP; 1 USFP; 2 SP; 8 AP
Collaboration: Patrick Foy, Alan Holoubek, George Holzer, Tom Pruitt, Donald Saff, with Tim Amory, Greg Burnet, Wendy Elias, Ken Elliott, Eleanor Erskine, Richard Karnatz, Kelly Medei, Johntimothy Pizzuto, Eric Vontillius

Lichtenstein's Brushstroke Figures, a series of eight images produced at Graphicstudio between 1987 and 1989 using an inventive combination of print processes, continue the figure and portrait compositions the artist had been creating on canvas at this time.[1] Considered as a whole, the series is almost kaleidoscopic in effect, involving the rearrangement of similar components to develop entirely new images.

Overlapping but distinctly individual brushstrokes form the building blocks for Lichtenstein's Brushstroke Figures, which incorporate the staples of the artist's vocabulary—the benday dots, diagonal stripes, swirls of "real" brushstrokes and hard-edged "cartoon" brushstrokes. The techniques used to render each of the elements vary from print to print, thus in one print the benday dot brushstrokes may be woodcut, whereas in another they are waxtype. Lichtenstein approached all of his Brushstroke Figures with the wit and humor characteristic of his oeuvre. Perhaps the most playful, seemingly spontaneous image in the series is *Roads Collar*, where the subject sports a round, clownlike nose with a white dot at the center—a humorous counterpoint to the red benday

dots surrounded by white in the neighboring brushstroke. The yellow brushstroke outlined in black that forms the shock of blonde hair and the gestural spontaneity of the bronze "collar" add to the playfulness of this image.

Brushstroke Figures were the first works to use the waxtype process devised by Graphicstudio. Conceived as a printmaking equivalent to encaustic painting and developed by Patrick Foy and others at the workshop under Donald Saff's direction, waxtype is a screenprint process, but instead of ink, pigmented beeswax is squeegeed through a specially prepared steel screen.[2] Once on the page, the wax can be "burned in," that is, heated with a microtorch, resulting in a glossy, translucent encaustic surface: "the screened wax formula is melted with a torch and buffed in a number of successive overlays that create a kind of sheen enhancing the luminosity, translucency, and intensity of color saturation of the medium, while building up the soft-edge impasto effects of true encaustic brushstrokes."[3] The wax can also be left unheated, thereby retaining a matte surface with a fabriclike texture that results from the contact of the wax with the screen.

Saff has described his visit to the artist's studio, with preliminary wax-type samples in hand:

> At that time, Mr. Lichtenstein was in the midst of a painting frenzy. Several paintings were being worked on and a number of his well-known brush-stroke forms were spread out on the studio floor. I picked up one of the smaller forms and asked if I could return to Tampa with it for the purpose of conducting experiments in a variety of media and materials. . . . The form was executed in glass, plastic, and wood sculptural forms and used in lithography, woodblock, waxtype, and screenprinting experiments. When presented with the results of this experimentation, it was a relatively short time before the ideas for the *Brushstroke Figures* suite fell into place.[4]

While exploiting the tactile properties of waxtype, Lichtenstein created a dialogue of textures on the surface of each of the Brushstroke Figure prints by combining the new process with lithography, woodcut, and screenprint. Each process yields a different nuance of texture: the smooth, crisp screenprinted images; the soft, dry opacity of the litho-graphic stroke (created by applying Xerox toner and alcohol to the plate with a rag, then heating the plate to fuse the toner for further processing and printing); the lush, wet, shimmering quality of the "burned in" en-caustic; the matte, fabriclike surface of the wax that has not been fixed with heat; and the wood grain variations produced by the woodblock.

Three different methods were employed for cutting the woodblocks in this series: hand-cutting, routing, and the Graphicstudio heliorelief pro-cess.[5] The woodcut element for *Roads Collar* was hand-cut. Lichtenstein had previously explored the humor in the apparent paradox of using a rigid woodblock to produce the image of a fluid mark (the brushstroke) when he incorporated woodcut brushstrokes in a series of apple still lifes published by Petersburg Press in 1982. In the Petersburg Press prints suc-cessive printings (four to six) were deliberately used to reduce or elimi-nate the appearance of wood grain.[6] In the Graphicstudio prints, where texture plays an integral role, Lichtenstein varied the prominence of the wood grain, minimizing it in some areas by using a fine-textured birch wood, and maximizing it in others with a high-grained walnut block.

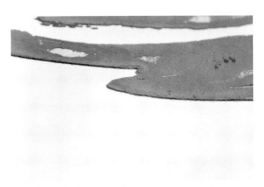

81a. Detail of screened wax on paper, prior to "burning in"

1. See, for example, *Portrait* (1986), re-produced in *American Masters,* New York 1990, 31. For related sculpture, see *Roy Lichtenstein: Bronze Sculpture 1976–1989* [exh. cat., 65 Thompson Street] (New York, 1989), cats. 28–31.
2. The screen must be coated with silicon to facilitate release of wax, and pres-surized air was periodically forced through the screens to clean them during proofing and editioning.
3. Saff, in *Lichtenstein,* Gothenburg 1989.
4. Saff, in *Lichtenstein,* Gothenburg 1989.
5. Lichtenstein's interest in woodcut dates back to the 1950s. Living and working in Columbus and Cleveland, Ohio, he ex-plored the process along with intaglio and lithography. In 1951 he received the Pur-chase Prize in the Fifth National Print Annual at the Brooklyn Museum for a woodcut entitled *The Battle*. Phillips 1982, 93, notes that during the three years preceding 1982 virtually all of the artist's prints had been woodcuts. Lich-tenstein is considered to have played a major role in the revival of the technique during the last decade.
6. See *PCN* 13, no. 6 (Jan.-Feb. 1983), 218, for a description of how the apple woodcuts were produced.

a

These photographs provide an overview of the methods used by Graphicstudio staff to produce Lichtenstein's multimedia prints: a) the artist drawing a lithographic plate; b) carving a woodblock to the artist's specifications; c) mixing wax for the waxtype process; d) examining a proof; e–f) applying gold pigment to printed wax and removing the excess; g) buffing a wax mark; and h) the artist (second from left) signing an edition

b

c

d

e

f

g

h

82 Portrait, 1987–1989

Color lithograph, woodcut, screenprint, and waxtype on 638 g/m² cold-pressed
Saunders Waterford paper
52⁹/₁₆ x 34¹/₄ (133.5 x 87)
Edition: 60; 1 BAT; 2 PP; 2 PrP; 1 NGAP; 1 GP; 1 USFP; 2 SP; 8 AP
Collaboration: Patrick Foy, Alan Holoubek, George Holzer, Tom Pruitt, Donald Saff, with
Tim Amory, Greg Burnet, Wendy Elias, Ken Elliott, Eleanor Erskine, Richard Karnatz,
Kelly Medei, Johntimothy Pizzuto, Eric Vontillius

Lichtenstein began using the brushstroke motif during the 1960s, but it
was two decades later that it was to become, along with the renowned
benday dots, a signature of his style. His brushstroke imagery has
evolved from his fairly simple, straightforward (Franz Kline-like) brushstroke compositions of the 1960s, rendered in a cartoon manner, to the
increasingly complex interwoven systems of benday dots, diagonals,
"real" and "cartoon" brushstrokes that can be seen in the Graphicstudio
prints. In his Brushstroke Figures, Lichtenstein continues the exploration
of the brushstroke, that fundamental artist's mark, by combining real
and cartoon strokes as he had in still-life and landscape paintings and
prints of the 1980s.[1]

Lichtenstein exploits the inherent tension between the associations
of a representational image and the physical reality of pigment on a
ground. His brushstrokes simultaneously suggest movement—the act of

creating the brushstroke, the gesture—as well as the physical, static two-dimensional mark itself. Often in the Graphicstudio prints the combination of diverse means of rendering the brushstroke—the benday dots, diagonal stripes, and cartoonlike images that are the aesthetic vocabulary out of which the artist constructs his visual language—creates a feeling of metamorphosis, as if the image as a whole is transmogrifying from one existence to another. This is especially true of Lichtenstein's *Green Face* (fig. 82a), where a face in the mirror seems to be dissolving (or is it forming?). The figure in *Green Face* is a fleeting, ephemeral, protean image—not unlike what one sees with a glance in a mirror.[2]

In images like the Brushstroke Figures, Lichtenstein seems to have traveled full circle from his early work in the abstract expressionist style. The sinuous, roving red stroke that wraps around the "face" in *Portrait* and meanders downward to meet the horizontal bronze stroke near the bottom of the composition has an expressive, gestural quality that is reminiscent of the cartoon images the artist executed in an abstract expressionist style during the late 1950s. But the hesitancy of the early pop gestural works, now distilled and refined by Lichtenstein's formal pop vocabulary (dots, diagonals, the cartoon idiom), is, in works like the Brushstroke Figures, replaced with a sureness that reflects the intercession of the pop style.

Lichtenstein's interest in exploring new textural possibilities is another component of his aesthetic that has its roots early in his career—in his use of Rowlux, for example, during the 1960s.[3] The artist has mixed sand and mica into paint to create the Entablature paintings of the 1970s; he also used metallic foils, along with both embossing and debossing, to achieve the interplay of surface textures in a series of Entablature prints produced during those years. Lichtenstein has commented that part of his fascination with the benday dots—which have come to be synonymous with his art—is the interplay of the textures of paint and canvas set up by the intermittent spacing of crisp circles of pigment.[4]

The waxtype process was therefore of special interest to Lichtenstein, offering as it does lush, translucent color and numerous textural possibilities not obtainable with other printing processes. The large green vertical stroke in *Portrait* was produced using successive layers of wax—screened and then separately burned in to control both texture and tonality. In other Graphicstudio prints dry pigment was brushed through the screen over the burned in wax, yielding a unique depth of color, and an iridescence, as in the print *Blonde* (app. 134), where gold pigment has been printed over the dark blue wax and then slightly burned in to create a shimmering stroke. Metallic inks as used in *Portrait*, the mirrored mylar elements in *The Mask* (app. 138), and the aluminum powder rubbed into the wet wax of the gray background in *Grandpa* (cat. 83) add further tactile/textural interest.

82a. *Green Face*, 1987–1989 (app. 137)

1. See also Castleman 1991, 89–93, for additional discussion of Lichtenstein's brushstroke motif and the Brushstroke Figures.
2. The incorporation of the mirror in *Green Face* is an expressionistic return to the subject of the mirror explored by Lichtenstein in both paintings and prints during the early 1970s in his hard-edge, cartoon style. See Cowart 1981, 16–30.

3. For a brief comment by the artist on his use of Rowlux, see Waldman 1971, 28.
4. Tuchman 1974, 27, records the following statement by the artist concerning texture and the benday dot: "Well, one thing might be the texture: areas of dots next to unmodulated color. It created meanings which I didn't really understand—except that it moved me."

83 Grandpa, 1987–1989

Color lithograph, woodcut, screenprint, and waxtype on 638 g/m² cold-pressed
Saunders Waterford paper
57 x 41¹/₈ (144.8 x 104.4)
Edition: 60; 1 BAT; 2 PP; 2 PrP; 1 NGAP; 1 GP; 1 USFP; 2 SP; 8 AP
Collaboration: Patrick Foy, Alan Holoubek, George Holzer, Tom Pruitt, Donald Saff, with
Tim Amory, Greg Burnet, Wendy Elias, Ken Elliott, Eleanor Erskine, Richard Karnatz,
Kelly Medei, Johntimothy Pizzuto, Eric Vontillius

Lichtenstein is able to achieve a wonderfully poignant expression in the image of *Grandpa* using masterfully few "strokes." The lyrical, flowing quality of the the red "nose" stroke is contained by its own hard, wood-cut edges, over which rides a horizontal stroke of violet and under which lies a controlled field of benday dots. Tightly interlocked compositional elements—for example, the small yet essential dark blue dot above Grandpa's right eye—are characteristic of each of the images in the Brushstroke Figures series. The seemingly spontaneous appearance of

I also don't think color relationships mean any-thing if they're independent of form relationships.
Roy Lichtenstein, in Tuchman 1974

the arrangement, with its large, sweeping brushstrokes, belies the reality of the complex visual organization.

Each of the Brushstroke Figure compositions began as a collage specifically created for this project. In their interlocking patterns of shape and color, the prints retain a collagelike appearance—an association that is reinforced by the fabriclike, tactile density of the waxtype. Master printer Patrick Foy has commented: "The Lichtenstein project was definitely [one of] the most satisfying, simply because it was the most challenging. [It was the] most complicated [project] in terms of the combination of all the elements. . . . We spent five weeks just printing that gray background on *Grandpa*. That's a long time. So, we were still figuring things out when we were editioning."[11]

The pigmented wax used in the process was a precise mixture of beeswax, solvent, and either dry or concentrated pigments. Obtaining the precise hues required by the artist added further complexity to the project: "We were trying to do something that hadn't been done and do it quickly, and get specific colors, not just a red that was a suitable red. It had to be exactly his red or his green. And the colors react differently with the wax. When you mix them with the wax they go different ways than they typically would. You couldn't just use a cadmium yellow [pigment] to come up with cadmium yellow. You'd have to modify it in different ways. It took a lot of refinement."

The mixing of the colors required exact measurements of all the ingredients and precise control of the temperature of the melted wax; a slight variation would affect the color saturation. Even the rate the wax was stirred during the mixing process played a role in the resulting color. As Foy recalls: "For the first proof I was working in a classroom at the music school, with my hot plate and my mixer, trying to develop the palette of colors for all of the prints. . . . The very first tests of the waxes were [thus] hand-mixed. . . . You had to stir it until it cooled to the point that [the mixture] was thick enough that the pigment wouldn't settle out. Then we figured out we could use an electric mixer to do that part, but that changed everything because the harder and faster you mixed some of the pigments, the more intense the color becomes, so you had to specifically time how long. . . . if you mixed it for two minutes longer it came out a different color."

83a. Roy Lichtenstein (kneeling), with Don Saff (rear) and Lichtenstein's assistant James de Pasquale examining collages for prints in New York, February 1987

1. Foy, telephone conversation with Corlett, 4 November 1990.

Other quotations are taken from this conversation.

NANCY GRAVES

Born in Pittsfield, Massachusetts, 1940
Lives and works in New York City

BY THE AGE OF TWELVE NANCY GRAVES knew she was going to be an artist. Her interest was fed by repeated visits to the Berkshire Museum in her hometown, where her father was assistant to the director. The combination of art and natural history in that museum's collection was a formative influence in the approach to art she later developed, merging disciplines such as the natural sciences, history, and cultural studies.

Graves took art classes at Vassar College, but majored in English literature (B.A. 1961). She was awarded a scholarship to the Yale Summer School of Music and Art in Norfolk, Connecticut (1959), which led to her enrollment at the Yale School of Art and Architecture (B.F.A. 1962; M.F.A. 1964). There she studied painting with Jack Tworkov, Alex Katz, and Al Held, among others. In 1964 she was awarded a Fulbright-Hayes Fellowship to study painting in Paris. The following year she traveled to Florence, where she discovered in the wax models of the seventeenth-century anatomist Clemente Susini, housed in La Specola, the combination of visual aesthetics and the natural world that was to become a leitmotif in her own art. Her first camel sculptures were produced in Florence in 1966.

Working in New York, Graves made three camels (now in the collection of the National Gallery of Canada), which composed the first one-woman exhibition held at the Whitney Museum of American Art. (Two subsequent camels are in the Neue Galerie der Stadt Aachen, Germany.) Graves explored paleontological and anthropological imagery in her sculpture until 1971, when she returned to painting. In 1976 a commission from the Museum Ludwig in Cologne to create a bronze version of one of her fossil sculptures provided the opportunity for her to explore the possibilities of that medium, first using the lost-wax process of bronze casting, then moving into direct casting techniques at the Tallix Foundry in Peekskill, New York.

During the early 1970s Graves also explored filmmaking, producing five films between 1970 and 1974, two of which, shot on location in Morocco, featured camels (*Goulimine*, 1970; *Izy Boukir*, 1971). In a 1985 collaboration with choreographer Trisha Brown, she created the set and costume for *Lateral Pass*, which brought Graves a New York Dance and Performance Bessie Award (1986). Other honors include the Skowhegan Medal for Drawing/Graphics (1980) and an honorary degree from Skidmore College in 1989.

Graves has executed prints since the 1970s, exploring lithography, screenprint, monotype, and the intaglio processes, including aquatint and drypoint. In addition to Graphicstudio, she has worked with Landfall Press in Chicago, with Iris Editions, Simca Print Artists, and Tyler Graphics, Ltd., in New York, and with 2RC in Rome.

Graves' first one-person exhibition was held at the Berkshire Museum in 1964. Other important solo exhibitions include those at the National Gallery of Canada, Ottawa (1971, 1973), Neue Galerie der Stadt Aachen (1971), Museum of Modern Art, New York (1971), Institute of Contemporary Art of the University of Pennsylvania (1972), La Jolla Museum of Contemporary Art (1973), Albright-Knox Art Gallery, Buffalo (1980), and Vassar College Art Gallery (1986). In 1987 the Fort Worth Art Museum organized a sculpture retrospective, accompanied by a catalogue raisonné.

Nancy Graves working on the clay model for the fish element of *Canoptic Legerdemain* (cat. 84), November 1989

84 Canoptic Legerdemain, 1990

Brushed stainless steel, aluminum mesh, cast resin, cast paper, aluminum (Hexcel) panels, cast epoxy with sand and marble dust, and a color lithograph on Arches White 300 gr. with chine collé on Sekishu rice paper

Overall: 85 x 95 x 37 (215.9 x 241.3 x 94)

Edition: 7; 1 BAT; 1 NGAP; 1 PrP; 1 GP; 1 USFP; 2 AP

Collaboration: Donald Saff, Nick Conroy, Ken Elliot, Alan Holoubek, Tom Pruitt, Conrad Schwable, Eric Vontillius, with Alan Eaker, Patrick Foy, George Holzer, Kelly Medei, Deli Sacilotto, and Tim Baker, George Byers, Jack Casey, Brian Eddleman, Elizabeth Hagy, John Morgan, Charles Parkhill, Dealey Settlemyre

Gift of Graphicstudio/University of South Florida and the Artist in Honor of the Fiftieth Anniversary of the National Gallery of Art

Canoptic Legerdemain, Nancy Graves' first edition sculpture, expands the painting explorations that the artist began about 1983 in which she extended a complex two-dimensional arrangement of superimposed imagery into the third dimension by attaching aluminum elements to the canvas. Recently Graves has asserted, "I don't feel that I've given up painting when I make sculpture, because all kinds of optical and physical transformations can occur in three-dimensional form."[1] These transformations are clearly evident in *Canoptic Legerdemain*, in which seemingly opposing forces are juxtaposed or merged: visual weight is pitted against buoyancy, transparency against opacity, linearity against solidity, while interior merges with exterior, and a sense of stability and balance is suggested along with an implicit energy and movement.

In 1979 Graves described the importance of layering in her painting, which can be easily applied to this work as well:

The paintings exist as a sequence of layers or levels of space which must read intellectually and visually. Scale in the traditional sense as a referent to

84a. Maquette for *Canoptic Legerdemain*, c. 1990, acrylic, watercolor, gold leaf, and graphite on cut and pasted paper mounted on foam core, 17 x 15½ x 2½ (43.2 x 39.3 x 6.3), 1991.75.178

space is contradicted—i.e. large does not necessarily mean "up front" but equally can be read "behind" or as "middle ground." A figure/ground tension occurs which varies or shifts with the painting depending on what or where the eye focuses. Emphasis on layering is an exposure of "process" as a formal ingredient of the *making* of the painting. The *making* in this sense (or the layering) can be understood as the *meaning* of the painting.[2]

In *Canoptic Legerdemain* color and line—which interlock in the two-dimensional composition of the lithographic element at the back of the piece—acquire physical depth in the overall composition, the equivalent of a three-dimensional drawing in space. The openness of the sculpture, enhanced by the transparency of some of the overlapping elements, belies its tightly interwoven, interactive structure. The shifting planes of the relief elements, extending outward at various angles, twisting and turning in and around each other, heighten the work's complexity and dynamism. The multiple images, overlapping, folding in and around each other, generate rhythmic shifts as the eye follows first one form, then another: "The boundary between figure and ground and the inverse relations I can create between the two have also preoccupied me a great deal recently."[3]

The profusion of imagery further reflects an ongoing concern in Graves' work with the passage of time and with the relationship of time to the process of viewing a work of art. The longer one studies Graves' imagery, the more fully the vision unfolds. Every element in *Canoptic Legerdemain* leads a double life, serving an iconographical as well as compositional function. The imagery reflects the artist's continuing study of art history, culture, and archeology: "In the last two or three years I've selected figurative images or paradigms from Japanese, Korean, Egyptian, and Greek [sources], which configure with Renaissance, medieval, and baroque imagery."[4]

Canoptic Legerdemain brings together complex and varied iconographical references from Byzantine, Egyptian, and Christian sources, while interweaving male and female historical and mythological roles. The "hand of God," seen in the lithograph and again as a relief element, appears in other recent works by Graves.[5] Its obvious source was Michelangelo's *Creation of Adam* fresco on the ceiling of the Sistine Chapel. A related Sistine fresco served as the basis for the face of Eve (printed in red on the lithograph), from which the hand of God extends. The snake has cross-cultural associations, including its role in the Garden of Eden story. Like many of Graves' iconographic elements, the creature appears here more than once: on the lithographic element it is an image borrowed from an offset engraving from a book; and it is reincarnated in three dimensions with a transparent mesh skin that reveals the skeletal structure within.

On the left side of the composition Graves rendered the sixth-century Byzantine Empress Theodora in an intricate and open design that recalls the tesserae of the mosaic in San Vitale (Ravenna) on which it is based. The shimmering gold leaf of Theodora's crown emphasizes her royal stature. Interwoven with this image are references to the Egyptian astrological calendar—blue stars, and a sunburstlike design superimposed on circular forms. Other references to ancient Egyptian culture include the fishing scene, cut from stainless steel with a laser that had been digitally programmed from the artist's drawing. The scene, as Graves has explained, "is a composite of a number of different images from Theban tombs that we found in the library at the university." The ducks on the left side of the lithographic element are also based on images from Theban tombs, as are the canopic (burial) jars referred to in the work's title, located beneath the ducks. On the lithograph's right side Graves has included images of wailing Theban women (from the Tomb of Ramose, Thebes), whose arms are raised in official mourning.

In 1983 Graves had introduced classical Greek forms as well as references to Greek culture in her work, seen here in the resin bust of Aphrodite, a positive from a secondary cast in the artist's collection, originally taken from the Elgin Marbles, that has recently been featured in her work. A portion of a Hellenistic Greek robe has also been featured in the lithograph (executed in gray and brown tones and superimposed on the

84b. *Canoptic Prestidigitation*, 1990 (app. 117)

ducks and canopic jars), an image that was chosen, the artist noted, in part "for its graphic configuration and the way it would contrast with the laser cut."

The laser-cut line drawing of the Egyptian fishing image echoes the blue line drawing of a related scene on the lithograph. The red waves beneath Theodora, based on a Korean source,[6] create a colorful, opaque, staccato counterpart to the translucent, fluid, three-dimensional river that winds through the opposite side of the composition. Interaction of the various surface textures and patterns are an integral part of Graves' aesthetic. She noted, for example, that "the contrast of light and dark in the surface incident of the snake scales is related [to the laser cut as well as to] the painterly gesture on the hand of God which reaches out from the face of Eve."

In creating her unique bronze sculptures, Graves does not usually work from a sketch or mock-up, but for *Canoptic Legerdemain* she produced a maquette (fig. 84a), the overall dynamism and energy of which informs the sculpture as well. Certain elements, such as the snake and the hand of God, are common to both, but the maquette served as a visual reference and a source upon which the artist could improvise, rather than as a model intended for direct translation.

A number of innovative processes were employed to achieve the remarkable interplay of color, pattern, and texture in this work. Graves commented admiringly of the Graphicstudio staff that "with Don Saff as the innovational *modus vivendi*, techniques seemed to be coming out of their pores, and for anything I would think of, they would come up with ten solutions. This was due to the strengths of each individual who responded to Don's gutsy go-ahead to unrestricted experimentation." Saff, says Graves, is "the Diaghilev of the print world." The lithographic element, mounted on an aluminum Hexcel panel at the back of the piece, was printed from eighteen plates, as was the edition print *Canoptic Prestidigitation* (fig. 84b) produced during the same period as the sculpture. Graves employed diverse materials to achieve the varied lines and tones in the lithograph, including lithographic crayon and washes of tusche, toner, and turpenoid. The hand of God, printed in royal purple on Sekishu rice paper applied by chine collé, provides further variation in texture and transparency, as the images beneath the hand appear as ghostlike lines and shapes.[7] A cast-paper falcon, mounted on a shaped aluminum panel and suspended in front of the print, echoes the applied cast-paper image in the edition print.

The Theodora panel is epoxy mixed with sand and marble dust, created in a rubber mold made from a clay original on which palm leaves dipped in wax, wax stars, and wax-covered styrofoam chips had been added. The sunken relief of the fish elements[8] to the immediate right of Theodora's face were also produced from a clay original, but in order to replicate the engraved surface, it was necessary to produce a reverse mold in wax first, from which a rubber mold could then be made. The entire panel was sandblasted before painting, creating the gritty surface texture.

Both the skeletal structure and the skin of the snake are actually "found" materials; the diamond-shaped aluminum mesh of its skin was manufactured for use on screen doors, whereas its internal armature is a section of prefabricated aluminum grating. The resin and milled fiberglass river was cast from a rubber mold made over styrofoam that had been cut to form the sinuous curves of its course. The styrofoam had been covered with Plasticine, which the artist manipulated with her fin-

"Canoptic" is an integration of the volumetric versus the pictorial. As in my painting and sculpture, distinctions between the two are questioned through permutations of traditional processes. Figuration and abstraction are pursued through the actuality or illusion of line, color, gravity, mass, and subject matter or content.

Nancy Graves, correspondence with Mary Lee Corlett, 1991

gers and other tools; rope and wire were also pressed into the clay. After casting, the perforated areas were cut out. The Aphrodite bust, cast in clear resin, had its color applied with an airbrush. As Graves noted: "when [it was determined] that we were going to use [resin], I wanted light to reflect and refract the color of the different interfacing forms. When the snake, for example, is lit properly, the blue of the resin in the Aphrodite bust is reflected on the body of the snake, and the silver of the snake reflects into the stainless steel of the Egyptian fishing image."[9]

Throughout her career, Graves has consistently pursued technical alternatives for their expressive potential, and *Canoptic Legerdemain* is a tour de force in this regard.

1. Graves 1990, 32. Graves' recent paintings have featured a remarkable layering of images, overlapping yet transparent, interwoven into a complex web of line, color, and figure. For examples, see *Brushstrokes Cut Loose* (1990) or *Probability and Naturalism* (1990), both oil on canvas and aluminum, reproduced in *Graves*, Gothenburg 1990.

2. Graves 1979, 40.

3. Graves 1990, 32.

4. Graves, telephone conversation with Corlett, 25 October 1990. Unless otherwise noted, all other Graves quotations come from this conversation. Graves is well traveled, having been to Egypt twice, once in 1981 to the Fayum region, and again c. 1988 to Luxor.

5. See, for example, *Brushstrokes Cut Loose* (1990), cited above. It is only recently, in the late 1980s, that the figure began to appear in Graves' work.

6. Graves, conversation with Corlett, 1990.

7. The purple hand of God also seems to function as a shadow of the black version mounted separately and extending outward from the print. In fact, shadows have intermittently played a role in Graves' sculpture. See, for example, her comments about *Calipers* (1969), in Wasserman 1970, 44. As pointed out in Bourdon 1985, Graves will occasionally paint a shadow on the canvas beneath the attached element in her recent paintings with attached aluminum elements. The actual shadow cast by *Canoptic Legerdemain* is certainly an active element in the piece.

8. The fish have their source in Theban tomb imagery and have appeared in other recent works by Graves; see *Probability and Naturalism* (1990).

9. Graves has further noted: "I suppose the light of Florida, it being so diffuse and constant, was an [influence] in this process, causing my thinking to be so much involved with the way color played upon other colors."

TECHNICAL NOTE

Most print processes mentioned in this catalogue are discussed in the technical references listed in the bibliography. Heliorelief and waxtype, however, have been recently developed at Graphicstudio.

Heliorelief
Heliorelief is a photomechanical process for creating a woodblock. It involves first adhering to wood a light-sensitive water-soluble film emulsion of the type used for screenprinting. A high-contrast photonegative or image drawn on mylar is then transferred to the film emulsion by placing it in close contact with the sensitized block and exposing them to light. The block is then washed, and the emulsion dissolved in the places protected by the dark areas of the negative or mylar (areas to be cut away), leaving the film emulsion where it was hardened by exposure to light in the open areas of the negative or mylar (areas to be printed). The remaining emulsion acts as a stencil of the image. After the block has dried fully, the uncovered areas are cut away by a sandblasting process that leaves the emulsion-covered printing areas in relief. The amount of pressure required by the sandblasting varies with the type of wood. When the sandblasting is completed, the film emulsion stencil is removed with water and the block allowed to dry again. It is then ready for printing by the same methods used for traditional woodcuts.

Waxtype
Waxtype is a screenprinting process in which pigmented beeswax rather than traditional printing ink is pressed through the stencil-covered screen. It is possible to achieve printed surfaces of great variety using this method. Printed wax may be left unmodified, revealing the woven texture of the screen, or "burned-in" with a torch, for a smooth surface with a more fluid, encaustic-like appearance, and burnished to a high sheen. Consecutive layers of wax may be forced through the screen to create a multilayered surface of low relief.

APPENDIX

All works listed here are in the Graphicstudio Archive, National Gallery of Art, Washington, and are the Gift of Graphicstudio / University of South Florida and the Artist, unless otherwise designated. Works in the exhibition are marked with an asterisk. Artists are listed alphabetically. Under each artist, works are arranged chronologically by the year in which the project was begun; within each year, entries are listed alphabetically. Exceptions are the series and portfolios, which are listed in the order established by the artists.

Except for works studied for this exhibition, all information is based on Graphicstudio documentation sheets. Except where indicated, this checklist includes only those works for which editions were printed. Proofs generally include a *bon à tirer*, printers' proofs, various presentation and special proofs, artists' proofs, and trial proofs, which may be unique. Numbers preceded by a *B.* (following titles) refer to Baro 1978.

VITO ACCONCI

1. **End Mask**, 1983
One-color photoetching with embossing
8⁵/₈ x 7⁷/₈ (21.9 x 20.0)
Edition: 60 (1/30–30/30; I/XXX–XXX/XXX) plus 25 proofs
1986.26.1

2. **People Mask**, 1983
Photoetching with embossing
8⁵/₈ x 7⁷/₈ (21.9 x 20.0)
Edition: 60 (1/30–30/30; I/XXX–XXX/XXX) plus 23 proofs
1986.26.3

3. **Red Mask**, 1983
One-color photoetching with embossing
8⁵/₈ x 7⁷/₈ (21.9 x 20.0)
Edition: 60 (1/30–30/30; I/XXX–XXX/XXX) plus 22 proofs
1986.26.2

* 4. **Building-Blocks for a Doorway**, 1983–1985
  Color hardground, softground, photoetching, and aquatint
  Two panels: 93^7/8 x 47^1/4 (238.4 x 120.0) each
  Edition: 8 plus 8 proofs
  1986.26.4
  51 sheets of related sketches and notes are in the Graphicstudio Archive

RICHARD ANUSZKIEWICZ

5. **Clearwater**, 1972–1973 (B. 88)
  Color lithograph
  30 x 22 (76.2 x 55.9)
  Edition: 70 (1/50–50/50; I/XX–XX/XX) plus 11 proofs
  1986.26.5

6. **Largo**, 1972–1973 (B. 89)
  Color lithograph
  30 x 22 (76.2 x 55.9)
  Edition: 70 (1/50–50/50; I/XX–XX/XX) plus 10 proofs
  1986.26.7

* 7. **Sun Coast** (triptych), 1972–1973 (B. 92)
  Color lithograph
  Three panels: 30 x 22^1/2 (76.2 x 57.2) each
  Edition: 70 (1/50–50/50; I/XX–XX/XX) plus 12 proofs
  1986.26.8–10

8. **Tampa Summer**, 1972–1973 (B. 90)
  Color lithograph
  31 x 22^1/2 (78.7 x 57.2)
  Edition: 65 (1/45–45/45; I/XX–XX/XX) plus 8 proofs
  1986.26.246

* 9. **Tampa Winter**, 1972–1973 (B. 91)
Color lithograph
31 x 22½ (78.7 x 57.2)
Edition: 70 (1/50–50/50; I/XX–XX/XX) plus 11 proofs
1986.26.6

ARAKAWA

"No!" Says the Signified, 1973–1974
Six prints plus screenprinted title page and lithograph colophon, housed in a
gray, fabric-covered box with a screenprinted title; 72 boxes including proof sets
were issued
Copublished with Multiples, Inc.

* 10. **Untitled 1** (B. 93)
Color lithograph with collage
Verso: lithograph
22½ x 30¹/₁₆ (57.2 x 76.4)
Edition: 60 (1/40–40/40; I/XX–XX/XX) plus 15 proofs
1986.26.189

* 11. **Untitled 2** (B. 94)
Color lithograph with screenprint
Verso: lithograph
22¼ x 30¼ (56.5 x 76.8)
Edition: 60 (1/40–40/40; I/XX–XX/XX) plus 16 proofs
1986.26.190

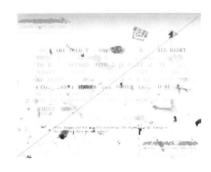

* 12. **Untitled 3** (B. 95)
Color lithograph
22½ x 30¹/₈ (57.2 x 76.5)
Edition: 60 (1/40–40/40; I/XX–XX/XX) plus 16 proofs
1986.26.191

* 13. **Untitled 4** (B. 96)
  Color lithograph with collage
  22¹/₂ x 30¹/₄ (57.2 x 76.8)
  Edition: 60 (1/40–4/40; I/XX–XX/XX) plus 16 proofs
  1986.26.192

* 14. **Untitled 5** (B. 97)
  Color lithograph with screenprint
  22¹/₂ x 30¹/₁₆ (57.2 x 76.4)
  Edition: 60 (1/40–40/40; I/XX–XX/XX) plus 15 proofs
  1986.26.193

* 15. **Untitled 6** (B. 98)
  Color lithograph
  22¹/₂ x 30¹/₈ (57.2 x 76.5)
  Edition: 60 (1/40–40/40; I/XX–XX/XX) plus 19 proofs
  1986.26.194

* 16. **The Sharing of Nameless**, 1984–1986
  Color lithograph and screenprint with embossing
  36⁵/₈ x 56¹¹/₁₆ (93.1 x 144)
  Edition: 60 plus 20 proofs
  1987.77.1
  Six related sketches are in the Graphicstudio Archive

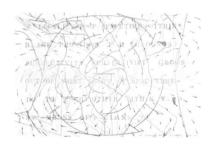

* 17. **The Sharing of Nameless**, 1984–1986
  Color aquatint and etching with embossing
  31¹³/₁₆ x 47⁷/₁₆ (80.8 x 120.5)
  Edition: 60 plus 20 proofs
  1987.77.2

ALICE AYCOCK

* 18. **How to Catch and Manufacture Ghosts: Collected Ghost Stories from the Workhouse**, 1981
Photoetching with pastel additions
29 x 38¹³/₁₆ (73.7 x 98.5)
Edition: 60 (1/30–30/30; I/XXX–XXX/XXX) plus 19 proofs
1986.26.12

19. **How to Catch and Manufacture Ghosts: Collected Ghost Stories from the Workhouse**, 1981
Etching with watercolor additions
28¹/₂ x 38³/₄ (72.4 x 98.4)
Edition: 30 (1/15–15/15; I/XV–XV/XV) plus 18 proofs
1986.26.11

OSCAR BAILEY

20. **Asheville, North Carolina**, 1982–1983
Color Cirkut photograph
8 x 60 (20.3 x 152.4)
Edition: 50 (1/20–20/20; I/XXX–XXX/XXX) plus 10 proofs
1986.26.16

21. **Biltmore Gardens, North Carolina**, 1982–1983
Color Cirkut photograph
8 x 60³/₄ (20.3 x 154.3)
Edition: 50 (1/20–20/20; I/XXX–XXX/XXX) plus 10 proofs
1986.26.15

* 22. **Tampa X 2**, 1982–1983
Color Cirkut photograph
10 x 68¹¹/₁₆ (25.4 x 174.5)
Edition: 45 (1/15–15/15; I/XXX–XXX/XXX) plus 10 proofs
1986.26.14

* 23. **Woods, North Carolina,** 1982–1983
Color Cirkut photograph
10 x 66¼ (25.4 x 168.3)
Edition: 50 (1/20–20/20; I/XXX–XXX/XXX) plus 10 proofs
1986.26.13

LARRY BELL

24. **Untitled #1,** 1974 (B. 99)
Color screenprint with flocking
84 x 42 (213.4 x 106.7)
Edition: 80 (1/60–60/60; I/XX–XX/XX) plus 18 proofs
1986.26.17

25. **Untitled #2,** 1974 (B. 100)
Color screenprint with flocking
84 x 42 (213.4 x 106.7)
Edition: 80 (1/60–60/60; I/XX–XX/XX) plus 15 proofs
1986.26.18

26. **Untitled #3,** 1974 (B. 101)
Color screenprint with flocking
84 x 42 (213.4 x 106.7)
Edition: 60 plus 18 proofs
1986.26.19

27. **Untitled #4,** 1974 (B. 102)
Color screenprint with flocking
84 x 42 (213.4 x 106.7)
Edition: 80 (1/60–60/60; I/XX–XX/XX) plus 15 proofs
1986.26.20

28. **Untitled #5**, 1974 (B. 103)
Color screenprint with flocking
84 x 42 (213.4 x 106.7)
Edition: 70 (1/60–60/60; I/X–X/X) plus 16 proofs
1986.26.21

29. **Untitled #6**, 1974 (B. 104)
Color screenprint with flocking
84 x 42 (213.4 x 106.7)
Edition: 80 (1/60–60/60; I/XX–XX/XX) plus 16 proofs
1986.26.22

SANDRO CHIA

* 30. **Father and Son Song**, 1987–1989
Color heliorelief and hand-carved woodcut with painted oak and gum plywood
frame
85³/₄ x 75⁵/₈ x 4¹/₄ (217.8 x 192.1 x 10.8)
Edition: 12 plus 12 proofs
Gift of Graphicstudio/University of South Florida and the Artist in Honor of the
Fiftieth Anniversary of the National Gallery of Art, 1990.72.01
A related two-part drawing on mylar is in the Graphicstudio Archive

31. **Flowers Fight**, 1987
Basswood heliorelief, acrylic paint, gum plywood, gold leaf
35⁹/₁₆ x 23⁷/₈ x 7 (90.3 x 60.6 x 17.8)
Edition: 12 plus 13 proofs
1989.90.1
A related drawing on mylar is in the Graphicstudio Archive

32. **Surprising Novel: Chapter One**, 1987–1989
Color heliorelief woodcut with painted additions
18¹/₂ x 16¹/₄ (47.0 x 41.3)
Edition: 50 plus 10 proofs
1991.75.58
Six drawings on mylar related to this series are in the Graphicstudio Archive

33. Surprising Novel: Chapter Two, 1987–1989
Color heliorelief woodcut with painted additions
18¹/₂ x 16¹/₄ (47.0 x 41.3)
Edition: 50 plus 10 proofs
1991.75.59

34. Surprising Novel: Chapter Three, 1987–1989
Color heliorelief woodcut with painted additions
18¹/₂ x 16¹/₄ (47.0 x 41.3)
Edition: 50 plus 10 proofs
1991.75.60

35. Surprising Novel: Chapter Four, 1987–1989
Color heliorelief woodcut with painted additions
18¹/₂ x 16¹/₄ (47.0 x 41.3)
Edition: 50 plus 10 proofs
1991.75.61

36. Surprising Novel: Chapter Five, 1987–1989
Color heliorelief woodcut with painted additions
18¹/₂ x 16¹/₄ (47.0 x 41.3)
Edition: 50 plus 10 proofs
1991.75.62

37. Surprising Novel: Chapter Six, 1987–1989
Color heliorelief woodcut with painted additions
18¹/₂ x 16¹/₄ (47.0 x 41.3)
Edition: 50 plus 10 proofs
1991.75.63

38. Surprising Novel: Chapter Seven, 1987–1989
Color heliorelief woodcut with painted additions
18¹/₂ x 16¹/₄ (47.0 x 41.3)
Edition: 50 plus 10 proofs
1991.75.64

CHUCK CLOSE

39. **Georgia**, 1984–1986
Direct gravure
41 x 26 (104.1 x 66)
Edition: 12 plus 8 proofs
1986.26.25
Published by Pace Editions, Inc.

40. **Georgia/Fingerprint I**, 1984–1985
Direct gravure
30 x 22¹/₂ (76.2 x 57.2)
Edition: 30 plus 21 proofs
1986.26.23
Published by Pace Editions, Inc.

41. **Georgia/Fingerprint II**, 1984–1985
Direct gravure
30³/₁₆ x 22¹/₄ (76.7 x 56.5)
Edition: 35 plus 20 proofs
1986.26.24
Published by Pace Editions, Inc.

* 42. **Emily/Fingerprint**, 1986
Direct gravure
54¹/₁₆ x 40⁷/₈ (137.3 x 103.8)
Edition: 45 plus 16 proofs
1987.77.3
Published by Pace Editions, Inc.

43. **Emily/Fingerprint/Silk Collé**, 1986
Direct gravure with silk collé
54¹/₈ x 40³/₄ (137.5 x 103.5)
Edition: 10 plus 10 proofs
1987.77.6
Published by Pace Editions, Inc.

* 44. **Leslie/Fingerprint**, 1986
Direct gravure
54¼ x 40¾ (137.8 x 103.5)
Edition: 45 plus 16 proofs
1987.77.5
Published by Pace Editions, Inc.

45. **Leslie/Fingerprint/Silk Collé**, 1986
Direct gravure with silk collé
54¼ x 40¼ (137.8 x 102.3)
Edition: 10 plus 11 proofs
1987.77.8
Published by Pace Editions, Inc.

46. **Marta/Fingerprint**, 1986
Direct gravure
54⅛ x 41⅜ (137.5 x 102.6)
Edition: 45 plus 17 proofs
1987.77.4
Published by Pace Editions, Inc.

* 47. **Marta/Fingerprint/Silk Collé**, 1986
Direct gravure with silk collé
54⅛ x 40½ (137.5 x 102.9)
Edition: 10 plus 10 proofs
1987.77.7
Published by Pace Editions, Inc.

48. **John I**, 1986–1990
Color direct gravure
30 x 23 (76.2 x 58.4)
Edition: 40 plus 21 proofs
1991.75.179
Published by Pace Editions, Inc.

49. **John II**, 1986–1991
Color direct gravure
30 x 23 (76.2 x 58.4)
Edition: 40 plus 21 proofs
Published by Pace Editions, Inc.
Not yet accessioned

HARRISON COVINGTON

50. **Yellow Arch**, 1970 (B. 18)
Color lithograph
31 x 22 (78.7 x 55.9)
Edition: 20 plus 12 proofs
1991.75.76

JIM DINE

* 51. **The Tampa Tool Reliefs**, 1973–1974 (B. 113)
Five-part aluminum sculpture
Approximately 27 x 29 x 2 (68.6 x 73.7 x 5.1), each part
Edition: 9 (A-I)
Gift of Jim Dine, 1990.45.1–5
Published by Petersburg Press Ltd.
See cat. 9A-E for illustrations of all five parts

* 52. **Metamorphosis of a Plant into a Fan**, 1974 (B. 110)
Five-part aluminum sculpture
Approximately 26 x 16 x 12 (66.0 x 40.6 x 30.5), each part
Edition: 26 (A-Z)
Gift of Jim Dine in Honor of the Fiftieth Anniversary of the National Gallery of
Art, 1990.130.1–5
Published by Petersburg Press Ltd.

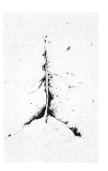

* 53. **The Plant Becomes a Fan #1**, 1974–1975 (B. 105)
Lithograph with screenprint varnish
36 x 24¼ (91.4 x 61.6)
Edition: 80 (1/60–60/60; I/XX–XX/XX) plus 25 proofs
1986.26.212
Copublished with Petersburg Press Ltd.

* 54. **The Plant Becomes a Fan #2**, 1974–1975 (B. 106)
Lithograph with screenprint varnish
36 x 24¼ (91.4 x 61.6)
Edition: 80 (1/60–60/60; I/XX–XX/XX) plus 25 proofs
1986.26.213
Copublished with Petersburg Press Ltd.

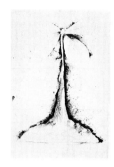

* 55. **The Plant Becomes a Fan #3**, 1974 (B. 107)
Lithograph with screenprint varnish
36 x 24½ (91.4 x 62.2)
Edition: 80 (1/60–60/60; I/XX–XX/XX) plus 25 proofs
1986.26.214
Copublished with Petersburg Press Ltd.

* 56. **The Plant Becomes a Fan #4**, 1974–1975 (B. 108)
Lithograph with screenprint varnish
36 x 24⅜ (91.4 x 61.9)
Edition: 80 (1/60–60/60; I/XX–XX/XX) plus 25 proofs
1986.26.215
Copublished with Petersburg Press Ltd.

* 57. **The Plant Becomes a Fan #5**, 1974–1975 (B. 109)
Lithograph with screenprint varnish
36 x 24½ (91.4 x 62.2)
Edition: 80 (1/60–60/60; I/XX–XX/XX) plus 25 proofs
1986.26.216
Copublished with Petersburg Press Ltd.

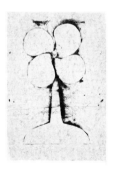

* 58. **The Woodcut Bathrobe**, 1974–1975 (B. 111)
Color woodcut and lithograph
36¼ x 24½ (92.1 x 62.2)
Edition: 80 (1/60–60/60; I/XX–XX/XX) plus 27 proofs
1986.26.217
Copublished with Petersburg Press Ltd.

59. **Black and White Bathrobe**, 1974–1975 (B. 112)
Color lithograph (white on black)
36 x 24 (91.4 x 61.0)
Edition: 80 (1/60–60/60; I/XX–XX/XX) plus 22 proofs
1986.26.218
Copublished with Petersburg Press Ltd.

60. **Untitled Cast Concrete**, 1981–1985
Cast concrete and aluminum, one head with painted additions
Head: 19 x 12 x 4¹/₂ (41.3 x 30.5 x 11.4)
Stand: 50¹/₂ x 15 x 15 (128.3 x 38.1 x 38.1)
Edition: 4 proofs, 3 of them spray-painted
1986.26.27–28

* 61. **The Heart and the Wall**, 1983
Color softground and spitbite etching with power tool drypoint and sanding in
four parts
Top quarters: 43⁵/₈ x 34³/₄ (110.8 x 88.3) each
Bottom quarters: 45³/₄ x 34³/₄ (116.2 x 88.3) each
Edition: 28 plus 15 proofs
1986.26.240–243
Published by Pace Editions, Inc.
A related drawing is in the Graphicstudio Archive

62. **The Robe Goes to Town**, 1982–1983
Color aquatint and screenprint
57 x 36 (144.8 x 91.4)
Edition: 59 plus 19 proofs
1986.26.219
Published by Pace Editions, Inc.

* 63. **Swaying in the Florida Night**, 1982–1983
Etching and aquatint
Framed: 47 x 70¹/₂ (119.4 x 179.1)
Edition: 65 plus 20 proofs
1986.26.26
Published by Pace Editions, Inc.

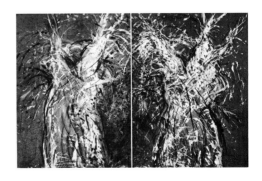

64. Black and White Blossom, 1985–1986
Direct gravure, hardground etching, spitbite aquatint, and power tool drypoint
62⅛ x 39¹/₁₆ (157.8 x 99.1)
Edition: 60 plus 16 proofs
1987.77.16
Published by Pace Editions, Inc.

65. Hand Painting on the Mandala, 1986
Color direct gravure and power tool drypoint with painted additions
49¾ x 40⅛ (126.3 x 101.9)
Edition: 60 plus 23 proofs
1987.77.12
Published by Pace Editions, Inc.

66. My Nights in Santa Monica, 1985–1987
Direct gravure, hardground and softground etching, spitbite aquatint, and
power tool drypoint
35⁵/₁₆ x 72¼ (90.2 x 183.5)
Edition: 20 plus 17 proofs
1987.77.13
Published by Pace Editions, Inc.

67. My Nights in Santa Monica (The Bistre Version), 1985–1987
Direct gravure, etching, and power tool drypoint
35½ x 72⅜ (90.2 x 183.8)
Edition: 20 plus 16 proofs
1987.77.14
Published by Pace Editions, Inc.

68. Shellac on a Hand, 1985–1986
Direct gravure, spitbite aquatint, and power tool drypoint with painted
additions
57⅞ x 40 (147.0 x 101.6)
Edition: 30 plus 15 proofs
1987.77.15
Published by Pace Editions, Inc.

69. **A Side View in Florida**, 1985–1987
Hardground and softground etching and power tool drypoint with painted
additions
51¹/₂ x 40 (130.8 x 101.6)
Edition: 15 plus 26 proofs, including 6 on silk collé
1987.77.9
Published by Pace Editions, Inc.

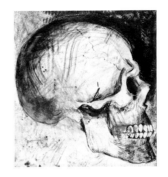

70. **Two Florida Bathrobes**, 1985–1987
Color lithograph and etching
31³/₄ x 46¹/₂ (80.7 x 118.1)
Edition: 70 plus 20 proofs
1987.77.17
Published by Pace Editions, Inc.

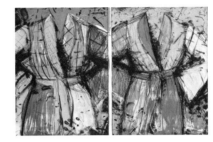

71. **Yellowheart and a Devil**, 1985–1987
Color direct gravure and softground etching
39¹/₄ x 59¹/₂ (99.7 x 151.1)
Edition: 11 plus 7 proofs and 1 unique, hand-painted impression
1987.77.11
Published by Pace Editions, Inc.
* *A related drawing and the hand-painted impression are in the Graphicstudio
Archive*

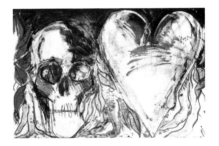

* 72. **The Foreign Plowman**, 1987–1989
Color heliorelief, hand-cut woodcut, and spitbite etching with painted additions,
in five panels
Panel 1: 70⁷/₈ x 24⁵/₁₆ (180.0 x 61.8); panel 2: 70⁷/₈ x 25⁹/₁₆ (180.0 x 64.9);
panel 3: 70⁷/₈ x 24⁹/₁₆ (180.0 x 62.4); panel 4: 70⁷/₈ x 23⁹/₁₆ (180.0 x 59.9);
panel 5: 70⁷/₈ x 24⁹/₁₆ (180.0 x 62.4)
Edition: 10 plus 9 proofs, 1 adhered to maple as a folding screen
1991.75.78–82
Copublished by Pace Editions, Inc., and Waddington Graphics

73. **The Mead of Poetry #1**, 1987–1989
Woodcut
59³/₄ x 41 (151.8 x 104.1)
Edition: 34 plus 1 proof
1991.75.174
Copublished by Pace Editions, Inc., and Waddington Graphics

74. **The Mead of Poetry #1**, 1987–1989
Woodcut with chine collé
59³/₄ x 41 (151.8 x 104.1)
Edition: 15 plus 7 proofs
1989.56.1
Copublished by Pace Editions, Inc., and Waddington Graphics

75. **The Mead of Poetry #2**, 1987–1989
Woodcut
59³/₄ x 41 (151.8 x 104.1)
Edition: 34 plus 1 proof
1991.75.175
Copublished by Pace Editions, Inc., and Waddington Graphics

76. **The Mead of Poetry #2**, 1987–1989
Woodcut with chine collé
59³/₄ x 41 (151.8 x 104.1)
Edition: 15 plus 7 proofs
1989.56.2
Copublished by Pace Editions, Inc., and Waddington Graphics

77. **The Mead of Poetry #3**, 1987–1989
Woodcut
41³/₈ x 32 (105.1 x 81.3)
Edition: 34 plus 1 proof
1991.75.176
Copublished by Pace Editions, Inc., and Waddington Graphics

78. **The Mead of Poetry #3**, 1987–1989
Woodcut with chine collé
41³/₈ x 32 (105.1 x 81.3)
Edition: 15 plus 7 proofs
1989.56.3
Copublished by Pace Editions, Inc., and Waddington Graphics

* 79. **The Oil of Gladness**, 1987
Color heliorelief woodcut and spitbite and softground etching
79¹/₈ x 37³/₄ (201 x 95.9)
Edition: 50 plus 18 proofs
1989.56.4
Copublished by Pace Editions, Inc., and Waddington Graphics

80. **Ravenna in November**, 1987–1989
Color heliorelief woodcut and spitbite and softground etching with painted
additions
78¹¹/₁₆ x 51⁵/₁₆ (199.9 x 130.3)
Edition: 14 plus 12 proofs
1991.75.83
Copublished by Pace Editions, Inc., and Waddington Graphics

81. **Red Dancer on the Western Shore**, 1987–1989
Color woodcut and spitbite etching
78⁵/₈ x 47⁵/₁₆ (199.7 x 120.2)
Edition: 14 plus 11 proofs
1991.75.77
Copublished by Pace Editions, Inc., and Waddington Graphics

* 82. **Youth and the Maiden**, 1987–1989
Color heliorelief and hand-cut woodcut, spitbite and softground etching, and
drypoint with painted additions
Left and right panels: 78⁵/₈ x 24⁵/₁₆ (199.8 x 61.8) each
Center panel: 78⁵/₈ x 91¹/₂ (199.8 x 232.4)
Edition: 16 plus 9 proofs
Gift of Graphicstudio/University of South Florida and the Artist in Honor of the
Fiftieth Anniversary of the National Gallery of Art, 1990.72.2–4
Copublished by Pace Editions, Inc., and Waddington Graphics

ROBERT FICHTER

83. **Atom Struck Tile the Explosion Center Hiroshima Shade/Light**, 1984
Etching and offset lithograph
26¹/₂ x 34 (67.3 x 86.4)
Edition: 65 plus 19 proofs
1986.26.29

* **84. Dürer with Red Flower**, 1984
  Cibachrome
  35 x 27¹/₄ (88.9 x 69.2)
  Edition: 5 plus 6 proofs
  1986.26.35

* **85. Frog Biology**, 1984
  Cibachrome
  34⁷/₈ x 27¹/₄ (88.6 x 69.2)
  Edition: 5 plus 7 proofs
  1986.26.33

* **86. Hurricane Signal**, 1984
  Cibachrome
  20 x 24 (50.8 x 61.0)
  Edition: 33 plus 4 proofs
  1986.26.30

87. Mutant Magic #1: Baby Gene Pool Takes the Stage, 1984
Color lithograph
32 x 23 (81.3 x 58.4)
Edition: 70 plus 27 proofs and 7 progressive proofs
1991.75.101

88. Nature Returns, Large Version, 1984
Cibachrome
58 x 46 (147.3 x 116.8)
Edition: 2 plus 3 proofs
1986.26.36

89. Nature Returns, Small Version, 1984
Cibachrome
30 x 24 (76.2 x 61.0)
Edition: 5 plus 7 proofs
1986.26.34

90. **Space Heater**, 1984
Cibachrome
24 x 30 (61.0 x 76.2)
Edition: 5 plus 6 proofs
1986.26.32

91. **Total Readymade, Large Version**, 1984
Cibachrome
44 x 57³/₄ (111.8 x 146.7)
Edition: 2 plus 4 proofs
1986.26.37

92. **Total Readymade, Small Version**, 1984
Cibachrome
24 x 30 (61 x 76.2)
Edition: 5 plus 7 proofs
1986.26.31

93. **Untitled**, 1984
Etching
16 x 15 (40.6 x 38.1)
Edition: 6
1991.75.100

LEE FRIEDLANDER

Photographs of Flowers, 1974–1975 (B. 114)
Fifteen photographs mounted on 16 x 20 (40.6 x 50.8) Harumi paper, plus title
page and colophon housed in a blue fabric-covered box
Edition: 90 (1/70–70/70; I/XX–XX/XX) plus 12 proof sets
Copublished with Haywire Press

* 94. **Wall of Potted Plants and Trees/Putney, Vermont**, 1972
Image: 6⁷/₈ x 10¹/₄ (17.5 x 26.0)
1986.26.195

* 95. Roses in Vase/New York City, 1974
  Image: 12^{15}/$_{16}$ x 8^{1}/$_{2}$ (32.9 x 21.6)
  1986.26.196

* 96. Rosebush with Leafy Background/Fort Lee, New Jersey, 1972
  Image: 9^{5}/$_{8}$ x 6^{1}/$_{2}$ (24.5 x 16.5)
  1986.26.197

* 97. Chrysanthemums at Flower Market/Paris, 1972
  Image: 6^{13}/$_{16}$ x 10^{1}/$_{4}$ (17.3 x 26.0)
  1986.26.198

* 98. Hollyhocks/Taos, New Mexico, 1972
  Image: 6^{15}/$_{16}$ x 10^{7}/$_{16}$ (17.6 x 26.5)
  1986.26.199

* 99. Roses with Eaten Leaves/Parc St. Cloud, France, 1973
  Image: 6^{11}/$_{16}$ x 10 (17.0 x 25.4)
  1986.26.200

* 100. Cactus/Brooklyn Botanical Gardens, 1973
  Image: 8 x 12 (20.3 x 30.5)
  1986.26.201

* 101. **Chrysanthemums in Garden Pots/Luxembourg Gardens, Paris, 1972**
  Image: 4³/₄ x 7¹/₂ (12.1 x 19.1)
  1986.26.202

* 102. **Kerria Japonica Shrub/New City, New York, 1974**
  Image: 7³/₈ x 11¹/₁₆ (18.7 x 28.1)
  1986.26.203

* 103. **Evergreen Tree/Northern France, 1972**
  Image: 6¹/₂ x 9⁷/₈ (16.5 x 25.1)
  1986.26.204

* 104. **Single Rose Bloom in Formal Garden/Bagatelle Gardens, Paris, 1973**
  Image: 10 x 6⁵/₈ (25.4 x 16.8)
  1986.26.205

* 105. **Potted Fern/Mariposa, California, 1972**
  Image: 7¹/₁₆ x 10⁵/₈ (17.9 x 27.0)
  1986.26.206

* 106. **Petunias/Salinas, California, 1972**
  Image: 9¹³/₁₆ x 6⁹/₁₆ (24.9 x 16.7)
  1986.26.207

* 107. **Climbing Rose Vines/Saratoga Springs, New York, 1973**
  Image: 7¹/₈ x 10³/₄ (18.1 x 27.3)
  1986.26.208

* 108. **Potted Rose/Putney, Vermont, 1972**
Image: 8¹¹/₁₆ x 5¹³/₁₆ (22.1 x 14.8)
1986.26.209

MICHAEL GLIER

* 109. **Men at Home: Entertaining**, 1984–1985
Direct gravure, aquatint, and drypoint
36 x 24⁷/₈ (91.4 x 63.2)
Edition: 60 plus 16 proofs
1986.26.41
Seven drawings on mylar related to the Men at Home series are in the Graphicstudio Archive

* 110. **Men at Home: Grooming**, 1984–1985
Direct gravure, aquatint, drypoint, and roulette
36 x 24⁷/₈ (91.4 x 63.3)
Edition: 60 plus 16 proofs
1986.26.40

* 111. **Men at Home: Mopping**, 1984–1985
Direct gravure, aquatint, drypoint, and roulette
35¹³/₁₆ x 24¹³/₁₆ (91.0 x 63.1)
Edition: 60 plus 16 proofs
1986.26.39

* 112. **Men at Home: Necking**, 1984–1985
Direct gravure, aquatint, drypoint, and roulette
36¹⁵/₁₆ x 24¹⁵/₁₆ (91.3 x 63.3)
Edition: 60 plus 16 proofs
1986.26.42

* 113. **Men at Home: Sitting,** 1984–1985
Direct gravure
35⅞ x 24⅞ (91.2 x 63.2)
Edition: 60 plus 16 proofs
1986.26.38

ROBERT GORDY

114. **Female Head,** 1984
Color aquatint
37⅛ x 28⅝ (94.6 x 72.4)
Edition: 60 plus 33 proofs
1986.26.54
A related drawing on tracing paper is in the Graphicstudio Archive

115. **Nude,** 1984
Color aquatint
27 x 23 (68.6 x 58.4)
Edition: 60 plus 27 proofs
1986.26.55
A related drawing on tracing paper is in the Graphicstudio Archive

NANCY GRAVES

116. **Canoptic Legerdemain,** 1990
Steel, resin, aluminum, cast paper, epoxy, sand and marble dust, acrylic paint,
lithography (and miscellaneous processes)
Approximately 85 x 95 x 37 (215.9 x 241.3 x 94.0)
Edition: 7 plus 7 proofs
Gift of Graphicstudio/University of South Florida and the Artist in Honor of the
Fiftieth Anniversary of the National Gallery of Art, 1990.72.05
A related maquette is in the Graphicstudio Archive

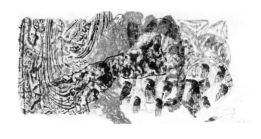

117. **Canoptic Prestidigitation,** 1990
Color lithograph with chine collé and cast paper collage
36½ x 74½ (92.7 x 189.2)
Edition: 40 plus 23 proofs
1991.75.177

CHARLES HINMAN

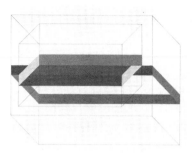

* 118. **Untitled**, 1969 (B. 7)
Color lithograph
22½ x 29⅛ (52.1 x 74.0)
Edition: 70 (1/60–60/60; I/X–X/X) plus 6 proofs
Gift of Ruth and Don Saff, 1990.133.1
*A second impression, Gift of the Graphicstudio/University of South Florida and
the Artist, 1986.26.57, and a related drawing are in the Graphicstudio Archive*

119. **Untitled**, 1969 (B. 8)
Color lithograph with embossing
20 x 29 (50.8 x 73.7)
Edition: 70 (1/60–60/60; I/X–X/X) plus 4 proofs
1986.26.56
A related drawing is in the Graphicstudio Archive

120. **Untitled**, 1969–1970 (B. 9)
Embossing
19 x 29 (48.3 x 73.7)
Edition: 33 (1/25–25/25; I/VIII–VIII/VIII) plus 8 proofs
1986.26.58

121. **Untitled**, 1969–1970 (B. 10)
Embossing
20 x 28 (50.8 x 71.1)
Edition: 33 (1/25–25/25; I/VIII–VIII/VIII) plus 8 proofs
1986.26.59

JEFF KRONSNOBLE

122. **Truck**, 1970 (B. 20)
Color lithograph
22 x 31 (55.9 x 78.7)
Edition: 25 (1/20–20/20; I/V–V/V) plus 6 proofs
1991.75.119

NICHOLAS KRUSHENICK

* 123. **Untitled**, 1970 (B. 24)
Color lithograph
$28^{1}/_{2}$ x $21^{15}/_{16}$ (72.4 x 55.7)
Edition: 40 (1/30–30/30; I/X–X/X) plus 9 proofs
1986.26.60

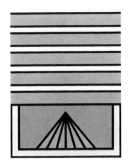

* 124. **Untitled**, 1970 (B. 25)
Color lithograph
22 x $57^{1}/_{16}$ (55.9 x 144.9)
Edition: 40 (1/30–30/30; I/X–X/X) plus 9 proofs
1986.26.143

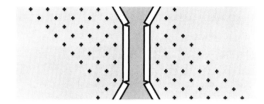

125. **Untitled**, 1970 (B. 26)
Color lithograph
$28^{1}/_{2}$ x 22 (72.4 x 55.9)
Edition: 40 (1/30–30/30; I/X–X/X) plus 10 proofs
1986.26.62

126. **Untitled**, 1970 (B. 27)
Color lithograph
$28^{1}/_{2}$ x 22 (72.4 x 55.9)
Edition: 19 (1/10–10/10; I/IX–IX/IX) plus 5 proofs
1986.26.63

127. **Untitled, State II**, 1971 (B. 28)
Color lithograph
$28^{1}/_{2}$ x 22 (72.4 x 55.9)
Edition: 40 (1/30–30/30; I/X–X/X) plus 7 proofs
1986.26.64

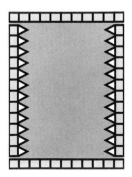

* 128. **Untitled**, 1970 (B. 29)
Color lithograph
28¹/₂ x 21¹⁵/₁₆ (72.4 x 55.7)
Edition: 23 (1/13–13/13; I/X–X/X) plus 8 proofs
1986.26.61

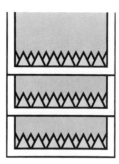

129. **Untitled, State II**, 1971 (B. 30)
Color lithograph
28¹/₂ x 22 (72.4 x 55.9)
Edition: 40 (1/30–30/30; I/X–X/X) plus 8 proofs
1986.26.65

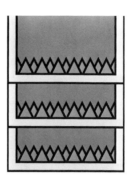

130. **Untitled**, 1971 (B. 31)
Color lithograph
28¹/₂ x 22 (72.4 x 55.9)
Edition: 40 (1/30–30/30; I/X–X/X) plus 6 proofs
1986.26.66

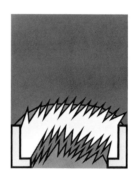

ALFRED LESLIE

* 131. **Folded Constance Pregnant**, 1985–1986
Color softground etching
106⁷/₈ x 73¹/₂ (271.5 x 186.7)
Edition: 30 plus 10 proofs
1987.77.18

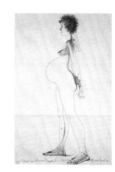

310

ROY LICHTENSTEIN

* 132. **Brushstroke Chair, Wood,** and **Brushstroke Ottoman, Wood,** 1986–1988
Wood with painted sections
Chair: 70^{11}/$_{16}$ x 18 x 27^{1}/$_{4}$ (179.6 x 45.7 x 69.2)
Ottoman: 20^{3}/$_{4}$ x 17^{3}/$_{4}$ x 24 (52.7 x 45.1 x 61.0)
Edition: 12 (1/12–8/12 without ottomans; 9/12–12/12 with ottomans) plus
6 proofs
1988.55.1–2

* 133. **Brushstroke Chair, Bronze,** and **Brushstroke Ottoman, Bronze,** 1986–1988
Bronze with painted sections
Chair: 68^{15}/$_{16}$ x 17^{3}/$_{4}$ x 25^{1}/$_{16}$ (175.1 x 45.1 x 63.7)
Ottoman: 20^{1}/$_{8}$ x 17^{9}/$_{16}$ x 24^{5}/$_{16}$ (51.1 x 44.6 x 61.8)
Edition: 5 plus 3 proofs
Not presently in Graphicstudio Archive

134. **Blonde,** 1987–1989
Color waxtype, lithograph, woodcut, and screenprint
57^{13}/$_{16}$ x 37^{3}/$_{8}$ (146.9 x 94.9)
Edition: 60 plus 18 proofs
1989.56.9
Copublished with Waddington Graphics

135. **Blue Face,** 1987–1989
Color waxtype, lithograph, woodcut, and screenprint
54 x 33^{1}/$_{2}$ (137.2 x 85.1)
Edition: 60 plus 18 proofs
1989.56.5
Copublished with Waddington Graphics

* 136. **Grandpa**, 1987–1989
Color waxtype, lithograph, woodcut, and screenprint
57 x 41¹/₈ (144.8 x 104.4)
Edition: 60 plus 18 proofs
1989.56.10
Copublished with Waddington Graphics

* 137. **Green Face**, 1987–1989
Color waxtype, lithograph, woodcut, and screenprint
58⁷/₈ x 41 (149.5 x 104.1)
Edition: 60 plus 18 proofs
Gift of Graphicstudio/University of South Florida and the Artist in Honor of the
Fiftieth Anniversary of the National Gallery of Art, 1990.72.6
Copublished with Waddington Graphics

138. **The Mask**, 1987–1989
Color waxtype, lithograph, woodcut, and screenprint with collage
46¹/₁₆ x 31¹/₄ (117.0 x 79.4)
Edition: 60 plus 18 proofs
1989.56.6
Copublished with Waddington Graphics

139. **Nude**, 1987–1989
Color waxtype, lithograph, woodcut, and screenprint
56¹/₈ x 32¹/₂ (142.6 x 82.6)
Edition: 60 plus 18 proofs
1989.56.11
Copublished with Waddington Graphics

* 140. **Portrait**, 1987–1989
Color waxtype, lithograph, woodcut, and screenprint
52⁹/₁₆ x 34¹/₄ (133.5 x 87.0)
Edition: 60 plus 18 proofs
1989.56.8
Copublished with Waddington Graphics

* 141. **Roads Collar**, 1987–1989
Color waxtype, lithograph, woodcut, and screenprint
52⁵/₈ x 28³/₄ (133.7 x 73.0)
Edition: 30 plus 18 proofs
1989.56.7

BRYN MANLEY

142. **A Predestined Meeting**, 1969
Color lithograph
31 x 21 (78.7 x 53.3)
Edition: 25 (1/20–20/20; I/V–V/V) plus 5 proofs
1991.75.127

ROBERT MAPPLETHORPE

* 143. **Untitled #1**, 1985
Color photogravure and screenprint
30¹/₄ x 24⁷/₈ (76.9 x 63.2)
Edition: 60 plus 18 proofs
1986.26.67

144. **Untitled #2**, 1985
Color photogravure and screenprint
30 x 24³/₄ (76.2 x 62.9)
Edition: 60 plus 18 proofs
1986.26.68

145. **Untitled #3**, 1985
Color photogravure with painted additions
30 x 24³/₄ (76.2 x 62.9)
Edition: 60 plus 18 proofs
1986.26.69

146. **Untitled #4**, 1985
Color photogravure with painted additions
30 x 24³/₄ (76.2 x 62.9)
Edition: 60 plus 18 proofs
1986.26.70

147. **Untitled #5**, 1985
Photogravure, screenprint, and flocking with painted additions
30 x 24³/₄ (76.2 x 62.9)
Edition: 60 plus 18 proofs
1986.26.71

148. **Tampa Orchid**, 1985–1986
Color photogravure and screenprint
21¹/₂ x 35¹/₄ (54.6 x 89.5)
Edition: 60 plus 15 proofs
1987.77.19

149. **Hyacinth**, 1986–1987
Photogravure
45 x 38 (114.3 x 96.5)
Edition: 30 plus 19 proofs
1987.77.22

* 150. **Hyacinth**, 1986–1987
Photogravure with silk collé
45¹/₄ x 38³/₈ (114.9 x 97.5)
Edition: 27 plus 7 proofs
1987.77.23

* 151. **Irises**, 1986–1987
Photogravure
45¹/₁₆ x 38³/₈ (114.5 x 97.5)
Edition: 30 plus 23 proofs
1987.77.20

152. **Irises,** 1986–1987
Photogravure with silk collé
45 x 38⅛ (114.3 x 96.8)
Edition: 27 plus 6 proofs
1987.77.21

* 153. **Orchid,** 1986–1987
Photogravure
45⅛ x 38⅛ (114.7 x 96.8)
Edition: 30 plus 19 proofs
1987.77.24

154. **Orchid,** 1986–1987
Photogravure with silk collé
45 x 38⅜ (114.3 x 97.5)
Edition: 27 plus 7 proofs
1987.77.25

BRUCE MARSH

155. **Untitled,** 1970–1971 (B. 23)
Lithograph
22 x 30 (55.9 x 76.2)
Edition: 40 (1/30–30/30; I/X–X/X) plus 14 proofs
1991.75.129

GEORGE PAPPAS

156. **Untitled,** 1969–1970 (B. 17)
Color lithograph
29½ x 20 (74.9 x 50.8)
Edition: 25 (1/20–20/20; I/V–V/V) plus 7 proofs
1991.75.130

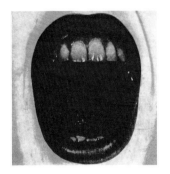

PHILIP PEARLSTEIN

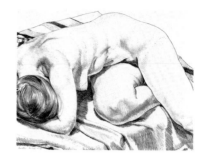

* 157. **Nude Curled Up**, 1969 (B. 1)
One-color lithograph
18¹/₄ x 23¹/₁₆ (46.4 x 58.6)
Edition: 30 (1/20–20/20; I/X–X/X) plus 3 proofs
1986.26.244
Six related drawings are in the Graphicstudio Archive

* 158. **Two Nudes**, 1969 (B. 2)
One-color lithograph
22³/₈ x 29¹/₈ (56.8 x 74.0)
Edition: 40 (1/30–30/30; I/X–X/X) plus 4 proofs
1986.26.245
Three related drawings are in the Graphicstudio Archive

159. **Nude on Folding Stool**, 1969 (B. 3)
One-color lithograph
22 x 15¹/₂ (55.9 x 39.4)
Edition: 30 (1/20–20/20; I/X–X/X) plus 4 proofs
1986.26.77

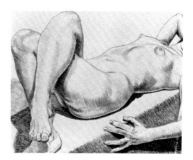

160. **Nude Lying with Crossed Legs**, 1969 (B. 4)
One-color lithograph
18 x 22 (45.7 x 55.9)
Edition: 30 (1/20–20/20; I/X–X/X) plus 3 proofs
1986.26.78

161. **Two Female Models on Rocker and Stool**, 1975 (B. 5)
Lithograph
36 x 74 (91.4 x 188.0)
Edition: 40 (1/20–20/20; I/XX–XX/XX) plus 15 proofs
1986.26.79

162. **Two Female Models on Rocker and Stool**, 1975 (B. 6)
Color lithograph
36 x 74 (91.4 x 188.0)
Edition: 40 (1/20–20/20; I/XX–XX/XX) plus 23 proofs
1986.26.80

* 163. **Models With Mirror**, 1983–1985
Color etching and aquatint
35⅝ x 54 (90.5 x 137.2)
Edition: 60 plus 20 proofs
1986.26.76
Copublished with 724 Prints

* 164. **View of Rome**, 1986
Color direct gravure, sugar-lift aquatint, and roulette
35⅝ x 47¼ (90.5 x 120.0)
Edition: 60 plus 24 proofs
1987.77.26
Four related drawings on mylar are in the Graphicstudio Archive

* 165. **Jerusalem, Kidron Valley**, 1987–1989
Color heliorelief and hand-carved woodcut
40⅛ x 119 (101.9 x 302.3)
Edition: 22 plus 21 proofs
1989.90.2
Ten related drawings on mylar are in the Graphicstudio Archive

166. **Jerusalem, Temple Mount**, 1987–1989
Color heliorelief and hand-carved woodcut
18½ x 27 (47.0 x 68.6)
Edition: 30 plus 27 proofs
1989.90.3
Nine related drawings on mylar are in the Graphicstudio Archive

MEL RAMOS

167. **Llama**, 1970 (B. 21)
Color lithograph
30 x 22 (76.2 x 55.9)
Edition: 38 (1/30–30/30; I/VIII–VIII/VIII) plus 9 proofs
1986.26.81

168. **Indian Rhinoceros**, 1970 (B. 22)
Color lithograph
22 x 30 (55.9 x 76.2)
Edition: 38 (1/30–30/30; I/VIII–VIII/VIII) plus 6 proofs
1986.26.82

FRANK RAMPOLLA

169. **Standing Man**, 1970 (B. 19)
Color lithograph
31 x 22 (78.7 x 55.9)
Edition: 25 (1/20–20/20; I/V–V/V) plus 7 proofs
1986.26.83

ROBERT RAUSCHENBERG

170. **Made in Tampa: Tampa 1**, 1972 (B. 58)
Color lithograph
36 x 33 (91.4 x 83.8)
Edition: 40 (1/20–20/20; I/XX–XX/XX) plus 10 proofs
1986.26.93

* 171. **Made in Tampa: Tampa 2**, 1972–1973 (B. 59)
Color lithograph and blueprint
29^{15}/$_{16}$ x 74^1/$_2$ (76.0 x 189.2)
Edition: 40 (1/20–20/20; I/XX–XX/XX) plus 12 proofs
1986.26.85

* 172. **Made in Tampa: Tampa 3**, 1972 (B. 60)
Color lithograph with collage and graphite
43⁷/₈ x 47 x ¹/₄ (111.5 x 119.4 x 0.6)
Edition: 40 (1/20–20/20; I/XX–XX/XX) plus 9 proofs
1986.26.87

173. **Made in Tampa: Tampa 4**, 1972 (B. 61)
Color lithograph
40 x 22 (101.6 x 55.9)
Edition: 40 (1/20–20/20; I/XX–XX/XX) plus 9 proofs
1986.26.89
The artist designated Tampa 4 *through* Tampa 7 *as the "Seasonbags." Housed in
a white paper-covered portfolio, they were issued with a screenprinted title page
and lithographed colophon*

174. **Made in Tampa: Tampa 5**, 1972 (B. 62)
Color lithograph and blueprint
40 x 22 (101.6 x 55.9)
Edition: 40 (1/20–20/20; I/XX–XX/XX) plus 9 proofs
1986.26.88

175. **Made in Tampa: Tampa 6**, 1972 (B. 63)
Color lithograph
40 x 22 (101.6 x 55.9)
Edition: 40 (1/20–20/20; I/XX–XX/XX) plus 9 proofs
1986.26.90

176. **Made in Tampa: Tampa 7**, 1972 (B. 64)
Color lithograph
40¹/₆ x 22¹/₈ (102.0 x 56.2)
Edition: 40 (1/20–20/20; I/XX–XX/XX) plus 12 proofs
1986.26.104

177. **Made in Tampa: Tampa 8**, 1972 (B. 65)
Color lithograph and screenprint with collage
38¹/₁₆ x 50 (96.6 x 127.0)
Edition: 40 (1/20–20/20; I/XX–XX/XX) plus 11 proofs
1986.26.105

* 178. **Made in Tampa: Tampa 9**, 1972–1973 (B. 66)
Color lithograph and blueprint
68 x 12⁷/₈ (172.7 x 32.7)
Edition: 40 (1/20–20/20; I/XX–XX/XX) plus 10 proofs
1986.26.94

179. **Made in Tampa: Tampa 10**, 1972–1973 (B. 67)
Color lithograph
34 x 118 (86.4 x 289.6)
Edition: 40 (1/20–20/20; I/XX–XX/XX) plus 14 proofs
1986.26.106

* 180. **Made in Tampa: Tampa 11**, 1972–1973 (B. 68)
Blueprint and sepiaprint
29⁵/₁₆ x 41³/₁₆ (74.5 x 104.6)
Edition: 40 (1/20–20/20; I/XX–XX/XX) plus 10 proofs
1986.26.95

181. **Made in Tampa: Tampa 12**, 1972–1973 (B. 69)
Color lithograph and sepiaprint
40 x 66 (101.6 x 167.6)
Edition: 40 (1/20–20/20; I/XX–XX/XX) plus 12 proofs
1986.26.86

* 182. **Made in Tampa Clay Pieces: Tampa Clay Piece 1**, 1972 (B. 72)
Clay and screenprinted decals
14^1/$_2$ x 15^1/$_2$ x ^{3}/$_4$ (36.8 x 39.4 x 1.9)
Edition: 20 (1/10–10/10; I/X–X/X) plus 13 proofs
1986.26.96
The cardboard prototype is in the Graphicstudio Archive

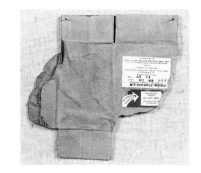

* 183. **Made in Tampa Clay Pieces: Tampa Clay Piece 2**, 1972 (B. 73)
Clay and screenprinted decal
15^1/$_2$ x 23^1/$_2$ x ^{3}/$_4$ (39.4 x 59.7 x 1.9)
Edition: 20 (1/10–10/10; I/X–X/X) plus 10 proofs
1986.26.97
The cardboard prototype is in the Graphicstudio Archive

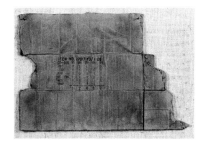

* 184. **Made in Tampa Clay Pieces: Tampa Clay Piece 3**, 1972–1973 (B. 74)
Clay, screenprinted decal, fiberglass, and epoxy
19^1/$_2$ x 24 x 5^1/$_2$ (49.5 x 61.0 x 14.0)
Edition: 20 (1/10–10/10; I/X–X/X) plus 11 proofs
1986.26.98
The cardboard prototype is in the Graphicstudio Archive

* 185. **Made in Tampa Clay Pieces: Tampa Clay Piece 4**, 1972 (B. 75)
Clay and screenprinted decals
9^1/$_2$ x 17 x 1^1/$_2$ (24.1 x 43.2 x 3.8)
Edition: 20 (1/10–10/10; I/X–X/X) plus 14 proofs
1986.26.107
The cardboard prototype is in the Graphicstudio Archive

* 186. **Made in Tampa Clay Pieces: Tampa Clay Piece 5**, 1972 (B. 76)
Clay and fiberglass with collage
34 x 18 x 3 (86.4 x 45.7 x 7.6)
Edition: 20 (1/10–10/10; I/X–X/X) plus 10 proofs
1986.26.108

187. **Homage to Picasso**, 1973 (B. 77)
Color screenprint and solvent transfer
30 x 22 (76.2 x 55.9)
Edition: 120 (1/90–90/90; I/XXX–XXX/XXX) plus 57 proofs
1986.26.101

* 188. **Crops: Cactus**, 1973 (B. 81)
Color screenprint and solvent transfer
60 x 38 (152.4 x 96.5)
Edition: 40 (1/20–20/20; I/XX–XX/XX) plus 10 proofs
1986.26.109

* 189. **Crops: Coconut**, 1973 (B. 79)
Color screenprint and solvent transfer
60¼ x 38 (153.0 x 96.5)
Edition: 40 (1/20–20/20; I/XX–XX/XX) plus 13 proofs
1986.26.100

* 190. **Crops: Mangrove**, 1973 (B. 78)
Color screenprint and solvent transfer
60 x 38 (152.4 x 96.5)
Edition: 40 (1/20–20/20; I/XX–XX/XX) plus 11 proofs
1986.26.99

191. **Crops: Peanuts**, 1973 (B. 80)
Color screenprint and solvent transfer
60 x 38 (152.4 x 96.5)
Edition: 40 (1/20–20/20; I/XX–XX/XX) plus 11 proofs
1986.26.102

192. **Crops: Watermelon**, 1973 (B. 82)
Color screenprint and solvent transfer
60 x 38 (152.4 x 96.5)
Edition: 40 (1/20–20/20; I/XX–XX/XX) plus 11 proofs
1986.26.110

* 193. **Airport Series: Cat Paws**, 1974 (B. 83)
Color relief and intaglio on fabric with collage
Framed: 42^{5}/$_{16}$ x 44^{5}/$_{16}$ x 1^{1}/$_{2}$ (107.5 x 112.6 x 3.8)
Edition: 40 (1/20–20/20; I/XX–XX/XX) plus 15 proofs
1986.26.103

194. **Airport Series: Room Service**, 1974 (B. 86)
Color relief and intaglio on fabric with collage
54 x 57^{1}/$_{2}$ (137.2 x 146.1)
Edition: 40 (1/20–20/20; I/XX–XX/XX) plus 20 proofs
1986.26.113

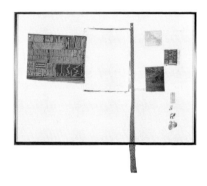

* 195. **Airport Series: Platter**, 1974 (B. 84)
Color relief and intaglio on fabric
Framed: 52^{1}/$_{4}$ x 35^{5}/$_{16}$ x 1^{1}/$_{2}$ (132.7 x 89.7 x 3.8)
Edition: 40 (1/20–20/20; I/XX–XX/XX) plus 16 proofs
1986.26.111

* 196. **Airport Series: Sheephead**, 1974 (B. 87)
Relief and intaglio on fabric with collage
Framed: 45^{3}/$_{8}$ x 60^{5}/$_{16}$ x 1^{1}/$_{2}$ (115.3 x 153.2 x 3.8)
Edition: 40 (1/20–20/20; I/XX–XX/XX) plus 19 proofs
1986.26.114

197. **Airport Series: Switchboard**, 1974 (B. 85)
Color relief and intaglio on fabric with collage
34^{1}/$_{2}$ x 36^{1}/$_{2}$ x 7^{1}/$_{2}$ (87.6 x 92.7 x 19.1)
Edition: 40 (1/20–20/20; I/XX–XX/XX) plus 18 proofs
1986.26.112

* 198. **Chinese Summerhall**, 1982–1983
Color photograph
29⁷⁄₈ x 1248¹⁄₄ (75.9 x 3170.6)
Edition: 5 (unnumbered)
1986.26.84
Copublished with Gemini G.E.L.
The original mock-up, 1991.75.180, is in the Graphicstudio Archive

detail

199. **Studies for Chinese Summerhall I**, 1982–1983
Color photograph
30 x 106 (76.2 x 269.2)
Edition: 25 plus 8 proofs
Gift of Gemini G.E.L. and the Artist, 1991.74.234
Copublished with Gemini G.E.L.

200. **Studies for Chinese Summerhall II**, 1982–1983
Color photograph
30 x 87⁷⁄₈ (76.2 x 223.0)
Edition: 25 plus 8 proofs
Gift of Gemini G.E.L. and the Artist, 1991.74.238
Copublished with Gemini G.E.L.

201. **Studies for Chinese Summerhall III**, 1982–1983
Color photograph
87⁷⁄₈ x 30 (223.0 x 76.2)
Edition: 25 plus 8 proofs
Gift of Gemini G.E.L. and the Artist, 1991.74.237
Copublished with Gemini G.E.L.

202. **Studies for Chinese Summerhall IV**, 1982–1983
Color photograph
30 x 94 (76.2 x 238.7)
Edition: 25 plus 8 proofs
Gift of Gemini G.E.L. and the Artist, 1991.74.235
Copublished with Gemini G.E.L.

203. **Studies for Chinese Summerhall V**, 1982–1984
Color photograph
30 x 94 (76.2 x 238.7)
Edition: 25 plus 8 proofs
Gift of Gemini G.E.L. and the Artist, 1991.74.236
Copublished with Gemini G.E.L.

204. **Studies for Chinese Summerhall** (series of 28 individual studies), 1982
Color photographs
Average sheet size: 40 x 30 or 24 x 20 (101.6 x 76.2 or 61.0 x 50.8)
Edition: 6 studies issued in edition of 60 (1/30–30/30; I/XXX–XXX/XXX)
plus 10 proofs; 22 studies issued in edition of 30 (1/30–30/30) plus 10 proofs
1986.26.115–142

* 205. **Araucan Mastaba/ROCI Chile**, 1985–1986
Screenprinted enamel with painted additions on polished natural aluminum over
a plywood substructure, with sterling silver and lapis lazuli
20⅝ x 22 x 22 (52.4 x 55.9 x 55.9)
Projected edition: 25 plus 17 proofs
1991.75.216
Copublished with Rauschenberg Overseas Culture Interchange

206. **Fifth Force**, 1985–1986
Bronze, acrylic paint, Xerox transfer on silk, waxed thread, painted shot with
stainless steel pin
83¼ x 15 x 45 (211.5 x 38.1 x 114.3)
Projected edition: 25 plus 16 proofs
Gift of Graphicstudio/University of South Florida and the Artist in Honor of the
Fiftieth Anniversary of the National Gallery of Art, 1990.72.7

* 207. **Tibetan Garden Song/ROCI Tibet**, 1985–1986
Cello, chrome-plated washtub, glycerine, Chinese scrollmaker's brush, mirrored
Plexiglas
Diameter: 43 x 18¼ (109.2 x 46.4)
Projected edition: 25 plus 16 proofs
1991.75.215
Copublished with Rauschenberg Overseas Culture Interchange

208. **Bamhue/ROCI Japan**, 1986–1987
Square bamboo, neon lights, and brass electrical box, fittings, and cable
90 x 4 x 10³/₄ (228.6 x 10.2 x 27.3)
Projected edition: 25 plus 16 proofs
1991.75.217
Copublished with Rauschenberg Overseas Culture Interchange

JAMES ROSENQUIST

209. **Art Gallery**, 1971 (B. 45)
Color lithograph
30 x 22 (76.2 x 55.9)
Edition: 40 (1/30–30/30; I/X–X/X) plus 16 proofs
1986.26.150

* 210. **Cold Light**, 1971 (B. 44)
Color lithograph
22⁹/₁₆ x 30¹/₈ (57.3 x 76.5)
Edition: 100 (1/70–70/70; I/XXX–XXX/XXX) plus 11 proofs
1986.26.158

211. **Delivery Hat**, 1971 (B. 39)
Color lithograph
6¹/₄ x 4¹/₂ (15.9 x 11.4)
Edition: 100 (1/70–70/70; I/XXX–XXX/XXX) plus 13 proofs
1986.26.156

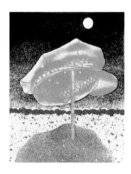

212. **Earth and Moon**, 1971 (B. 48)
Color lithograph with Plexiglas face and plastic beads
18¹/₂ x 17¹/₂ x ³/₈ (47.0 x 44.5 x 0.9)
Edition: 100 (1/70–70/70; I/XXX–XXX/XXX) plus 14 proofs
1986.26.159

213. **Fedora**, 1971 (B. 40)
Color lithograph
6³/₁₆ x 4³/₈ (15.7 x 11.1)
Edition: 100 (1/70–70/70; I/XXX–XXX/XXX) plus 9 proofs
1986.26.147

* 214. **Mastaba**, 1971 (B. 47)
Color lithograph with Plexiglas face and styrene beads
32¹/₄ x 24¹/₄ x ³/₈ (81.9 x 61.6 x 0.9)
Edition: 100 (1/70–70/70; I/XXX–XXX/XXX) plus 14 proofs
1986.26.149

215. **Mirrored Flag**, 1971 (B. 41)
Color lithograph
29 x 22 (73.7 x 55.9)
Edition: 100 (1/70–70/70; I/XXX–XXX/XXX) plus 13 proofs
1986.26.145

216. **Moon Beam Mistaken for the News**, 1971 (B. 42)
Color lithograph
22 x 30 (55.9 x 76.2)
Edition: 100 (1/70–70/70; I/XXX–XXX/XXX) plus 11 proofs
1986.26.146

217. **Moon Box**, 1971 (B. 43)
Color lithograph
16¹/₂ x 19¹/₈ (41.9 x 48.6)
Edition: 100 (1/70–70/70; I/XXX–XXX/XXX) plus 11 proofs
1986.26.157

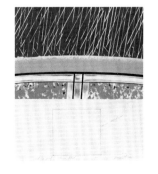

218. **Music School**, 1971 (B. 46)
Color lithograph
34¹/₂ x 30 (87.6 x 76.2) (2 sheets hinged together)
Edition: 100 (1/70–70/70; I/XXX–XXX/XXX) plus 11 proofs
1986.26.148

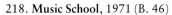

219. **Water Spout**, 1971 (B. 49)
Color lithograph
30 x 22 (76.2 x 55.9)
Edition: 60 (1/30–30/30; I/XXX–XXX/XXX) plus 13 proofs
1986.26.160

220. **Iris Lake**, 1975 (B. 51)
Color lithograph
36 x 74 (91.4 x 188.0)
Edition: 60 (1/40–40/40; I/XX–XX/XX) plus 9 proofs
1986.26.152

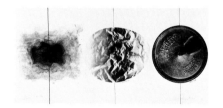

221. **Miles**, 1975 (B. 54)
Color screenprint with painted additions
30 x 22 (76.2 x 55.9)
Edition: 200 plus 58 proofs
1986.26.154

* 222. **Mirage Morning**, 1975 (B. 52)
Color lithograph with window shades, stones, string, and Plexiglas face
36¼ x 74¼ x 2¾ (92.1 x 188.6 x 7.0)
Edition: 60 (1/40–40/40; I/XX–XX/XX) plus 9 proofs
1986.26.161

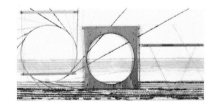

* 223. **Pale Cradle**, 1975–1976 (B. 55)
Color lithograph and screenprint with collage
41¾ x 29¹¹/₁₆ (106.0 x 75.4)
Edition: 60 (1/40–40/40; I/XX–XX/XX) plus 9 proofs
1986.26.153

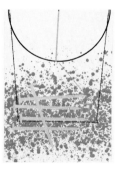

* 224. **Rails**, 1976 (B. 53)
Color lithograph and screenprint
34¾ x 71³/₁₆ (88.3 x 180.8)
Edition: 60 (1/40–40/40; I/XX–XX/XX) plus 10 proofs
1986.26.162

225. **Miles II**, 1975–1977 (B. 56)
Color screenprint
30 x 22 (76.2 x 55.9)
Edition: 35 (1/25–25/25; I/X–X/X) plus 6 proofs
1986.26.155

226. **Tampa—New York 1188**, 1975 (B. 50)
Color lithograph
36 x 74 (91.4 x 188.0)
Edition: 60 (1/40–40/40; I/XX–XX/XX) plus 9 proofs
1986.26.151

227. **Quarter Century**, 1981
Color lithograph
30 x 22 (76.2 x 55.9)
Edition: 90 (1/45–45/45; I/XXXXV–XXXXV/XXXXV) plus 4 proofs
1986.26.144

* 228. **Crosshatch and Mutation**, 1986
Color monoprint and lithograph collage
42¼ x 51⁷⁄₁₆ (107.3 x 130.7)
Edition: 29 plus 9 proofs
1989.56.13
Monoprint template on mylar is in the Graphicstudio Archive

229. **Flowers and Females**, 1986
Color monoprint and lithograph collage
60⅛ x 70¾ (152.8 x 179.7)
Edition: 29 plus 9 proofs
1989.90.5
Monoprint template on mylar is in the Graphicstudio Archive

* 230. **The Kabuki Blushes,** 1986
Color lithograph and monoprint collage
39³/₈ x 41⁵/₈ (100.0 x 105.7)
Edition: 59 plus 9 proofs
1989.56.12
Monoprint template on mylar is in the Graphicstudio Archive

* 231. **Shriek,** 1986
Color monoprint and lithograph collage
42¹/₄ x 71⁵/₈ (107.0 x 181.9)
Edition: 29 plus 9 proofs
1987.77.27

* 232. **The Prickly Dark,** 1987–1989
Aquatint
66³/₈ x 67 (168.6 x 170.2)
Edition: 55 plus 15 proofs
1989.90.4

* 233. **Sister Shrieks,** 1987–1989
Color monoprint and lithograph collage
48 x 80 (121.9 x 203.2)
Edition: 39 plus 12 proofs
1989.90.6
Monoprint template on mylar is in the Graphicstudio Archive

* 234. **Welcome to the Water Planet,** 1987
Aquatint
75¹³/₁₆ x 59⁷/₈ (192.6 x 152.1)
Edition: 55 plus 15 proofs
Gift of Graphicstudio/University of South Florida and the Artist in Honor of the
Fiftieth Anniversary of the National Gallery of Art, 1990.72.8

EDWARD RUSCHA

235. **Crackers**, 1970 (B. 34)
Lithograph
16 x 20 (40.6 x 50.8)
Edition: 40 (1/30–30/30; I/X–X/X) plus 12 proofs
1986.26.165

* 236. **Nine Swimming Pools**, 1970 (B. 37)
Lithograph
16^1/$_8$ x 20^1/$_{16}$ (40.9 x 51.0)
Edition: 40 (1/30–30/30; I/X–X/X) plus 11 proofs
1986.26.166

* 237. **Real Estate Opportunities**, 1970–1971 (B. 33)
Color lithograph
16^1/$_8$ x 20^1/$_8$ (40.9 x 51.1)
Edition: 40 (1/30–30/30; I/X–X/X) plus 11 proofs
1986.26.164

* 238. **Some Los Angeles Apartments**, 1970 (B. 35)
Lithograph
16^1/$_4$ x 20^3/$_{16}$ (41.3 x 51.3)
Edition: 40 (1/30–30/30; I/X–X/X) plus 8 proofs
1986.26.167

* 239. **Twentysix Gasoline Stations**, 1970–1971 (B. 38)
Color lithograph
16^1/$_{16}$ x 20^1/$_8$ (40.8 x 51.1)
Edition: 40 (1/30–30/30; I/X–X/X) plus 17 proofs
1986.26.168

240. **Various Small Fires**, 1970 (B. 32)
Lithograph
16 x 20 (40.6 x 50.8)
Edition: 40 (1/30–30/30; I/X–X/X) plus 11 proofs
1986.26.163

DONALD SAFF

241. **Untitled**, 1971 (B. 57)
Color lithograph
22 x 30 (55.9 x 76.2)
Edition: 57 (1/42–42/42; I/XV–XV/XV) plus 8 proofs
1986.26.169

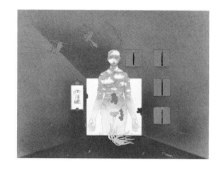

MIRIAM SCHAPIRO

* 242. **Children of Paradise**, 1984
Color lithograph and collage
31⁷/₈ x 48 (80.9 x 121.9)
Edition: 60 plus 23 proofs
1986.26.170
A related collage is in the Graphicstudio Archive

HOLLIS SIGLER

243. **If She Could Free Her Heart to Her Wildest Desires**, 1982
Lithograph in folded format with pop-up elements
Open: 12³/₁₆ x 18³/₄ (31.0 x 47.6)
Closed: 12³/₁₆ x 9³/₈ (31.0 x 23.8)
Edition: 90 (1/45–45/45; I/XXXXV–XXXXV/XXXXV) plus 23 proofs
1986.26.172

RICHARD SMITH

* 244. **Evergloom**, 1969 (B. 11)
Color lithograph printed on both sides of paper and then folded
Sheet dimensions as folded: 15¹/₈ x 22¹/₂ (38.4 x 57.2)
Edition: 70 (1/60–60/60; I/X–X/X) plus 6 proofs
Gift of Ruth and Don Saff, 1990.133.2
A second impression, Gift of Graphicstudio/University of South Florida and the Artist, 1986.26.173, and a related drawing are in the Graphicstudio Archive

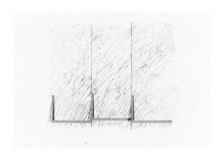

* 245. **Everglad**, 1969 (B. 12)
Color lithograph printed on both sides of paper and then folded
Sheet dimensions as folded: 15¹/₈ x 22¹/₂ (38.4 x 57.2)
Edition: 70 (1/60–60/60; I/X–X/X) plus 2 proofs
Gift of Ruth and Don Saff, 1990.133.3
A second impression, Gift of Graphicstudio/University of South Florida and the Artist, 1986.26.174, and a related drawing are in the Graphicstudio Archive

MARK STOCK

246. **Shovel**, 1984–1985
Color lithograph
31¹/₂ x 48¹/₂ (80.0 x 123.2)
Edition: 60 plus 13 proofs
1986.26.171

JOEL-PETER WITKIN

* 247. **Harvest**, 1985
Photogravure
22⁵/₈ x 19³/₄ (57.4 x 50.2)
Edition: 10 proofs
1986.26.180
This proof of an uneditioned project is inscribed "N.A.T." and is in the Graphicstudio Archive

248. **Helena Fourment**, 1985
Photogravure
22^1/$_2$ x 19^3/$_4$ (57.2 x 50.2)
Edition: 10 proofs
1986.26.181
This proof of an uneditioned project is inscribed "N.A.T." and is in the
Graphicstudio Archive

249. **Man Without Legs**, 1985
Photogravure
22^1/$_2$ x 19^3/$_4$ (57.2 x 50.2)
Edition: 10 proofs
1986.26.178
This proof of an uneditioned project is inscribed "N.A.T." and is in the
Graphicstudio Archive

* 250. **Portrait of Nan**, 1985
Photogravure
22^5/$_8$ x 19^3/$_4$ (57.4 x 50.2)
Edition: 10 proofs
1986.26.179
This proof of an uneditioned project is inscribed "N.A.T." and is in the
Graphicstudio Archive

* 251. **Ragazzo con quattro bracci** (The Boy with Four Arms), 1985
Photogravure
22^9/$_{16}$ x 19^3/$_4$ (57.3 x 50.2)
Edition: 10 proofs
1986.26.176
This proof of an uneditioned project is inscribed "N.A.T." and is in the
Graphicstudio Archive

252. **The Result of War: The Cornucopian Dog**, 1985
Photogravure
22^1/$_2$ x 19^3/$_4$ (57.2 x 50.2)
Edition: 10 proofs
1986.26.177
This proof of an uneditioned project is inscribed "N.A.T." and is in the
Graphicstudio Archive

253. **Venus, Pan, and Time**, 1985
Photogravure
22¹/₂ x 19³/₄ (57.2 x 50.2)
Edition: 10 proofs
1986.26.182
This proof of an uneditioned project is inscribed "N.A.T." and is in the Graphicstudio Archive

THEO WUJCIK

254. **Jasper Johns**, 1984–1985
Relief etching
30 x 37 (76.2 x 94.0)
Edition: 60 plus 13 proofs
1986.26.183

ADJA YUNKERS

255. **Aegean IX 69**, 1969 (B. 15)
Color lithograph
23 x 32 (58.4 x 81.3)
Edition: 38 (1/30–30/30; I/VIII–VIII/VIII) plus 6 proofs
1986.26.184

256. **La Maison Dieu 69**, 1969 (B. 16)
Color lithograph
32¹/₂ x 23¹/₂ (82.3 x 59.7)
Edition: 38 (1/30–30/30; I/VIII–VIII/VIII) plus 6 proofs
1986.26.185

257. **Untitled**, 1969 (B. 14)
Color lithograph
30 x 22 (76.2 x 55.9)
Edition: 38 (1/30–30/30; I/VIII–VIII/VIII) plus 5 proofs
1986.26.175

BIBLIOGRAPHY

This highly selective bibliography includes books, exhibition catalogues, periodical articles, and essays. Section one documents recent relevant publications on the graphic arts; section two is restricted to citations specifically concerned with Graphicstudio; section three provides references to the individual artists.

LAMIA DOUMATO
Head, Reader Services
National Gallery of Art Library

SECTION I: GENERAL

Ackley, Clifford S. *70s into 80s: Printmaking Now*. Exh. cat., Museum of Fine Arts. Boston, 1986.

Adams, Clinton. *American Lithographers, 1900–1960*. Albuquerque, 1983.

American Women Printmakers. Exh. cat., University of Missouri. St. Louis, 1976.

Antreasian, Garo Z. "Some Thoughts about Printmaking & Print Collaboration." *Art Journal* 39 (Spring 1980), 180–188.

———, and Clinton Adams. *The Tamarind Book of Lithography: Art and Techniques*. New York, 1971.

Armstrong, Elizabeth. *First Impressions: Early Prints by Forty-Six Contemporary Artists*. Exh. cat., Walker Art Center. Minneapolis, 1989.

———. "First Impressions." *Print Collector's Newsletter* 20 (May–June 1989), 41–46.

Baro, Gene. *Thirty Years of American Printmaking*. Exh. cat., Brooklyn Museum. New York, 1977.

———. *Twenty-Second National Print Exhibition*. Exh. cat., Brooklyn Museum. Brooklyn, 1981.

Big Prints. Exh. cat., Arts Council of Great Britain. London, 1980.

Boyce, J. M. *Contemporary Mezzotints*. Exh. cat., Williams College of Art. Williamstown, MA, 1978.

Carey, Frances, and Anthony Griffiths. *American Prints, 1879–1979*. Exh. cat., British Museum. London, 1980.

Castleman, Riva. *American Impressions: Prints since Pollock*. New York, 1985.

———. *Printed Art: A View of Two Decades*. Exh. cat., Museum of Modern Art. New York, 1980.

———. *Prints from Blocks: Gauguin to Now*. New York, 1983.

———. *Seven Master Printmakers: Innovations in the Eighties*. Exh. cat., Museum of Modern Art. New York, 1991.

Cohen, Ronny H. "Jumbo Prints: Artists Who Paint Big Want to Print Big." *ARTnews* 83 (Oct. 1984), 80–87.

———. "New Abstraction V." *Print Collector's Newsletter* 18 (March–April 1987), 9–13.

———. "The New Graphic Sensibility Transcends Media." *Print Collector's Newsletter* 14 (Nov.–Dec. 1983), 157–159.

———. "Paper Routes." *ARTnews* 82 (Oct. 1983), 78–85.

———. "Prints about Art." *Print Collector's Newsletter* 16 (Nov.–Dec. 1985), 164–168.

Cohrs, Timothy. "Hudson River Editions, Pelavin Editions—A Report Back From the Other-World of Printmaking." *Arts* 61 (Nov. 1986), 41–43.

The Combination Print: 1980's. Exh. cat., New Jersey Center for Visual Arts. Summit, NJ, 1988.

Conrad, Barnaby, III. "A Stroll down Fifty-Seventh Street." *Horizon* 24 (April 1981), 26–34.

Contemporary American Monotypes. Exh. cat., Chrysler Museum. Norfolk, VA, 1985.

Crimp, Douglas. "On the Museum's Ruins." *October* 13 (Summer 1980), 41–58.

Dückers, Alexander. *Von Beuys bis Stella*. Exh. cat., Staatliche Museen Preussischer Kulturbesitz. Berlin, 1986.

Field, Richard S. "The Painterly Print: Monotypes from the Seventeenth to the Twentieth Century." *Print Collector's Newsletter* 11 (Jan.–Feb. 1981), 202–204.

———. *Recent American Etching*. Exh. cat., Davidson Art Center, Wesleyan University. Middletown, CT, 1975.

———. "On Recent Woodcuts." *Print Collector's Newsletter* 13 (March–April 1982), 1–6.

———, and Ruth E. Fine. *A Graphic Muse: Prints by Contemporary American Women*. Exh. cat., Mount Holyoke College Art Museum. South Hadley, MA, 1987.

Fine, Ruth E. *Gemini G.E.L.: Art and Collaboration*. Exh. cat., National Gallery of Art. Washington, 1984.

Friedman, Martin, et al. *Tyler Graphics: The Extended Image*. Exh. cat., Walker Art Center, Minneapolis. New York, 1987.

Gambrell, Jamey. "All the News That's Fit for Prints: A Parallel of Social Concerns of the 1930s & 1980s." *Print Collector's Newsletter* 28 (May–June 1987), 52–55.

Gilmour, Pat. *Ken Tyler, Master Printer, and the American Print Renaissance*. Canberra, 1986.

———. *The Mechanized Image: An Historical Perspective on Twentieth Century Prints*. Exh. cat., Arts Council of Great Britain. London, 1978.

Goldman, Judith. *American Prints: Process and Proofs*. Exh. cat., Whitney Museum of American Art. New York, 1981.

———. "Printmaking: The Medium Isn't the Message Anymore." *ARTnews* 79 (March 1980), 82–85.

———. "Woodcuts: A Revival?" *Portfolio* 4 (Nov.–Dec. 1982), 66–71.

Heartney, Eleanor. "'Images and Impressions' at the Walker Art Center: Belief in the Possibility of Authenticity." *Arts* 59 (Dec. 1984), 118–121.

Henry, Gerrit. "The Artist and the Face: A Modern American Sampling." *Art in America* 63 (Jan.–Feb. 1975), 41.

Hunter, Sam. "Post-Modernist Painting." *Portfolio* 4 (Jan.–Feb. 1982), 46–53.

Images and Impressions: Painters Who Print. Exh. cat., Walker Art Center. Minneapolis, 1984.

Johnson, Una E. *American Prints and Printmakers*. Garden City, NY, 1980.

Krasnow, Iris. "Profiles in Passion." *Museum & Arts Washington* 3 (Sept.–Oct. 1987), 44–49.

Larson, Philip. "New Expressionism." *Print Collector's Newsletter* 15 (Jan.–Feb. 1985), 199–200.

Lovejoy, Margot. "Innovations in American Printmaking: 1956–1981." *Print Review* 13 (1981), 38–54.

Mirrors of the Mind. Exh. cat., Castelli Graphics. New York, 1975.

The Modern Art of the Print: Selections from the Collection of Lois and Michael Torf. Exh. cat., Williams College Museum of Art, Williamstown, MA, and Museum of Fine Arts, Boston, 1984.

Monumental Drawing: Works by 22 Contemporary Americans. Exh. cat., Brooklyn Museum. Brooklyn, 1986.

The Monumental Image. Exh. cat., University Art Gallery, Sonoma State University. Rohnert Park, CA, 1987.

Owens, Craig. "The Allegorical Impulse: Toward a Theory of Postmodernism (Part 2)." *October* 13 (Summer 1980), 58–80.

The Painterly Print: Monotypes from the Seventeenth to the Twentieth Century. Exh. cat., Metropolitan Museum of Art. New York, 1980.

Paperworks from Tyler Graphics. Exh. cat., Walker Art Center. Minneapolis, 1985.

Phillips, Deborah C. "Definitely Not Suitable for Framing." *ARTnews* 80 (Dec. 1981), 62–67.

———. "Looking for Relief? Woodcuts Are Back." *ARTnews* 81 (April 1982), 92–96.

Photographer as Printmaker: 140 Years of Photographic Printmaking. Exh. cat., Arts Council of Great Britain. London, 1981.

Photography and Art: Interactions since 1946. Exh. cat., Los Angeles County Museum of Art. Los Angeles, 1987.

Print Collector's Newsletter (1970–).

Process and Print. Exh. cat., Sarah Lawrence College Art Gallery. Bronxville, NY, 1988.

Radierungen im 20. Jahrhundert. Exh. cat., Staatsgalerie. Stuttgart, 1987.

Ross, Conrad H. "The Monoprint and the Monotype: A Case of Semantics." *Art Voices South* 2 (July–Aug. 1979), 89–91.

Sacilotto, Deli. *Photographic Printmaking Techniques*. New York, 1982.

Saff, Donald J. *Modern Masters of Intaglio*. Exh. cat., Paul Klapper Library, Queens College. New York, 1965.

———, ed. "Printmaking: The Collaborative Art." *Art Journal* 39 (Spring 1980), 167–201.

———, and Deli Sacilotto. *Printmaking: History and Process*. New York, 1978.

———. *Screenprinting: History and Process*. New York, 1979.

Saft, Carol. "The Growth of Print Workshops and Collaborative Printmaking since 1956." *Print Review* 13 (1981), 55–68.

Smagula, Howard J. "Printmaking: Art in the Age of Mechanical Reproduction." In *Currents: Contemporary Directions in the Visual Arts*, 99–133. Englewood Cliffs, NJ, 1983.

Sparks, Esther. *Universal Limited Art Editions: A History and Catalogue, The First Twenty-Five Years*. Chicago and New York, 1989.

Stasik, Andrew, ed. *American Prints and Printmaking, 1956–1981*, issued as *Print Review* 13. New York, 1981.

———. "Toward a Broader View and Greater Appreciation of America's Graphic Artist: The Printmaker." *Print Review* 14 (1981), 24–37.

Stein, Donna. "Photography in Printmaking." *Print Review* 16 (1983), 4–20.

Stretch, Bonnie Barrett. "Prints and Photographs: A Rich Mix of Mediums." *ARTnews* 87 (Feb. 1988), 56, 62.

A Survey of Prints, 1970–1977. Exh. cat., Museum of Contemporary Art. Chicago, 1977.

Tallman, Susan. "The Woodcut in the Age of Mechanical Reproduction." *Arts* 65 (Jan. 1989), 21–22.

Tamarind 25 Years: 1960–1985. Exh. cat., Art Museum, University of New Mexico. Albuquerque, 1985.

Tyler, Kenneth E. *Tyler Graphics: Catalogue Raisonné, 1974–1985*. Minneapolis and New York, 1987.

Velasco, Frances, and Suzanne Fried. "Combining Color Xerography with the Techniques of Silkscreen and Intaglio." *Leonardo* 17 (Spring 1984), 27–31.

Vermillion Publications 1978–1983. Minneapolis, 1983.

Volmer, Suzanne. "Drawings and Prints: As the Twain Meet." *Arts* 57 (Feb. 1983), 84–85.

Walker, Barry. *The American Artist as Printmaker: 23rd National Print Exhibition*. Exh. cat., Brooklyn Museum. Brooklyn, 1983.

———. *Public and Private: American Prints Today*. Exh. cat., Brooklyn Museum. Brooklyn, 1986.

Walker, Richard W. "Advice to Investors: Look 'Beyond the Familiar.'" *ARTnews* 82 (Summer 1983), 101–103.

Watrous, James. *A Century of American Printmaking, 1880–1980*. Madison, WI, 1984.

Wye, Deborah. "Collaboration East and West: A Discussion." *Print Collector's Newsletter* 16 (Jan.–Feb. 1986), 196–205.

———. *Committed to Print*. Exh. cat., Museum of Modern Art. New York, 1988.

———. "Printing Today: Eight Views." *Print Collector's Newsletter* 13 (Jan.–Feb. 1983), 189–200.

SECTION II: GRAPHICSTUDIO

Baro, Gene. *Graphicstudio U.S.F.: An Experiment in Art and Education*. Exh. cat., Brooklyn Museum. Brooklyn, 1978.

Benbow, Charles. "Graphicstudio Concept Is Expanded at USF." *St. Petersburg Times*, 12 April 1980, 8B.

Fine, Ruth E. "Donald Saff: A Life in Art." In *Donald Saff: Mixed Metaphor, 1956–1989*. Exh. cat., Tampa Museum of Art. Tampa, 1989.

Henry, Gerrit. "Donald Saff." *ARTnews* 83 (Summer 1984), 191–193.

Kelder, Diane. "Prints: Made in Graphicstudio." *Art in America* 61 (March–April 1973), 84–85.

Rauschenberg at Graphicstudio. Exh. cat., University of South Florida, Library Gallery. Tampa, 1974.

Rodriquez, Joanne M. "Extra Money Ignites Visual Arts." *Tampa Tribune Times*, 20 April 1980, 1–3.

Roy Lichtenstein: New Prints and Sculpture from Graphicstudio. Exh. cat., Wetterling Gallery. Gothenburg, Sweden, 1989.

Saff, Donald J. "Graphicstudio U.S.F." *Art Journal* 34 (Fall 1974), 10–18.

Graphicstudio Archive, National Gallery of Art: copies of thirty-two videotapes documenting various aspects of projects produced at Graphicstudio between 1985 and 1990.

Graphicstudio Archive, National Gallery of Art: six photocopied volumes of miscellaneous papers, including *Institute for Research in Art: Annual Report to the Provost, 1986/87, Graphicstudio U.S.F.*, vol. 3, *Bibliography;* and *Selected Memoranda, May 1982–March 1988;* as well as *Institute for Research in Art: Graphicstudio U.S.F., July 1, 1988–February 15, 1990*, vols. 1–4 (which include bibliography, documentation sheets, reports, exhibition reviews, etc.).

Graphicstudio Archive, National Gallery of Art: transcripts of twelve interviews with Graphicstudio artists conducted by University of South Florida student Jade Dellinger between 1987 and 1989.

SECTION III: ARTISTS

Acconci

Adams, Brooks. "Public Address Systems: Public Places, Museum of Modern Art, New York." *Art in America* 76 (Oct. 1988), 162–167.

Assembled: Works of Art Using Photography as a Construction Element. Exh. cat., Art Galleries, Wright State University. Dayton, OH, 1990.

Avgikos, Jan. "Interview: Vito Acconci." *Art Papers* 5 (Jan.–Feb. 1981), 1–5.

Diacono, Mario. *Vito Acconci: dal testo-azione al corpo come testo*. New York, 1975.

Lotringer, Sylvère. "Interview: Vito Acconci." *Flash Art* 147 (Summer 1989), 124–128.

Machineworks: Vito Acconci, Alice Aycock, Dennis Oppenheim. Exh. cat., Institute of Contemporary Art. Philadelphia, 1981.

"Making Shelter: Exhibit and Symposium, Graduate School of Design, Harvard University." *Harvard Architecture Review* 7 (1989), 8–53.

McFadden, Sarah. "Acconci's Home Works." *Connoisseur* 217 (June 1987), 26, 30.

Onorato, Ronald J. *Vito Acconci: "Domestic Trappings."* Exh. cat., La Jolla Museum of Contemporary Art. La Jolla, CA, 1987.

"Prints and Photographs Published." *Print Collector's Newsletter* 16 (March–April 1985), 18–21.

"Prints and Photographs Published." *Print Collector's Newsletter* 17 (March–April 1986), 16–18.

"Projections of Home." *Artforum* 26 (March 1988), 126–128.

Visions of Paradise. Exh. cat., Hayden Gallery, Massachusetts Institute of Technology. Cambridge, MA, 1984.

Vito Acconci: The House and Furnishings as Social Metaphor. Exh. cat., University of South Florida. Tampa, 1986.

Vito Acconci: Interview by Robin White. Oakland, CA, 1979.

Vito Acconci: Photographic Works 1969–1970. Exh. cat., Rhona Hoffman Gallery. New York, 1988.

Walker, Samuel, and Larry J. Feinberg. *Acid and Light: Contemporary Photo-Etchings*. Exh. cat., Allen Memorial Art Museum, Oberlin College. Oberlin, OH, 1987.

Anuszkiewicz

Anuszkiewicz: Acrylic Paintings 1966–1974. Exh. cat., Israel Museum. Jerusalem, 1976.

Anuszkiewicz, Richard. "A Study in the Creation of Space with Line Drawing." Master's thesis. Yale University, 1955.

Baker, Kenneth. "Abstractions a la Pop." *Christian Science Monitor,* 16 March 1970.

Corbino, Marcia. "Square Roots: Richard Anuszkiewicz Takes a Four-Sided Approach to Art." *Sarasota Herald Tribune,* 23 March 1980, 20.

Eichenberg, F. "Playing Cards." *Print Collector* 12 (March–April 1975), 14–16.

Gruen, John. "Richard Anuszkiewicz: A Beautiful Discourse with Space." *ARTnews* 78 (Sept. 1979), 68–69.

Lunde, Karl. *Anuszkiewicz.* New York, 1977.

———. "Richard Anuszkiewicz." *Arts Magazine* 49 (March 1975), 56–57.

Paintings and Graphics by Josef Albers, Richard Anuszkiewicz, Vincent Mariane. Exh. cat., Robinson Galleries. Houston, 1976.

Richard Anuszkiewicz. Exh. cat., La Jolla Museum of Contemporary Art. La Jolla, CA, 1976.

Richard Anuszkiewicz: Prints and Multiples, 1964–1979. Exh. cat., Sterling and Francine Clark Art Institute. Williamstown, MA, 1979.

Richard Anuszkiewicz: Recent Paintings. Exh. cat., Andrew Crispo Gallery. New York, 1975. Includes interview with Anuszkiewicz by Gene Baro.

Varian, Elayne H., and Albert Stewart. *Richard Anuszkiewicz: Prints.* Exh. cat., Fine Arts Gallery, Florida State University. Tallahassee, 1981.

Arakawa

Alloway, Lawrence. "Arakawa's Paintings: A Reading." *Arts* 44 (Nov. 1969), 26–29.

Arakawa. "Some Words." *Artfinder* (Winter 1986), 62.

Arakawa and Madeline H. Gins. *The Mechanism of Meaning.* New York, 1979.

Arakawa. "Notes on My Paintings—What I Am Mistakenly Looking For." *Arts* 44 (Nov. 1969), 29.

Arakawa. Exh. cat., Arts Club of Chicago. Chicago, 1981.

Arakawa. Exh. cat., Padiglione d'arte contemporanea. Milan, 1984.

Arakawa. Exh. cat., Städtische Kunsthalle. Düsseldorf, 1977.

Arakawa: Recent Drawings. Exh. cat., Aldrich Museum of Contemporary Art. Ridgefield, CT, 1984.

Calvino, Italo. "The Arrow in the Mind." *Artforum* 24 (Sept. 1985), 115–117.

Gins, Madeline H. "Forum: Arakawa's 'The Sharing of the Nameless' 1982–83." *Drawing* 6 (Jan.–Feb. 1985), 103–104.

———. "Interview with Arakawa." *Flash Art* 133 (April 1987), 64–68.

Larson, P. "Words in Print." *Print Collector's Newsletter* 5 (July–Aug. 1974), 53–56.

The Prints of Arakawa. Exh. cat., Williams College Museum of Art. Williamstown, MA, 1979.

Restany, Pierre. "Arakawa: Blank il colore della mente." *Domus* 669 (Feb. 1986), 68–69.

Aycock

After Years of Ruminating on the Events that Led up to His Misfortune. Exh. cat., Muhlenberg College Center for the Arts. Allentown, PA, 1978.

Alice Aycock: Retrospektive der Projekte und Ideen 1972–1983. Exh. cat., Württembergischer. Stuttgart, 1983.

Alice Aycock Projects, 1979–1981. Exh. cat., University of South Florida. Tampa, 1981.

Benbow, Charles. "Graphicstudio Concept Is Expanded at USF." *St. Petersburg Times,* 12 April 1980, 8B.

Complex Visions: Sculpture and Drawings by Alice Aycock. Exh. cat., Storm King Art Center. Mountainville, NY, 1990.

Fry, Edward. "The Poetic Machines of Alice Aycock." *Portfolio* 3 (Nov.–Dec. 1981), 60–65.

Halley, Peter. "The Crisis in Geometry." *Arts Magazine* 58 (June 1984), 111–115.

Machineworks: Vito Acconci, Alice Aycock, Dennis Oppenheim. Exh. cat., Institute of Contemporary Art. Philadelphia, 1981.

Poirier, Maurice. "The Ghost in the Machine: Alice Aycock's Constructions." *ARTnews* 85 (Oct. 1986), 78–85.

Rosen, Carol. "Sites and Installations: Outdoor Sculpture Revisited." *Arts Magazine* 64 (Feb. 1990), 65–70.

Sondheim, Alan, ed. *Individuals: Post-Movement Art in America.* New York, 1977.

Bailey

Found Objects: Mid Century Genre. Exh. cat., Upton Gallery, State University College at Buffalo. Buffalo, 1965.

Portfolio. Exh. cat., Upton Gallery, State University College at Buffalo. Buffalo, 1964.

Chia

Aronson, Steven M. "Sandro Chia in Tuscany." *Architectural Digest* 47 (Jan. 1990), 136–141.

Berger, D. "Sandro Chia in His Studio: An Interview." *Print Collector's Newsletter* 12 (Jan.–Feb. 1982), 168–169.

Fischer, Wolfgang. "Sandro Chia in Camera: Interview." *Studio International* 201 (April 1988), 8–13.

Hawthorne, Don. "Prints from the Alchemist's Laboratory." *ARTnews* 85 (Feb. 1986), 89–95.

Hughes, Robert. "Doing History as Light Opera." *Time* (16 May 1983), 79.

Marzorati, Gerald. "The Last Hero." *ARTnews* 82 (April 1983), 58–66.

"Prints and Photographs Published." *Print Collector's Newsletter* 17 (Sept.–Oct. 1986), 140–144.

Rassegna internazionale d'arte Acireale turistico-termale: Opere fatte ad arte: Acireale. Exh. cat., Palazzo di Citta. Florence, 1979.

Ratcliff, Carter. "On Iconography and Some Italians." *Art in America* 70 (Sept. 1982), 152–159.

Sandro Chia. Exh. cat., Chiesa di San Nicolò. Spoleto, Italy, 1988.

Sandro Chia. Exh. cat., Stedelijk Museum. Amsterdam, 1983.

Sandro Chia: Five Poems for Five Works on Paper and One Sculpture. Exh. cat., Akira Ikeda Gallery. Tokyo, 1987.

Sandro Chia: Juli 1985. Exh. cat., Galerie Thaddeus J. Ropac. Salzburg, 1985.

Sandro Chia: Novanta Spine al vento. Exh. cat., Museum Modernerkunst. Salzburg, 1989.

Sandro Chia, Francesco Clemente, and Enzo Cucchi. Exh. cat., Die Kunsthalle. Bielefeld, 1983. Includes interview with Chia.

Sandro Chia Prints 1973–1984. Exh. cat., Metropolitan Museum of Art. New York, 1984.

Waldman, Diane. *Italian Art Now: An American Perspective.* Exh. cat., Solomon R. Guggenheim Museum. New York, 1982.

Wei, Lilly. "Making Art, Making Money." *Art in America* 78 (July 1990), 132–141.

Weisner, Ulrich. *Passione per l'arte: Sandro Chia.* Bielefeld, 1986. Includes writings by Chia.

Close

Chuck Close. Exh. cat., Pace Gallery. New York, 1983.

Chuck Close: Dot Drawings 1973 to 1975. Exh. cat., Laguna Gloria Art Museum. Austin, 1975.

Chuck Close, Editions: A Catalog Raisonné and Exhibition. Exh. cat., Butler Institute of American Art. Youngstown, OH, 1989.

Chuck Close: Recent Work. Exh. cat., Pace Gallery. New York, 1986. Includes an interview with Close by Arnold Glimcher.

Copie Conforme? Exh. cat., Centre Georges Pompidou. Paris, 1979.

Cottingham, Jane. "An Interview with Chuck Close." *American Artist* 47 (May 1983), 62–67, 102–105.

Curtis, Verna Posever. "The Photograph and the Grid." *Chuck Close: Handmade Paper Editions—David Hockney: Photo-Composites*. Exh. cat., Milwaukee Art Museum. Milwaukee, 1984.

Deloach, Douglass. "Up Close: An Interview with Chuck Close." *Art Papers* 6 (March–April 1982), 1–3.

Diamonstein, Barbaralee. "Chuck Close: I'm Some Kind of Slow-Motion Cornball." *ARTnews* 79 (Summer 1980), 113–119.

Finch, Christopher. "Color Close-Ups." *Art in America* 77 (March 1989), 112–119.

Handmade Paper Editions. Exh. cat., Pace Editions. New York, 1982.

Harshman, Barbara. "An Interview with Chuck Close." *Arts Magazine* 52 (June 1978), 142–145.

Johnson, Ken. "Photographs by Chuck Close." *Arts Magazine* 61 (May 1987), 20–23.

Levin, Kim. "Chuck Close: Decoding the Image." *Arts* 52 (June 1978), 146–149.

Lyons, Lisa, and Martin Friedman. *Close Portraits*. Exh. cat., Walker Art Center. Minneapolis, 1980.

Lyons, Lisa, and Robert Storr. *Chuck Close*. New York, 1987.

Nemser, Cindy. "Photography as the Naked Truth." *Louisiana Revy* 13 (Feb. 1973), 30–33. Interview with Chuck Close.

"New York in the Eighties: A Symposium." *New Criterion* 4 (Summer 1986), 12–14.

"Prints and Photographs Published." *Print Collector's Newsletter* 17 (May–June 1986), 58–62.

Sandback, Amy B., and Ingrid Sischy. "A Progression by Chuck Close: Who's Afraid of Photography." *Artforum* 22 (May 1984), 50–55.

Shapiro, Michael. "Changing Variables: Chuck Close and His Prints." *Print Collector's Newsletter* 9 (July–Aug. 1978), 69–73.

Simon, Joan. "Close Encounters." *Art in America* 68 (Feb. 1980), 81–83.

Steiner, Wendy. "Postmodernist Portraits." *Art Journal* 46 (Fall 1987), 173–177.

Westerbeck, Colin. *Chuck Close*. Exh. cat., Art Institute of Chicago. Chicago, 1989.

Dine

Ackley, Clifford S. *Etchings by Jim Dine: Nancy Outside in July*. New York, 1983.

Beal, Graham W. J. *Jim Dine: Five Themes*. Exh. cat., Walker Art Center. Minneapolis, 1984.

Billeter, Erika. "Jim Dine: Zeichnung Als Totalitat." *Du* 7 (1988), 82–89.

Bonin, Wibke von, and Michael Cullen, eds. *Jim Dine: Complete Graphics*. Berlin, 1970.

D'Oench, Ellen, and Jean E. Feinberg. *Jim Dine Prints, 1977–1985*. Exh. cat., Davis Art Center and Cecile Zilkha Gallery, Wesleyan University. New York, 1986.

Glenn, Constance. *Jim Dine Drawings*. New York, 1985. Includes conversations with Dine.

Jim Dine: Gemälde, Aquarelle, Objecte, Graphik. Exh. cat., Kunsthalle Bern. Bern, 1971.

Jim Dine: The Hand-Coloured Viennese Hearts 1987–90. Exh. cat., Waddington Graphics/Pace Prints. New York and London, 1990.

Jim Dine: Oeuvres sur papier 1978–1979. Exh. cat., Galerie Alice Pauli. Lausanne, 1979.

Jim Dine: Paintings, Drawings, Etchings, 1976. Exh. cat., Pace Gallery. New York, 1977.

Jim Dine: Paintings, Drawings, Sculpture. Exh. cat., Pace Gallery. New York, 1986.

Jim Dine: Recent Graphics. Exh. cat., Hopkins Center Art Galleries, Dartmouth College. Hanover, NH, 1974.

Jim Dine: Sculpture and Drawings. Exh. cat., Pace Gallery. New York, 1984.

Jim Dine: Youth and the Maiden. Exh. cat., Waddington Graphics, London, 1989.

Krens, Thomas. *Jim Dine Prints, 1970–1977*. New York, 1977.

"Prints and Photographs Published." *Print Collector's Newsletter* 15 (July–Aug. 1984), 103–108.

"Prints and Photographs Published." *Print Collector's Newsletter* 17 (July–Aug. 1986), 95–98.

Shapiro, David. *Jim Dine: Painting What One Is*. New York, 1981.

Fichter

Berendt, John. "Modern Icons by a Masterful Iconoclast." *American Photographer* 9 (Dec. 1982), 70–78.

Fichter, Robert. *After Eden: An Exhibition and Book of Images*. Exh. cat., University of South Florida. Tampa, 1984.

———. *Know Where to Look*. Chicago, c. 1977.

———, and James R. Hugunin. *A X Cavation/RWF: A Weapon to Meet the Terrible Needs*. Boulder, CO, 1988.

Hicks, E. "Asking Political Questions." *Artweek* 14 (24 Dec. 1983), 11.

Hugunin, James R. "Fichter and Other Questions." *Afterimage* 12 (Nov. 1984), 6–8.

Invented Images. Exh. cat., Art Museum, University of California. Santa Barbara, 1980.

Jenkins, William. "Robert Fichter," *Northlight* 14 (1983), 4–15.

Murray, Joan. "Images of Protest." *Artweek* 15 (29 Sept. 1984), 11–12.

National Endowment for the Arts/Fellowship Artists, Florida 1983–1984. Exh. cat., Fine Arts Gallery, Florida State University. Tallahassee, 1985.

9 Critics, 9 Photographs. Carmel, CA, 1980.

Sobieszek, Robert A., ed. *Robert Fichter: Photography and Other Questions*. Albuquerque, 1983.

Friedlander

Allison, Sue. "Lee Friedlander." *American Photographer* 12 (March 1984), 60–61. Interview with Friedlander.

Friedlander, Lee. *The American Monument*. New York, 1976.

———. *Cray at Chippewa Falls*. Minneapolis, 1987.

———. *Factory Valleys: Ohio and Pennsylvania*. New York, 1982.

———. *Flowers and Trees*. New York, 1981.

———. *Fourteen American Monuments*. New York, 1977.

———. *Like a One-Eyed Cat: Photographs by Lee Friedlander 1956–1987*. Exh. cat., Seattle Art Museum. New York, 1989.

———. *Self Portrait*. New York, 1970.

———. *Three on Technology: New Photographs*. Cambridge, MA, 1988.

———. *Work from the Same House*. London, 1969.

Di Pietro, W. S. "Notes on Photography." *New Criterion* 6 (Oct. 1987), 16–27.

Ehrlich, Richard. "Lee Friedlander: The Uses of Confusion." *Creative Camera* 9 (1986), 16–17.

Green, Jonathan. *American Photography: A Critical History, 1945 to the Present*. New York, 1984.

Holborn, Mark. "Lee Friedlander Portraits." *Aperture* 104 (Fall 1986), 84–86.

Kenner, Hugh, and Rob Kenner. "The First Photo." *Art and Antiques* 6 (May 1989), 69–79.

Lee Friedlander, Photographs. Exh. cat., Hudson River Museum. New City, NY, 1978.

Rosler, Martha. "Lee Friedlander's Guarded Strategies." *Artforum* 13 (April 1975), 46–53.

Whelan, Richard. "Man of Irony" *Portfolio* 4 (Sept.–Oct. 1982), 106–111.

Woodward, Richard B. "Lee Friedlander: American Monument." *ARTnews* 88 (Nov. 1989), 140–145.

Glier

Allthorpe-Guyton, M. "Jenny Holzer, A-One, Mike Glier, Lady Pink." *Arts Review* 35 (27 May 1983), 283.

Art and Social Change, U.S.A. Exh. cat., Allen Memorial Art Museum, Oberlin College. Oberlin, OH, 1983.

Drawn to Scale: Cynthia Carlson, Michael Glier, and Randy Twaddle. Exh. cat., Addison Gallery of American Art, Phillips Academy. Andover, MA, 1990.

Damsker, Matt. "Glier's World View on Four Walls." *Los Angeles Times*, 5 Feb. 1984, 89–90. Statements by Glier.

"Expressionism Today: An Artist's Symposium." *Art in America* 70 (Dec. 1982), 72. Text based on interview with Glier by Sarah McFadden.

Face It: 10 Contemporary Artists. Exh. cat., Ohio Foundation on the Arts. Columbus, 1982.

Glier, Mike. "Working Watteau." *Artforum* 26 (April 1988), 99–100.

Hatton, B. "Urban Kisses." *Artscribe* 38 (Dec. 1982), 16–21.

Kuspit, Donald B. "Gallery Leftism." *Vanguard* 12 (Nov. 1983), 22–25.

Miller, Charles V. "A Viney Pastoral: Mike Glier Drawing from Nature." *Artforum* 25 (April 1987), 114–115.

Ratcliff, Carter. "Art and Resentment." *Art in America* 70 (Summer 1982), 9, 11, 13.

Wallworks. Exh. cat., John Weber Gallery. New York, 1986.

Weinstock, Jane. "A Lass, a Laugh, and a Lad." *Art in America* 71 (Summer 1983), 7–10.

Graves

Balken, Debra B. *Nancy Graves: Painting, Sculpture, Drawing, 1980–1985.* Exh. cat., Vassar College Art Gallery. Poughkeepsie, NY, 1986.

Berman, Avis. "Nancy Graves' New Age of Bronze." *ARTnews* 85 (Feb. 1986), 56–64.

Bourdon, David. "Lady Bountiful." *Vogue* (Feb. 1985), 82, 84.

Collins, Amy F., and Bradley Collins. "The Sum of the Parts." *Art in America* 76 (June 1988), 112–119.

DeVuono, Frances. "Knoedler and Company Exhibit." *ARTnews* 89 (Feb. 1990), 152–153.

Frank, Elizabeth. "Her Own Way: The Daring and Inventive Sculptures of Nancy Graves." *Connoisseur* 216 (Feb. 1986), 54–61.

Kelder, Diane. "New Editions by Nancy Graves." *Arts Magazine* 64 (Oct. 1988), 17–18.

Morgan, Robert C. "American Sculpture and the Search for a Referent." *Arts Magazine* 62 (Nov. 1987), 20–23.

Nancy Graves. Exh. cat., Wetterling Gallery. Gothenburg, Sweden, 1990.

"Nancy Graves: Between Painting and Sculpture." *Art International* 11 (Summer 1990), 29–33. Statements by the artist.

"Nancy Graves: Excerpts from Notebooks." *Artscribe* 17 (April 1979), 39–41.

Nancy Graves: Prints 1972–1988. Exh. cat., Associated American Artists. New York, 1988.

Nancy Graves: Sculpture, Drawings, Films, 1969–1971. Exh. cat., Neue Galerie im Alten Kurhaus. Aachen, Germany, 1971.

Nancy Graves: A Survey 1969–1980. Exh. cat., Albright-Knox Art Gallery. Buffalo, NY, 1980.

"Prints and Photographs Published." *Print Collector's Newsletter* 16 (March–April 1985), 18–21.

"Prints and Photographs Published." *Print Collector's Newsletter* 16 (July–Aug. 1985), 99–102.

The Sculpture of Nancy Graves: A Catalogue Raisonné. New York, 1987.

Shapiro, Michael E. "Nature into Sculpture: Nancy Graves and the Tradition of Direct Casting." *Arts Magazine* 59 (Nov. 1984), 92–96.

Wasserman, Emily. "A Conversation with Nancy Graves." *Artforum* 9 (Oct. 1970), 42–47.

Hinman

Charles Hinman. Exh. cat., Denise René. New York, 1972.

Charles Hinman. Exh. cat., Galleri Bellman. New York, 1983.

Charles Hinman: Current Works. Exh. cat., Everson Museum of Art. Syracuse, 1980.

Gilbert-Rolfe, J. "Charles Hinman, Denise René Gallery." *Artforum* 12 (Jan. 1974), 67–72.

Hinman, Charles. In "New Talent in U.S.A." *Art in America* 54 (July–Aug. 1966), 36.

Johnson, Ellen H. "Three New, Cool, Bright Imagists." *ARTnews* 64 (Summer 1965), 42–44.

Masheck, Joseph. "Hinman." *Artforum* 10 (June 1972), 81–82.

Olsen, S. "A Conversation with Charles Hinman." *Midwest Art* 3 (Nov. 1976), 24.

"Prints and Photographs Published." *Print Collector's Newsletter* 12 (May–June 1981), 49.

Krushenick

Battcock, Gregory. "Krushenick's Cultural Revelations." *Arts* 43 (April 1969), 26–27.

Krushenick. Exh. cat., Galerie Ileana Sonnabend. Paris, 1967.

Nicholas Krushenick. Exh. cat., Galerie Beyeler. Basel, 1971.

Nicholas Krushenick. Exh. cat., Jaffe-Friede Gallery, Hopkins Center, Dartmouth College. Hanover, NH, 1969.

Nicholas Krushenick. Exh. cat., Kestner-Gesellschaft. Hannover, 1972.

Nicholas Krushenick. Exh. cat., Walker Art Center. Minneapolis, 1968.

Perreault, John. "Krushenick's Blazing Blazons." *ARTnews* 66 (Mar. 1967), 34, 72–73.

Robins, Corinne. "The Artist Speaks: Nicholas Krushenick." *Art in America* 57 (May–June 1969), 60–65.

———. "Nicholas Krushenick: New Paintings." *Arts Magazine* 50 (Dec. 1975), 86–87.

Strohl, Audrey W. "Nicholas Krushenick Blends Canvases with Campuses." *Art Voices South* 1 (July–Aug. 1978), 11–12.

Leslie

Action Precision: The New Direction in New York, 1955–1960. Exh. cat., Newport Harbor Art Museum. Newport Beach, CA, 1984.

Alfred Leslie. Exh. cat., Allan Frumkin Gallery. New York, 1975. Statement by the artist.

Alfred Leslie. Exh. cat., Museum of Fine Arts. Boston, 1976.

Alfred Leslie: Drawings. Exh. cat., Flynn gallery, New York, 1991.

Arthur, John. "Interview: Alfred Leslie Talks with John Arthur." *Drawing* 1 (Nov.–Dec. 1979), 81–85.

Baker, Kenneth. "Second Generation: Mannerism or Momentum." *Art in America* 73 (June 1985), 102–111.

Goodyear, Frank H., Jr. *Contemporary American Realism since 1960.* Exh. cat., Pennsylvania Academy of the Fine Arts. Philadelphia, 1981.

———. *Eight Contemporary American Realists: Alfred Leslie. . . .* Exh. cat., Pennsylvania Academy of the Fine Arts. Philadelphia, 1977.

Jouffroy, Alain. "Al Leslie: de l'abstraction gestuelle à l'hyperréalisme." *XXᵉ Siècle* 37 (Dec. 1975), 98–102.

Leslie, Alfred. *100 Views along the Road.* Exh. cat., Oil and Steel Gallery. New York, 1983.

"Prints and Photographs Published." *Print Collector's Newsletter* 17 (Sept.–Oct. 1986), 140–144.

Sources of Light: Contemporary American Luminism. Exh. cat., Henry Art Gallery, University of Washington. Seattle, 1985.

"Watercolors that Transport." Excerpt from Leslie's book *100 Views along the Road.* In *American Artist* 53 (April 1989), 66–69, 96–102.

Westfall, Stephen. "Then and Now: Six of the New York School Look Back." *Art in America* 73 (June 1985), 112–121. Includes interview with Leslie.

Lichtenstein

Alloway, Lawrence. *Roy Lichtenstein.* New York, 1983.

American Masters of the 60's. Exh. cat., Tony Shafrazi Gallery. New York, 1990.

Coplans, John, ed. *Roy Lichtenstein.* New York, 1972.

———. "Talking with Roy Lichtenstein." *Artforum* 5 (May 1967), 34–39.

Cowart, Jack. *Roy Lichtenstein 1970–1980.* Exh. cat., Saint Louis Art Museum. New York, 1981.

Glenn, Constance. *Roy Lichtenstein: Ceramic Sculpture.* Exh. cat., Art Galleries, California State University. Long Beach, CA, 1977. Includes conversation with Lichtenstein.

Phillips, Deborah C. "Looking for Relief? Woodcuts Are Back." *ARTnews* 81 (April 1982), 92–96.

"Prints and Photographs Published." *Print Collector's Newsletter* 20 (July–Aug. 1989), 101–104.

Rose, Bernice. *The Drawings of Roy Lichtenstein.* Exh. cat., Museum of Modern Art. New York, 1987.

Roy Lichtenstein: A Retrospective of Prints, 1962–1971. Exh. cat., John Berggruen Gallery. San Francisco, 1971.

Roy Lichtenstein: Drawings and Prints. New York, 1971.

Roy Lichtenstein: Drawings and Prints. Secaucus, NJ, 1988.

Roy Lichtenstein: Graphics, Reliefs, and Sculpture, 1969–1970. Exh. cat., Art Gallery, University of California, Irvine. Los Angeles, 1970.

Roy Lichtenstein: New Prints and Sculptures from Graphicstudio. Exh. cat., Wetterling Gallery. Gothenburg, Sweden, 1989.

Taylor, Paul. "Roy Lichtenstein: Interview." *Flash Art* 148 (Oct. 1989), 87–93.

Tuchman, Phyllis. "Pop." *ARTnews* 73 (May 1974), 24–29. Interview with Lichtenstein and others.

Waldman, Diane. *Roy Lichtenstein.* Exh. cat., Solomon R. Guggenheim Museum. New York, 1969.

———. *Roy Lichtenstein.* Milan, 1971.

Mapplethorpe

Allen, Jane A. "The Sacred and the Profane." *New Art Examiner* 17 (Summer 1990), 18–22.

Bondi, I. "The Yin and the Yang of Robert Mapplethorpe." *Print Letter* 19 (Jan.–Feb. 1979), 9–11. Interview with Mapplethorpe.

Bourdon, David. "Robert Mapplethorpe." *Arts* 5 (April 1977), 7.

Celant, Germano. *Artmakers.* Milan, 1984.

The Collection of Robert Mapplethorpe. Auction catalogue, Sotheby Parke Bernet. New York, 1982.

Evans, Tom. "Photographer in Focus." *Art and Artists,* no. 210 (March 1984), 16–19. Interview with Mapplethorpe.

Henry, Gerrit. "Robert Mapplethorpe: Collecting Quality." *Print Collector's Newsletter* 13 (Sept.–Oct. 1982), 128–130. Interview with Mapplethorpe.

Jones, Bill. "Born Again: Seeing the End of Photography." *Arts Magazine* 64 (Oct. 1989), 72–77.

Kardon, Janet. *Robert Mapplethorpe: The Perfect Moment.* Exh. cat., Institute of Contemporary Art. Philadelphia, 1988.

Koch, Stephen. "Guilt, Grace, and Robert Mapplethorpe." *Art in America* 74 (Nov. 1986), 144–151.

Larson, Kay. "How Should Artists Be Educated." *ARTnews* 82 (Nov. 1983), 87.

Manegold, C. S. "Robert Mapplethorpe: The Latest Wave." *Artscribe* 45 (Feb.–April 1984), 36–40.

Mapplethorpe, Robert. *Certain People: A Book of Portraits.* Pasadena, CA, 1985.

———. *Flowers.* Boston, 1990.

———. *Lady, Lisa Lyon.* New York, 1983. Text by Bruce Chatwin.

———. *Some Women.* Boston, 1989.

———. *Ten by Ten.* Munich, 1988. Text by Els Barents.

Mapplethorpe Portraits: Robert Mapplethorpe Photographs, 1975–87. Exh. cat., National Portrait Gallery. London, 1988.

Marshall, Richard. *Robert Mapplethorpe.* Exh. cat., Whitney Museum of American Art. New York, 1988.

"The Masters." *American Photo* 1 (Jan.–Feb. 1990), 62–77.

Morgan, Stuart. "Something Magic." *Artforum* 25 (May 1987), 118–123.

Robert Mapplethorpe. Exh. cat., Stedelijk Museum. Amsterdam, 1988.

Robert Mapplethorpe, fotographie. Exh. cat., Museo Fortuny. Venice, 1983.

Sekula, Allan. "Issues and Commentary." *Art in America* 78 (Feb. 1990), 39–43.

Smith, Patti. "Transfiguration Configuration: Mapplethorpe." *Camera* 56 (Sept. 1977), 4–13, 33.

Sokolowski, Thomas W. "Iconophobics Anonymous." *Artforum* 28 (Summer 1990), 114–119.

Tully, Judd. "Mapplethorpe: Self-Portraits Hot Sellers at Sotheby's." *Washington Post,* 3 Nov. 1980, C1, C6.

Weiley, Susan. "Prince of Darkness, Angel of Light." *ARTnews* 87 (Dec. 1988), 106–111.

Pearlstein

Adrian, Dennis. "The Prints of Philip Pearlstein." *Print Collector's Newsletter* 4 (July–Aug. 1973), 49–52.

"An Artist's Case." *Art in America* 78 (May 1990), 61.

Bowman, Russell. *Philip Pearlstein: The Complete Paintings.* New York, 1983.

Cummings, Paul. *Artists in Their Own Words: Interviews by Paul Cummings.* New York, 1979.

Dückers, Alexander. *Philip Pearlstein: Zeichnungen und Aquarelle, die Druckgraphik.* Exh. cat., Staatliche Museen Preussischer Kulturbesitz. Berlin, 1972.

Field, Richard S. *Philip Pearlstein: Prints, Drawings, Paintings.* Exh. cat., Davison Art Center, Wesleyan University. Middletown, CT, 1979.

Gardner, Paul. "The Electronic Palette." *ARTnews* 84 (Feb. 1985), 66–73.

Goldman, Judith. "The Proof Is in the Process: Painters as Printmakers." *ARTnews* 80 (Sept. 1981), 148–151.

Hurwitz, Laurie. "Artists and Computers." *American Artist* 51 (Oct. 1987), supp. 2–4.

Landwehr, William C. *The Lithographs and Etchings of Philip Pearlstein.* Exh. cat., Springfield Art Museum. Springfield, MO, 1978. Essay by Richard S. Field.

Mainardi, Pat. "Philip Pearlstein: Old Master of the New Realists." *ARTnews* 75 (Nov. 1976), 74.

Pearlstein, Philip. "Process Is My Goal." *New York Times,* 31 Oct. 1976, D29.

———, Lawrence Alloway, and Peter Schjeldahl. "Andy Warhol." *Art in America* 75 (May 1987), 137–143.

Perreault, John. *Philip Pearlstein: Watercolors and Drawings.* New York, 1988. Foreword by Pearlstein.

Philip Pearlstein. Exh. cat., Georgia Museum of Art, University of Georgia. Athens, GA, 1970. Essay by Linda Nochlin.

Philip Pearlstein: Landscape Aquatints 1978–1980. Exh. cat., Brooke Alexander Gallery. New York, 1981. Essay by Jerome Viola.

Philip Pearlstein: Paintings, Drawings, Prints. Exh. cat., Donald Morris Gallery. Detroit, 1972.

Philip Pearlstein: Paintings and Watercolors. Exh. cat., John and Mable Ringling Museum. Sarasota, FL, 1981.

Philip Pearlstein: A Retrospective. Exh. cat., Milwaukee Art Museum. New York, 1983. Essays by Russell Bowman, Philip Pearlstein, and Irving Sandler.

Pomeroy, Ralph. "Pearlstein Portraits." *Art and Artists* 8 (Sept. 1973), 38–43. Interview with Pearlstein.

"Prints and Photographs Published." *Print Collector's Newsletter* 16 (Sept.–Oct., 1985), 139–142.

Shaman, Sanford S. "An Interview with Philip Pearlstein." *Art in America* 69 (Sept. 1981), 120–126, 213–215.

———. "Philip Pearlstein: Painting to Watercolors." *Arts Magazine* 59 (Oct. 1984), 134–136.

Storr, Robert. "Pearlstein Today: Upping the Ante." *Art in America* 72 (Feb. 1984), 90–99.

Viola, Jerome. *The Painting and Teaching of Philip Pearlstein.* New York, 1982.

Rauschenberg

Ashton, Dore. *Rauschenberg: XXXIV Drawings for Dante's "Inferno."* Exh. cat., Galerie Gerald Cramer, Geneva. New York, 1968.

Bernstock, Judith E. "A New Interpretation of Rauschenberg's Imagery." *Pantheon* 46 (1988), 149–164.

Feinstein, Roni. "The Early Work of Robert Rauschenberg: The White Paintings, the Black Paintings, and the Elemental Sculpture." *Arts* 61 (Sept. 1986), 28–37.

Forge, Andrew. *Rauschenberg.* New York, 1969.

Ginsburg, Susan. "Rauschenberg's Dialogue." *Print Collector's Newsletter* 6 (Jan.–Feb. 1976), 152–155.

Gruen, John. "Robert Rauschenberg: An Audience of One." *ARTnews* 76 (Feb. 1977), 44–48.

Herrera, Hayden. "Rauschenberg's Scroll." *Connoisseur* 213 (Jan. 1983), 57–61.

Kotz, Mary Lynn. *Rauschenberg/Art and Life.* New York, 1990.

———. "Robert Rauschenberg's State of the Universe Message." *ARTnews* 82 (Feb. 1983), 54–61.

McCullagh, Janice. "Image to Collage." *Arts Magazine* 60 (Dec. 1985), 80–85.

Ormond, Mark. *Robert Rauschenberg: Works from the Salvage Series.* Exh. cat., John and Mable Ringling Museum of Art. Sarasota, FL, 1985.

Perry, Arthur. "A Conversation between Robert Rauschenberg and Arthur Perry." *Artmagazine* 41 (Nov.–Dec. 1978), 31–35.

Prints from the Untitled Press, Captiva, Florida. Exh. cat., Wadsworth Atheneum. Hartford, 1973.

Ratcliff, Carter. "Rauschenberg's Solvent-Transfer Drawings." *Print Collector's Newsletter* 18 (May–June 1987), 49–51.

Rauschenberg, Robert. "The Boy from Port Arthur." *Art and Antiques* 3 (Feb. 1986), 58–61.

———. *Photos In + Out City Limits: Boston.* West Islip, NY, 1981.

———. *Photos In + Out City Limits: New York C.* West Islip, NY, 1982.

Rauschenberg at Graphicstudio. Exh. cat., Library Gallery, University of South Florida. Tampa, 1974.

Rauschenberg Currents. Exh. cat., Dayton's Gallery 12. Minneapolis, 1970.

Rauschenberg Graphic Art. Exh. cat., Institute of Contemporary Art. Philadelphia, 1970.

Rauschenberg Overseas Culture Interchange. Exh. cat., National Gallery of Art. Washington, 1991.

Robert Rauschenberg. Exh. cat., National Collection of Fine Arts. Washington, DC, 1976.

Robert Rauschenberg: Bilder, Zeichnungen, Lithos. Exh. cat., Amerika-Haus. Berlin, 1965.

Robert Rauschenberg: Graphik. Exh. cat., Kunstverein. Karlsruhe, 1971.

Robert Rauschenberg: Paintings, Drawings, and Combines, 1949–1964. Exh. cat., Whitechapel Art Gallery. London, 1964.

Robert Rauschenberg: Photographs. New York, 1981. Includes interview with Rauschenberg by Alain Sayag.

Robert Rauschenberg: Prints 1948–1970. Exh. cat., Minneapolis Institute of Arts. Minneapolis, 1970.

Robert Rauschenberg: Werke 1950–1980. Exh. cat., Staatliche Kunsthalle. Berlin, 1980.

Robert Rauschenberg: Work from Four Series. Exh. cat., Contemporary Arts Museum. Houston, 1985.

Robert Rauschenberg in Black and White: Paintings 1962–1963, Lithographs 1962–1967. Exh. cat., Newport Harbor Art Museum, Newport Beach, CA. Balboa, 1969.

Rose, Barbara. *Rauschenberg.* New York, 1987. Interview.

Seckler, Dorothy G. "The Artist Speaks: Robert Rauschenberg." *Art in America* 54 (May 1966), 72–85.

7 Characters: Rauschenberg. Los Angeles, 1983. Essay by Donald Saff.

Smith, Graham. "Photos In + Out City Limits." *Print Collector's Newsletter* 14 (Nov.–Dec. 1983), 183–184.

Solomon, Alan R. *Robert Rauschenberg.* Exh. cat., Jewish Museum. New York, 1963.

Swenson, Gene R. "Rauschenberg Paints a Picture." *ARTnews* 62 (Apr. 1963), 24–27.

Tomkins, Calvin. *The Bride & the Bachelors.* New York, 1965.

———. *Off the Wall: Robert Rauschenberg and the Art World of Our Time.* Garden City, NY, 1980.

Tyler, Kenneth, and Rosamund Felson. "Two Rauschenberg Paper Projects." *Paper Art and Technology* (1979), 81–86.

Young, Joseph E. "Pages and Fuses: An Extended View of Robert Rauschenberg." *Print Collector's Newsletter* 5 (May–June 1974), 25–30.

Rosenquist

Barnett, Catherine. "Wise Men Fish Here." *Art and Antiques* 5 (Feb. 1988), 43–44, 91.

Battcock, Gregory. "James Rosenquist." *Arts Magazine* 46 (May 1972), 49–52.

Bernstein, Roberta. "Rosenquist Reflected: The Tampa Prints." *Print Collector's Newsletter* 4 (March–April 1973), 6–8.

Cotter, Holland. "Advertisements for a Mean Utopia." *Art in America* 75 (Jan. 1987), 82–89.

Charbonneaux, Catherine. "Le Pop paie." *Connaissance des arts* 420 (Feb. 1987), 26–27.

Goldman, Judith. *James Rosenquist.* New York, 1985.

Heartney, Eleanor. "Rosenquist Revisited." *ARTnews* 85 (Summer 1986), 98–103.

James Rosenquist. Exh. cat., Fine Arts Gallery, Florida State University. Tallahassee, 1988. Essay by Craig Adcock.

James Rosenquist at USF. Exh. cat., University of South Florida. Tampa, 1988. Essay by Donald Saff.

James Rosenquist: Gemälde, Räume, Graphik. Exh. cat., Kunsthalle. Cologne, 1972.

James Rosenquist: Nevermind, from Thought to Drawing. Exh. cat., Universal Limited Art Editions. New York, 1990.

James Rosenquist Graphics Retrospective. Exh. cat., John and Mable Ringling Museum of Art. Sarasota, FL, 1979.

James Rosenquist: Welcome to The Water Planet and House of Fire, 1988–1989. Mount Kisco, NY, 1989. Essay by Judith Goldman.

Lippard, Lucy. *Changing: Essays in Art Criticism.* New York, 1971.

"Prints and Photographs Published." *Print Collector's Newsletter* 16 (Nov.–Dec. 1985), 176–179.

"Prints and Photographs Published." *Print Collector's Newsletter* 17 (Sept.–Oct. 1986), 140–144.

"Prints and Photographs Published." *Print Collector's Newsletter* 21 (March–April 1990), 24.

Ratcliff, Carter. "Rosenquist's Rouge." *Artforum* 23 (Summer 1985), 92–94.

Siegel, Jeanne. "An Interview with James Rosenquist." *Artforum* 10 (June 1972), 30–41.

Tucker, Marcia. *James Rosenquist.* Exh. cat., Whitney Museum of American Art. New York, 1972.

Ruscha

Antin, Eleanor. "Reading Ruscha." *Art in America* 61 (Nov.–Dec. 1973), 64–71.

Barendse, Henri Man. "An Interview with Ed Ruscha." *Afterimage* 8 (Feb. 1981), 8–10.

Bourdon, David. "A Heap of Words about Ed Ruscha." *Art International* 15 (Nov. 1971), 25–28, 38.

———. "Ruscha as Publisher [or ALL BOOKED UP]." *ARTnews* 71 (April 1972), 32–36, 68–69.

Coplans, John. "Concerning 'Various Small Fires,' Edward Ruscha Discusses His Perplexing Publications." *Artforum* 3 (Feb. 1965), 24–25. Interview with Ruscha.

Edward Ruscha. Exh. cat., Albright-Knox Art Gallery. Buffalo, NY, 1976.

Edward Ruscha. Exh. cat., Centre Georges Pompidou, Paris. Barcelona, 1990.

Edward Ruscha. Exh. cat., Stedelijk Museum. Amsterdam, 1976.

Edward Ruscha: Prints and Publications, 1962–74. Exh. cat., Arts Council of Great Britain. London, 1975.

Ed Ruscha: Recent Works on Paper. London, 1988.

Edward Ruscha: Young Artist. Exh. cat., Minneapolis Institute of Arts. Minneapolis, 1972.

Failing, Patricia. "Ed Ruscha, Young Artist: Dead Serious about Being Nonsensical." *ARTnews* 81 (April 1982), 74–81.

Fehlau, Fred. "Ed Ruscha." *Flash Art* 138 (Jan.–Feb. 1988), 70–72.

4x6: Zeichnungen von Edward Ruscha. Exh. cat., Westfälischer Kunstverein. Münster, 1986.

Graphic Works by Edward Ruscha. Exh. cat., Auckland City Art Gallery. Auckland, New Zealand, 1978.

Kangas, Matthew. "Just an Average Guy." *Vanguard* 8 (Oct. 1979), 16–17.

Larson, Philip. "Ruscha in Minneapolis." *Print Collector's Newsletter* 3 (July–Aug. 1972), 52–54.

Lloyd, G. "A Talk With Ed Ruscha." *Dumb Ox* 4 (Spring 1977), 5–7.

Mitchum, Trina. "A Conversation with Ed Ruscha." *Journal of the Los Angeles Institute of Contemporary Art* 21 (Jan.–Feb. 1979), 21–24.

Pindell, Howardena. "Words with Ruscha." *Print Collector's Newsletter* 3 (Jan.–Feb. 1973), 125–128. Interview with Ruscha.

Radice, Barbara. "Interview with Ed Ruscha." *Flash Art* 54/55 (May 1975), 49.

Ruscha, Edward. *Real Estate Opportunities.* Los Angeles, 1970.

———. *Some Los Angeles Apartments.* Los Angeles, 1965.

———. *Twentysix Gasoline Stations.* Los Angeles, 1963.

The Works of Edward Ruscha. Exh. cat., San Francisco Museum of Modern Art. New York, 1982. With essays by Dave Hickey and Peter Plagens.

Schapiro

At Home. Exh. cat., Museum of Art. Long Beach, CA, 1983.

Bradley, Paula W. "Miriam Schapiro: The Feminist Transformation of an Avant-Garde Artist." Ph.D. diss., University of North Carolina. Chapel Hill, 1983.

Cecil, Sarah. "New Editions." *ARTnews* 83 (Oct. 1984), 102.

Degener, Patricia. "Artist's Messages from the Heart." *St. Louis Post Dispatch,* 17 May 1985.

Garver, Thomas H. *Paul Brach and Miriam Schapiro: Paintings and Graphic Works.* Exh. cat., Newport Harbor Art Museum, Newport Beach, CA. Balboa, 1969.

Gill, Susan. "From 'Femmage' to Figuration." *ARTnews* 85 (April 1986), 95–101.

Gouma-Peterson, Thalia. *Miriam Schapiro: A Retrospective, 1953–1980.* Exh. cat., College of Wooster Art Museum. Wooster, OH, 1980.

———. "The Theater of Life and Illusion in Miriam Schapiro's Recent Work." *Arts Magazine* 60 (March 1986), 38–43.

Humanism: An Undercurrent. Exh. cat., University of South Florida. Tampa, 1984.

Lyons, Harriet. "Woman's Art: It's the Only Goddam Energy Around." *Ms* 6 (Dec. 1977), 40–43. Interview with Schapiro.

Miriam Schapiro: Anatomy of a Kimono. Exh. cat., Reed College Art Gallery. Portland, OR, 1978.

Miriam Schapiro: Femmages 1971–1985. Exh. cat., Brentwood Gallery. St. Louis, MO, 1985. With an essay entitled "Femmage," by Schapiro and Melissa Meyer.

"Prints and Photographs Published." *Print Collector's Newsletter* 15 (Sept.–Oct. 1984), 42–45.

Robinson, Charlotte, ed. *The Artist and the Quilt.* New York, 1983. With an essay by Schapiro, "Geometry and Flowers."

Ruddick, Sara, and Pamela Daniels, eds. *Working It Out.* New York, 1977.

Sanford, Christy, and Enid Shomer. "An Interview with Miriam Schapiro." *Women Artists News* 11 (Spring 1986), 22–26.

Schapiro, Miriam. "Recalling Womanhouse." *Women's Studies Quarterly* 15 (Spring–Summer 1987), 25–30.

———. *Rondo.* San Francisco, 1989.

The Shrine, the Computer, and the Dollhouse. Exh. cat., Mandeville Art Gallery, University of California. San Diego, 1975. Includes a interview with Schapiro by Moira Roth.

Smith

Barrett, Cyril, S.J. "Richard Smith: Sculptor or Painter?" *Art International* 8 (20 Oct. 1967), 35–38.

Castle, T. "Richard Smith in New York." *Art Monthly* 29 (Sept. 1979), 8–9.

Denvir, Bernard. "A Double Reality: The Work and Career of Richard Smith." *Art International* 14 (Summer 1970), 78–82.

4 Jonge Engelse Schilders: ... Richard Smith. XXXIII Biennale Venetië 1966. Exh. cat., Museum Boymans-van Beuningen. Rotterdam, 1967.

Gilmour, Pat. "Richard Smith: Printmaker." *Art and Artists* 5 (June 1970), 23.

Lippard, Lucy. "Richard Smith: Conversations with the Artist." *Art International* 8 (25 Nov. 1964), 31–34.

Packer, W. "Radical and Elegant." *Art and Artists* 8 (March 1974), 20–23.

Paginas Amarillas. Exh. cat., Fundacion museo de arte contemporáneo de Caracas. Caracas, 1975. Text by Richard Smith.

Richard Smith: Neue Arbieten. Exh. cat., Ulm Museum. Ulm, 1980.

Richard Smith: Paintings, 1958–1966. Exh. cat., Whitechapel Art Gallery. London, 1966.

Richard Smith: Recent Work 1972–1977. Exh. cat., Hayden Gallery, Massachusetts Institute of Technology. Cambridge, MA, 1978.

Richard Smith: A Retrospective Exhibition of Graphics & Multiples. Exh. cat., British Council. London, 1979.

Richard Smith: Seven Exhibitions 1961–75. Exh. cat., Tate Gallery. London, 1975.

Rose, Barbara. "Richard Smith: An Interview with Barbara Rose." *Studio International* 190 (Sept.–Oct. 1975), 165–167.

Seymour, Ann. "Richard Smith." *Studio* 179 (June 1970), 256–261.

Smith, Richard. "Ideograms." *Ark* 16 (1956), 52–56.

———. "New Readers Start Here." *Ark* 32 (Summer 1962), 37–43.

———. "Preoccupations: Richard Smith Talks with Ann Seymour." *Art and Artists* 5 (June 1970), 18–23.

———. "Printing Paintings, Painting Prints." *Print Collector's Newsletter* 6 (Jan.–Feb. 1976), 156–157.

———. "Richard Smith Discusses His Latest Work." *Studio* 178 (Dec. 1969), 242.

———, and Kenneth E. Tyler. *Richard Smith: Cartouche Series.* Exh. cat., Norman MacKenzie Art Gallery, University of Regina. Regina, Canada, 1980.

Solomon, Elke. "New Editions." *ARTnews* 74 (March 1975), 64–65.

Witkin

Chris, Cynthia. "Witkin's Others." *Exposure* 26 (Spring 1988), 16–26.

Edwards, Owen. "Dancing With Death." *American Photographer* 11, no. 2 (Aug. 1983), 29–30.

———. "Joel-Peter Witkin." *American Photographer* 15 (Nov. 1985), 40–53.

Fahey, David. "Joel-Peter Witkin." *Interview* 15 (July 1985), 103–105.

Fontanella, Lee. "From Matters of Fact to Matters of Value." *Photo Vision* 19 (n.d.), 7–63.

"Joel-Peter Witkin." In *Contemporary Photographers.* Chicago, 1988.

Joel-Peter Witkin. Exh. cat., Centre national de la photographie, Palais de Tokyo. Paris, 1989.

Joel-Peter Witkin. Exh. cat., Centro de Arte Reina Sofia. Madrid, 1988.

Joel-Peter Witkin. Exh. cat., Stedelijk Museum. Amsterdam, 1983.

Joel-Peter Witkin: Forty Photographs. Exh. cat., San Francisco Museum of Modern Art. San Francisco, 1985. Introduction by Van Deren Coke.

Joel-Peter Witkin: Gods of Earth and Heaven. Pasadena, CA, 1989.

Kozloff, Max. "Connection between Two Critics about a Disagreeable Beauty." *Artforum* 22 (Feb. 1984), 45–53.

Lotringer, Sylvère. "Embracing Death: An Interview with Joel-Peter Witkin." *Journal: A Contemporary Arts Magazine* 5 (Spring 1987), 47–49.

Photo-Derived. Exh. cat., School of Fine Arts Gallery, Indiana University. Bloomington, 1989.

Witkin, Joel-Peter. "Divine Revolt." *Aperture* 100 (Fall 1985), 34–41.

———. Interview with Robin Brailsford. *Photo Metro* (Sept. 1988), 14–21.

INDEX

Page numbers for illustrations are set in boldface italic type

PHOTO CREDITS

Photographs of works of art in the Graphicstudio Archive have been taken by Dean Beasom, Philip A. Charles, Lorene Emerson, Peter Foe, Edward Owen, and George Holzer. Other photographs have been provided by Stephanie Anuszkiewicz, Courtesy of Richard Anuszkiewicz, p. 99; Oscar Bailey, p. 125; Bruce Beeken, Courtesy of Graphicstudio, University of South Florida, figs. 80a, 80b; Russ Blaise, Courtesy of James Rosenquist, fig. 60b; Ken Cohen, fig. 78a; Bevan Davies, Courtesy of The Pace Gallery, fig. 37a; Courtesy of Elvehjem Museum of Art, University of Wisconsin-Madison, fig. 51a; EEVA, Courtesy of Ronald Feldman Fine Arts, New York, fig. 19c; Courtesy of Robert W. Fichter, p. 161; Ruth Fine, fig. 61b; Courtesy of Graphicstudio, University of South Florida, figs. 4, 5, 6, 8, 12, 14, 17, 19, 21a, 38b, 66a, 68a, 69a, 56a, 62a, and pp. 98, 104, 119, 168; Gridley/Graves, Courtesy of Castelli Graphics, fig. 56b; Courtesy of Charles Hinman, p. 116; Courtesy of Hirschl & Adler Modern, New York, fig. 3a; George Holzer, Courtesy of Graphicstudio, University of South Florida, figs. 1, 2, 22, 23, 24, 25, 26, 27, 28, 29, 30, 31, 33, 34, 35, 36, 5a, 13a, 15a, 20a, 44a, 47a, 58a, 58b, 60a, 76a, 76b, 77a, 79a, 81b, and pp. 54, 70, 140, 141, 149, 153, 178, 183, 201, 208, 230, 260, 261, 265, 272–273, 278; Courtesy of John Weber Gallery, New York, p. 145; Toby Lewis and Brenda Black, Courtesy of Feigen Incorporated, Chicago, p. 134; Tom Lopez, Courtesy of Graphicstudio, University of South Florida, p. 196; Colin McRay, Courtesy of Crown Point Press, San Francisco, fig. 32a; Courtesy of Multiples, Inc., fig. 28a; Eric Pollitzer, Courtesy of James Rosenquist, fig. 61a; Tom Pruitt, Courtesy of Graphicstudio, University of South Florida, fig. 81a; Paul Ruscha, Courtesy of Edward Ruscha, fig. 26a; Deli Sacilotto, Courtesy of Graphicstudio, University of South Florida, p. 187; David Yager, Courtesy of Graphicstudio, University of South Florida, figs. 21, 11a.